Social Theory
for a
Changing Society

Social Theory
for a
Changing Society

EDITED BY

Pierre Bourdieu
and
James S. Coleman

Westview Press
BOULDER • SAN FRANCISCO • OXFORD

Russell Sage Foundation
NEW YORK

Published in 1991 in the United States of America by Westview Press, Inc., 5500 Central Avenue, Boulder, Colorado 80301, and in the United Kingdom by Westview Press, 36 Lonsdale Road, Summertown, Oxford OX2 7EW

Library of Congress Cataloging-in-Publication Data
Social theory for a changing society / edited by Pierre Bourdieu and
  James S. Coleman.
    p. cm.
  Includes bibliographical references.
  ISBN 0-8133-1193-4. — ISBN 0-8133-1194-2 (pbk.).
  1. Social change. 2. Social structure. 3. Social control.
I. Bourdieu, Pierre. II. Coleman, James Samuel, 1926–
HM101.S69348 1991
303.4—dc20   91-12563
                                                                              CIP

Printed and bound in the United States of America

The paper used in this publication meets the requirements
of the American National Standard for Permanence of Paper
for Printed Library Materials Z39.48-1984.

10   9   8   7   6   5   4   3   2   1

Contents

Prologue:
Constructed Social Organization

James S. Coleman

There is in modern society a structural change that underlies many of the social changes with which the conference was concerned. My argument here will be that this is a qualitative change in the way society is organized, a change with many implications.

I will call this a change from primordial and spontaneous social organization to constructed social organization (see Coleman 1990, Chapters 2, 3, and 24 for an extended examination of this change). The common definitions of these terms contain some hint of what I mean, but I will describe the change more fully to ensure that it is clearly understood.

By primordial social organization I mean social organization that has its origins in the relationships established by childbirth. Not all these relations are activated in all cultures, but some subset of these relations forms the basis for all primitive and traditional social organization. From these relations, more complex structures unfold. For example, from these relations come families; from families come clans; from clans, villages; and from villages, tribes, ethnicities, or societies.

The primordial relations generate more than a great network: Supra-individual *actors* come into being. Depending on the society, the nuclear family may be the smallest, with other kin-based units such as the household or the clan as larger, more encompassing actors. These corporate bodies were regarded as actors in primitive law and sometimes also in codified legal systems: They were held corporately responsible for the actions of their members, and they took actions corporately, as in a vendetta or a feud. But as corporate actors, they had one special property: Unlike the modern corporation, the corporate actor was not distinct from the persons

This book is based on a conference, "Social Theory and Emerging Issues in a Changing Society," held at the University of Chicago, April 5–8, 1989, under the auspices of the Russell Sage Foundation and the Maison des Sciences de l'Homme.

of whom it was composed. Such bodies ordinarily had authority structures with a single person at the head, often the patriarch of the family or the clan.

The contrast between primordial and constructed social organization does not mean, of course, that the organization that I describe as primordial (such as family, clan, ethnic group, religious group) has no purposive component; it means, rather, that the purposive or constructed elements all took as the starting point the primordial relations generated by birth. Being based on primordial relations, this social organization tends to have a particular character. In terms of Talcott Parsons's (1951) pattern variables, primordial organization is *diffuse*, not specific; *ascriptive*, not achievement oriented; *particularistic*, not universalistic; and *affectively expressive* rather than affectively neutral.

There are, to be sure, many variations in primordial social structure. But the central element is that the larger structures are based on the relations established by birth. The birth-generated relations constitute the basis on which religious bodies grow, and both law and government in most traditional societies are not distinct from religious organization. In this volume, Thomas Luckmann describes the diffusion of religious sanctions throughout the social structure of archaic societies and the later development of a differentiation between religious and other institutions, a differentiation that was not complete until the modern period.[1]

One consequence of this basis for social structure is that the structure grows incrementally, as does any organic entity. New relations are generated by new births, and the society develops by accretion. There may be revolutions or other social convulsions that fracture the structure, but these are the fractures of an organic entity. (This, of course, is the reverse of Emile Durkheim's (1947 [1902]) use of the term *organic*, which he used to represent a society characterized by an extensive division of labor.)

This primordial basis for social organization has, with variations, been characteristic of the human race throughout its history. It has always been supplemented by what may be called spontaneous social organization. Spontaneous social organization is social organization generated from two-person transactions, in which the transaction itself provides sufficient incentive for both parties' actions. No third parties are necessary in order for the relation to be established or maintained. Spontaneous social relations are exemplified by economic exchange but also by friendship relations and by other stable long-term relations voluntarily entered into. The ideology that embodies such a structure is nineteenth-century liberalism; the social structure is individualistic rather than communitarian or hierarchical, and classical economic theory expresses this structure.

Primordial social organization has been broadly supplemented by spontaneous social organization; but it is now coming to be supplanted by a differently based structure that I will call constructed social organization. The expansion of constructed social organization became the preoccupation of Max Weber, who described it as the progressive "rationalization" of society. Constructed social organization is, as the term signifies, social organization constructed for either a single purpose or a narrow range of purposes. The prototype is the formal organization, composed of positions established by the person or persons who constructed the organization. The rules, the expectations and obligations between positions, and the incentive structures that individuals confront do not arise spontaneously. They are fixed in place by the designer of the organization.

The distinction between spontaneous and constructed social organization can be described by distinguishing between two types of relations between actors. I will call the two types of relations simple and complex.

Simple social relations are self-sustaining in the sense that incentives to both parties to continue the relation are intrinsic to the relation. The incentives are generated by the relation itself, and continuation of the relation depends on its generating sufficient incentives for both parties. Examples are such social relations as relations of friendship, "informal" social relations of all sorts, and authority relations such as those of master and servant. These relations can be seen as building blocks for much of social organization. Social organization that grows, as in a community or a sprawling social network, is an amalgam of such relations. These may be called simple relations to distinguish them from a second class of relations.

The second class of social relations consists of those that are not self-sustaining but that are dependent on a third party for their continuation. Incentives to one or both of the two parties to continue the relation are not intrinsic to the relation but must be supplied from the outside. This is the kind of relation on which formal organizations are built. Social organization consisting of such relations does not just "grow"; one (or both) of each pair of parties has no incentive to establish such a relation. This kind of organization must be *built* because it is based on more complex structures of incentives, involving three or more parties for each two-actor relation. The organization is a structure of relations made up of obligations and expectations, but there is no requirement—as there is in a social organization composed of simple relations—that each person's obligations and expectations bring about a positive account balance in each of the person's relations. Each person need have only one positive account balance covering the total set of actors involved in this complex structure of incentives. I will call this form of social relation a complex relation.

Friedrich Hayek (1973), in the very first pages of his sweeping *Law, Legislation, and Liberty,* makes the spontaneous versus constructed distinction I have described here. He does not distinguish what I have called primordial social organization, regarding it as merely a component of spontaneous social order. Hayek's thesis in general is that spontaneous social order gives outcomes superior to those resulting from purposively constructed social organization and is therefore to be encouraged. He argues that constructed organization necessarily implies centralized power and must be monolithic, authoritarian, and totalitarian in character. He sees the emergent, spontaneous, multi-source social order as the protection against such an overarching authority system. My argument here will be that constructed social organization is not coincident with monolithic authority systems but is compatible with dispersed and competing centers of power and that the relation between constructed, spontaneous, and primordial social organization is more complex than Hayek would have it. Further, I will argue that modern society could not exist without an extensive component of constructed social organization and that constructed social organization will be an even larger part of societies of the twenty-first century.

To see the difference between primordial and constructed social organization, it is useful to examine the first stirrings of modern constructed organization. These occurred beginning in the thirteenth century with the emergence of a new form of person in English common law. From the thirteenth through nineteenth centuries in Europe, a new kind of corporate actor came into being in society with no single individual at its head; it was not based on family or kin group but nevertheless was able to take goal-directed action and to be recognized as a subject and object of action in a court of law. The English historian, Frederick W. Maitland, was perhaps the most prominent theoretician of this new form, although Otto von Gierke, who examined these developments in central Europe, was Maitland's predecessor. Towns chartered by the English king were among the first examples of the new nonfamily based corporations; the East India Company and the Virginia Company were among the first commercial enterprises of this form. The joint-stock corporation, as it took legal shape in the nineteenth century, has come to be the most prominent type, but there are many others as well: nonprofit corporations, trade unions, professional associations, trade associations, and purposive associations of other types.

Several distinguishing characteristics mark this form of organization as distinctive from the social organization that had preceded it. One is the fact that the corporation, or corporate actor, had a legal personality separate from that of the persons who brought it into being—its incorporators. The principle of limited liability separated the legal self of the corporate actor from the legal selves of the incorporators.

A second distinguishing property of the new corporation was that its elements were not persons but positions. The prototypical structure was that of the formal organization, with a structure composed of positions and with persons as replaceable occupants of those positions.

A third property of the new corporation was that it grew through a different process than did spontaneous or primordial organization. It grew through creation of a new position, or a new set of positions (for example, a department), that has complex relations to existing positions in the organization. Only then was the position filled by a person. Both primordial and spontaneous social organization grow through individual actions in establishing new simple relations with new persons.

The rise of modern purposive corporate actors—the prototype of Hayek's constructed social order—is, paradoxically from Hayek's perspective, coincident with the rise of liberalism, free social relations, and open societies.

What I have described as spontaneous social organization could flow only after the tightly interwoven organic structure of primordial social organization was broken apart. But this occurred at the hand of the constructed social organization, the new purposive corporate actors, the corporations. They exemplified a new freedom, especially apparent in England but also on the Continent, of persons to engage freely in relations not dictated by their positions in society.

This new corporate actor, which began on the periphery of social systems as a way of organizing otherwise infeasible activities, has come to occupy the center of modern social organization. Productive activities once carried out within the household migrated to these new corporate actors. With the growth of commercial leisure, consumption activities have also come to be carried out in the context of these modern corporate actors—whether music recording companies, fast food restaurants, or commercial amusement parks. In the meantime, the unit that had been the nucleus of social organization from which much of the rest of society was constructed—the family—has been crowded into a peripheral position in society.

It is possible to believe that these changes are trends that will reverse themselves in cyclical fashion as some unseen pendulum swings back. Alternatively, it is possible to see these changes as the first stages in the replacement of primordial social organization with social organization that is purposively constructed.

This alternative view carries extensive implications. By this view, the social organization of the future is neither that of unbridled individualism nor overwhelming communitarianism. It is social organization by design, social organization as a creation of human intelligence.

Constructed social organization has parallels in other areas of activity. Chronologically first among these parallels is the constructed physical environment, with Newtonian mechanics as its scientific base and civil engineering and architecture as its practical tools. In its early manifestations, the constructed physical environment consisted of little more than fixed dwelling structures created as former hunters and gatherers began to engage in cultivation. In its current manifestations, it is the creation of whole cities of glass and concrete, with transportation networks using mechanical modes of locomotion and communication networks based on electronic transmission.

Another parallel is in constructed chemical organization, organic compounds that never existed in nature but that are constructed for a purpose. These include medical drugs, pesticides and herbicides, and the "designer drugs" that replace natural psychoactive compounds. Still another parallel is the construction of new radioactive elements through nuclear fission and, sometime in the future, nuclear fusion. The most recent parallel is constructed biological organization. We are now beginning to have the genetic tools for constructing biological organisms, modifying the genes at particular sites to design an organism to fulfill a specific purpose.

In all these realms of activity, construction that makes use of human intelligence and knowledge increasingly supplants organization more closely tied to nature. But the use of man-made constructions—whether physical, chemical, biological, or social—can have undesired and unanticipated consequences. Our knowledge is fragmentary and partial. We fail to recognize that bacteria will evolve to become resistant to a chemical designed to kill them or that DDT will accumulate and concentrate in the food chain until the shells of the eggs of aquatic birds become too thin to function. We fail to recognize, until the process is far along, that the widespread combustion of fossil fuels increases the carbon dioxide level to an extent that may bring about climatic changes or that the burning of high-sulfur coal can acidify distant lakes through acid rain. We fail to recognize that a large electrical grid designed to increase efficiency of electricity distribution can, if overloaded, propagate a local breakdown to cover the whole geographic region touched by the grid.

We fail to recognize that high-rise apartment buildings, which can compress many middle-class families onto a small land area without disaster, cannot do so for lower-class families whose internal organization is weak, until the high crime rates in high-rise public housing force abandonment of the buildings. We fail to recognize that piecework systems among production workers in large plants, designed to maximize production per unit cost, may generate a secondary collective response that will reduce production. We fail to recognize that the modern corporate actors cannot only bring us material welfare through efficient production but, through their extraction of functions from the family, can destroy the very institution that creates the new generation of workers on which they themselves depend.

We fail to recognize that large high schools, designed for efficiency and diversity of offerings, can become inefficient through an expansion of administrative staff and ineffective through the superficiality of relations between teachers and students. We fail to recognize that when the welfare functions carried out by the family for the aged, the physically infirm, the young, and others incapable of economic self-sufficiency are taken over by the state, what is introduced is not only equality of treatment but also two less benign outcomes: caregivers with little incentive to provide humane and responsible care, and a reduced self-sufficiency. The state action may thus exacerbate the very condition it is instituted to remedy. We fail to recognize that when narrow-purpose corporations, designed to exploit market opportunities, come into being, some will have an incentive to develop a youth market and, like modern-day pied pipers, to lead youth away from parent-generated norms and from school-imposed goals. We fail to recognize that increased progressivity in income taxes will generate an increase in taxpayer tactics to reduce reported income. We fail to recognize that centrally planned economies lack the incentives on which productivity depends. We fail to recognize that states or other organizations governed without mechanisms through which diverse interests can affect corporate action will be oppressive in the short run and unstable in the long run.

All these things are unintended consequences of the use of human knowledge to substitute constructed physical, chemical, biological, or social organization for that which arose naturally through evolutionary or other incremental processes. Are these consequences sufficiently harmful to lead us to stop this use of knowledge? The answer may differ in different cases, but I think the usual answer must be no. The benefits we derive from this greater control of the physical, biological, and social worlds are sufficiently great that we would not relinquish this control and return to a past that was in many ways a dark and dreary one.

These unintended consequences are nevertheless important, for they exemplify several general points. When bacteria become resistant to a drug, when state-provided welfare increases welfare dependency, or when new taxes generate new strategies to escape taxes, the cause is similar and is also similar to a principle in chemistry enunciated by a French chemist in 1885 and named after him as Le Chatelier's principle: "If a change occurs in one of the factors, such as temperature or pressure, under which a system is in equilibrium, the system will tend to adjust itself so as to annul, as far as possible, the effect of the change." The principle, also known as the principle of mobile equilibrium, expresses the recognition that interventions in an ongoing system do not merely have an effect where applied; the effect is spread through the system, shifting the equilibrium slightly but any one element very little.

The mechanism through which the systemic reaction occurs differs in different cases. It may be mutation and natural selection, as in the case of antibiotic-resistant bacteria, or it may be persons seeing an opportunity to obtain benefits with reduced effort, as in the case of welfare-generated dependency, or to offset a tax increase through increased exemptions, as in the case of income taxes.

Other cases of indirect effects of the substitution of constructed organization for natural or primordial organization follow a different principle, which differs sharply from Le Chatelier's principle. This is a principle that may be called system overload. Sometimes the system overload is generated by a tragedy-of-the-commons process in which each individual's pursuit of self-interests imposes negative externalities on all others, resulting in suboptimal collective outcomes. Some of the environmental consequences of constructed physical organization—such as acid rain, ozone depletion, and carbon dioxide accumulation—are of this type. But the potential for the tragedy of the commons also occurs in primordial social organization. In the classic commons setting of an English village, there was no tragedy because informal norms regulated usage. The potential for the tragedy is realized only when primordial social organization is no longer stable and self-contained, when it can no longer support the informal social controls on which it depends.

There are other sources of system overload, as exemplified by the social disorganization found in high-rise public housing projects. To pack together in a vertical column people who have no functional interdependencies and who do have time on their hands creates a setting in which norms of social control cannot easily grow and in which a household has no proprietary space that it can protect, beyond the four walls of its living quarters. System overload can also be created with centralization, as can occur when a large high school replaces several small ones. There will be excess demand for certain facilities and resources, while others will be in excess supply. If there are no mechanisms in the administrative bureaucracy to allow adjustments in staff supply to meet demand, there will be a continued system overload at certain points combined with underutilization at others. This is a simple point, but one that is frequently ignored in constructed social organization, designed without a mechanism for reconfiguring itself as demand differs.

Centralization, or creating a single system from what had been several, can also produce an increase in inequality. Again, I will use high schools as an example: Large high schools have greater variance in participation in extracurricular activities than do small ones, as Barker and Gump (1964) have shown. A higher fraction of students does not participate at all, and a few students are leaders in everything. The tendency is sufficiently strong that some large high schools have established rules that restrict the number of offices in extracurricular programs that a student can simultaneously hold.

The same phenomenon can be seen elsewhere. The centralizing effect of television on viewing sports led to much greater inequality (of income, attention, status) among athletes than was true before the centralization; some professional athletes are now almost the highest salaried persons in society, while other athletes, whose counterparts once enjoyed the attention of a local audience, have no such audience.

Increased inequality is one of several types of problems that arise when a large number of independent or weakly interdependent socioeconomic systems become a single system with extensive interdependencies. Another problem is instability resulting from specialization of function. As demand for a product changes, a component of the system, specialized to provide that product, will experience wild economic fluctuations. If a region or nation is thus specialized, changes in demand will lead to economic instability of the region or nation.

IMPLICATIONS FOR SOCIAL THEORY

The implications for social theory of the view of the world I have expressed here are extensive. The view implies that social theory must concern itself with the problems of constructed social organization, not merely with the problems that have occupied it throughout its short existence. Social theory, in this view, must be not merely theory that would allow us—as William Graham Sumner would have it—to understand "the cake of custom," not merely theory that distinguishes *gemeinschaft* and *gesellschaft* nor that which distinguishes charismatic, traditional, and rational modes of authority. It should be not merely theory that describes the transition from societies with a minimal division of labor to those with an extensive division of labor. It should be theory developed to aid in the construction of social organization.

This position is closer to that of Karl Marx than to that of Friedrich Hayek. Yet the vision of society to which that theory should be directed is, I would claim, closer to that of Hayek than to that of Marx.

Social Control in Primordial
and Constructed Social Organization

Much of social theory is concerned with social control. And much of the theoretical work on social control is concerned with those control mechanisms characteristic of primordial social organization. Chief among these are norms and values. Social control is exercised through norms by means of sanctions, either externally imposed or internally held. Social control exercised through values is control at the very fountainhead of action, leading individuals to want to do that which realizes some socially beneficial outcome. Values, like internal sanctions, are established in the socialization process, which can operate at any stage in life but is most extensive in childhood.

The question of whether stable and traditional societies exercise social control over their members principally through shaping their values or principally through sanctions that constrain action is not a settled one among anthropologists (see Schweder 1987), but these two mechanisms of social control are characteristic of primordial social organization. Formal law may come into being, but if it does, it is an accumulation of the rules and principles generated by the norms and values that hold for this social system.

What is true of norms and values, however, is that they grow slowly and only in stable social systems. The imposition of external sanctions is subject to free-rider problems. When there is not stability but continuing change in social systems, the potential future retribution that can overcome the free-rider problem is gone, and, as a result, external sanctions that make norms effective vanish. The creation of internal sanctions through socialization is in the socializer's interest only when relations are sufficiently stable to make it possible to reap the benefits of the socialization effort. It is characteristic of primordial social organization that relations are long term, with the stability that gives adults the incentive to invest in socializing children. But as primordial social organization is replaced by constructed social organization (as when parental care is replaced by marketed day care), the relations no longer have the stability that provides an incentive to the caregivers to invest in the creation of internal sanctions through socialization.

Thus, as primordial social organization is replaced by *either* the spontaneous social organization of an individualistic society *or* by constructed social organization, or, as must necessarily exist, by some combination of the two, the question arises as to what form of social control will replace the primordial mechanisms—that is, norms and values. The immediate answer, of course, is law, together with formal means of law enforcement.

This is not a sufficient answer, however, for formal law enforcement is a poor substitute for a well-functioning normative system, with a mix of internalized sanctions and informal external sanctions. There are other answers, some to be found in practice and others merely potential theoretical developments. First, however, I will give a sense of the import of the problem through an example: A highly stratified rural society has a primordial base for social organization, supporting a normative structure in which family socialization is reinforced by a strong set of external sanctions. These external sanctions are in turn held in place by the upper strata of the system. When lower-strata families from such a society migrate to urban areas without strong neighborhood organization, the external sanctioning structure is gone, and the social control exercised by the family no longer has the support of an external informal sanctioning system. If there were a well-developed system of social control for constructed social organization, then there would be no increase in crime with the move from the rural society to the urban one. The magnitude of crime in urban areas, where primordial social organization beyond the family is largely absent, compared to that in rural areas, where such organization is present, indicates just how poorly the problem of social control in constructed social organization is solved in practice.

Some of the solutions to problems of social control in constructed organization—beyond the simple answer of law enforced by policing—can be seen in formal organizations. Here there are rules, and the highly articulated structure of the organization is in part constructed that way in order to police (or supervise) obedience to the rules. Yet the problem of social control is hardly solved in such organizations, as attested by the ubiquity of what is called in economics the principal-agent problem—the principal's problem of providing the appropriate combination of policing and incentives that will lead the agent to act in ways desired by the principal.

In different organizations, the principal-agent problem is addressed in different ways. For example, U.S. automobile companies use a high component of hierarchical supervision of workers, while Japanese companies engaged in similar production use a higher component of production incentives and a higher component of work-group collective supervision. The latter is an importation into the firm of the structural conditions that facilitate the growth of norms backed by effective sanctions.

The examples suggest that an examination of practices related to social control in formal organizations might be a useful starting point for a theory of social control in constructed social organization. These practices may include the establishment of structural conditions that allow the growth of spontaneous social organization that will accomplish the principal's goal, as the example of work-group collective supervision suggests. These examples also suggest the possible value of extending the aims of principal-agent theory to include not merely the accomplishment of productive goals for a formal organization but, beyond that, the general problem of social control in social organization where the conditions for classical social control (internalized values, norms enforced by internalized sanctions and informal external sanctions) do not obtain.

The Problem of Distribution
of the Social Product

In the shift that has occurred in the past century from subsistence economies of households to a single interdependent exchange economy, the society has moved from one in which each household maintained independent viability or something close to it to a society in which the criterion of viability is met only at the societal level. In the subsistence economy, the units (essentially households) that engaged in transactions fulfilled the requirements of independent viability in that both parties to the transaction showed a gain from the relation. If individuals within the household were net liabilities, the losses were made up by the household as the principal welfare institution. If households themselves were net liabilities, these losses were made up by the next-larger economic unit, the extended family, the village, or (where the employment relation had a feudal quality) the employer.

The criterion of independent viability at the household level is no longer met when most economic exchanges of goods and services have moved outside the household in a double-exchange economy. (The first exchange is labor for money, the second is money for consumption goods and services.) Persons have replaced households as the units engaged in economic transactions with the larger society, and the welfare activities of the family have come to be taken over by the state. The liabilities that made persons economically dependent are no longer absorbed by the corporate bodies most proximate to them (just as the economic exchanges of which they are a part are no longer with actors most proximate to them). The state itself has jumped over all these bodies to become a major welfare institution.

The question that may be asked is whether such a structure has long-run viability. This is a structure in which the money wage can be regarded as a drawing right on the aggregate product of all the society's productive activity. But in an economy of abundance and a society not organized in families, a distribution of these drawing rights through productive work leaves a large fraction of society without drawing rights. A second set of drawing rights—welfare rights, broadly defined—is provided by redistribution through the political system. This makes viability of the system precarious, for the second set of drawing rights—the welfare rights—may reduce the value of the first set: rights to earned income on the basis of productive activity. If so, disincentives to contribute are created.

For whatever reason, there has come to be an increasingly large economic dependency in the exchange economy. Attempts to repair this dependency have been made almost entirely through redistribution by the state. Taxation for redistribution can be seen, as Arthur Okun (1975) has described it, as a second-round redistribution that follows the first-round distribution through the market, which allocates wages and other income. Seen in this way, taxation-and-redistribution implies a set of preferences, on the part of those holding political decision-making rights, for a greater degree of equality than the market, left to function freely, provides.

Okun's description of state-organized taxation and redistribution as a "second-round redistribution" suggests its functional correspondence to the communal redistribution that has traditionally occurred through the family, the household, the village chief, and the ethnic group. Yet unlike that redistribution, the social structure necessary to suppress the disincentive to contribute is missing. An underclass is created that is not only permanent but that gains new recruits without restraint. The redistribution creates incentives that tend to defeat the first round of distribution through wages for productive activity (see Charles Murray 1984, 1988, for arguments about the importance of this effect in the United States).

What has not been attempted is a consideration of alternative systems under which these drawing rights are provided, in such a way that disincentives to contribute to the aggregate product are less. To begin with, we may ask the question: How has the family, as a communal unit, solved the problem of disincentives to contribute to its aggregate product? If the family can be seen as the one social unit that has successfully carried out distribution principally on the basis of need rather than principally on the basis of contribution, then how has it done so? One answer is that it has done so only very imperfectly. There are wives who see their husbands as ne'er-do-wells and spend their lives struggling to provide an income that the husband will not. There are husbands who see their nonworking wives as sloths, interested only in consuming. Families often have difficulties in inducing their children, employed and living at home, to contribute to the family budget. The extended families of the past often contained an uncle or a cousin who was said to spend his life sponging off relatives.

Nevertheless, families appear to overcome the disincentive, or free-rider, problem better than do other social units. The means by which they do so appear to be largely tangible and intangible incentives: stigmatizing noncontributors and giving status, power, and extra resources within the family to those who contribute more than their share.

These are kinds of incentive structures that appear to be effective only in very small social units. In fact, it may be that the size of the unit within which there is communal redistribution on the basis of need has been limited primarily by the size of the unit within which these social psychological benefits and costs can be effective. This size will, of course, be larger if the unit within which stigma, reputation, deference, and power are effective is larger.

Yet the social structure of a corporate economy of abundance (a social structure in which persons need one another less and thus have less opportunity to accumulate social capital) is one in which the size of such social psychologically effective units is small and becoming smaller. There may be means of reconstituting such groups, whether through the family or by way of a new institution, thus reviving communal redistribution as a robust complement to primary distribution through the double-exchange economy. Yet apart from scattered and generally short-lived experiments by the young with urban communes, there is little to suggest how such units might be constituted.

One possible approach to the distribution problem in a double-exchange economy with abundance is to accept that there is a necessity for a "second round" of distribution, but not of the sort that Okun envisioned. There has always been a second round in the form of the family and its derivative institutions. This approach would attempt to bring into being institutions proximate to the individual that would have the resources necessary to shoulder the liabilities of dependent persons and the capacity to produce social psychological incentives of the form that have proved effective in the family: stigma, status, deference, power. This approach would be, as in the previous section, to create around the individual new forms of social capital—microsocial institutions whose power would grow at the expense of the state as they took over its redistributive activities.

Questions are raised by this approach, however. How can such bodies be brought into being, and what would they be like? What does "proximity" mean in modern society? Most such "proximate" bodies are physically proximate; yet a decreasing fraction of persons' relations are based on physical proximity. And what kind of reallocation of rights in society (away from the state or away from the individual) can provide sufficient resources to these proximate bodies so they can absorb welfare functions once the province of the family and now the province of the state? What is the loss in equality created by the devolution of resources and responsibility to microsocial institutions?

CONCLUSION

As primordial corporate bodies wither away and as the social capital on which societal functioning has depended is eroded, the purposive social organization that replaces them presents both opportunities and problems. I have tried, in examining social control and distributional questions, to give a glimpse of these opportunities and problems. I want to give a sense of the necessity for development of social theory and pursuit of social research if society is to realize the opportunities and avoid the problems.

These opportunities and problems are posed by changes in the very basis of social organization. They constitute a demand for social science, a demand that increases with this transformation of social organization. This requires a social science that consists both of applied social research and social theory. The theory, if it is to be of value for this task, crosses the traditional bounds of the disciplines within which knowledge is ordered, for the transformation of society has changed the linkages between these institutional areas. In so doing, it becomes a new social science, appropriate to the new social structure.

NOTES

1. There are some people who would say that there is no fundamental difference between the primitive social organization that relies on informal norms and modern social organization composed of formal organization that uses highly formalized

means of social control. These are the same people who would say that there is no difference between the primitive Ringtausch of the Trobriand Islands involving exchange of woven mats, and the complex stock, bond, and futures markets that occur on the London, New York, or Tokyo stock exchanges. When Joan Robinson (1956, p. 236), an iconoclastic economist throughout her life, said that economic theory cannot be more precise than the economic transactions to which it refers, she was evidently thinking of differences like these. The obverse of her statement is that as the economic transactions become more precise and formally designed, economic theory must mirror these changes if it is to be useful for analytical or policy purposes. The same is true of social theory. Failure to do so will result in social theory possibly appropriate for the Trobriand islanders but not for modern society.

REFERENCES

Barker, R. G., and P. V. Gump. 1964. *Big School, Small School*. Stanford: Stanford University Press.
Coleman, J. S. 1990. *Foundations of Social Theory*. Cambridge, MA: Harvard University Press.
Durkheim, Emile. 1947. *The Division of Labor*. New York: The Free Press.
Hayek, F. A. v. 1973. *Law, Legislation, and Liberty*, vol. 1. London: Routledge and Kegan Paul.
Murray, C. 1984. *Losing Ground*. New York: Basic Books.
_____ . 1988. *In Pursuit of Happiness and Good Government*. New York: Simon and Schuster.
Okun, A. 1975. *Equality and Efficiency: The Big Tradeoff*. Washington, DC: Brookings.
Parsons, Talcott. 1951. *The Social System*. New York: The Free Press.
Robinson, Joan. 1956. "The Industry and the Market." *Economic Journal* 66:360–364.
Schweder, Richard A. 1987. "Ghostbusters in Anthropology," unpublished paper. The University of Chicago.

Comments

Michael Hechter

The major point of this chapter is that social theory should pay greater attention to the problem of attaining social control in constructed orders, as against primordial ones. Constructed orders should have theoretical pride of place not merely because they have been gaining at the expense of alternative kinds of orders but also because control is both harder to attain and harder to explain in large, consciously designed organizations than it is in small, primordial groups.

This point has two implications, only one of which is explicitly mentioned in the chapter. The explicit implication is meant for sociologists. Jim Coleman believes that by placing too much emphasis on primordial orders, sociological theorists have overstressed the importance of internalized norms and values as control mechanisms. Whereas these elements are central to the explanation of control in primordial orders, their effectiveness rests on conditions that tend not to hold in constructed orders. For the most part, control in constructed orders is due not to internalized norms and values but rather to consciously designed monitoring and sanctioning systems: Hence formal organizations, which offer a wealth of evidence concerning the strengths and weaknesses of these systems of control, should be more common objects of theoretical concern than communal structures.

One of the basic challenges posed by constructed orders is to discover how they can be set up so as to economize on control costs. Clearly, bringing social theory to bear on this problem is a task of the highest priority. As an aside, Coleman's idea of establishing organizations intermediate between the state and the family that can motivate and sanction individuals on the basis of their performance in a cost-effective way is one that recalls Durkheim's rather truncated discussion of occupational communities in *Suicide.*

There is also a second message here, one that is directed toward those rational-choice theorists who see in repeated game theory a sufficient explanation for all control in all types of social orders. The point that is not made explicit in the paper—but perhaps should be—is that explanations of social control in constructed orders that are based on repeated game theory suffer from many of the same kinds of limitations that plague normative explanations in these settings. Both arguments work best in small groups where monitoring is unproblematic and exit costs are high. But the efficacy of internalized norms on the one hand and repeated exchange on the other rapidly deteriorates as group size increases and exit costs decrease.

By and large, these lessons have not yet been assimilated into social or political theory, but they should be. Still, other parts of the argument raise questions.

In the first place, I do not understand why the various forms of social organization—primordial, spontaneous, and constructed—are defined according to their origins when surely it is no easy matter to figure out the origins of any given order or institution. Too often, the historical cupboard is uncomfortably bare.

This leads to a question about the historical sequence of the spontaneous and constructed organizational forms. The chapter's general claim seems to be that spontaneous orders precede constructed ones in history, but is this always true? The discussion of the origins of the joint-stock corporation suggests that under certain conditions constructed orders may precede spontaneous ones, such as liberal institutions. And is it possible to devise endogenous explanations of these shifts in social orders?

Much of the effort in the chapter goes toward a comparison of control in constructed and primordial orders, but this highlights a curious omission. For Hayek, who first introduced the basic distinction, the critical comparison was that between constructed and *spontaneous* orders. Hayek had reasons to favor spontaneous orders over constructed ones, reasons having to do with the alleged consequences that these different kinds of orders have for economic performance. Hayek believed that spontaneous orders permitted a much more efficient flow of information—and, hence, superior economic performance—than constructed orders could ever provide. (It is not my intention to discuss the adequacy of Hayek's claims here.)

Coleman implies that social forms arising from evolutionary selection differ from those arising from conscious planning on account of their unanticipated consequences. That constructed orders have unanticipated consequences is true, but it is also an artifact of the distinction between these types of orders: Since constructed orders are the only social forms that are established by human design, they alone can be properly described as having unanticipated consequences.

The key issue the chapter raises is not really about unanticipated consequences. Rather, it is about the relative optimality of different institutional designs for various kinds of social outcomes, be they economic or otherwise. Yet the concept of optimality only makes a subliminal appearance here. Thus, there can be a tragedy of the commons when the primordial system grows too large, and welfare institutions can dampen incentives for productivity among those who are dependent.

I suspect that few of us would be attracted to social science if we did not believe that social theory could, in principle, enable us to design better institutions, if not optimal ones. Even Hayek's radical strictures against planning and state intervention in the economy can be read in this light.

But what are the ends these institutions should be designed to attain? Economists often assume that institutions should foster maximum economic growth; sociologists place greater emphasis on social solidarity. But different incentive structures are required to bring about these different outcomes. Who decides on the relative priority of competing ends, and on what basis are the decisions to be made?

Successful institutional design can never be simply a matter of engineering, although good engineering may well be a necessary condition for good institutional design. Individual values, however they are revealed and aggregated, will always affect institutional design, to a greater or lesser extent. Therefore, perhaps some theoretical attention should be devoted to understanding the sources of these values in the social theory of the future.

Comments

Susan P. Shapiro

It is only fitting, or at least not surprising, that an exercise to develop a new social theory for the late twentieth and early twenty-first centuries should borrow a device from classical social theory—the state of nature. But just as there is no "real" state of nature, there is no "natural," or "primordial," social organization. All social organization is socially constructed. The "primordial" social organization into which one is born in stereotypic Western middle-class nuclear families composed of some combination of mothers, fathers, stepparents, siblings and stepsiblings, and child-care providers is no less socially constructed than that into which one is born in hunting and gathering societies where biological fathers are often physically distant from their offspring who, with siblings and nonsiblings, are reared by several women and often socialized by their peers. Nor is the old-fashioned primordial family of the arranged marriage, imposed by third parties, any less socially constructed than the futuristic family hauntingly portrayed in Margaret Atwood's (1986) *The Handmaid's Tale* of child bearing and rearing as highly specialized roles in an occupational stratification system conceived and brutally enforced by the state. And these child-rearing arrangements are no less socially constructed than a form of social organization that is now awakening several miles to the north in which men and women, dressed in multi-colored coats, yell and scream and gesticulate wildly with elaborate hand signals in order to spend billions of other people's dollars to secure the future right to buy commodities of which these clients never intend to take possession. These are all constructed forms of social organization.

So I take Coleman's distinctions between primordial, spontaneous, and constructed social organization as ideal types, painted with a very broad brush, and use his chapter as an invitation to

- Decompose the ideal types and explore the ways in which and dimensions along which we construct social organization
- Make problematic his evolutionary argument that primordial forms of social organization are being irreversibly forced out by constructed ones
- Reconsider the implications of constructed social organization for social control

First, what are the ways in which we construct social organization? One can unearth from Coleman's chapter at least eight themes that suggest continua from simple-"primordial" to complex-"constructed" organizational forms:

1. The size or scale of social units
2. The proximity or physical distance across which parties to an exchange or transaction are joined
3. The familiarity of interactional partners; the extent to which exchanges join intimates, acquaintances, or strangers
4. The social distance spanned by a social relationship—Are interactions face-to-face or are they instead separated by chains of intermediaries (markets, stock exchanges, labor unions, brokers, agents, and the like)?
5. Temporal features of relationships:
   a. Are they stable, ongoing, episodic, long term, or short term?
   b. What is the permanence or impermanence of relational membership; how much turnover characterizes the relationship; how replaceable are those who fill its positions?

    c. Do relationships represent a kind of "futures transaction" (such as insurance, credit, investment, or pensions) in which one party makes a commitment far in advance of return, payoff, or the exercise of obligation by the other?

6. The units of action in constructed social organization: Are they persons, positions, organizations created by third-party individuals (what Coleman means by "constructed social organization"), organizations created by other organizations, or networks of organizations engaging in interdependent relationships?

7. Roles:
    a. Do individuals or organizations occupy single or multiple roles simultaneously or serially; what is the potential for role conflict?
    b. What is the density of role relationships? Borrowing from the legal anthropologist Max Gluckman (1967), one can differentiate between multiplex relationships, in which actors are joined together by a network of intersecting roles (based on kinship, work, community, and ethnic, religious, or political ties), and simplex ones, which join actors in single-interest relationships.

8. The properties or commodities of exchange: In addition to the tangible resources that Coleman identifies with the primordial family, there are what Charles A. Reich (1964) calls the "new properties"—licenses, franchises, entitlements, royalties, contracts, grants, pensions, financial instruments, and the like.

These eight themes, among others, are arrayed like columns on a Chinese menu from which those constructing social organization pick and choose, yielding a vast multidimensional matrix. If one is wedded to Coleman's labels, I suppose one could think of a more "primordial" or "spontaneous" social organizational region of the matrix in which individual actors holding multiplex roles engage in stable, ongoing, small-scale, proximate, face-to-face relationships, exchanging tangible property with familiar partners. But to treat the vast remaining multidimensional space as simply "constructed social organization" is to dump radically dissimilar organizational forms into a colossal melting pot, to obliterate significant variations among them, and thereby to straitjacket future sociological theory. A brief discussion of the evolutionary strands of Coleman's argument and its speculations about social control illustrates some of my concerns.

Coleman suggests that constructed social organization is a relatively recent development, its earliest stirrings dating to the thirteenth century (notwithstanding early armies, churches, and other religious organizations, which he seemingly overlooks or assumes to be primordial), that inexorably seems to be replacing or crowding into peripheral positions primordial and spontaneous forms of organization.

Yet these broad brush strokes tend to obscure the finer detail that illuminates contradictory—and theoretically interesting—trends. First, they underplay Mark Granovetter's (1985) finding of the powerful impulse of individuals and organizations to embed complex activity within concrete personal relations and structures of relations—in short, the impetus to constitute primordial arrangements (what Coleman elsewhere describes as "microsocial" institutions) within constructed organizational forms. Second, they ignore the possibility that constructed organizations may have primordial-like or spontaneous relationships among themselves. For example, in a piece that has considerable bearing on Coleman's discussion of the role of law, Marc Galanter (1974) argues that when "repeat-players" (typically constructed social organizations) have disputes with other repeat-players with which they have dense, ongoing relationships (the simple end of continuum #5a [long term] and to some extent of continua #2 [proximate], #3 [familiar], and #4 [face-to-face] as well), they tend to avoid law as a dispute-settlement alternative. Stewart Macaulay (1963) makes a similar argument about the (non)use of contract among business firms with ongoing relationships. By focusing on the proliferation of constructed social organizations and the extent to which they seem to be appropriating the traditional functions of primordial or spontaneous ones, Coleman may be missing the most intriguing development of all—the variable proliferation of primordial forms within and in the relationships between purposively constructed social organizations.

That brings me to the theme of social control, about which there is space to make only a few comments. First, I echo Granovetter's (1985) observation in a different context when I note that Coleman has a profoundly over-socialized view of life (and an overly consensual view of the emergence of norms and values) in primordial social organizations and an undersocialized one of that in constructed social organizations. Second, he offers law and law enforcement as the alternatives where the conditions for classical social control (internalized values, norms enforced by internalized sanctions and informal external sanctions) do not obtain in constructed social organization. Ironically, though, these are the very settings where Christopher D. Stone (1975) argues that "the law ends"—where legal strategies of deterrence and social control are ineffective in shaping and constraining complex organizational behavior.

The sociology of law of the late twentieth century is increasingly a sociology of the retreat from law—to alternative dispute resolution, self-regulation, insurance schemes, no-fault systems, bargaining in the shadow of the law, formal tinkerings with organizational design, authority relations, communication structures, and the like—as social control systems struggle with the structural difficulties of regulating complex organizational arrangements. In addition to the system overload and free-rider problems, which Coleman links to constructed social organization, regulatory systems must also find ways to respond to asymmetries of and unequal access to information, power, expertise, resources, property, and opportunity; to futures transactions, long-latent injuries, and the remote consequences of complex temporal relationships; to the domino-like linked interdependencies of complex networks of organizations; and to systemic role conflicts that coexist with these organization forms.

This leads me to a point about which Coleman and I agree—that sociological theory might fruitfully look to rules and structural arrangements in formal organizations (Coleman), institutional arrangements associated with the undersocialized conception of "man" (Granovetter 1985), the corporation's decision structure and processes (Stone 1975), or the "guardians of trust" (Shapiro 1987) in trying to understand the problems (and possible solutions) of social control in complex societies. Incidentally, this interest in the construction of new forms of social capital and microsocial institutions deemed central to the "new social science" of the twenty-first century can also be found in Emile Durkheim's (1958 in translation) nineteenth-century lectures on *Professional Ethics and Civic Morals*.

In closing, I find the distinction between primordial and constructed social organization artificial, obscuring fascinating variations that occur within these ideal typical categories and important properties they sometimes share. But my discomfort is largely one of labels, for Coleman's chapter contains within it intriguing (if somewhat buried) suggestions of how to decompose the broad categories and of the perplexing theoretical questions such an exercise unearths. As sociologists explore and fill in the subtle detail captured by Coleman's bold strokes, they will discover a canvas worthy of a social theory for the coming century.

REFERENCES

Atwood, Margaret. 1986. *The Handmaid's Tale*. Boston: Houghton Mifflin.

Durkheim, Emile. 1958. *Professional Ethics and Civic Morals*. Glencoe: Free Press.

Galanter, Marc. 1974. "Why the 'Haves' Come Out Ahead: Speculations on the Limits of Legal Change." *Law and Society Review* 9:95–160.

Gluckman, Max. 1967. *The Judicial Process Among the Barotse of Northern Rhodesia*. Manchester: Manchester University Press.

Granovetter, Mark. 1985. "Economic Action and Social Structure: The Problem of Embeddedness." *American Journal of Sociology* 91:481–510.

Macaulay, Stewart. 1963. "Non-contractual Relations in Business: A Preliminary Study." *American Sociological Review* 28:55–67.

Reich, Charles A. 1964. "The New Property." *Yale Law Journal* 73:733–787.

Shapiro, Susan P. 1987. "The Social Control of Impersonal Trust." *American Journal of Sociology* 93:623–658.

Stone, Christopher D. 1975. *Where the Law Ends: The Social Control of Corporate Behavior*. New York: Harper & Row.

PART ONE

Changes in Technology and Organizational Responses

1

Moebius-Strip Organizations and Open Labor Markets: Some Consequences of the Reintegration of Conception and Execution in a Volatile Economy

Charles Sabel

THE VICISSITUDES OF THE SOCIOLOGY OF WORK

Not so long ago, but in an easily forgotten time, the sociology of work was often seen as an academic master key to understanding industrial society. Grasp of the controlling logic of higher throughput, capital intensive, and intricately connected production systems was thought a necessary and sufficient condition for understanding the changing organization of work and the corporation and their effects—reformist or revolutionary, according to the angle of analysis—on the way managers, workers, and trade unions of various kinds formulated their respective claims to authority. So pervasive was the belief in the connection between a determinate logic of technological progress on the one hand and organizational change and self-understanding on the other that business historians canonizing the rise of a new science of corporate management and Marxists conjecturing the emergence of collective revolutionary subjects—now skilled, now unskilled—in the same

In writing this chapter, I have profited from discussions with Fabrizio Barca, Joshua Cohen, James Coleman, Ronald Dore, Gary Herrigel, Carlo Jaeger, Horst Kern, Richard Locke, Toshihiro Nishiguchi, Arthur L. Stinchcombe, Jonathan Zeitlin, and, especially, Michael Piore. The usual exculpations apply, although my debts are greater than usual. An earlier version of this chapter was presented as an address to the First Plenary Session of the British Sociological Association, April 2, 1990, University of Surrey, Guilford.

corporations understood that they were speaking a differently accented version of a single lingua franca.[1]

Today that lingua franca is fast becoming a dead language, for obvious reasons. Technology is commonly regarded as permissive rather than constraining: as much a tool for the realization of changing human ends as a machine imposing its rhythms on its tenders. Corporations, buffeted by markets that have become more volatile in part because technology is proving so malleable, are desperately trying to reduce their risks by transforming dedicated or special-purpose resources into general-purpose ones—whenever, that is, they cannot simply transform fixed into variable costs. In the process, they are inventing organizational forms whose complexity and mutability often threaten to overwhelm those who design and execute them as well as the sociologists and economists who struggle to understand their constitutional principles. *Work* now refers to such disparate and rapidly changing experiences that it is at least as reasonable to treat the word as a popular shorthand for survival as to regard it as a category of activity that gives similar contours to our different understandings of life.

There have been two contrary responses to the breakdown of the linguistic whole. One is an effort to articulate separate languages for understanding at least some of the pieces. These investigations of diverse technological trajectories, patterns of work, and forms of corporate governance often produce a vertiginous experience of diversity as the constitutive fact of social life.[2] Caricatured, the view is that societies consist of contradictory institutions whose historically specific heterogeneity is a precondition for survival in a changing environment. Context and contingency—national, local, or corporate—suddenly explain most things in a world with no grand rhythm or reason.

The second response is the search for new generalities amidst the apparent ruins of the old. The task here is to understand which parts of—and to whose benefit—the mass-production system and the vast areas of state and quasi-public institutions on which it rested would have to change in order to accommodate the demands of any of the many variously probable economic and political environments. This response can end in the intoxicating vision of a world not gone to pieces but, rather, stood on its head. In this view, universal materializing machines replace product-specific capital goods; small and effortlessly recombinable units of production replace the hierarchies of the mass-production corporation; and the exercise of autonomy required by both the machines and the new organizations produces a new model producer whose view of life confounds the distinction between the entrepreneurial manager and the socialist worker-owner.[3] Contingency and context determine only whether and in what precise way particular nations, regions, or firms manage the necessary handstands.

The aim of this chapter is to adumbrate a sociology of work or production that does justice to the prudent version of these caricatures: to account, that is, for the diversity and similarity of efforts to adjust to the new competitive environment. It advances two principal arguments. The first is that a strategy of responding to turbulent markets by deploying general-purpose resources (or, in an equivalent formulation, the reintegration of conception and execution) must itself be hedged and complemented by deployment of less flexible ones. It is the shifting relationship between the core strategy and its hedges and complements, the argument runs, that creates the impression of unruly variety. One consequence of these risk redistribution strategies is the emergence of production structures that blur hierarchical distinctions within firms, the boundaries between them, and the boundary between firms in a particular area and the public and private institutions of the local society. I will call such production structures meta-corporations or Moebius-strip organizations: meta-corporations because they are designed to be easily redesigned[4] and Moebius-strip organizations because, as with a looped ribbon twisted once, it is impossible to distinguish their insides from their outsides. Another consequence is a constant reordering of versatile and rigid technologies that reflects, among other things, guesses about the longevity of the parts of a product in relation to the whole as well as uncertainty about those guesses.

The second argument concerns the effects of these organizational and technological ambiguities on the labor market. The claim is that the spread of the new production structures creates demand for skilled labor while undermining the fixity of any particular job. Workers under these circumstances must acquire skills, including the ability to cooperate in particular settings in order to be employable, yet cannot rely on long-term relations with any single employer. To learn what they need to learn in order to move from job to job in an economy in which boundaries between firms and between firms and society are blurring, they must join various networks that cross company lines and reach from the economy into social and family life. I will call this situation an open labor market to distinguish it from craft labor markets, which are based on traditional connections to particular materials or processes, and the internal labor markets of the mass-production industry, which are based on long-term employment in clearly bounded corporations. Because of Groucho Marx's notorious fascination with ambivalent attractions, I will refer to the employees' experience of open labor markets as the creation of Groucho Marx identities.

So great are the mutual benefits of flexibility in the world of fluid organizations and open labor markets I am about to describe that it may almost seem as if coercion in any form has no place within it. But flexibility, of course, creates or depends on vulnerability of the most diverse kinds, and vulnerability invites the exercise of power by the less vulnerable. Nor is there any reason to think that those excluded from the emergent flexible economies will accept exclusion without a fight. In the conclusion, therefore, I underscore the novel aspects of conflicts within the new economy and between its beneficiaries and others—above all, the significance of the radical disjuncture between these two kinds of struggle.

THE META-CORPORATION:
RECONCILING LEARNING
AND MONITORING

This section begins with a sketch of a new form of organization that hedges its risks not through portfolio diversification into unrelated activities but by learning to move rapidly from declining markets or market segments to prosperous ones in the same or related industries. The precondition of this strategy is increased internal flexibility, and its consequence is the opening of the borders between corporations and between the economy and local society. But flexibility and openness create new problems of coordination. The second part of the section, therefore, argues that responses to these vulnerabilities are consistent with the reintegration of conception and execution and depend on overcoming the distinction—traditional in theories of organization of the firm—between learning and monitoring or trust and control. For reasons of space, I limit discussion in this section to large firms in the manufacturing sector.[5] But the argument developed here applies to large service-sector firms, particularly in banking, insurance, and retail merchandising.[6] Nor is it vitiated by the current wave of mergers and acquisitions. On the contrary: Incomplete as it is, the evidence to date suggests that in the United States, at least, the redeployment of assets expedites the redistribution of operating authority described below.[7] Elsewhere I have presented convergent arguments regarding the organization of small- and medium-sized firms (Sabel 1989).

Market Fragmentation and the Logic
of Development Costs

Imagine a world in which technology and consumer tastes are in continual but not spasmodic flux. Consumers are always wanting new kinds of cars but are unlikely to abandon them all in favor of bicycles. Products and processes constantly appear that are superior to current ones in many ways, but it is rare for the improvements to be so great that existing goods simply lose all utility. Consumers are willing to pay a premium above the price for standard goods for differentiated products that satisfy their particular wants. Implicitly, they evaluate their purchases as would users of investment goods: not by considering absolute cost but by comparing the ratio of price to performance, understood precisely as the capacity to meet particular wants. Because of advances in flexible process technologies, it is possible to reduce the cost differential between standard and specialized goods so much that increasing numbers of investment-minded consumers are willing and able to pay the premium for the latter. As they do so, they reduce the market for standard goods, raising costs to mass producers and forcing them ultimately to find ways to differentiate their own products—thus aiding in the improvement of flexible process technologies, further reducing the cost differential for customized goods, and setting the stage for further repetitions of the cycle.

In a world of stable markets, firms use dedicated or product-specific resources—special-purpose machines and semi-skilled workers—to mass produce standard goods. Their chief problem is the amortization of the fixed costs of these resources. But under the circumstances just described, the corporation's main problem is the reduction of development time and costs.[8] By assumption, product runs are short, and physical investment goods (as opposed to the computer programs that often control them) can be reused because their flexibility dramatically reduces retooling expenses. Hence, development costs are a rapidly increasing share of production costs. By the same assumption, goods are only marketable for a short period before successor products reduce their value. By any comprehensive accounting measure, therefore, it is pointless to reduce development costs unless development times can be reduced as well.

To reduce the burden of development costs, it is necessary to reintegrate the conception and execution of production plans in the sense of redefining both as joint problems that must be solved simultaneously. Designs are only commercially viable if they facilitate manufacture at acceptable costs; profitable investment in small-batch manufacturing depends on an understanding of design sufficient to make well-informed estimates of the range of flexibility required to produce several generations of a product in all its variants. Because the problems are linked in this way, solutions to one suggest solutions to the other, and the expense of solving the joint problem can be reduced. From this, it follows that conception and execution must be concurrent rather than sequential activities, with efforts to realize plans leading to their refinement and these refinements facilitating their realization. Development costs and time can thus be simultaneously reduced because the same process that makes possible more efficient use of underutilized expertise also speeds its flow. A good illustration of these principles is the production of low-budget, or—as they are called in the trade—fast-track, Hollywood films. Shooting often begins before the screenplay is complete; each day's work on the set advances the story line for the text. In the mid-1980s, average development time for a new car was 48.2 months for Japanese producers and 60.4 months for U.S. car makers. Development work in Japanese automobile firms proceeds analogously (see Clark et al. 1987, pp. 729–776; Fujimoto 1989).

At the limit, the drive to reduce development costs will lead to a blurring of the boundaries between, and the hierarchical distinctions within, firms. The first step is the administrative decentralization of the corporation. Responsibility for design, manufacture, and sale of a narrowly defined range of products (small copiers, headlights as opposed to taillights, large turbines, and the like) is assigned to quasi-independent operating units. The corporation often becomes, in effect, a holding company that makes strategic decisions, raises capital, allocates it among the operating units, and periodically monitors general performance. By rotating promising managers through different kinds of jobs in different operating units, headquarters also forms a corporate elite that understands the needs of the concern as a whole. The corporate planning, accounting, research, and technical staffs are cut to the bone, if not disbanded or reorganized as wholly owned subsidiaries that must sell their services to other operating units or outside firms. Thus, the corporation becomes more a federation of companies than a single organizational entity.[9]

A typical next step is for the operating units to reduce the risk, cost, and time of designing new products by seeking partners who take substantial responsibility for defining and manufacturing key components or aggregates of companies—modules—of the final product. Collaborative arrangements allow the firm to learn from its partners' experiences in their own and other industries without assuming responsibility for their survival; make it possible to shift direction rapidly should there be a truly revolutionary technical breakthrough; and—above all—concentrate scarce investment funds on exploring those technologies that at any moment define the integrity of the firm and its products.[10]

Prominent examples of this kind of collaborative manufacturing are computer "systems" firms such as Sun Microsystems, a leading California maker of engineering workstations. Sun designs its own microprocessor (which is manufactured by several "process specialists"), writes software linking many commercially available components, and assembles the final product.[11] Many major automobile firms now develop the electronic control mechanisms that regulate engines, brakes, and the relationship between these and other components of the car in collaboration with external suppliers. Many plan to or already enlist suppliers in the design and production of modules such as seats, instrument panels, brakes, doors, or bumpers.[12]

At the limit, problems of reducing development costs for successive models shade into the problem of maintaining the firm's long-term innovative capacity: its ability to learn of and profit from ideas that do not square with its organizational habits. Collaborative manufacturing grows out of and reinforces the assumption that it is no longer possible to distinguish between incremental improvements in product and process technologies and radical breakthroughs or even to determine the relevance of research in one specialized area for work in another. Clues to great advances in one field can be found in apparently routine development work or apparently distant research in another area. A large firm might, therefore, complement its new supplier relationships with a minority stake in some of its key partners (a way of symbolically transforming repeated contractual exchanges into an enduring relationship between entities with mingled identities and shared destinies). It might supplement these relationships by diversifying and decentralizing its own core research and development facilities. This can be done by investing in firms experimenting in potentially relevant but unproven technologies, hiring a venture-capital firm to assemble a portfolio of such investments, creating internal ventures to develop interesting ideas, or establishing design departments in the operating units. In the extreme case, which I will call collaborative manufacturing, producing a component or conducting research in a particular area become ways of learning what needs to be known to choose and monitor the external partners who assume the full burden of production and investigation.

By the same logic, hierarchical distinctions within corporations blur as conception and execution are integrated to encourage projects that can be rapidly produced and production set-ups that can accommodate new projects. *Integrated engineering* is the U.S. term for the interpenetration of design and production engineering just described. Closer to the shop floor, supervisors and the work groups they lead assume responsibility for many of the residual industrial engineering tasks required to complete the translation of design into efficient manufacturing practice. Within the work team, increasingly skilled workers assume some of the responsibilities for set-up, maintenance, logistics (particularly control of work flow), and quality control that were parceled out to specialized departments in the mass-production system.

The explosive proliferation of project groups or teams in firms of all sizes and branches is perhaps the best expression of the blurring of internal hierarchical distinctions and company boundaries. Whereas the aim of interdisciplinary committees in the mass-production corporation was to harmonize the application of standard operating procedures in different parts of the organization, the role of the new project teams is almost the reverse: to introduce new procedures, production methods, and products in precisely those situations where current practice inhibits innovation. The teams are typically composed of specialists from a variety of disciplines and companies and are distinguished by large nominal differences in hierarchical rank. Thus, a team responsible for introducing a flexible manufacturing system for one family of components might include design and production-planning engineers, programmers, skilled workers, and representatives from sales and marketing as well as from the vendors of the capital goods and network software to be used in the new system. Teams of this sort often undertake projects lasting five or more years; and many managers, technicians, and workers develop their careers by moving to successively more responsible jobs in different teams. To the extent that the project teams are empowered to combine disciplines in ways that produce analogous but otherwise unachievable changes in the larger organization, they are the institutional emblem and indispensable agent of the meta-corporation.

A final consequence of the reintegration of conception and execution, one that further blurs the boundary between firms and between the economy and society, is the formation of regional economies: clusters of firms with different specialties working in various combinations to serve common markets.[13] First, the more volatile markets become, the riskier it becomes to hold inventory—hence, the need for just-in-time logistics, which require that suppliers put production units, warehouse facilities, or transportation hubs close to their major customers' plants. Second, the more volatile the markets and technology, the more likely it is that timely knowledge is embodied in everyday experience—the more likely it is, in other words, that knowledge becomes local knowledge. Living together in the sense of learning to speak a common technical or commercial language becomes a precondition for working together. Once firms value such conviviality, they must be present where this expertise is grounded. Call this the localization effect of firms—or of members of a community of producers—on each other. Third, the more specialized a firm becomes, the more it depends on the collective provision of training, research, hazardous-waste disposal, supplemental unemployment or medical protection, environmental monitoring, market information, or warehousing that it cannot provide itself. Many such services can be supplied by private vendors, but, in any particular case, some are almost certain to be provided by, or in partnership with, local authorities. If firms rely on public provision of crucial services, however, they become part of the local political community. Their survival depends on its prosperity. Call this the localization effect of providing a public exoskeleton to specialized firms.

Note, however, that the foregoing does not require all key operations needed to manufacture a complex product to be located in a single region. Some must be, for the reasons just given. But a company often prefers to collaborate with a supplier in a distant network rather than work with a local producer of a key subassembly. Hence, regionalization and internationalization of production may proceed hand in hand; the more robust a local economy, the more it attracts and is attracted to complementary foreign localities. The decisive point is that, whatever the regional distribution of activities, firms in each region have similar relationships to their neighbors and local institutions.

Trust and Mistrust
in the Meta-Corporation

What is, of course, missing from this account of the meta-corporation is reference to the conflicts that make such organizations so hard to construct and maintain. Imperiled corporate staffs can raise the self-interested but legitimate question: What, in their absence, will secure the integrity and coordination of the decentralized operating units? In the same spirit, design engineers, plant managers, and workers told to collaborate with outsiders in the production of subassemblies for which they previously had exclusive responsibility may, in their own self-interest, caution their superiors against the dangers of being too dependent on a collaborator of unproven loyalty. The subcontractor has ample reason to fear closer relations with an overbearing partner. Or a plant manager asked to contribute to a local training program may prefer an in-house program that directly benefits only the company and company employees. And even when there is agreement in principle to decentralize authority, collaborate with outsiders, or share the costs of public goods, fights over who wins and loses from the application of the principle—or even squabbles over how much and by what rules the winners will be paid—are often violent enough to undo the agreement. The upshot is that the benefits of collective learning may be unobtainable because of considerations of factional or personal vulnerability and advantage.

The practical problems are theoretically vexing as well because innovation in general and the meta-corporation in particular seem to depend on the fusion of two well-established but contrary principles of organization. Indeed, given the available theories, the puzzle about the meta-corporation is not that it is ramshackle but that it can stand at all. In the rest of this section, therefore, I suggest how learning organizations address their vulnerabilities by creating novel forms of governances that create the impression of a fusion of opposites.

As all those familiar with debates in this area have already guessed, the contrary principles in question are those of markets and hierarchies (Williamson 1975). On the one hand, innovation seems to require that the actors, individual or institutional, enjoy the entrepreneurial autonomy to act as they see fit and reap the full rewards of their initiative. Otherwise, they will have neither the ability nor the motive to create something novel. On the other hand, insofar as innovation requires complementary, project-, or product-specific investments, success seems to depend on organizational coordination of all the necessary activities. Otherwise, each potential investor would be paralyzed by the fear that, having dedicated resources to the common project, he or she would be at the mercy of partners who might decide to abandon the enterprise, seek other collaborators, or use the threat of doing either as a weapon in renegotiating the bargain. The problem, therefore, is how to induce the coordination without stifling the initiative.

One school of thought, originating in the work of Ronald H. Coase and Oliver E. Williamson, argues that autonomy can be organized if the form of organization is supple enough. In the simplest variant, which virtually no one believes adequate to the case of innovative institutions, control is achieved by means of hierarchical authority: Do as I say because, as my subordinate, you have agreed to follow my instructions.[14] In a second variant, principals control their agents by means of complex incentive systems: Do what I would want you to do if I had your knowledge of the situation because your performance is observable and success will be rewarded.[15]

A still more general variant emphasizes the ownership of property as a means of control. Property owners have a double hold on their agents. First, the agents' skill or human capital is typically useful only when combined with the sort of physical assets the owner possesses. Second, the ownership of assets confers the residual rights of control on the owner: the authority to use or command the use of the physical assets in any way not inconsistent with the applicable laws, contracts, or customs. Thus, the property holder can in effect enjoin collaborators: Exercise your freedom in my interest, or else I will deny you the use of my physical capital without which your autonomy is useless (Hart 1989, pp. 1757–1774).

But just as every new tax produces unintended consequences, including new forms of tax evasion, so every control strategy produces surprises, including elaboration of a counterstrategy. That bureaucratic rules can be used as instruments of individual or group privilege at the expense of the institutional good is among the most common sociological commonplaces.[16] But elaborate incentive schemes are hardly a solution. It can also be shown that in complex situations, defined by multiple and often-conflicting goals, incentive schemes concentrate efforts on activities that the principal regards as less important than those self-interest has led the agents to pursue (Holmstrom and Migrom 1990). Finally, the history of innovative, small-firm start-ups in industries as diverse as steel, semiconductors, and computers suggests that, given broad capital markets, it is hard to control collaborators by holding hostage the physical capital they use (Saxenian 1990).

A contrary school of thought resolves the problem of coordination by observing that, under certain conditions, all potential collaborators rightly assume that each will forebear from exploiting the others' vulnerability. The assumption of mutual forbearance is called trust. Once trust has been established, the parties can assume that they will fairly share the burdens of problems that arise by definition whenever economic exchange is also an occasion for reciprocal learning. Hence, they have nothing to lose and everything to gain from engaging in such exchanges. The origins of trust are obscure in this analysis. Where it is not treated as a social datum, it is regarded as the result of the historical, hard-fought formation of a national, ethnic, religious, or political identity; and the limits of trust in economic affairs coincide with the boundaries of these collective identities. Some of the Nordic analyses of economic networks[17] and many discussions of relations among groups of small- and medium-sized firms in the Italian industrial districts are examples of this line of argument (see Becattini 1990, pp. 37–51). If the maxim of the first school is something close to Lenin's view that trust is good but control is better, the maxim of the second, especially in its Italian variant, is that trust is enough.

The difficulty of this line of argument is that by drawing such a firm distinction between trust and mistrust, it overstates both the robustness of trust relations and the difficulty of establishing them in the first place. But those who depend on trust relations are also most aware of their fragility and most vigilant in protecting them. The vitality of industrial districts—in Italy and elsewhere, today as in the nineteenth century—depends on their ability to establish arbitration boards and joint councils to resolve the constant conflicts that arise between labor and capital, large firms and small, and public providers of collective goods and the firms.[18] The Nordic networks of firms are under the collective tutelage of the trade unions, government, political partners, and—increasingly—local authorities. Conversely, the rapidity with which Japanese managers and U.S. managers following their lead have been able to establish trust relations within plants and between customers and suppliers in the United States strongly suggests that, given the right incentives, trust can be built where it was not previously found.[19] Pursuit of self-interest, in sum, can lead out of but also into relations that are not purely self-regarding; arguments that see control as a substitute for trust or vice versa fail to do justice to that fact and therefore fail as solutions to the coordination problem of innovation.

Between these two positions are, however, intermediate ones that take better account of the complex relationship between trust and self-interest. The simplest of these positions resolves the difficulties of the other two by creating a category—often called the relational contract—that combines descriptive features of the first two while purging them of their troubling theoretical connections. The result is a more believable account of the mixture of vigilance and vulnerability that, in fact, characterizes long-term collaborative exchanges. But here description is a substitute for analysis. Stripped of all local color, the argument is reduced to the unhelpful assertion that relational contracts work when and because they work. Pressed to explain, proponents of this view typically use the kinds of culturalist or group identity explanations characteristic of the trust school. Ronald Dore's analysis of subcontracting relations in the Japanese textile industry or William G. Ouchi's discussions of the network clans that occupy the typological space between markets and hierarchies are examples (see Dore 1983, pp. 459–482; Ouchi 1980, pp. 129–141).

Another strand of the intermediate position, the one I will follow, cuts deeper by attacking the distinctions between trust and mistrust and the corresponding forms of governance. One theme, as developed by Jeffrey L. Bradach and Robert G. Eccles, is that the shortcomings of one form of governance can be overcome if that form is combined with another possessing compensating strengths. A fast-food chain, for example, can learn much from its franchisees, but it finds their behavior hard to monitor. The situation is the reverse with its wholly owned outlets. By owning some outlets and franchising others, therefore, the company learns both how to innovate and how to monitor the risks of innovation (Bradach and Eccles 1989, pp. 97–118). A related theme in their work and in that of Arthur L. Stinchcombe is that apparently distinct governance structures can make use, albeit in different forms, of the same features or institutions. The existence of a market can thus facilitate the creation of trust relations by providing price information that serves as a self-evident, mutually agreeable boundary condition on an exchange that is already subject to strain through constant renegotiation of its other aspects (Stinchcombe 1985, pp. 121–171). This deconstruction of governance structures and the categories of trust and mistrust explains why, for example, in Dore's characterization of large Japanese firms, "cooperative pursuit of common goals" goes hand in hand "with vigilant monitoring to ensure that the costs and benefits of achieving those goals are fairly shared" (Dore 1989, p. 6). The argument can also be extended historically to show how trust relations can be built and destroyed, although I will not do so here.[20]

What I want to claim here is that the meta-corporation is pressing this intermediate argument toward its radical conclusion. The effort to group governance structures with complementary strengths is accompanied by an effort to create institutions in which the distinction between learning and monitoring is reduced to the point of imperceptibility. Thus, as noted earlier, production in a system of collaborative manufacturing is both a means of learning how to make things better and a way of learning how to select and monitor partners. The transformation of central technical staffs into quasi-independent companies serves the same double end. The rotation of managers through different jobs in different operating units is a variation on this theme. It forms a corporate elite that is good at monitoring complex tasks because of the variety of tasks it has learned and that has learned the importance of learning through its diverse experiences in monitoring. Notice, however, that the creation of institutions and careers that blend learning and monitoring does not imply the end of corporate conflict. There will still be more or less self-interested fights about organizational integrity, vulnerability, and equity. The meta-corporation's hope, I believe, is simply that the new governance structures increase the likelihood that the parties to the disputes will have come to an understanding of themselves and the organization that favors a resolution in the latter's interest.

The meta-corporation is in its infancy, and study of it has hardly begun. But for present purposes, I think, baby steps will do. If the foregoing suggests how organizations' reintegration of conception and execution converges with their reconciliation of monitoring and learning, the stage is set for another aspect of the argument: consideration of the way Moebius-strip organizations use technology.

TECHNOLOGICAL DIVERSIFICATION

Whereas almost all students of organizational behavior or corporate strategy agree that something fundamental is going on and then proceed to argue about the interpretation of widely agreed, stylized facts, observers of technology are divided as to whether there is much new to talk about and whether the apparently new is truly novel. At issue is the interpretation of the variety of production forms intermediate between mass production and the caricature of universal materializing machines. Are they renovations of the former? Anticipations or variants of the latter? Or hybrids that reflect market conditions that are themselves intermediate between mass and specialized production? As in the previous section, the claim is that the actors have realized the dangers of pursuing either of two strategies long regarded as mutually exclusive and exhaustive—monitoring or control versus learning and trust, and the use of rigid, dedicated equipment versus flexible, programmable machines—and have discovered how to combine elements drawn from both.

Three Views of Flexible Technologies

Three views of the deployment of new technologies dominate current debate. The first of these emphasizes the continuing primacy of the large firms, either because technological innovation is being assimilated by existing organizations and patterns of authority (see, for example, Hirsch 1985, pp. 160–182) or because technical or economic barriers block diffusion of flexible automation equipment (or networks of such equipment) to smaller firms.[21] These arguments regarding the limitations of small firms simply do not stand up to close empirical scrutiny, as we will see. The problem with the others is that in their haste to answer the undoubtedly important question of who is in control, they overlook the possibility that the new system might operate according to a logic of its own (Amin and Roberts 1990, pp. 185–219).

The second view in the debate purports to show the plasticity of technology and the way its use depends on the economic and organizational setting into which it is introduced. Sociologists such as Hans-Jürgen Ewers, Carsten Becker, and Michael Fritsch (1989) as well as Arndt Sorge and his colleagues (Sorge et al. 1982) find that—other things being equal—small-batch specialized production favors the use of versatile, programmable equipment operated by skilled workers, whereas high-volume production favors more rigid uses of such equipment by much less skilled workers. In conjunction with Eckart Hildebrandt and Rüdiger Seltz's monograph on the West German machine-tool industry (1989), this work establishes the capacity of small firms to adopt single pieces of flexible technology and increasingly to connect them by computer into networks.[22] The limitation of these studies is that in emphasizing local situations—particularly the extreme ones—they obscure the crucial influence of the whole of any production system on the formulation of each of its parts.

A third, business school view describes best-practice cases and draws conclusions about the relationship of skill and sophisticated technology for managers. The surprising result of the work of Ramchandran Jaikumar (1986, pp. 69–76) and John F. Krafcik and John Paul MacDuffie (1989) is that the rigid, low-skill use of the new technology appears to be much more expensive—perhaps prohibitively so—than the context school's finding suggested. These scholars argue that the *real* choice firms face is between a high-productivity, high-quality, flexible, high-skill system and a low-productivity (because frequently broken), low-quality, low-skill one. But here, too, the focus on a general lesson—that skill is a precondition for the effective use of the new technologies in all settings—has distracted attention from the ways different uses of technologies influence one another.

Mechanizing Flexible Production

There are two principal methods of mechanizing flexible production. Each can be deployed to produce a fixed number of variants of a single product (flexible mass production) to accommodate an unpredictable number of variants of related products (what I will call fully flexible manufacturing or flexible specialization). In some situations, the two methods are fungible, and firms choose the one with which they have had the most experience. In many other situations, however, considerations of cost in relation to various kinds of uncertainty lead firms to prefer one method over the other or a combination of both to either by itself.

The first method of mechanizing flexible production is by means of versatile or programmable equipment. At its most rigid, this system resembles a programmable variant of the traditional mass-production transfer line: a sequence of single-purpose machines linked by an automatic conveyance system operating at a fixed rhythm. If the individual machines are more versatile and less rigidly coupled, the set-up becomes what is typically called a flexible manufacturing system. These systems are capable of manufacturing a range of parts defined by, say, a common size and prismatic geometry. At their most versatile, automation systems of this first type consist of general-purpose capital goods linked by reroutable transfer mechanisms.

In machining operations, flexibility in this type of automation is typically achieved with programmable machining centers, which literally transform themselves from one type of machine tool to another through automatic tool changes: a lathe becomes a mill, which becomes a borer, and so on. In assembly, the latest robotics makes possible equally versatile equipment that might, by analogy, be called assembly centers. These are batteries of from ten to thirty independently programmable robots that together position, clamp, weld, or otherwise fasten an extraordinary variety of complex parts or subassemblies. They, too, transform their mechanical identity through tool changes. Conveyance is by systems that route parts individually from workstation to workstation, either by automatically guided vehicles (robot carriers) controlled by magnetized strips buried under the factory floor or by self-powered monorail carriers moving along an overhead track system. By decoupling the progress of the work pieces, these systems make it easy to manufacture different models in arbitrary sequences, reconfigure the flows of production when new models are introduced, and divert parts from disabled to operating machines or to buffer stations.

The second method of mechanizing flexible manufacturing is by what I will call snap-on capital goods. By these I mean machines and machine attachments such as jigs or dies that can be incorporated in a matter of minutes, if not seconds, into the production process as the need arises. Snap-on machines typically occupy an intermediate position between dedicated and versatile equipment. One example would be a press with a restricted operating range but not optimized for production of a particular part at a given speed and pressure; another would be a small spray-painting unit capable of covering pieces of a given size with a limited number of coatings. Snap-on machine attachments are built according to norms that facilitate their rapid substitution and lower their production costs. Dies for stampings, for example, will be of a standard height to speed insertion into the press, and design elements common to a family of dies will be inventoried by computer and reused as needed in the construction of new attachments. Here, too, conveyance among machines ranges from a rigid conveyor to a reroutable mechanical transfer system to a push cart.

Used most restrictively, snap-on capital goods simply reduce the set-up times necessary to change from one variant of a product to another on a traditional mass-production manufacturing line. If many different, easily substitutable specialized machines are grouped so that by altering the flow of the work piece it is possible to perform a wide range of constantly varying operations, the system becomes a snap-on variant of fully flexible manufacturing. Between these extremes are what the Japanese call U-shaped, or horseshoe, lines (see Ikeda et al. 1980). These are sequences of easily replaced or retooled specialized machines. The number of machines exceeds the number of persons serving them. Operators select those machines required to manufacture particular pieces, and the composition of the machine part changes as the product range is altered. The horseshoe configuration simply reduces the effort required to move the work pieces through the appropriate sequence. The U-shaped line is the snap-on equivalent of the flexible manufacturing system.

The choice between versatile and snap-on technologies depends on expectations about the volatility of product mix and the length of model life as well as the relative prices of machinery of each type. These, in turn, are related to certain principles of product design and investment characteristics of the two types of flexible automation in ways that pattern the deployment of technology in a flexible economy.[23]

Take first the question of product design. In the previous section, we saw that modularity—the conception of products as a system of systems—emerged as an answer to the problem of cutting development costs and time. But modularity is also a means of reducing the costs of producing many variants of a single product by, in effect, extending the life of some of its components. The greater the range of end products, the greater the benefits in reduced production costs of creating variety through combinations of parts drawn from a limited number of parts families[24] (components of different dimensions but with closely related geometric characteristics and produced with the same equipment) or subassemblies, each of which can be varied without compromising its compatibility with the others. Subassemblies, moreover, can be decomposed into easily recombinable subunits or components. But, of course, the expected longevity of particular parts or modules varies greatly with respect to the life expectancy of the end products of which they are components, and, in a world of short product life cycles, these differences determine whether a particular component is provided in high or low volumes. Barring a truly revolutionary technological breakthrough, for example, a family of car engines produced in one facility might be expected to power two or three model generations over the course of fifteen to twenty years. A brake family might be expected to equip one generation of models in all its variants during a seven-year life. A door or seat assembly might change every year or two to accommodate new styles in interior design.

Take next the investment profiles of versatile versus snap-on mechanization. All else being equal, programmable equipment requires greater initial investment per unit output than does a snap-on system. Decisions regarding the moment-to-moment choice of machines and tools are made manually in the latter and by a combination of hard- and software in the former. And what is true moment to moment is all the more true for long periods. The product range of all snap-on systems can be modified piecemeal as needed. Programmable systems must be able to perform operations for which demand may emerge near the end of the productive life of the capital equipment. (The fully flexible variant of professional automation is an exceptional case because it is anticipated that machines with new characteristics will be introduced into the system.) The higher initial costs of programmable systems are offset by lower operating costs, but whether the initial difference in investment can be recouped depends on total production during the lives of the respective installations.

Hence, two simple rules of thumb emerge. First, the longer the life of the parts family or module, the more it is likely that it will be built by programmable rather than snap-on equipment. Second, the less predictable the range of output—the less tightly coupled—the closer either type of system will be to being fully flexible. Several examples will illustrate this double calculation at work.

One point of reference is the engine plant. The product, however variable by comparison to earlier standards (when a change in the number of cylinders meant junking a whole production line), is still relatively homogeneous. Output levels are high; thus, rapid operations are of the essence. Investments in sophisticated capital goods that are both versatile and fast can be amortized over a long period. Under these conditions, the preferred solution is flexible mass production: a line of programmable but specialized machines—programmable boring machines, not machine centers—linked by a fast-moving conveyance system.[25]

Final assembly facilities illustrate the opposite pole in the application of programmable technologies. The final assembly is the module of all modules, and the plant that can connect all subassemblies should be usable for all modules of any current generation and for many successive generations of a product. What we should expect here is precisely what we see, as anticipated in the preceding discussion: the rapid introduction of programmable assembly cells or loosely coupled sequences of programmable workstations. FIAT managers, for example, estimate that they will be able to reuse at least 80 percent of the capital goods in the new Cassino plant south of Rome in the manufacture of cars yet to be designed. They are confident, moreover, that it will be possible to use flexible routing systems and shift work to introduce new models into the plant without ceasing production of currently salable ones. They, like Volkswagen managers at Emden, also claim on the basis of experience to date that all of the firm's current models could be produced in any desired combination at their respective plants.

Headlight production illustrates the typical setting in which snap-on technology dominates. The product will be altered every year or two to give a more stylish look to a range of models and variants that will be fundamentally renewed only once every seven or eight years. In addition, the number of variants of the subassembly produced for any type of car is likely to be large because, for example, the trim and other design elements of the subassembly must match those of the rest of the car. Total production volumes will be high, and ideally the subassemblies will be produced and delivered in the sequence in which they will be installed on the final assembly line. Hence, the headlight producer needs high-volume production facilities whose capacity to vary the mix of current products does not limit the capacity to change the components of that mix at short intervals.

The U-shaped line meets these requirements. Some stations are bays of two or three machines of the same type, equipped to produce production of a different variant of the subassembly. A single worker loads the appropriate machine as required. Other stations consist of scaled-down versions of continuous process equipment—machinery for heat treatment or for applying coatings or finishes—that has been adapted in-house to suit the requirements of the materials being worked. By reducing the size (and generally the operative range) of, for example, the general-purpose painting equipment and painting the subassembly in the production line rather than in a distinct painting department, the firm reduces the complexity of its logistics. This arrangement also creates the optimal conditions for learning how to improve this kind of manufacturing operation. Given that the basic principles of miniaturization (and much of the necessary hardware) in any particular process area are likely to change rather slowly, the costs of developing successive generations of equipment are modest.[26]

Similar considerations govern the choice of technology used to manufacture the various types of capital goods themselves. Thus, versatile, programmable machines tend to be produced by flexible manufacturing systems, whereas snap-on machines or machine attachments are produced with versatile equipment deployed as in the fully flexible factory. The more flexible the capital goods, the smaller the risk to owning them and, thus, the greater the manufacturer's potential market. General-purpose machines, particularly if they are lower- or medium-priced, will therefore tend to be produced in relatively long runs with a limited range of variants. Various flexible manufacturing systems are well suited to producing the different geometrically defined families of parts from which successive generations of such equipment are built. And in fact, Japanese producers of large numbers of programmable lathes or machining centers for small- to medium-sized job shops typically favor such systems for their high-volume products.

Taken as a whole, the discussion so far illustrates one cross section of the technological strata of an economy in which products are short-lived but demand is still stable enough to make confident guesses about the relationship between average product life and the longevity of its chief components. In the automobile industry, to continue with our dominant example, the top stratum—the one closest to the final consumer—consists of flexible assembly plants using a combination of robotic assembly cells and sequences of discrete, programmable equipment, the balance between the two depending on the design of the car. At the next level are the suppliers of high-volume modules. Producers of relatively long-lived modules favor flexible mass production; producers of short-lived modules favor snap-on equipment arranged in U-shaped or horseshoe lines. At a still lower stratum are the capital goods suppliers. Some of these will be using flexible manufacturing systems to produce versatile equipment such as assembly robots and the machining centers. Other capital goods producers will be using fully flexible technologies to produce snap-on machines and machine attachments. A more complete cross section would, of course, have to include references to the technological choices of the high- and low-volume su-bassemblers' own suppliers, including those in steel and other process industries.

But even if it were thus extended, a fundamental limitation would remain to this attempt to match types of flexible technology to positions in a production system governed by a global logic of market diversification and technological malleability. Firms are, in fact, often not as certain in their estimates of product and component longevity as I have assumed. Nor are they as sure about the relative costs, much less *trends* in the relative costs, of versatile compared with disposable technologies.

The consequence of these additional uncertainties is that the technological hedging strategies—the firm's choice of a particular type of mechanized flexibility as the least risky given the concurrent choices of other firms in the same economy—are themselves hedged. An obvious way to accomplish such second-order hedging is to create hybrid solutions: production systems that combine, say, versatile and snap-on technologies in a way that facilitates subsequent changes in the balance between them. Such hybrids can be observed in the constitution of individual machines, the composition of single production lines, or the simultaneous pursuit of different technological strategies by different plants making similar products in the same firm. It is more and more common, for example, to see presses or complex grinding machines that are both programmable and designed for use with snap-on attachments. The U-shaped line, with its characteristic combination of loosely coupled, disposable machinery and scaled-down, general-purpose equipment, is—in principle—also such a hybrid, although I have emphasized the dominant role of the easily replaceable specialized machines. FIAT plans to build several plants on the Cassino model to accommodate short-run models and fluctuations in demand. The cars that can be sold in higher, more predictable volumes will be produced at less flexible facilities. In practice, U.S. firms seem to arrive at these hybrids as they try to eliminate the defects in technologically thoroughbred systems or correct unambiguous and incorrect bets on the future. Western European and Japanese firms, in contrast, arrive at them by combining—as in the U-shaped line—isolated pieces of diverse technologies and strategies, each introduced for reasons of its own.

But in any case, there is now substantial agreement in all three advanced manufacturing zones that, with regard to choices of technology or orga-nizational design, there are guiding principles—those, namely, that follow from hedging guesses about the implications of the logic of flexibility—but few principled solutions in the sense of the thoroughbred models presented thus far. And even when firms *do* choose thoroughbred solutions, they tend to hedge the choices by making sure that they have access to alternatives through contact with suppliers, other divisions of the company, or consultants. This kind of virtual diversification ensures that, at a minimum, no sequence of decisions in favor of one type of technology accidentally becomes irre-versible.

Looked at from afar, therefore, the technologies deployed in a flexible economy will seem to be an assortment of hybrids, with only loose associations between types of equipment and types of production. Looked at from the inside, however, any one of the hybrids or selected clusters of them will appear to result from the application of straightforward principles of technical choice under uncertainty to a limited set of equipment types, all more flexible than traditional mass-production machinery and more productive than the repertoire of traditional flexible machines.

This is the place, finally, to discuss skill. Studies done at the Soziologisches Forschungsinstitut in Göttingen and the Institut für Sozialwissenschaftliche Forschung in Munich document clearly the extent to which workers operating versatile capital equipment require increasing fundamental knowledge of a greater variety of disciplines to do their jobs.[27] In the case of workers who program their own equipment or maintain complex systems, traditional distinctions between blue- and white-collar work are breaking down. It is plain that workers tending machines in the bays of U-shaped lines are less skilled than workers programming machining centers, although in some cases they may be as skilled as the operators of flexible manufacturing systems. But it is easy to make too much of these absolute differences in skill level. What is perhaps more interesting is the fact that, whatever their current jobs, workers in different positions in these production systems are plainly having to extend their skills in overlapping ways. The worker in the U-shaped line must start off adept at several jobs and learn to set up or program several pieces of equipment and to manage the ever-changing work flow in his or her area.[28] The craft worker using a versatile machine has to become more adept at managing logistics when that machine is linked with others, and so on. What workers face in common is the continuing need to augment and adapt their skills to the changing needs of the workplace. Peer Hull Kristensen's studies of work in small- and medium-sized Danish metalworking plants show a similar pattern as well (1987).

The need for skilled adaptability of this kind is, furthermore, the common finding of recent studies of emergent types of employees in a variety of work settings and countries. Research by Thierry J. Noyelle (1987), Larry Hirschhorn (1988, pp. 19–38), and Lauren Benton and colleagues (Benton et al. 1989) on the reorganization of the service sector calls attention to the abandonment of internal job ladders in banking, insurance, and retailing firms. As part of a strategy of permanent innovation, these internal labor markets are being replaced by a system of "horizontal" recruitment into project groups of generally trained persons with various specialties; extensive programs of continuing education equip the group members for new tasks. "We want to hire people who have a general capacity to become specialists, over and over again," a bank official told Benton and her collaborators (Benton et al. 1989, p. 49). The work of Eckart Hildebrandt and Ruediger Seltz (1989, p. 149) on the introduction of computer-controlled machinery in the West German machine-tool industry shows that design and production engineers are making "spiral" careers by advancing from project group to project group in different firms, rather than by the traditional climb up the hierarchy of a single firm. Rosabeth Moss Kanter's study (1989) of managerial career patterns in recently reorganized U.S. corporations uncovered a great variety of ways of getting ahead, including some similar to the one revealed by Hildebrandt and Seltz, all predicated on the impossibility of progressing step-by-step up a hierarchy—typically because hierarchies of the familiar type no longer existed.

The limitations of such studies are well known.[29] But they are all we have, and they tell a common story. In the next section, therefore, I will draw out the implications of the need to constantly acquire new skills in an uncertain institutional environment for the employee's relationship to work.

OPEN LABOR MARKETS
AND GROUCHO MARX IDENTITIES

The characteristics of labor markets and the experience of work in the world of the meta-corporation are shaped by two related paradoxes that follow directly from the drive to reintegrate conception and execution. The first is that the same considerations that lead to an increasing demand for skill make it increasingly difficult to fix the definition of particular jobs and give them a secure institutional place. Skill is the ability to execute incomplete or indicative instructions, and the meta-corporation's reintegration of conception and execution plainly depends on the cooperation of skilled persons in sales, design, and manufacturing and the outside suppliers—all with an intimate, almost instinctive, knowledge of the corporation's needs. But reliance on the skills of outsiders, especially the constantly shifting but more intimate relationship to subcontractors (the systems suppliers) and consultants (the former staffs reconstituted as independent firms, or complete outsiders operating on the open market), makes it impossible to say what will go on inside and outside the firm: Just as the outer edge of a Moebius strip flows into its inner edge, so activities inside these organizations can move outside, and vice versa.[30] And when the status of entire production or research units can change in a matter of months, or when everyone anticipates this possibility, production workers, technicians, and engineers must constantly wonder how they will survive if they are looking for a job.

Hence, a characteristic ambiguity exists in employees' identity. They must be loyal to the work-group or corporation in order to execute concepts while reconceptualizing them. But to whom, in the Moebius-strip organization, is this loyalty owed? Conversely, the meta-corporation owes its employees *its* loyalty. Why else would employees accept the uncertainty of permanent reorganization? But given permanent reorganization, to whom is the meta-corporation promising this loyalty? Recall Groucho Marx's observation that he would not want to be a member of any club that would want him for a member. As it tries to retain the freedom to recombine resources without destroying its employees' loyalty, the meta-corporation is becoming the kind of club Groucho Marx would always *consider* joining.[31]

The second distinguishing paradox of the open labor market is this: Work in the restructured economy simultaneously increases and limits the employees' autonomy in the world of life outside it. Employees who are encouraged to think of themselves as entrepreneurs, to treat their employer as a market, and to pay attention to hazardous materials are forced to manage resources and risks in ways that make it easier to imagine changing the conditions of their lives. The conceivable changes range from going into business for themselves to becoming much less tolerant of environmental threats at home. But this enhanced autonomy is simultaneously qualified by the same situation that produced it. Just as the firms form networks with one another and their environment in order to keep abreast of local knowledge, so do individuals secure their long-term employability through participation in neighborhood groups, hobby clubs, or other professional and social networks outside the firm. Only those who participate in such multiple, loosely connected networks are likely to know when their current jobs are in danger, where new opportunities lie, and what skills are required in order to seize these opportunities. The more open corporate labor markets become, the greater the burden these networks will have to bear and the greater will be the economic compulsion to participate in the social activities they organize.

Hence, just as it is becoming harder to say for whom one works, it is becoming harder to say when one is working. Activities at work become preparation for turning the family into a family enterprise that absorbs all leisure; family and leisure activities become preconditions of employability. Anticipation of these possibilities undermines the distinctions between *work, leisure,* and *family.* A limiting case is the two-earner household, which could not enter the labor market at all if it did not participate in the community life of day care centers, schools, or neighborhood improvement associations and whose double dependence on the local labor market can only be managed by careful use of all the information about employment this participation provides.

IN SEARCH OF A NEW
LANGUAGE OF POWER

At the outset, I said that power might almost seem to disappear from the world of the meta-corporation but that this appearance would be deceiving. As a conclusion, I will distinguish the power struggles within the restructured economy from power struggles between it and the persons and firms it excludes. My purpose is to underscore the novelty of the relation between these two kinds of conflicts and to point toward an understanding of that relation by showing how it escapes traditional categories of analysis.

The discussion of trust and governance structures has foreshadowed the analysis of conflicts within the meta-corporation. Wherever there are bilateral monopolies—wherever, that is, two parties benefit from an exchange relation that neither can easily carry on with a third—the party that ultimately depends less on the relation can extract the greater share of the total benefits. To do so is to exercise power in the familiar sense of bargaining power.

By making everyone dependent on the expertise of everyone else, the meta-corporation creates a web of bilateral monopolies. Governance structures that simultaneously encourage learning and monitoring limit these conflicts but do not eliminate them. The many open questions in this regard are obvious. Will suppliers be able to use their growing expertise to augment their margin of maneuver by establishing independent relations with the market? Will managers put their expertise at the service of outside stakeholders or their coworkers? If the latter, will employees use their increasing skills to play a sustained and concerted role in shaping the large questions of corporate strategy or even national economic policy? Certainly, the disparities in labor's power in different systems of mass production—compare the roles of trade unions in Sweden and the United States in the 1960s and 1970s—strongly suggest that nothing in the logic of any particular industrial order determines the outcome of such bargaining conflicts or the composition of the alliances to which they give rise. In this sense, context and contingency—local, regional, and national—matter.

The conflicts between those inside and those excluded from the world of the meta-corporation are different. These groups are not mutually dependent in the sense that each requires the cooperation of the other to achieve its ends. In a learning economy, workers must possess substantial skills to acquire more. The unskilled, therefore, have little chance to set foot in the factory; they do not have value as a labor reserve or even as a reservoir of purchasing power. Markets are more likely to be international than national. Without global management of aggregate demand, a skilled worker or engineer will have a greater interest in the earning power of his or her counterparts in other countries than in that of an unskilled neighbor. As conflict becomes disentangled from the possibility of mutually advantageous exchange, the exercise of power becomes a clash of wills, an existential struggle between friends and foes in which the control of resources is seen as a precondition of collective survival.

In the traditional sociology of work, there was a clear connection between the two kinds of power: The exercise of bargaining power ended in existential struggle. The archetypal case was, of course, Marxism, in which the proletariat is dispossessed, deskilled, immiserated, and emarginated before rising up against the investor class to reclaim its possessions, prowess, and social place. Even absent a determining logic of technological development and despite the differences between mass-production and Moebius-strip corporations, it is tempting to categorize potential conflicts in the new economy by analogy to these familiar tropes.

The first possible outcome evokes the idea of proletarianization. The ins stay in and the outs stay out, maintained by welfare systems and casual employment that guarantee their physical survival while sapping their capacity to change their situation. In the meta-corporations, small groups of workers use their market power to extract privileges at the expense of the excluded or their coworkers, further decreasing the chance of any redistribution of rights in favor of the outsiders. The suggestion is that if there is any justice in this world, the social tensions these divisions produce will eventually lead to chaos or to the effort to construct a more inclusive alternative.

This second, inclusive outcome corresponds to the classic idea of the socialization of the means of production. In this alternative, the struggles for power in both senses are linked in a way that weakens the grip of the owners of capital on the meta-corporation while widening the circle of the flexible economy to include more and more of the unskilled. The key to this solution is the formation of a new kind of labor movement, born of the existing trade unions or other organizational experiences. Instead of directly regulating conditions of work in firms or industries, this labor movement would help employees acquire the skills and knowledge of the labor market they need to move from job to job, while also enabling them to manage the changing relationship between work and the rest of life. By providing these services, this movement would become as indispensable to the meta-corporation as other systems suppliers, while encouraging older firms—daunted by skill shortages—to reorganize as meta-corporations. To succeed nationally, the new labor movement would seek allies by pressing for legislation facilitating the redistribution of resources from prosperous regions to those that needed to restructure. It would also have to build a popular constituency by pressing for the protection of individual and group rights to self-determination at the workplace and becoming the paladin of an educational and vocational training system open to all. Here is a new bloodless version of the revolutionary victory of reason and solidarity.

Many now argue that we in the United States have already begun to inhabit the first world (see National Center on Education and the Economy 1990). There is a widening debate with the West European labor movement directed toward achieving some version of the second.[32] Yet despite this verisimilitude, I think these evocative analogies obscure what is most novel and conceptually disorienting about the new economy: the chasm between insiders and outsiders and the amorphous relationship of insiders to one another.

Thus, to associate exclusion from the meta-corporations with proletarianization is to invite confusion of abandonment with exploitation. The association suggests that the losers in the new economy are insufficiently compensated for their contribution to production, whereas we have seen that what they are losing is the possibility to make *any* contribution to the economy. Throughout the history of industrialization, the unskilled were recruited from farming, petty commerce, or artisan workshops into the factories. They—or, more likely, their children—learned the skills they needed by doing successively more demanding jobs. Whether such employees were justly compensated for their contributions is, of course, open to debate. That the barriers between the high-skill economy and the subsistence borderlands have been raised is not. Exclusion may be more inhuman than exploitation insofar as the winners' absolute indifference to the losers is more brutalizing than even a master's twisted reliance on a slave. But to raise that possibility, it is necessary to acknowledge the difference between the two. Surely, one task of a new sociology of work will be to inquire into the connections— if any—that family ties, political allegiances, welfare rights, and other circuitous exchange relations create between insiders and outsiders in the new economy. Or, to put the point the other way around, what barriers will questions of gender, ethnicity, and social origins create between them?

Association of the second, inclusive outcome to the idea of the socialization of the means of production likewise tends to foreclose discussion of troubling questions. The association suggests not only that the more inclusive economy would be less vulnerable to social conflict than the exclusive one (which seems plausible) but also that it might lack *any* significant conflict (which hardly follows). The world of inclusive meta-corporations might be a world of cabals and cliques in which the struggle for an honorable place *within* the community of production constantly threatens the forms of cooperation on which productive flexibility depends.[33] Or to avoid this danger, it might be a world in which workplace autonomy was combined with, even dependent on, forms of social conformity persons of my generation once associated with the post-war U.S. suburbs and those in the United States now associate with Japan. What would be the role of women in either of these societies? Of men? Or the meaning of citizenship?

Notice, however, that this inclusive world does not correspond to the idea of a pluralist society, at least in its U.S. variant. Pluralists believe the identity of each individual is the composite of the vector of his or her attachments to groups of different kinds.[34] But the identities of these groups are fixed by ethnicity, religion, or place in the division of labor. In the meta-corporate world I am describing, individuals form and reform identities by reference to groups whose own identities are constantly in flux. Individuals are thus not the "natural" result of the accidental combination of "natural" collective self-understandings. Surely, a second pressing task for a new sociology of work is, therefore, to better characterize the substance of solidarity within the meta-corporation.

A world in which the boundaries within and among firms and between the public and private are blurring is not a world without boundaries. New boundaries, indeed new kinds of boundaries, are being drawn as the old fade. To detect them, we need not only a new language of analysis but new concepts of equality and fairness. And by the oldest paradox in the book, once we have such a language and such concepts, we will begin to change the very boundaries we discuss.

NOTES

1. The most comprehensive version of the thesis that the rationalization of work deskilled almost all those active in production is Braverman (1974). For a view of continuous process control workers as potential revolutionaries, see Mallet (1963). For the view that the acquisition of new skills by such workers will lead to novel

forms of cooperation, rather than conflict, with management, see Blauner (1964). For a history of the modern corporation consistent with the assumptions regarding technological development underpinning the work of Braverman and Mallet, see Chandler (1977).

2. Two excellent studies that illustrate this tendency are Jones (1990, pp. 293–309); and Salais and Storper (1990).

3. Michael Piore and I have been cited enough as victims of this fantasy so that I would not dream of pointing the finger at someone else. Although many persons hold some part of the views caricatured in the text, no one—ourselves included—comes close to holding them all. But see Piore and Sabel (1984) and judge for yourself.

4. For an early discussion of institutions with related capabilities, see Stinchcombe (1965, pp. 34–35).

5. When not otherwise indicated, the following composite account of the meta-corporation is based on interviews with managers in more than thirty U.S., French, Italian, Japanese, Swedish, Swiss, and West German multinationals conducted between 1985 and 1990. The firms are leaders in the automobile, automotive parts, computer, chemical, electrical equipment, food processing, garment, machine-tool, opto-electric, telecommunications, and textile machinery industries. Interviews with capital goods manufacturers in Baden-Württemberg (conducted with Gary Herrigel) in July 1986, with U.S. and West German automobile and automotive parts manufacturers (conducted with Herrigel and Horst Kern) in January and July–August 1989, and with managers of a large Italian manufacturer of men's and women's clothing (with Richard Locke) between 1988 and 1990 were especially important in forming my views. For more on the firms surveyed and the results, see Sabel, Herrigel, and Kern (1990); and Kern and Sabel (1990, pp. 144–166).

Many of the features of the meta-corporation have been described at length in the management literature. For representative references, see Sabel (1989, pp. 17–70, fn. 65). Of the many recent portraits of large-firm reorganization, including decentralization of authority to quasi-independent units with responsibility for particular product lines or markets, intensified collaboration with outside suppliers, and elimination of staff or its reintegration with line operations, one of the best is "Small Earthquake: IBM Slightly Hurt," which appeared in the *Financial Times* in installments on April 24, 25, 27, and May 2, 1990. A more rigorous analysis of this ensemble of changes is the Harvard Business School case study of the reorganization of Allen Bradley's Industrial Computer and Communication Group. See Harvard Business School, "Allen Bradley's ICCG: Repositioning for the '90's" (Case N9-491-066, December 20, 1990).

6. For restructuring in the service industry, see Bailey (1989), Benton et al. (1989), Hirschhorn (1988), Noyelle (1987), and Oberbeck (1986).

7. A recent and comprehensive study finds, first, that acquirers of the unbundled assets of firms that are taken over are already expert in the use of the assets they are buying. This suggests that companies are concentrating their efforts in particular lines of production, not diversifying risk through acquisition of unrelated businesses. The study finds, second, that the new owner companies tend to close the headquarters of firms they acquire and to lay off white-collar, but not blue-collar, workers. This suggests that the acquirers' aim is to eliminate bureaucracy in general and to push responsibility for decisions down to the operating units in particular. Third, whereas headquarters are closed, production facilities are not. This suggests that the acquirer is not seeking to achieve economies of scale in production through consideration of plants. See Bhagat et al. (1990).

8. In a recent survey, approximately four hundred chief executives of U.S. companies cited "shortened product-development cycles" as their first priority. See Kleinfield (1990, pp. 1–6).

9. The reduction in size of corporate headquarters is documented in a recent study of the New York City economy, where 74 of the Fortune 500 companies were based in 1988. In one case presented as typical, a corporation with $2 billion in sales and 25,000 employees in 1989 reduced its headquarters staff from 500 in 1980 to 90 in 1989. Of those who left headquarters, 300 were "dispersed to line companies," and 110 were victims of "downsizing." For this and other examples, see Telesis (1989).

10. For an analysis of new subcontracting strategies regarding the U.S. manufacturing industry, see Helper (forthcoming, 1991). For subcontracting in Japan, and especially the growth in the subcontractors' autonomy in relation to the customers' efforts to increase flexibility, see Nishiguchi (1989).

11. On Sun and similar firms, see Saxenian (1990).

12. An extreme is BMW, which pays 75 percent of the total cost of components to outside suppliers and, but for considerations of prestige, would have subcontracted construction of cylinder heads, one of the most sophisticated components of its engines.

13. For more on the formation of such economies, see Sabel (1989).

14. For a nuanced presentation of this view, see Williamson and Ouchi (1981, pp. 347–370).

15. For examples of this kind of argument, see Pratt and Zeckhauser (1985).

16. For one of the best statements of the view, see Crozier (1964).

17. Laage-Hellman (1987, pp. 26–83); and Johanson and Mattsson (1987, pp. 34–48). But note that the network school has an ambivalent view regarding the origins of trust. It is treated both as a datum—the result, essentially, of "a similar cultural and educational background"—and as the outcome of increasingly complex and demanding exchanges with various partners. See, for both views, Laage-Hellman (1987, pp. 63–64).

18. For the role of such organizations in modern Italian industrial districts, see Trigilia (1990, pp. 160–184). For an example of the importance of regulatory institutions in the industrial districts of nineteenth-century Europe, see Boch (forthcoming).

19. For an evaluation of the striking success of the Japanese transplants and U.S. firms applying Japanese organizational principles, see Womack et al. (1990, pp. 85–87).

20. A related argument derived from the theory of repeated games shows how firms can lower the cost of establishing trust relations by acquiring a reputation for reliability through forebearing behavior; how fear of jeopardizing this reputation also checks opportunism; and even how the need to ensure that all employees act accordingly leads to formulation of a corporate "culture" understood as the injunction not to exploit the vulnerability of partners. In a fuller treatment of the problem of the passage from mistrust to trust and back, it would be necessary to connect this last variant to the second. See Kreps (1990, pp. 90–143).

21. Cainarca et al. (1987). Yet another variant asserts that large firms will dominate the economy because of the need to coordinate innovation through hierarchy. For this view, see Antonelli (1989, pp. 33–45). The preceding discussion suggests that if "big" firms are needed to solve complex coordination problems, they will be big in a sense radically different from the traditional understanding of the large firm that informs this line of argument.

22. "The introduction of the newest computer technologies depends ever less on the financial strength and organization potential of large firms. The building blocks of systems rationalization [the connection into networks of discrete pieces of computer-controlled equipment] are also affordable for middle-sized firms" (Hildebrandt and Seltz, pp. 439–440).

23. Notice, however, that the cost estimates in turn depend on the relationship between the design of the final product and the firm's automation strategy. The added cost of the complex cells performing many operations is compensated, in theory, by the relaxation of design constraints needed to assure efficient manufacture in a greater number of simpler steps.

24. A good discussion of "parts family" or "group" technologies is Brödner (1990).

25. There is, however, nothing immutable about such a solution. If the cost of versatile capital goods sinks rapidly enough, it may prove efficient to build smaller, more dedicated facilities serving one assembly plant rather than many, or more flexible, plants that dramatically increase the range of engine variants offered by any one company. See Hervey (1987–1988, pp. 15–19).

26. Managers typically acknowledge the dangers associated with dedicated equipment but argue that in many cases of module production, rewards in efficiency more than outweigh the risks.

27. Two good examples of the current research are Düll and Lutz (1989); and Baethge et al. (1989).

28. For a good discussion of the relationship between increased flexibility in routing work in progress and the need to "cross train" operators in a variety of jobs, see Bailey (1989).

29. There is little aggregate evidence of increased inter-firm mobility of skilled workers, technicians, or managers in the large-firm sector in those countries, notably the Federal Republic of Germany and Japan, where these firms are expanding. And much of the scanty evidence that exists, moreover, is contradictory.

A recent test of human capital theory, for example, found that both U.S. and Japanese firms with high levels of training did not have low levels of turnover. Companies that rewarded workers with longer tenure also did not have lower turnover rates. At the least, these findings do not support the view that increases in training are leading to a closure of corporate boundaries. See Levine (1990).

Other studies show that the large firms are hoarding their most qualified employees because they value their scarce skills. But the studies do not explore the possibility that the firms are retaining skilled personnel precisely by offering them opportunities for self-development normally achievable only through job changes. A high official of a leading Japanese opto-electronics firm told me, for example, that in his company, engineers collaborated in project teams with outsiders and entered into joint ventures with them. To offset these fissiparous tendencies, the company planned to turn itself into the center of opto-electronic research in Japan, not least by creating a kind of internal research university. "If we succeed in that," he said, "anyone who wants to realize a technological dream in this industry will have to maintain an institutional association with us." In any case, surveys report that the newest entrants to the work force seem more disposed to change jobs than their counterparts in earlier cohorts. See generally, Büchtemann (1990); and Dore et al (1989, pp. 55–66). It is worth noting, finally, that the business press is beginning to advise managers to acquire a portfolio of skills that make them marketable outside as well as inside the large corporation throughout their entire working lives. See Handy (1990).

30. One of the limiting cases of this kind of labor market is found in the software conversion industry. Converters rewrite software developed for one type of computer

so that it will run on another machine. A successful conversion firm must organize work so that its employees are integrated into its clients' organizations (otherwise the programmers will not acquire the necessary expertise), and it must advertise its success in achieving this result. But what is a firm that can only succeed on the condition that it enables its employees to move on to other firms and that is known for doing so? For whom are its employees working? For a wide-ranging discussion of this case, see Stinchcombe and Heimer (1988, pp. 179–204).

For an argument that the gains in learning this kind of career mobility makes possible can outweigh such costs as additional training and disruption of authority, see Rochlin et al. (1987, pp. 76–90). There is an almost 100 percent turnover of the crews of the U.S. Navy's aircraft carriers every 40 months. Service tradition prescribes constant rotation of sailors and officers. Because almost everyone except a small core of senior enlisted specialists is constantly learning a new job, the situation encourages the general willingness to collaborate in mastering surprises necessary to maintain high-tempo flight operations under conditions that, given changes in technology and sea conditions, could not be stabilized in any case. The more general point is that if everyone in the aircraft carrier fleet knows how to learn from each other, it does not matter—and may even be a benefit—that the crews of individual ships are not fixed. For the economy, the analogous units would be craft or professional communities and firms.

31. In discussing their attachments to their work, middle managers in U.S. corporations are beginning to speak of "commitment" (to particular projects or work-groups) rather than loyalty (to an imprecisely defined corporate entity). This change reflects fear that they could be the next victims of restructuring. But in part, it may also reflect a change in the way obligations to employers as persons and institutions are conceptualized generally. See Heckscher (1990).

32. For a fuller statement of the argument and further references, see Kern and Sabel (1990).

33. See Mauss (1990, pp. 7–8; 35–37) for the view that the struggle for honor can be as socially disruptive as the struggle for wealth in a monetary economy.

34. On pluralism as defined in U.S. political science, see Truman (1953). British pluralists had a view of the reciprocal constitution of individual and group closer to the one suggested above. See Hirst (1989).

REFERENCES

Amin, Ash, and Kevin Roberts. 1990. "Industrial Districts and Regional Development: Limits and Possibilities." Pp. 185–219 in Frank Pyke, Giacomo Becattini, and Werner Sengenberger, *Industrial Districts and Inter-Firm Cooperation in Italy*. Geneva: International Labour Organisation.

Antonelli, Cristiano. 1989. "Capitalismo Flessibile o Capitalismo Organizzato?" *Politica ed Economia* 6:33–45.

Baethge, Martin, and Herbert Oberbeck. 1986. *Zukunft der Angestellten. Neue Technologien und Berufliche Perspektiven in Büro und Verwaltung*. Frankfort: Campus Verlag.

Baethge, Martin, Rolf Dobischat, Rudolf Husemann, Antonius Lipsmeies, Christiane Schiersmann, and Doris Weddig. 1989. "Gutachten über Forschungstand und Forschungsdefizite im Bereich Betrieblicher Weiterbildung Unter Besonderer Berücksichtigung der Belange der Mitarbeiter und Darguf Aufbauend Erarbeitung Einer Zukunftsweisenden Forschungskonzeption." Göttingen: Soziologisches Forschungsinstitut Research Report.

Bailey, Thomas. 1989. "Technology, Skills, and Education in the Apparel Industry." Technical Paper No. 7, Conservation of Human Resources, Columbia University.

Becattini, Giacomo. 1990. "The Marshallian Industrial District as a Socio-Economic Notion." Pp. 37–51 in Werner Sengenberger et al., eds., *Industrial Districts and Inter-Firm Cooperation in Italy*. Geneva: International Labour Organisation.

Benton, Lauren, Thomas Bailey, Theirry J. Noyelle, and Thomas M. Stanback, Jr. 1989. "Training and Competitiveness in U.S. Manufacturing and Services: Training Needs and Practices of Lead Firms in Textile, Banking, Retailing, and Business Services." New York: Conservation of Human Resources, Columbia University.

Bhagat, Sanjai, Andrei Shleifer, and Robert W. Vishny. 1990. "Hostile Takeovers in the 1980s: The Return to Corporate Specialization." Brookings Paper, Graduate School of Business, University of Chicago.

Blauner, Robert A. 1964. *Alienation and Freedom*. Chicago: University of Chicago Press.

Boch, Rudolf. Forthcoming. "The Rise and Decline of 'Flexible Production': The Solingen Cutlery Industry Since the Eighteenth Century." In Charles F. Sabel and Jonathan Zeitlin, eds., *Worlds of Possibility: Flexibility and Mass Production in Western Industrialization*.

Bradach, Jeffrey L., and Robert G. Eccles. 1989. "Price, Authority, and Trust: From Ideal Types to Plural Forms." *Annual Review of Sociology* 15:97–118.

Braverman, Harry. 1974. *Labor and Monopoly Capital: The Degradation of the Work in the Twentieth Century*. New York: Monthly Review Press.

Brödner, Peter. 1990. "Computersysteme: Ersatz oder Hilfsmittel des Menschen in der Produktion." Working Paper, Institut Arbeit und Technik, Gelsenkirchen.

Büchtemann, Christoph. 1990. "Employment Security Policy in Europe: Some Lessons from the West German Experience." Paper prepared for the International Labour Organisation/International Institute for Labour Studies/Wissenschaftszentrum Berlin International Conference on Workers' Protection and Labor Market Dynamics, Berlin, May 16–18, 1990.

Cainarca, Giancarlo, Massimo G. Colombo, and Sergio Mariotti. 1987. "Innovazione e Diffusione: Il Caso dell Automazione Flessibile." *L'Industria* 4:251–299.

Chandler, Alfred D., Jr. 1977. *The Visible Hand: The Managerial Revolution in American Business*. Cambridge, MA: Harvard University Press.

Clark, Kin B., Takahiro Fujimoto, and W. Bruce Chew. 1987. "Product Development in the World Auto Industry." *Brookings Papers on Economic Activity* 3:729–776.

Crozier, Michel. 1964. *The Bureaucratic Phenomenon*. Chicago: University of Chicago Press.

Dore, Ronald. 1989. "The Management of Hierarchy." Paper presented to the Nomisma Conference "Industrial Policy: New Issues and New Models: The Regional Experience," Bologna, Italy, November 16–17, 1989.

————. 1983. "Goodwill and the Spirit of Market Capitalism." *The British Journal of Sociology* 34:459–482.

Dore, Ronald, Jean Bounine-Cabalé, and Kari Tapiola. 1989. *Japan at Work: Markets, Management and Flexibility*. Paris: Organization for Economic Community and Development.

Düll, Klaus, and Burkart Lutz, eds. 1989. *Technikentwicklung und Arbeitsteilung im Internationalen Vergleich*. Frankfort: Campus Verlag.

Ewers, Hans-Jürgen, Carsten Becker, and Michael Fritsch. 1989. "Der Kontext Entscheidet: Wirkungen des Einsatzes Computer-Gestützter Techniken in Industriebetrieben. Pp. 25–63 in Schettkat, R., and M. Wagner, *Arbeitsmarktwirkungen Moderner Technologien*. Berlin: Walter de Gruyter.

Fujimoto, Takahiro. 1989. *Organizations for Effective Product Development: The Case of the Global Motor Industry*. Ph.D. dissertation, Graduate School of Business Administration, Harvard University.

Handy, Charles. 1990. *The Age of Unreason*. Cambridge: Harvard Business School Press.

Hart, Oliver. 1989. "An Economist's Perspective on the Theory of the Firm." *Columbia Law Review* 89:1757–1774.

Heckscher, Charles. 1990. "The Managerial Community." Manuscript, Graduate School of Business Administration, Harvard University.

Helper, Susan. Forthcoming. "Strategy and Irreversibility in Supplier Relations: The Case of the U.S. Auto Industry." *Business History Review*.

———. 1990. "Supplier Relations at a Crossroads: Results of Survey Research in the U.S. Auto Industry." Program Paper, Center for Regional Economic Issues, Case Western Reserve University.

Hervey, Richard P. 1987–1988. "Engine Manufacturing Strategies for the 1990s." *AiM Newsletter*, Michigan Modernization Service, Winter: 15–19.

Hildebrandt, Eckart, and Ruediger Seltz. 1989. *Wandel Betrieblicher Sozialverfassung Durch Systemische Kontrolle? Die Einführung Computergestützer Produktionsplanungs-und-Steuerungs-Systeme im Bundesdeutschen Maschinenbau*. Berlin: Edition Sigma.

Hirsch, Joachim. 1985. "Fordismus und Postfordismus: Die Gegen-Wärtige Gesellschaftliche Krise und ihre Folgen." *Politische Vierteljahresschrift* 26(2):160–182.

Hirschhorn, Larry. 1988. "The Post-Industrial Economy: Labour, Skills and the New Mode of Production." *The Service Industries Journal* 8(1):19–38.

Hirst, Paul, ed. 1989. *The Pluralist Theory of the State: Selected Writings of G.D.H. Cole, J.N. Figgis, and H.J. Laski*. London: Routledge.

Holmstrom, Bengt, and Paul Milgrom. 1990. "Multi-Task Principal-Agent Analyses." Manuscript, Yale School of Management, Yale University.

Ikeda, Masayoshi, Shoichiro Sei, and Toshihiro Nishiguchi. 1980. "U-Line Auto Parts Production." International Motor Vehicle Program Paper, M.I.T.

Jaikumar, Ramchandran. 1986. "Postindustrial Manufacturing." *Harvard Business Review* 64:69–76.

Johanson, Jan, and Lars-Gunnar Mattsson. 1987. "Interorganizational Relations in Industrial Systems." *International Studies of Management and Organization* 17(1):34–48.

Jones, Bryn. 1990. "New Production Technology and Work Roles. A Paradox of Flexibility Versus Strategic Control?" Pp. 293–309 in R. Loveridge and M. Pitt, eds., *The Strategic Management of Technological Innovation*. New York: John Wiley and Sons.

Kanter, Rosabeth Moss. 1989. *When Giants Learn to Dance*. New York: Simon and Schuster.

Kern, Horst, and Charles F. Sabel. 1990. "Gewerkschaften in Offenen Arbeitsmärkten: Überlegungen zur Rolle der Gewerkschaften in der Industriellen Reorganisation." *Soziale Welt* 2:144–166.

Kleinfield, N.R. 1990. "How 'Strykforce' Beat the Clock." *New York Times*, Business section, March 25, 1990:1, 6.

Krafcik, John F., and John Paul MacDuffie. 1989. "Explaining High-Performance Manufacturing: The International Automotive Assembly Plant Study." Working Paper, International Motor Vehicle Program, M.I.T.

Kreps, David M. 1990. "Corporate Culture and Economic Theory." Pp. 90–143 in James E. Alt and Kenneth A. Shepsle, *Perspectives on Positive Political Economy*. Cambridge: Cambridge University Press.

Kristensen, Peer Hull. 1987. "Udkanternes Industrielle Miljo." Manuscript, Institute of Economic and Social Policy, Copenhagen.

Laage-Hellman, Jens. 1987. "Process Innovation Through Technical Cooperation." Pp. 26–83 in IHåkan Håkansson, ed., *Industrial Technological Development*. London: Croom Helm.

Levine, David. 1990. "Tests on Human Capital Theory in the United States and Japan." Manuscript, School of Business Administration, University of California at Berkeley.

Mallet, Serge. 1963. *La Nouvelle Classe Ouvriere*. Paris: Editions du Seuil.

Mauss, Marcel. 1990. *The Gift*. Trans. W. D. Halls. New York: W. W. Norton.

National Center on Education and the Economy. 1990. *America's Choice: High Skills or Low Wages*. Rochester: National Center on Education and the Economy.

Nishiguchi, Toshihiro. 1989. *Strategic Dualism: An Alternative in Industrial Societies*. Ph.D. dissertation, Subfaculty of Sociology, Nuffield College, Oxford University.

Noyelle, Thierry J. 1987. *Beyond Industrial Dualism: Market and Job Segmentation in the New Economy*. Boulder: Westview Press.

Ouchi, William G. 1980. "Markets, Bureaucracies, and Clans." *Administrative Science Quarterly* 25:129–141.

Piore, Michael J., and Charles F. Sabel. 1984. *The Second Industrial Divide: Possibilities for Prosperity*. New York: Basic Books.

Pratt, John W., and Richard J. Zeckhauser, eds. 1985. *Principals and Agents: The Structure of Business*. Boston: Harvard Business School Press.

Rochlin, Gene I., Todd R. La Porte, and Kathlene H. Roberts. 1987. "The Self-Designing High-Reliability Organization: Aircraft Carrier Flight Operations at Sea." *Naval War College Review* 40:76–90.

Sabel, Charles F. 1989. "Flexible Specialization and the Re-emergence of Regional Economies." Pp. 17–70 in Paul Hirst and Jonathan Zeitlin, eds., *Reversing Industrial Decline? Industrial Structure and Policy in Britain and Her Competitors*. Oxford: Berg.

Sabel, Charles F., Gary Herrigel, and Horst Kern. Forthcoming 1991. "Collaborative Manufacturing: New Supplier Relations in the Automobile Industry and the Redefinition of the Industrial Corporation." In H. G. Mendius and U. Wendeling-Schröder, eds., *Zulieferer im Netz-Zwischen Abhängigkeit und Partnerschaft*. Cologne: Bund Verlag.

Salais, Robert, and Michael Storper. 1990. "One Industry, Multiple Rationalities: Flexibility and Mass Production in the French Automobile Industry." Working Paper No. D901, School of Architecture and Urban Planning, University of California at Los Angeles.

Saxenian, Annalee. 1990. "The Origins and Dynamics of Production Networks in Silicon Valley." Working Paper No. 516, Institute of Urban and Regional Development, University of California at Berkeley.

————. 1990. "Regional Networks and the Resurgence of Silicon Valley." *California Management Review* 33:89–112.

Sorge, Arndt, Gert Hartmann, Malcolm Warner, and Ian Nichols. 1982. *Mikroelektronik in der Industrie: Erfahrungen beim Einsatz von CNC-Maschinen in Grossbritannien und der Bundesrepublik Deutschland*. Frankfort: Campus Verlag.

Stinchcombe, Arthur L. 1965. "Organization-Creating Organizations." *Trans-Action* 2(2):34–35.

————. 1985. "Contracts as Hierarchical Documents." Pp. 121–171 in Arthur L. Stinchcombe and Carol A. Heimer, eds., *Organization Theory and Project Management*. Oslo: Norwegian University Press.

Stinchcombe, Arthur L., and Carol A. Heimer. 1988. "Interorganizational Relations and Careers in Computer Software Firms." *Research in the Sociology of Work* 4:179–204.

Telesis. 1989. "A Strategic Audit of Manufacturing in the New York–New Jersey Metropolitan Region." Report prepared for the Port Authority of New York and New Jersey. N.p.

Trigilia, Carlo. 1990. "Work and Politics in the Third Italy's Industrial Districts." Pp. 160–184 in Pyke, et al., *Industrial Districts.*

Truman, David B. 1953. *The Governmental Process: Political Interests and Public Opinion.* New York: Alfred A. Knopf.

Williamson, Oliver E. 1975. *Markets and Hierarchies. Analysis and Anti-Trust Implications.* New York: The Free Press.

Williamson, Oliver E., and William G. Ouchi. 1981. "The Markets and Hierarchies Program of Research: Origins, Implications, Prospects." Pp. 347–370 in Andrew Van de Ven and William Joyce, eds., *Perspectives on Organizational Design and Behaviors.* New York: John Wiley and Sons.

Womack, James P., Daniel T. Jones, and Daniel Roos. 1990. *The Machine That Changed the World.* New York: Rawson Associates.

Comments

Richard Biernacki

Charles Sabel has presented us with a set of bold conjectures from which our enterprise of social inquiry can certainly benefit. My comments will cover two sets of issues. The first concerns the status of the model and the way we ought to use this model to carry out further research. The second concerns the way we should situate the model of changes in the use of technology in a broader picture of social change.

In presenting a model of flexible manufacturing, Sabel intended to outline only a highly stylized portrait of an emergent trend. He has given us what Max Weber would have termed an *ideal type,* as he is not concerned with the question of whether any firm exhibits *all* the characteristics described— flexible specialization, subcontracting, the merger of product design and production, and so forth. I would like to ask whether we can chisel this portrait down to a set of criteria that will let us place any given firm in the sector of flexible manufacturing. Is a definition of flexibility always relative to other firms in the same industry, or can we make cross-industrial comparisons in flexibility to measure the degree of flexibility in the economy as a whole? This may not be possible. If not, we will have difficulty convincing skeptics that we are indeed experiencing an emergent trend and that an increasing number of firms conform in some way to a new ideal type.

This seems especially important if one considers the circumstance that employment in the manufacturing sector, to which Sabel confines himself, is shrinking both relatively and absolutely. Less than one-fifth of the labor force is now engaged in manufacturing. It seems relevant to ask whether the trends sketched in manufacturing are paralleled by changes in the service sector. It might be that the use of technology and the identities of the manufacturing workers as corporate actors are changing in the manner he describes. But if the changes are unique to that sector, and if they affect only a small portion of those employed, what importance ought we attach to this for our society as a whole?

The question of whether we can clearly differentiate between flexible versus Fordist styles of production is important not only for deciding where the core industrial countries are headed in the future, but for deciding where they were in the past. Just how widespread *was* Fordist-style mass production in the past? It is no surprise that many investigators—including Sabel— have found that in the Wuppertal in Germany or in the silk mills of Lyons, textile factories that concentrated on the production of short runs of specialized fabrics do not fit the model of Fordist production.

What *is* surprising, however, is that social and industrial historians who study the late nineteenth and early twentieth centuries find examples of flexible specialization in the most unexpected places: in the core mass-production industries. Consider the British cotton textile industry of Lancashire, which is often taken as the first quintessential mass-production industry. Recent research on spinning by William Lazonik has characterized the industry as a short-batch enterprise, in which entrepreneurs attempted to take advantage of short-term fluctuations in the costs of raw materials. Richard Marsden traced the way in which many towns in Yorkshire installed looms that could rapidly change the patterns they wove to match trends in fashion. Heavy investment in the creation of new fabric designs and trial and error experimentation with new finishes of cloth were essential for the survival of firms. Newspaper reporters in the 1850s in Lancashire commented on the way individual towns in Lancashire retained independent definitions of fashion and on the way these definitions could change rapidly within a locality without affecting an adjacent town. In other words, flexible specialization in textiles was not confined to a few pockets: It characterized the textile trade as a whole.

By citing such examples I mean to suggest only that inflexible, standardized mass production may always have been the exception rather than the rule. It seems as though we assume that what we have not investigated historically must have been inflexible mass production. Yet, every time a social or industrial historian investigates an industry, he or she finds it is more flexible than previously supposed. Unless we come up with a clear measure of flexible manufacturing, we may mislead ourselves into thinking we are entering a new age when we are only becoming more aware of alternatives that have not merely survived in a few niches in the past but have always flourished in the mainstream of industrial development.

This brings me to the second set of questions. If we are indeed experiencing a change in forms of manufacturing, can we situate this in a broader picture of social change? I do not disagree with the core assumptions of the model Sabel presented; I only ask how we ought to go about placing it in a larger context.

Sabel mentioned that the shift to flexible manufacturing was caused in part by the diversification of consumer preferences. Is this diversification only a consequence of higher consumer incomes, which allow consumers to pay a premium for custom goods? Does it result from greater inequality in the distribution of income? Perhaps the willingness of consumers to pay a premium for more customized goods reflects cultural changes in the way people use goods to construct their social identities.

Sabel offers some conjectures as to how changes in manufacturing will affect people's identities as producers. I wonder if we can go on to link changes in people's identities as producers to their identities as consumers. We could thus situate Sabel's picture of flexible specialization in an overall model of social change.

Comments

David Stark

In *The Second Industrial Divide*, Michael Piore and Charles Sabel argued that advanced industrial societies are posed at the edge of an epochal transformation from an era of mass production to one of flexible specialization. Whereas the period of mass production was characterized by the use of specialized machines to make standardized products, flexible specialization would be the use of standardized machines to make specialized products. In the current chapter, Sabel makes an important modification of that analysis, arguing that it is unlikely that the corporation of the future will assume a form of totally flexible production. The new forms of flexible production are, in fact, calling forth new forms of mass production—for example, quasi-mass production of the standardized machines themselves or mass production of modules and components to be flexibly assembled. Rather than a uniform system of total flexibility, Sabel sees on the near horizon a complex interplay of fully flexible machines, dedicated machines, and disposable machines.

The problem is how to combine these technologies to the greatest advantage. Under circumstances of extraordinarily rapid technological change and extreme volatility of products and markets, it seems there is no one best solution. Or, if one could be rationally chosen and resources locked in to it alone, the benefits of its fleeting superiority would not compensate for the costs of subsequent missed opportunities. Because managers hedge against these uncertainties, the outcomes, Sabel observes, are hybrid forms. Managers do not simply commit themselves to the array that keeps the most options open, but they create an organizational space open to the perpetual redefinition of what might constitute an option itself. Rather than a rational choice among an array of knowable options, we find practical action fluidly, unself-consciously, redefining what might be an option.

Organization becomes the art of deconstructing organizations that can reorganize themselves.

Managers in such an organizational configuration act not with a theoreticist orientation to a discreetly calculable future but with their practical reason as the temporal dimension within which a given project does not proceed from beginning to middle to end. Rather, production can begin even before product design is completed—with this design itself being modified in the course of production. All of this is predicated upon the elimination (or, at least, the mitigation) of the separation of design and execution. If the industrial world in which we are stepping combines flexible and mass productions, it nonetheless breaks decisively with the Taylorist principles governing mass production in its paradigmatic phase.

Consistent with Sabel's earlier writing on distinct notions of work, honor, and self, in this chapter he also steps beyond *The Second Industrial Divide* in analyzing the relationship between worker identities and systems of flexible production. But I was left to puzzle about this relationship because the version of the chapter I received ended with the cryptic heading "Moebius-Strip Identities and Groucho Marx Clubs," followed by the author's notation, "To be supplied." With this Rorschach test before me, I imagined two possible lines of argument.

In the first of these, flexible production systems would require flexible identities. The shorter the production runs, the more transient the identities; the more varied the work activities, the more kaleidoscopic the personality structures—a postmodern composite of interchangeable traits. Like the Moebius strip with neither inside nor outside, or like a Pynchon novel where the more we try to get inside a character the more we find there is nothing there, in the world of flexible manufacturing we would find disposable identities to run the disposable machines.

In the second possible line of argument, we would more closely follow Sabel's lead in the first part of the chapter and abandon the naive illusion of total flexibility in the sphere of identities no less than in the sphere of production. In such a view, the flexible allocation of labor will indeed require a more fluid worker identity—less attached, for example, to enterprises and occupations. But this maleability in work may in turn require relatively stable identities anchored in larger work-related communities or in spheres outside production altogether. As in the field of production, so in the realm of identities would we find mixes of fluidity and fixity, of flexibility and stability, of the disposable and the dedicated.

Moreover, the institutional prerequisites of a system of flexible manufacturing will require political bargains that establish rules of the game with relative stability. If these political bargains are to have any legitimacy, the parties to them must have relatively stable constituencies—that is, people must identify with social groupings or at least with collective representations of those collective actors. Thus, through this institutional mediation we can again argue that flexible production may require relatively stable identities—in this case, political identities.

It follows that the institutional and worker identity prerequisites of flexible manufacturing cannot be socially engineered. Dynamic flexibility requires a richer social life of voluntary association and more, rather than less, democracy.

I turn now to a related set of issues in a different political and economic context. As my own research is on problems of work, identities, and political transformation in state socialist societies, in reading Sabel's chapter I am led to ask whether the processes of flexible manufacturing he has analyzed have any prospects in socialist economies as we know them today.

Answering this question would require specifying with some analytic precision the characteristic differences between the two social systems. Time does not permit such an explication, but we can evoke some of these differences by briefly comparing the two great organizational theorists at the turn of this century, Frederick Winslow Taylor and Vladimir Lenin. Such comparison typically suffers from a misplaced concreteness focusing on Lenin's fascination with Taylor's scheme as Lenin hoped it could be applied *inside* the new Soviet factories. A more interesting comparison is that, whereas Taylor's followers attempted a rationalizing project of increasingly calculable, predictable, standardized control at the level of the firm, Lenin's followers directed their efforts to the macro-sphere as they attempted to bring an entire national economy under rational control through the budgetary instruments of central planning. Captivated by the technical and organizational accomplishments of the industrial engineers, Lenin sought to engineer the social environment. Both projects, moreover, were tied to knowledge claims. But whereas the scientific management of the firm claimed legitimacy on the basis of "laws" derived from "time and motion studies," the ability to manage an economy scientifically rested on claims to knowledge of the "laws of motion of history."

The irony is that the scientific management of society precluded scientific management at the level of the firm. Rather than eliminating uncertainties, the Leninist project produced new uncertainties from a bureaucratic environment that blocked bureaucratization and routinization on the shop floor. To solve or mitigate the daily uncertainties of supply bottlenecks, forced substitution, and disruptions to production caused by redistributive planning, plant and shop-level supervisors depend on the cooperation of workers within the production process. To secure this cooperation, they engage in selective rather than collective bargaining in ad hoc arrangements that circumvent central wage guidelines and coordinate the flexible allocation of labor within the firm. In short, not by design but by necessity, central planning produces a labor force with broader skills for more flexible allocation.

If, at the level of the socialist shop floor, we find not Taylorism but flexible allocation of labor, might it not be the case that an unintended consequence of central planning (the bureaucratic uncertainties of which, in such an argument, would correspond to the technological uncertainties facing the capitalist firm in Sabel's account) has been to produce organizational forms and worker identities that could form the basis for the kinds of dynamic flexibility Sabel is analyzing? The simple answer is probably no.

The patterns we see are limited to the shop floor as a static flexibility. These are adaptive features, not innovative ones; stopgaps, not breakthroughs. The more complex answer is that there is a germ, however small, of such a possibility. But one thing is clear: The major obstacle to the realization of such dynamic flexibility is the long-standing project of broad social engineering. Its dismantling is on the agenda—whether in efforts to gain recognition of the property rights (and, hence, new identities) of private producers in Hungary or in the recent struggles to gain recognition of the civic rights of union members (and, hence, new collective identities) in Poland—but this dismantling is far from accomplished in the societies of state socialism.

It is in this context—that is, the lessons I take from Sabel's chapter and from existing socialisms—that I feel obliged to state my disagreement with one of the assumptions of this conference: that the task of social theory should be to emulate theory of the physical world to guide the rational engineering of the social world. Sabel, I think, shows that this project is impossible and, moreover, unnecessary. Existing socialism shows that it is a failure. One might argue, of course, that the socialist project was guided by Marxism—a false science—but that its errors will not be duplicated when guided by a true one. I would suggest that any project of social engineering contains the causes of its failure because it is inherently un-democratic and rather than reknitting, it so badly tears the social fabric that its damage can take decades to repair.

With corporate managers rejecting in their practice Taylor's program, and with socialist managers questioning Lenin's, it would be a great irony if, as social theorists, we turn to projects of rationalist engineering from our century's beginning to serve as models for our practice at its close.

POSTSCRIPT

The above comments were written in April 1989, only months before the "revolutions of 1989" in Eastern Europe that brought a non-Communist government to office in Poland, opened the Hungarian border to the West, toppled the Berlin Wall, swept Vaclav Havel into the Czechoslovakian presidency, and executed Nicolae Ceausescu in Romania. This postscript is being written almost a year after those events, in a period in which the initial exhilaration at the speed of the demise of authoritarian regimes gives way to more somber reflection about the difficulties of consolidating dem-ocratic institutions and achieving far-reaching economic transformations in these transitions from state socialism.

There is little doubt that the installation of liberal democratic governments in East-Central Europe will have an important impact on the reorganization of the socialist corporation and the experience of work—for at the same time they are redrawing the boundaries of state and society in the political sphere, the citizens of Eastern Europe are also redrawing the boundaries of public and private in the economic sphere as they seek to transform the fundamental economic institutions and property relations of their societies. But considerable question remains about whether these changes will bear resemblance to the practices of flexible specialization Sabel describes. The socialist corporation is being reorganized, to be sure. In Czechoslovakia, Hungary, and Poland, efforts are underway to "privatize" the assets of the large public enterprises. Throughout the region, a vibrant debate can be heard about the scope and character of this privatization along a set of dimensions including: Should privatization be spontaneous or directed by some central agencies? Should ownership be concentrated or dispersed? And what should be the proportion of foreign ownership in the emerging system of transformed property relations?[1]

At first glance, it might seem that privatization would be a sure means to bring about a new structure of incentives lending themselves to flexible specialization—especially where the constraints of forced substitution in the recent past had produced a less specialized labor force and demanded its more flexible allocation within production. But the actual patterns of re-structured ownership are not promising in this regard. First, although there is much discussion about employee-share ownership and even about issuing privatization certificates (to be converted into shares in particular ventures) to all citizens, in the first waves of privatization the new private owners of the assets of the large public enterprises are most likely to be the former enterprise directors and party apparatchiks of the old regime. In these "nomenklatura buyouts," the old elite is converting its political capital into directly economic capital.

Second, in a situation in which the total private savings of the population are estimated to equal less than 5 percent of the total assets held in state ownership, privatization is most likely to take the form of "institutional cross ownership," in which socialist enterprises transform themselves into joint stock companies exchanging shares in the new companies with those of other reorganized socialist firms rather than being broken up and sold to natural owners. Such institutional ownership is, of course, not uncommon in the West. The problem in East-Central Europe, the critics of institutional cross-ownership charge,[2] is that the habits and modes of calculation of the senior managers of these "reorganized corporations" (who are mutually appointing each other to their new boards of directors) were forged in decades of bureaucratic infighting. With these deeply ingrained habits and practices, these managers will be more disposed to search for subsidies and favorable treatment from the still-powerful (although nominally liberal) state than to initiate organizational innovations.

Third, the kinds of corporate reorganization described by Sabel would require an enormous influx of capital to modernize the obsolete plant and equipment of the region. For the policy makers of East-Central Europe, the attraction of direct foreign investment is precisely this promise of capital for modernization. But despite some highly visible foreign buyouts, the record to date indicates that even bargain basement prices may not lure enough foreign capital to Czechoslovakia, Hungary, and Poland. In the crucial transition period of the coming years, it appears that the greater danger will be too little rather than too much direct foreign investment in these capital-poor economies.

In the long run, perhaps more promising than the reorganization of the large public enterprises are the prospects for economic renewal from the growth of the existing small-scale private producers of the "second economy" that emerged during the past decades in the shadow of the central plan. Can legalization and deregulation of this sector lead to dynamic, innovative, and perhaps flexible manufacturing? Here, too, the immediate prospects are not encouraging. First, despite no shortage of rhetorical proclamations about developing smaller-scale private entrepreneurship, the new governments' actual credit and taxation policies are as likely to damage as they are to promote employment and capital accumulation in this sector. Second, as Sabel and his colleagues have argued, dynamic flexible specialization requires not only competition but also cooperation among producers in specific locales. Research on the "Third Italy," for example, has traced such patterns of cooperation to long-standing institutions that protected society from complete penetration by the market.[3] The problem for contemporary Eastern Europe is that although state socialism prohibited the spread of the market in the past, it also virtually eliminated any institutions of civil society that might form the basis for such cooperation in the near future.[4] Thus, the most pessimistic scenario for East-Central Europe is for capitalism without capital and privatization without a private sector. In such a view, the craft-like skills of the industrial labor force and the entrepreneurial skills of small-scale producers would indeed remain skills without a place.

NOTES

1. For an extended analysis of this debate, see David Stark, "Privatization in Hungary: From Plan to Market or from Plan to Clan?" *East European Politics and Societies* 4 (1990):351–392.

2. See, for example, János Kornai, *The Road to a Free Economy: Shifting from a Socialist System* (New York: Norton, 1990).

3. Carlo Trigilia, "Small Firm Development and Political Subcultures in Italy." *European Sociological Review* 2 (1986):161–175. See also the collection of essays in a special issue of *Economy and Society* 18 (November 1989).

4. István Gábor, "On the Immediate Prospects for Private Entrepreneurship and Re-embourgeoisement in Hungary." *Working Papers on Transitions from State Socialism*, No. 90.3 (Ithaca: Cornell Project on Comparative Institutional Analysis, 1990).

2

The Future of Bureaucracy and Hierarchy in Organizational Theory: A Report from the Field

Rosabeth Moss Kanter

A principal tenet of modern social and economic theory has long been that a large proportion of the production and distribution of goods and services takes place through formal organizations constituted for this purpose and that these formal organizations are characterized by bureaucracy and hierarchy.

Bureaucracy as a concept is itself often used interchangeably with *formalization*; it involves the delineation of a set of positions or offices, with the duties, responsibilities, and rights devolving on the incumbents specified by formal, often written rules and procedures.

Hierarchy is a frequent companion to bureaucracy, as the positions are arrayed in terms of command rights or authority relationships; other privileges and perquisites stem from the position in a chain of command. As modern industrial bureaucracies have developed, hierarchy has developed with them. Business historian Alfred Chandler (1977) found the origins of the modern hierarchy in the mid-nineteenth century, when middle managers evolved to coordinate activities formerly handled by independent contractors in a market relationship. As companies grew in size and complexity, they created divisions that had their own internal hierarchy plus a hierarchy above to connect them to the corporation as a whole.

In the modern bureaucratic-hierarchical organization, level or status became the basis for compensation as well as authority, and the sets of statuses or grades comprising the hierarchy also tended to define the pathway for a career within the organization, from lower to higher positions. The

Portions of this paper were adapted from R. M. Kanter, *When Giants Learn to Dance: Mastering the Challenges of Strategy, Management, and Careers in the 1990s* (New York: Simon and Schuster, 1989).

promise of "promotion" up the hierarchy became a primary inducement for high performance; the alienated and disaffected often sought collective bargaining to improve their lot in a status from which they would not be promoted. Furthermore, there were incentives for the organization to proliferate its ranks and grades—to make more people feel they were "making progress." And there were incentives for getting larger and larger, for adding people; one widespread corporate job evaluation scheme, for example, gives higher compensation to positions with more people under them. The very size and complexity of the corporation itself required more people for purposes of coordination (middle managers) and more specialist staffs to develop the rules that would be administered uniformly throughout.

This brief description of the key components of the model of bureaucracy and hierarchy needs one more element to be complete: the assumption of a closed and bounded system with adequate control over the resources it needs to do its work.

Organizations were not born bureaucratic, of course, so both theory and practice recognized the existence of entrepreneurs and an entrepreneurial phase of organizational life. This was associated with new ventures—that is, organizations not yet institutionalized. Indeed, the initial phase of an organization's existence was assumed to be devoted to developing the bureaucratic administrative apparatus that would then be formalized and routinized—Max Weber's charismatic leader giving way to the administrator. Although some political economists such as Joseph Schumpeter (1942) recognized the vitality introduced into an economy by the "creative destruction" of the entrepreneur, for the most part social theorists devoted their attention to bureaucracy. Good or bad, it was bureaucracy and hierarchy that were thought to define modern economic organizations—even though empirical research found it hard to separate the effects of age (older), size (larger), complexity, and formalization on the organization structure called "bureaucratic" (see, for example, Aldrich and Auster 1986). It was bureaucracy that was at the center of the theory of organizations (and their discontents).

For several decades, at least since the end of World War II, organization theorists have been pointing to the dysfunctions of bureaucracy and hierarchy. In some cases, they have even been active in developing alternatives; Rensis Likert of the University of Michigan, for example, helped General Motors design its approach to greater teamwork and participation at the production level. For the most part, however, such alternatives involved reform within bureaucracy (for example, work units in which supervisors delegated more authority to workers) rather than a total reformulation of the model.

In recent years, the pace of change has accelerated, and the challenge to bureaucracy has entered new realms, especially in the United States but also in Western Europe. U.S. companies are confronting new economic realities of global competition, characterized by rapid technological change, often-constrained resources (due to capital market pressure, debt load, and higher costs of capital than in Japan), and a speed of information transmission and market reach that multiplies the number of competitors in nearly every industry—plus legal changes that create competition for former monopolies, such as the government-mandated breakup of AT&T, or help "upstarts" get a foot in the door, such as airline deregulation.

IN SEARCH OF THE EMERGING
ORGANIZATIONAL MODEL

Between 1983 and 1988, my research team and I conducted extensive descriptive fieldwork in over 80 companies, primarily in the United States but also in Canada and Western Europe, in order to document the ways corporations are responding to environmental challenges (Kanter 1989). Fieldwork was supplemented by a review of national statistical compilations, such as data about employment trends and surveys of corporate practices.

Three generic organizational strategies underlie the response of the companies studied: (1) restructuring to find synergies among pieces of the business—old ones or acquired ones; (2) opening their boundaries to form strategic alliances with suppliers, customers, and venture partners; and (3) developing explicit programs of investment and coaching to stimulate and guide the creation of new ventures from within. These three strategies form the core of a management that is neither purely bureaucratic nor purely entrepreneurial—an evolution of organizational forms that attempts to marry the flexibility, agility, creativity, and leanness of the entrepreneurial form to the large corporation. This shift in ideal corporate form (what Weber called an "ideal type") has major social and economic consequences—for the shape of the paycheck, the nature of the workplace, the connection between work life and personal life, the security of the job, and the form of a career.

For want of a better term, I call the new form *post-entrepreneurial* (Kanter 1989)—the addition of entrepreneurial elements to established companies, moving them away from bureaucracy in order to play effectively the new business "game." Rapid change in the business environment makes the game of business (to use a frequently invoked metaphor) sometimes resemble the croquet game in *Alice in Wonderland*. In that kind of game, every element is in motion—technology, suppliers, customers, employees, corporate structure, government regulation—and none can be counted on to remain stable for very long. It is impossible to win such a game by using bureaucratic and hierarchical forms: tall hierarchies and slow decision-making processes, an emphasis on adherence to formal procedures over achieving results, in-house rivalries and adversarial relationships with stakeholders, risk-averse officials who crush new ideas not directly related to the mainstream business, and rewards geared to climbing the ladder from position to position rather than to accomplishment or contribution.

Instead, corporations are getting in shape for their contests by developing flatter, more focused organizations stressing synergies, entrepreneurial enclaves pushing newstream businesses for the future, and strategic alliances or stakeholder partnerships stretching capacity by combining the strengths of several organizations. Together, these approaches constitute a new model of organization structure for the major corporation. I will summarize the elements of each and some of the evidence for their emergence, from field observations.

Synergies

The first major component of post-entrepreneurial strategy is to seek that combination of businesses, array of internal services, and the structure for organizing them that promotes synergies—a whole that multiplies the value of the parts. The goal is to design leaner, more cooperative, more integrated organizations with fewer layers of management and smaller corporate staffs. A key concept guiding the new corporate ideal corporation is focus: maximizing the core business competence. This contrasts sharply with a tendency to form diversified conglomerates in the period beginning around the 1960s.

At the same time that post-entrepreneurial companies are restructuring their lines of business through mergers, acquisitions, and divestitures in the search for focused combinations that build synergies, they are also reexamining their internal structure to ensure that all activities, all departments, "add value." For example:

- Interested in cutting costs as well as improving delegation downward, a telephone company—once among the most intricately graded of organizations—has almost eliminated an entire managerial level (promotions now jump people from level 3 to level 5 just below the officer ranks) and has doubled supervisory spans of control in its largest unit, which covers 75 percent of all employees.
- An auto giant took its first step toward streamlining by banning all one-to-one reporting relationships (a boss responsible for only one subordinate).
- A widely respected household products manufacturer has gradually thinned its line management ranks by creating "high commitment work systems" in which employee teams take full responsibility for production, without requiring managers.
- A pharmaceutical company is "delayering," as they put it, to reduce unnecessary levels that were indeed "delayers" of decisions and actions; it has distributed a kit of instructions to all departments on how to rearrange the organization chart to work without at least two levels of management.
- A gigantic oil company, calling itself an "elephant learning to dance," is trying to become more agile by collapsing several levels of the management hierarchy.

The principal targets of this kind of reorganization are corporate staffs and middle managers, groups that may have always been vulnerable to displacement in downturns of the business cycle. But restructuring to ensure that every management layer and every corporate service adds value to the organization's mission has also raised profound questions about how a corporation *should* be organized and what activities *should* be under its hierarchical umbrella, as opposed to being purchased on the market. In short, two kinds of roles are included in the "corporate" category: supporters and interveners. The questions about supporters are the more easily resolved. Some supporters are indeed facilitators and integrators who add value by improving the way business units operate or transferring knowledge and expertise among them. Supporters also include the vast armies of clerks and quasi-professionals whose role is to handle the paperwork and the documentation involved in business transactions. The ranks of supporters are being thinned already by two intertwined forces: information technology and the growth of specialist firms taking over corporate support functions. A leading electronics company, for example, anticipates that computer networks will reduce a purchasing staff of three thousand, largely doing routine work, to a mere one hundred professionals negotiating contracts and establishing systems. "Eighty percent of our transactions could be ordered directly through the requisition system on terminals, and bank-to-bank funds transfer could support them," a purchasing executive reported. For other companies, the road to smaller internal staffs is to turn routine transaction processing over to specialist firms that do nothing but handle the payroll or manage accounts receivable or keep the records.

Interveners are a different matter. They are considered the principal source of "fat" to be reduced in the post-entrepreneurial corporation. Over the years, corporate bureaucracies have come to include large numbers of people whose primary task is to check up on others, to ensure that "standards" are being met. These range from middle managers to staffs that establish procedures and then monitor how well other managers carry them out. As the same purchasing executive put it, "Controlling the number of purchase orders, checking up on how many parts were ordered, and nitpicking over which day we want [an order] to come in ends up being intervention rather than value-added." In short, interveners serve to slow down the work process by adding loops in the decision-making chain or hurdles to cross. The rationale for interveners is that they improve results. Some do. But the growing conviction is that most of them add costs without adding clear perceived value.

There are delicious ironies in the term "overhead" for administration and other corporate services. The original meaning of the word clearly involved the physical surroundings in which work took place—the roof over workers' heads. As corporations grew fat and complex, however, "overhead" began to signify something else to employees: "the people who can go over my head to second-guess my decisions." And looming first and foremost among those second-guessers, in the eyes of many producers, are corporate staffs. In most companies, "I'm from corporate and I'm here to help you" is considered as fraudulent a statement as "I'm from the IRS and I'm here to help you." In both cases, they feel they will be taxed.

A company can no longer afford to support anything that does not add value to its central business focus. Corporate services are either restructured to add value, or they are eliminated. Companies have a choice of methods:

• *Decentralizing and redeploying.* Putting more responsibility in the hands of unit managers and reducing the need for approvals or checkpoints make it possible to operate without so many layers of hierarchy and, by extension, with fewer people. Andrew Grove of Intel, for example, wants his company to be an "agile giant"—big enough to win global wars of products, technology, and trade while moving like a small company. To do this, he has decentralized approval and eliminated middle management layers.

• *Contracting out.* Of course, companies can decide not to manage certain activities themselves at all, and many are doing so in the name of "focus." The strategy here is to divest all but the solid core. Cut staff to the bone, do without some amenities altogether (who needs to manage a fleet of jet planes?), and contract out for everything else.

The ultimate extreme of the contracting-out strategy is represented by companies that are essentially marketing and financial shells working through vast networks of suppliers and dealers. Examples are found in publishing, apparel, and other fashion businesses that have long needed the flexibility to make changes quickly, effected by lean core organizations utilizing external specialist organizations for particular tasks. Benetton, an apparel producer, owns outright very little of the assets involved in bringing Benetton clothes to consumers; manufacturing is contracted out to numerous small factories, and retail outlets are licensees. Indeed, Benetton was part of a surge of entrepreneurship in northern Italy based on networks of small firms allying with each other, a development that economists Michael J. Piore and Charles F. Sabel considered the leading edge of an emerging industrial strategy of "flexible specialization" (Piore and Sabel 1984). In another sector, Lewis Galoob Toys, a toy producer, contracts out almost everything, including accounts receivable, running a company with over $50 million in sales with only about one hundred employees.

Raymond E. Miles calls this managerial style the "corporation as switchboard," the company acting as central information center and command point for a network of other organizations (see Miles and Snow 1984, 1986). This is clearly one strategy small companies can use to grow "big" in market scope and power very quickly. But it is also on the increase for much larger companies. It is not a long leap for companies that consider their manufacturing and sales functions to be "staffs" to business units that are essentially marketing arms to begin to think about whether it is efficient to continue to own so many plants and employ so many salespeople when working through contractors would give more flexibility.

• *Turning services into businesses.* In some cases, rather than divesting themselves of staff services, companies are converting them into profit centers that sell their services on the outside as well as inside. This is the nonhierarchical, nonbureaucratic, market-oriented response. Let those staff bureaucrats be entrepreneurs, and let the market decide if they add value or not. Among the companies thus deriving revenues from their own corporate services are Control Data, selling personnel services; Xerox, logistics and distribution services to customers; General Motors, employee training programs; and Security Pacific Bank, data processing and information systems.

Even when corporate staffs are not set loose in the outside market, companies are still starting to treat them as internal vendors who must compete with outside vendors to get their services purchased. General Foods recently put on a pay-as-you-use basis the "overhead" charges for corporate staff services, which were formerly assigned uniformly to users and nonusers. Of course, under the old system use was mandatory; for example, product managers in the past had to go through up to eight layers of management, including corporate staff, to get business plans approved. But now, those same staffs must prove to their internal customers' satisfaction that they add value. There are sometimes thorny questions of managing internal transfer payments and whether to set rates at market levels, but the principle is clear: Staffs are no longer considered "overhead" but potential sources of value; they are not watchdogs and interveners but suppliers serving customers.

In short, to use Oliver Williamson's language, companies are dismantling the very staffs that helped create the corporate hierarchy in the first place and replacing them with market-like relationships (Williamson 1975). Many employees are either being replaced with "outside" contractors or becoming contractors themselves.

Recent economic research data call into question the economic benefits of diversification. Increasingly, experts agree that the *economic* (as opposed to the *political*) justification for a multibusiness corporation is the achievement of synergy—a mix of *related* business activities that are stronger and more profitable together than they would be separately (Porter 1987; Montgomery 1985; Montgomery and Thomas 1988). The "portfolio" or "holding company" approach—in which each part stands alone and needs to be different in order to compensate for the weakness of other parts—has been increasingly discredited. Sometimes the delegitimizing of the diversified conglomerate has occurred for defensive reasons: the administrative costs of managing diversity or the vulnerability to takeovers engendered by the ease with which the business units can be unbundled and sold at a premium. But in addition, the quest for synergies comes from growth goals, especially in global technology companies, which face brutal, fast-paced competition and thus must transfer intelligence and innovation across the boundaries of business units and countries.

Thus, the new ideal is better integration: The post-entrepreneurial company also builds the connections between its various products or businesses, encouraging such cooperative efforts as cross-selling, product linkages in the marketplace, exchange of technological or market information, resource sharing to apply one unit's competence to another's problem, or letting one division serve as the lead for particular innovations to be used by the others. This means that the emerging company is itself more network-like—a federation of semi-autonomous divisions—than hierarchical. American Express, in particular, is moving in this direction.

Overall, the emphasis on synergies decreases the "vertical" dimension of organization—elaborate corporate hierarchies and large central staffs—and increases the "horizontal" dimension—the direct cooperation between peers across divisions and departments.

Alliances

The second major component of the new organizational strategy involves developing close working relationships with other organizations, extending the company's reach without increasing its size. Strategic alliances and partnerships are seen as a potent way to do more with less. They permit the company to remain lean, controlling costs while gaining access to more capacity than what is owned or employed directly. The traditional corporation was stuck with the limitations of do-it-oneself-or-don't-do-it-at-all mentalities. Partnerships are a flexible alternative to acquisition, with a more modest investment and the ability to remain independent. The leaner organization that contracts out for services depends on the suppliers of those services and therefore needs closer coordination with them. Furthermore, in a rapidly changing business environment, alliances with other organizations on which one company depends are a powerful way to ensure that all change in the same direction, thereby reducing uncertainty. The traditional corporation's mistrust of outsiders made it impossible to plan jointly with customers or suppliers.

Today, U.S. companies are collaborating in three ways. They can *Pool* resources in service consortia, *Ally* to exploit an opportunity in joint ventures, or *Link* systems in stakeholder or value-chain partnerships. In short, to coin a handy acronym, they are becoming *PALs* with other organizations.

Organizational sociologists have identified many of the conditions under which organizations handle uncertainty by seeking collaboration (for example, Thompson 1967), and these conditions increasingly hold not only for smaller, more "resource dependent" and "environmentally constrained" organizations but also for large, powerful corporations that once dominated their environments. For one thing, organizations have discovered the major strategic leverage to be found in their relationships with suppliers as well as customers, and they saw the virtues of emulating their formidable Japanese competitors. By 1980, for example, throughout all U.S. manfacturing, purchased materials and services accounted for 60 percent of the total cost of operations (indicating great economic benefits to be found here). Furthermore, the role of supplier relations in the superior quality of Japanese products had been noted. The Japanese model involves the supplier as "co-producer," fewer suppliers per customer and customers per supplier, long-term relationships, close interaction between all functions, physical proximity, and blanket contracts.

In the face of heightened competitive pressures, then, many U.S. firms have established new cooperative agreements with other organizations that involve unprecedented (for them) levels of sharing and commitment. In

1987, over forty coalitions between Ford Motor Company and outside commercial entities were identified by Harvard professor Malcolm Salter. There were over eight thousand person-visits by U.S.-based Ford employees to Japan—and so much traffic between Detroit and Tokyo in general that many U.S.-Tokyo flights now originate in Detroit rather than Chicago. Indeed, by 1986 General Electric had over one hundred cooperative ventures with other firms, and even IBM—long known as one of the "great independents"— had established formal partnerships with a number of other organizations, including Merrill Lynch and Aetna Life and Casualty. IBM was also trying to ally with potential competitors through agreements making them "value-added resellers"; McDonnell Douglas Automation, for example, would sell IBM products to its customers, adding its own to the package. In some sectors, more joint domestic ventures were announced in a single year in the 1980s than in the previous fifteen to twenty years combined. Furthermore, the number of R&D consortia involving collaboration in, or joint support for, basic research by companies within an industry that otherwise compete has grown dramatically to well over one hundred in part as a response to the loosening of anti-trust barriers through the National Cooperative Research Act of 1984. Overall, companies are seeking a number of benefits in association with other companies: information access, windows on technology, speed of action, and mutual accommodation to innovation that creates faster payback.

These relationships with "blurred boundaries," to use Joseph L. Badaracco's term (Badaracco 1988), overlay or even replace market relationships with organizational ones, often creating close, even intimate connections between separate organizations. Firms do not lose their legal identity; they retain their own culture and management structure; and they can pursue their own strategies. But they reduce their autonomy by strengthening their ties with other organizations, thus sharing authority over certain decisions. And sometimes the interpenetration makes it hard to distinguish employees of one organization from employees of the other. At Eastman Kodak, one of its suppliers staffs and runs Kodak's paper supply room.

Taking advantage of each other's capacities and coordinating their activities for mutual benefit require degrees of information-sharing unprecedented in the traditional corporation. And not only the external ally gets more information; the managers inside also have to know more in order to be intelligent representatives to the partnership. In general, effective alliances create multiple links between the allies: joint planning at the strategic level, technical data exchange at the professional level, and direct data linkages at the production level. The connections multiply. One partner company may make investments in the other that resemble the investments a corporation might make in one of its divisions, as Digital Equipment does with its suppliers: management conferences to review business plans, staff training programs, performance appraisal programs, and recognition events. The relationships may get even more intertwined when companies are both suppliers and customers to each other.

Successful partnerships imply a degree of equality among partners, as well as within each partnership, to which some companies and some managers are unwilling to move; they would rather try to duplicate traditional command conditions by manifesting less commitment than the partner, maintaining an imbalance of resources or information or starving the partnership by not supplying enough of these, and monopolizing the benefits. The partner, in turn, may have prematurely placed trust in the relationship, arousing so much resentment when the trust is violated that cooperation ceases. Or the domain for the alliance may be so circumscribed that effective action to derive benefits for all parties is impossible; the organizations fail to link their systems or plan together or find a framework for resolving differences; meanwhile, each has other loyalties that conflict with the partnership, including the pull of internal corporate politics.

Clearly, strategic alliances are not a casual matter. They should not be entered into casually, or else they absorb time and energy without bringing benefits and raise expectations only to frustrate them, which is more disappointing than never to have promised anything. For all the fanfare surrounding industry research consortia such as Bellcore for the regional telephone operating companies or the Microelectronics and Computer Corporation, experience suggests that the companies entering into those kinds of alliances are only weakly committed, and, in turn, the consortia produce little that they define as benefits—reinforcing their lack of commitment in a vicious circle. Being only casually a partner is like being only somewhat pregnant. Thus, partnerships ought to be formed only in those relationships that are sufficiently important so they will be entered into with full commitment and with a willingness to invest the resources and make the internal changes successful external partnerships entail—the sharing of information, the linking of systems, and the establishment of agreements for governing the partnership. What I have elsewhere termed the "six I's" of successful alliances—Importance, Investment, Interdependence, Integration, Information, Institutionalization—also require major shifts away from bureaucracy and hierarchy.

Newstreams

The third major organizational strategy is actively to promote what I call "newstreams"—a flow of new business possibilities within the firm, creating small business start-ups within large corporations. To do more with less in today's demanding competitive context means being able to capture and develop opportunities as they arise, to ensure that good ideas do not slip away and that new ventures are ready to join the mainstream business or lead the company in new directions. Thus, the domain for invention is extended well beyond the R&D department, and the domain for new venture formation is extended well beyond the acquisition department. Unlike the norm in traditional bureaucratic-hierarchical corporations, more people at more levels are given the chance to develop and lead newstream projects.

The very existence of channels for newstreams generates tensions and dilemmas because the requirements for nurturing a new venture conflict with bureaucratic management systems geared for running ongoing mainstream businesses—or at least better tolerated by the mainstream. "Planning" for a newstream start-up means placing bets rather than being able to predict a relatively assured set of results from a known line of business. Newstream ventures are not yet routinized; they are characterized instead by unexpected events, which makes scheduling difficult. Newstreams are uncertain in a number of respects; their course is bumpy, and they rock boats because they are controversial. Newstream projects are intense; they absorb more mental and emotional energy than established activities, generate new knowledge at a rapid rate, require excellent communication among those with fragments of the knowledge, and are thus more dependent on teamwork and more vulnerable to turnover. Finally, newstreams benefit from autonomy—perhaps a place of its own for the project, removed from the mainstream and allowing experimentation, but certainly a separation of style and procedures so the development project can move quickly without the constraints deemed necessary to control the mainstream business.

There is also a tension between the streams that makes traditional bureaucratic mainstream managers uneasy; the newstream quest for autonomy conflicts with the mainstream push for control. Mainstream people may resent the "privileges" newstream people have in being freed from traditional constraints; newstream people may argue, in turn, that they are more vulnerable, taking greater career risks. In numerous ways, the existence of newstreams flowing alongside the mainstream business loosens traditional hierarchical authority, undermines respect for bureaucracy, weakens corporate identification in favor of project identification, and teaches people they can rely on themselves, thereby reducing their dependence on the corporation to give them a career. The corporate "haves" become the people with the freedom to pursue their ideas; the "have-nots" are those still encumbered with the shackles of bureaucracy.

The Coming Demise
of Bureaucracy and Hierarchy?

The three postbureaucratic, postentrepreneurial organizational strategies are fundamentally different ways of organizing to get the work done. The corporation itself is being turned inside-out, like a reversible garment worn out on one side. Some executives I know are beginning to draw their organization charts upside-down, with managers at the bottom supporting the line employees at the top. But inside-out is an even more accurate image for the new organization. There is more "detachment" of what was once "inside" the corporation's protective shell (for example, employees being replaced by contingent workers, and staff departments being spun-off as independent contractors) and more "attachment" to what was once "outside" (for example, closer, more committed relationships with suppliers, customers, and even competitors). We are watching a simultaneous loosening of formerly strong relationships and a strengthening of formerly loose relationships. Those brought closer clearly benefit, but those cast out are often cast adrift.

The new corporate ideal involves a smaller fixed core but a larger set of partnerlike ties. There is less "inside" that is sacred—permanent, untouchable, unchangeable people, departments, business units, or practices—but more "outside" that is respected—representing opportunities for deal-making or leverage via alliances. This ideal represents a reversal of the old corporate imperative to get as big as possible in order to have power and control over the business environment. In times of turbulence and high uncertainty, vast size can instead produce rigidity and sluggishness.

Other analysts have noted this reversal in a number of different ways. TRW economist Pat Choate (1987) has heralded the coming of a "high-flex society," pointing to the new social policies required to increase business flexibility by helping individuals be more flexible in their job choices over their lifetimes. Michael J. Piore and Charles F. Sabel (1984), in *The Second Industrial Divide*, point to the competitive virtues of the small, focused company involved in a network of other companies providing complementary skills—a virtue they label "flexible specialization."

All of these developments represent a dramatic new corporate ideal, one very different from the old-style corporate bureaucracy:

- Bureaucracy tends to be position-centered, in that authority derives from position, and status or rank is critical. Post-bureaucratic, post-entrepreneurial organizations tend to be more person-centered, with authority deriving from expertise or from relationships.
- Bureaucratic management is repetition-oriented, seeking efficiency through doing the same thing over and over again. Post-entrepreneurial management is creation-oriented, seeking innovation as well as efficiency.
- Bureaucratic management is rules-oriented, defining procedures and rewarding adherence to them. Post-entrepreneurial management is results-oriented, rewarding outcomes.
- Bureaucracies tend to pay for status, in the sense that pay is position-based, positions are arrayed in a hierarchy, and greater rewards come from attaining higher positions. Post-entrepreneurial organizations tend to pay for contribution, for the value the person has added, regardless of formal position.

Thus, to use an overworked expression, the dominant business paradigm is changing.

Three principles emerge from observing the new organizational strategies in practice, intertwined post-entrepreneurial principles that create the flexibility required to meet the strategic challenge of doing more with less.

1. Minimize obligations, and maximize options. Keep filed costs low, and utilize as much as possible variable or contingent means to achieve corporate goals.

2. Seek leverage through influence and combination. Derive power from access and involvement, rather than from full control or total ownerships.
3. Encourage "churn." Keep things moving. Encourage continuous regrouping of people and functions and products to produce unexpected, creative new combinations. Redefine turnover as positive (a source of renewal) rather than negative, and seek a minimum level.

Still, in retrospect, each of the popular management buzz-words and fads of the last decade has been important in moving corporations toward challenging the old managerial assumptions, loosening their structures, and experimenting with new practices. One offshoot of many of these programs is the weakening of hierarchy and the reduction of levels of organization as employees are given more opportunities to influence decisions and exercise control.

Alongside the pro-people corporate policies popular in the last decade, however, are other business maneuvers often characterized as anti-people: financial manipulations and a takeover binge leading to involuntary restructuring and job displacement.

The post-entrepreneurial principles I have identified clearly contain both positives and negatives. At their best, they increase opportunity, giving people the chance to develop their ideas, pursue exciting projects, and be compensated directly for their contributions, and they encourage collaboration across functions, across business units, and even across corporations. But although they can increase the power and opportunity of some people, they can be disruptive and harmful to others, especially those who are displaced in the wake of restructuring or those who are victims of poorly implemented changes.

SOCIAL IMPLICATIONS:
THE CONTINGENT JOB AND THE DECLINE
OF THE BUREAUCRATIC CAREER

If we are indeed witnessing a crumbling of hierarchy—a gradual replacement of the bureaucratic emphasis on order, uniformity, and repetition with an entrepreneurial emphasis on creativity and deal-making—then we are also watching a new set of societal dilemmas arise in the wake of this change.

The post-entrepreneurial revolution not only changes the organization and management of the corporation; it changes the lives people lead in the business world. There are more contingencies, more uncertainties. Post-entrepreneurial strategies hold out the promise of more satisfaction and rewards for people, but more of those benefits are contingent on what the individual—and the team—does and not on what the corporation automatically provides.

For example, compensation systems are shifting away from a bureaucratic orientation in which *position*, not *performance*, determined pay and height in a hierarchy was the most significant determinant of earnings. The fixed portion of the paycheck is decreasing while the variable portion increases. Three forms of contribution-based pay—profit-sharing and gainsharing, performance bonuses, or a share of venture returns—give people the power to grow their own earnings, distribute the corporation's rewards more fairly to those who deserve them, and do not force people to wait in line for promotion as the only way to make progress (see Kanter 1989 for examples and evidence). The excitement of projects in which people are empowered to act on their own ideas makes work more satisfying and more absorbing, increasing the sense of accomplishment. The opportunity to be essentially in business for oneself, inside or outside the large corporation, puts more control in the hands of smaller goups. But this also means that incomes are more likely to fluctuate rather than steadily increase with promotions.

In many ways, the new corporate strategies are reshaping the relationship between employers and employees and causing a shift in the nature of work careers. As corporate jobs are changing in number, in mix, in substance, and in the characteristics of their incumbents, these changes affect career patterns. In fact, the traditional corporate ladder career may soon share the fate of the nuclear family: an oft-invoked ideal that applies to fewer and fewer people. Bureaucratic assumptions about a steady rise up a hierarchy, with people dependent on organizations for their careers, start to give way to more entrepreneurial assumptions about being, in effect, in business for oneself, even as an employee earning a paycheck. Reliance on organizations to give shape to a career is being replaced by reliance on self. The accumulation of "organizational capital" is being replaced by the accumulation of "reputational capital."

Restructuring. The increasing uncertainty and instability of corporate careers are direct results of restructuring. People at all levels, of course, are affected by the massive dislocations that accompany restructuring, and the costs are often much higher for those in lower-income and lower-skill categories. But the changes in the nature of managerial careers are most dramatic, for it is the administrative ranks that define a corporation, as opposed to a production system. Between 1981 and 1986, nearly 11 million people were classified by the Bureau of Labor Statistics as "displaced workers," almost 10 percent of the civilian labor force. Almost half again of these were experienced workers on the job for three or more years. The bureau further stated that more of this displacement was due to permanent separation rather than temporary layoffs as in previous recessions. While 56 percent of the displacement occurred in factory-related positions, almost 40 percent took place among white-collar groups most likely to have had safe corporate careers: 15 percent of the displacement was from the managerial and professional ranks; 22 percent was from technical, sales, and administrative support (Newman 1988).

Large firm managers and professional staff are disappearing, and with them goes a set of career expectations. In the 1980s, total employment in companies with 1,000 or more workers fell by 1.2 million. By 1986, only 11.88 percent of the U.S. labor force was employed by the *Fortune 500* companies, down from 15.4 percent in 1977. Numerous examples make clear why bureaucratic career ladders are crumbling even in the absence of mergers and acquisitions. After reducing total employment at Xerox by about 20 percent, CEO David Kearns still felt about another third of the jobs in management and administration could come out. At Exxon, the corporate headquarters staff went from 2,300 people in 1975 to 325 in 1987. Over 300 major companies cut back their work forces between January 1985 and June 1986, including Apple, which lost 1,200 employees (20 percent of the previous total), and Eastman Kodak, which lost 13,700 people (10 percent) by the end of 1985.

Many middle managers in bureaucratic companies have always felt powerless, squeezed between the demands of implementing strategies they do not influence and the ambitions of increasingly independent-minded employees (Kanter 1977). But at least they were well paid, had job security, and could expect a steady if slow rise upward. Now their privileges are eroding rapidly. They must cope with the classic difficulties of their positions while justifying why their positions exist at all. As Paul Hirsch (1987) put it, "Wall Street's advice to managers searching for excellence . . . has been to tell them to become excellent at searching for new jobs."

Contracting Out: Allying with Suppliers Instead of Employees. The second force influencing careers is the growth of what has been termed a "just-in-time work force," or the "externalization of employment"—in other words, hiring temporary help or replacing internal departments with external suppliers of services. There is ample evidence of the contracting out of jobs formerly done by full-time employees and the growth of "contingent" rather than "permanent" employment. Between 1963 and 1977, the number of temporary help service firms increased by 240 percent, payrolls by 468 percent, receipts by 469 percent in constant dollars, and employment by 450 percent. Between 1977 and 1981, there were increases of another 137 percent in payroll and 450 percent in employment. By 1986, 735,000 workers were employed by temporary help agencies, and the industry had almost doubled in size since 1982, growing 21 percent faster than the electronic computing equipment industry from 1979 to 1984 (Pfeffer and Baron 1988). For the United States as a whole, the number of people employed by temporary agencies rose from 400,000 to 804,000 between 1982 and 1986. At a time of dramatic declines in unemployment in general, temps were one of the fastest-growing segments of the labor force. And according to the Bureau of Labor Statistics data, the number of U.S. workers whose primary income was earned in temporary jobs rose from 471,800 to 835,000 from 1983 to 1986.

More than half of the new jobs created since 1980 have gone to contingent workers. The number of part-time workers in 1986 was 34.3 million, up from 28.5 million in 1980, and they are estimated to become 30 to 33 percent of the U.S. work force by 1990, according to a Conference Board economist, who argued that perhaps about half of these are involuntary part-timers. Eighty-five to 95 percent of U.S. corporations currently use temporary workers. By the year 2000, the Bureau of Labor Statistics indicates that about 80 percent of jobs will be in the service sector, which uses 75 percent of temporary employees (Forbes 1987; Wiggins 1988).

Furthermore, there has been a shift in the nature of temps from those doing routine work to those with professional skills for special projects. The temporary business is booming for legal and medical professionals, for example. Temporary agencies have themselves become big corporations. Norrell Corporation, number four in the industry in revenues, provides a variety of office and security services, staffing mail rooms, file rooms, cash receipts areas, and data processing departments, among others.

As contracting out continues and companies substitute supplier alliances for permanent employment, more people can expect to find their career in "producer service" industries, such as advertising, computer and data processing, personnel supply, management and business consulting, protective and detective services, building maintenance, legal services, accounting and auditing, and engineering and architecture—the fast-growing employment area. But this sector also offers, on average, more uncertainty and less security than the traditional corporate career. In 1986, 15 percent of the self-employed were found in producer services, and one of the most rapidly growing segments of the industry was personnel supply, accounted for by the dramatic expansion of temporary help agencies placing contingent workers (Tschetter 1987).

Innovation and Entrepreneurial Management: Newstream Projects. The third force altering the nature of careers is more positive. While traditional, perhaps more bureaucratic, managerial jobs are being eliminated at a record rate and managers face growing career uncertainty, changes in the content of jobs provide new kinds of opportunities. As corporations try to develop newstream business, they are establishing venture units or venture funds that allow managers to run their own businesses or get support for special projects—and earn a direct return. Furthermore, the general move toward contribution-based pay begins to eliminate the need for promotion up a career ladder in order to increase earnings.

Finally, the professionalizing of managerial work—the growth of specialized skills in such areas as financial analysis, strategic planning, compensation, or marketing—means that a manager's fate is no longer tied to a single corporation; most managers acquire a knowledge base and a set of skills that are transferable to other organizations. What economists call *firm-specific knowledge* derived from long experience with a single company is also declining in value relative to more generalizable expertise because of a rapidly changing business environment. When change and innovation are the issues, the skills to be flexible and to learn are more important as a way to build the future than long-term company experience, which helps to preserve traditions and routines.

In the most progressive in my fieldwork, workplace, opportunity, and recognition go to those who can *create* the job, not those who inherit a predetermined set of tasks defining a hierarchical position. At TIAA-CREF, for example, the Pinnacle newsletter exhorted employees who finished a project and had extra time on their hands to take the initiative to find another project to tackle because that would make them eligible for "Star" awards and Chairman's awards. Another example of how far this emphasis on inventing one's job extends is the suggestion made to me by an Apple manager after my first visit that I should "grow my own job"—and I was only a consultant. One Silicon Valley manager described it this way:

> In my position, the nature of the duties can change a lot depending on the expertise and interest of the individual. For example, if I were really anxious to travel and instruct, I could look around for some topics that aren't well documented and make myself an expert on those topics, and tell management that someone needed to go out and teach a course in that. In general, there's more work to do than people to do it, so you look at your position and you say, there are lots of things that would be appropriate for me to do. If I have a conscience I'll do what needs to be done. If I'm selfish, I'll do what I want to do. So there's a lot of flexibility. (Gregory 1984)

While full of opportunity, this workplace style is also full of uncertainty. The very chance to invent, shape, or grow a job puts career responsibility squarely in the hands of the individual. If jobs are fluid and created by their incumbents, then how is it possible for organizations to define orderly career paths? Making it possible for people to swim in newstreams, developing innovation projects, only underlines the idiosyncratic nature of the careers that evolve from individually determined jobs. Those working in corporate newstreams are not contingent employees in the same way that temps are; yet, they still may not be able to envision a future with the corporation beyond the current project.

The new business strategies thus alter the context in which careers take shape, especially for the white-collar elite of professionals and managers who once felt their careers were secured and assured. To understand the impact of this shift, it is important to consider how the traditional career paths are changing. I distinguish three principal "ideal types" of career patterns: bureaucratic (or administrative) careers; professional careers; and entrepreneurial careers. Field observations, coupled with some statistical evidence, suggest that the first is on the decline while the latter two are on the rise.

Bureaucratic Careers: Waning Forms

Bureaucratic careers are defined by the logic of *advancement*. The bureaucratic career pattern involves a sequence of positions in a defined hierarchy of other positions. "Growth" is equated with promotion to a position of higher rank that brings with it greater benefits; "progress" means advancement within the hierarchy. Thus, a "career" consists of formal movement from job to job—changing title, tasks, and often work-groups in the process. Indeed, these very characteristics were at the heart of Weber's original definition of bureaucracy.

The bureaucratic career type had its moments of historical dominance in the United States with the rise of the large twentieth-century industrial corporation based on mechanical technologies, U.S. hegemony, and a certain labor force. But as other nations come to the fore, as the global marketplace and international competition expand, as technology becomes more complex and more rapidly changing, as women and minorities seek access to the better jobs, and as growth slows (or reverses) in traditional industries, it is harder to sustain the assumptions on which the bureaucratic pattern was based. Those assumptions include:

- A limited pool of competitors for higher positions, with the "losers" accepting their place, thus permitting a pyramidal distribution of people and maintenance of the legitimacy of hierarchy
- Continuing organizational growth, so that opportunity could be offered through expanding the width of the pyramid
- Continuing employment security, so that eventually, over the life of the career, rewards foregone now would be received later, at higher ranks

In corporations today, more people at lower levels have *theoretical* access to promotion while the *actual* number of slots "above" is declining. If a company restructures to find synergies and ends up combining operations with an acquired company or downsizing and reducing management layers, there are fewer high-level jobs. If a company handles expansion by using temporary workers and contracting out to suppliers, then there are fewer chances for promotion, as promotion depends in part on expansion. And promotion chances decline precipitously if the company deliberately cuts back at higher levels. Overall, the corporate ladder is collapsing because it can no longer carry the weight of expectations for opportunity. Even the U.S. corporate welfare system—pensions and benefits offered to permanent employees of large companies—is rendered obsolete by the shift to the new post-entrepreneurial principles. Most of those corporate entitlements are based on an assumption of longevity—that one person sticks with one company (itself an assumed-to-be-unchanging entity). Instead, professional and entrepreneurial career forms are better suited to innovative organizations operating in an uncertain and turbulent environment with high demands for change.

Professional Careers: Waxing

The logic of professional career structures is defined by craft or skill, with the possession of valued knowledge the key determinant of occupational status and reputation the key resource for the individual. Career growth for professionals does not necessarily consist of moving from job to job, as it does for bureaucrats, and advancement does not have the same meaning. Instead, those on professional career tracks may keep the same title and the same nominal job over a long period of time. Opportunity in the professional form, then, involves the chance to take on ever-more demanding, challenging, important, or rewarding assignments that require greater exercise of the skills that define the professional's stock-in-trade. "Upward mobility" in the professional career involves the reputation for greater skill.

Professional careers are not automatically based in single organizations, although there is clearly a range within this category from professionals who are highly organizationally embedded (such as engineers and teachers) to those who are weakly organizationally embedded (for example, physicians in private practice affiliated with hospitals but not "employed" by them). The professional community may be a more important organizing factor in the professional career model than the employing organization. For example, consider the Hollywood film industry: a system of recurrent ties among major participants working under short-term contracts for single films (Faulkner and Anderson 1987). Those with performance records of success are then in a better bargaining position for the next round of contracting. Indeed, journalist Bruce Nussbaum observed that the model for work in big companies could soon be Hollywood, where producers move from one studio to another, loyal only to themselves and their profession, or television, where local news anchors jump from one station to another. Similar examples include professionals and entrepreneurs coming together for high-technology development projects, financial deals between bankers and international clients, and real estate development. One job-hopping manager commented that in biotechnology, "We are all gypsies. You work for an industry, not a company." His own career, for example, took him from a Ph.D. in chemistry to Polaroid to a medical diagnostics start-up. Computer professionals in Silicon Valley may also be part of a temporary work force, bouncing among companies to help with overload or provide specialized skill (Lozano 1989).

In such cases, careers are produced by *projects* rather than by the hierarchy of jobs in a single organization. And the key variable is reputation—of those pulling projects together so they can attract the best people, and of the professionals who want to find the best projects. Each project, in turn, adds to the value of a reputation as it is successfully completed. So people make their commitments to projects rather than to employers.

Entrepreneurial Careers:
Growing Dramatically

The third major career pattern is the entrepreneurial one. The term *entrepreneur* has come to be associataed with the formation of an independent business venture or with ownership of a small business, but these meanings are too restrictive. Instead, an entrepreneurial career is one in which growth occurs through the creation of new value or new organization capacity. If the key resource in a bureaucratic career is hierarchical position and the key resources in a professional career are knowledge and reputation, then the key resource in an entrepreneurial career is the ability to create a product or service of value.

Thus, for Kenneth Olsen, founder and chairman of Digital Equipment Corporation in 1957, career "growth" has involved no changes of title or job or position; yet, he has greatly increased his power, remuneration, and responsibilities by leading the growth of the organization around him to a much larger size—and reaping a direct return from the economic value he has created. This entrepreneurial career pattern is not restricted to the single founder. It occurs for everyone in the same organization who stays in place but leads the growth of the territory for which he or she is responsible. Recently formed and rapidly growing businesses often offer entrepreneurial careers in many areas to many people. In a small financial firm, the director of auto industry projects began with three people, and then—as the business grew—she found herself managing several levels of staff across several cities, with a bonus tied to the profits of her area.

Freedom, independence, and control over not only one's tasks (as the professional supposedly has) but also one's organizational surroundings are associated with the entrepreneurial career, accounting for some of its attractions. But also associated is greater uncertainty about the future, about how the career will unfold. The bureaucratic career is more predictable. There are ways to limit risks as an independent entrepreneur, of course, with franchising preeminent among them. The number of franchise-format businesses in the United States, over two thousand in 1986, is more than double what it was ten years earlier, according to Commerce Department data. A 5 percent discontinuance rate in the first year compares with a 30 to 50 percent rate of small business failures in the first year, according to Small Business Administration statistics. Commerce Department figures indicate a discontinuance rate in 1984 of 3.2 percent (not including franchises that are sold back to the parent, often at distress prices). Franchising has gotten a boost from the massive layoffs of middle managers, who use their severance pay to start businesses.

Whether forced out or opting out, big company managers and professionals are going into business for themselves in record numbers. Added to the restructuring victims, who have no choice because their jobs have disappeared, are the corporate escapees who see no chance for progress because entrenched managers are blocking their way up the ladder and the self-confident risk-takers who want more autonomy and the chance to capture the returns from their labors more directly. A spate of new service businesses in Boston, for example, has been formed by "stuck" middle managers who see fewer slots above them and those that do exist unlikely to be vacated soon. Going into business for themselves is thus a way to break loose. This version of the entrepreneurial dream revolves around autonomy rather than wealth, around "being my own boss" rather than building an empire. It is a response to the strains of subordinacy. One outplacement counselor, for example, claimed that 90 percent of her clientele of dismissed executives think of starting their own companies to avoid being in a position where they could be powerless and get fired again, although only 30 percent actually do.

The Coming Demise
of Bureaucracy and Hierarchy?

The overall impact of the new corporate strategies and forms is to delegitimize bureaucracy, weaken the power of hierarchy, and loosen the employment relationship. The impact of changes in the content and context of managerial jobs—corporate venture opportunities, rewards for contribution, and the professionalizing of managerial work—is to reduce the necessity for long-term employment with a single organization in a sequence of ever-"higher" jobs as the only way to earn increasing career rewards. At the same time, long-term employment is rapidly disappearing, leaving those who counted on it adrift in a sea of insecurity. Even for those who remain with one employer, the logic of their careers is less likely to resemble the bureaucratic pattern of an orderly progression of ever-higher levels and more remunerative jobs; instead, they are more likely to move from project to project, rewarded for each accomplishment, like professionals, or to create their own opportunity by developing newstream ideas and getting a piece of the action, like entrepreneurs.

The new career patterns are one more blow to the dominance of bureaucracy and hierarchy. Even inside large corporations, the nature of the managerial task changes when contingent career conditions prevail. Managing consultants, temporary employees, and suppliers requires an emphasis on different skills from those used to manage subordinates—negotiating terms and rates, coordinating across the boundaries of many organizations. Influence and persuasion must replace command and coercion. Furthermore, under traditional conditions, the pay and prestige of managers derived in part from the size of their staffs. Now, with an emphasis on shrinking internal staffs, the traditional indicators of importance decline. But skillful brokering among consulting firms and independent contractors clearly cannot produce the same benefit; instead, managers must demonstrate the value of their own expert contributions or risk being eliminated as just middlemen themselves. The meaning of a corporate career thus changes in substance as well as in promotion opportunities. Finally, there are losses of traditional values—of long-term employment security, of the mutual loyalty of employer to employee and employee to firm.

FROM SOCIAL CHANGE TO SOCIAL THEORY:
A FUTURE-ORIENTED MODEL OF ORGANIZATIONS

This review of developments in the corporate world suggests that the components of bureaucracy—and the theory underlying it—are being progressively reshaped, watered down, or reversed. Not yet entirely clear are the extent of this trend (although the diversity of the companies and countries in my fieldwork suggests it is extensive), the time frame over which it has emerged (managerial attention to nonbureaucratic organizational models such as the matrix can be traced at least as far back as to aerospace projects in World War II), or the precise language to use to describe the new organization forms. These are all matters for further empirical and theoretical attention. Still, one thing is clear. Claims that bureaucracy is the only rational (economically efficient) form of organization do not hold. The persistence of bureaucracy and hierarchy, where they persist, may lie in the realm of power and politics (the desire to retain the perquisites of superior status and the rights of command) rather than economics or may be attributed to inertia and lag (see, for example, Meyer and Zucker 1989). To increase their competitiveness in world markets because inertia is a luxury that can no longer be afforded, U.S. companies are moving away from the bureaucratic model. This very movement creates new managerial problems and organizational dilemmas, but movement it is.

The predominant twentieth-century critiques of bureaucracy (for example, by Alvin Gouldner, Robert Merton, and Herbert Simon) pointed to its "nonrational" side—the problems induced by such facts as that people bring interests and emotions with them into the workplace or that, despite formal inducements to meet high goals, their performance may be geared to the minimum acceptable standard. Therefore, classic social and economic theories of organizations were also flawed to the extent that they did not fully appreciate such human dynamics. James S. Coleman (1990) later pointed to other flaws in the Weberian assumptions in areas where corporate practice deviated from the classic model. The use of incentive payments at upper levels of corporations seemingly contradicted the idea that a well-designed position in an authority structure was sufficient to produce maximum performance; decentralization in large, complex organizations created additional centers of power, returning control to the managers thus empowered and engaging more of their interests than would occur if they were fully subordinated themselves in the chain of command.

At issue in most of these critiques were the *costs of subordination.* The theoretical perfection of bureaucracy was limited by the difficulties in inducing people to give up control over their own labor and in managing the complex dynamics that ensued—the coordination problem. Theory held, in short, that bureaucracy was still the most efficient mode for organizing complex purposive, repetitive economic activity (under conditions where market transactions would be too costly in their uncertainty); any limitations were *internal* to the firm and stemmed from the nature of the individuals comprising the firm.

Contingency theory looked *externally* in posing still another challenge to the classic model by arguing that the extent to which a particular form of organization was efficient was a function of the environment in which it operated (Lawrence and Lorsch 1967). The machine bureaucracy or mechanistic organization (Burns and Stalker 1961) defined by tall hierarchies, formal procedures, functional departments with clear and limited areas of activity, a reliance on written rules, and circumscribed communication could work well only in a stable and predictable environment. For an environment of rapid change requiring constant innovation, a more "organic" or "integrative" organization that defied the bureaucratic model would be more effective (Kanter 1983). Here the problem of bureaucracy stemmed from the *costs of conservatism and inertia.*

We must now go a step further in revising social theory to better address the realities of a changing world. The challenge to social theory posed by my report from the field is farther reaching. It suggests that global economic competition coupled with continuous technological change are hastening the evolution of an organizational model that not only separates ownership and control but also separates positions in an authority structure from influence over economic acts. The reification of the firm itself as a bounded entity is as misleading as the reification of internal status structures reflected in formal organization charts.

Instead, it is better to view economic activity in terms of *clusters of activity sets* whose membership composition, "ownership," and goals are constantly changing. Projects rather than positions are central. The bonds that ensue between actors are more meaningful and ongoing than those of single market transactions but less rigid and immutable than those of positions in authority structures. Action possibilities are neither as fully open as in a market transaction nor as fully constrained and circumscribed as in a bureaucracy. As Joseph L. Badaracco put it:

> As more firms introduce market relations within their boundaries while blurring their boundaries by replacing market relations with organizational ones, it becomes much more difficult and perhaps much less useful to think in terms of activities taking place either inside or outside of firms, of decisions being made either by firms or by markets, or of assets being owned by one firm or another. At the extreme, firms become evanescent—or, in the phrase of Michael Jensen and William Meckling—little more than "legal fictions which serve as a nexus for a set of contracting relationships among individuals." (Badaracco 1988, p. 87)

Furthermore, there is great variety in the relationships of individuals to organizational activity sets. While some actors are primarily defined by positions in a hierarchy of authority (for example, "employees" carrying out predefined tasks by specified procedures), others are defined by the ability to mobilize resources and develop commitment to new tasks (for example, "corporate entrepreneurs" [Kanter 1983] on the payroll as employees but also receiving additional economic and social inducements for initiative); others are defined by their "purely" economic motivation (such as subcontractors and contingent workers); and still others are defined by their dual position in several hierarchies, as a contributor to company X in a joint venture or alliance while "employed" by company Y.

More critically, perhaps, the activity sets do not exist or persist irrespective of the people occupying them. While the named entity under whose auspices activities occur (Corning Glass or Dow Corning) may have an existence independent of persons, the limited purpose associations (project teams) within it may come and go with the initiative and enthusiasm of particular people. This coalitional view of organizations suggests that perhaps social movement theory is more relevant to the emerging economic world than is bureaucratic theory.

The ultimate challenge is to move beyond static theories involving dualistic categorizations: either A or B. For example:

- Some firms are neither entrepreneurial start-ups nor bureaucracies; they combine elements of both.
- Some economic transactions are neither market-based nor hierarchical; they are hybrids, conducted by quasi-independent entities neither arm's length nor subject to the other's authority.
- Some key corporate actors are neither employees totally "inside" the firm and subject to its authority nor subcontractors totally "outside" the firm and subject to its whim.
- Some work is performed by neither full-time employees nor by self-employed entrepreneurs but by an "invisible work force" (Lozano 1989) of contingent workers bound by long-standing informal ties to the needs of a single organization.
- Even distinctions between work life and home life are blurred by the growth of telecommuters and a contingent work force with home offices.

Social and economic changes toward the close of the twentieth century, then, mean that organizational activity is less easily segmented into "types." Furthermore, both corporate actors and individual actors seem more likely to move across categories—change form, change location, change membership—more often.

Is the decline of "types," of rigid categorical distinctions and boundaries that firmly define membership in a set, itself a trend in the emerging global society? Are such bounded conceptions as "social status" or even "nation" themselves less relevant in a world of fluid boundaries and activities that span traditional categories (see Lodge 1989)? I leave such larger questions to others. But I reiterate my conclusion that global competition and ease of information access are transforming the organizational world so much that it would already be unrecognizable to classic social theorists and indescribable in their language.

REFERENCES

Aldrich, Howard, and Ellen R. Auster. 1986. "Even Dwarfs Started Small: Liabilities of Age and Size and Their Strategic Implications." *Research in Organizations Behavior* 8: 165–198.

Badaracco, Joseph L., Jr. 1988. "Changing Forms of the Corporation." Pp. 67–91 in J. R. Meyer and J. M. Gustafson, eds., *The U.S. Business Corporation, An Institution in Transition.* Cambridge, MA: Ballinger.

Burns, Tom, and G. M. Stalker. 1961. *The Management of Innovation.* London: Tavistock.

Chandler, Alfred. 1977. *The Visible Hand: The Managerial Revolution in American Business.* Cambridge, MA: Harvard University Press.

Choate, Pat, and J. K. Linger. 1987. *The High-Flex Society: Shaping America's Economic Future.* New York: Knopf.

Coleman, James S. 1990. "The Corporate Actor as a System of Action." *Foundations of Social Theory.* Cambridge, MA: Harvard University Press.

Faulkner, Robert R., and Andrew B. Anderson. 1987. "Short-Term Projects and Emergent Careers: Evidence from Hollywood." *American Journal of Sociology* 92 (January):879–909.

Forbes, Daniel. 1987. "Part-Time Work Force." *Business Month* (October):45–47.

Gregory, Kathleen L. 1984. *Signing Up: The Culture and Careers of Silicon Valley Computer People.* Ann Arbor, MI: University Microfilms (doctoral dissertation).

Hirsch, Paul. 1987. *Pack Your Own Parachute.* Reading, MA: Addison-Wesley.

Kanter, Rosabeth Moss. 1989. *When Giants Learn to Dance: Mastering the Challenges of Strategy, Management, and Careers in the 1990s.* New York: Simon and Schuster.

———. 1983. *The Change Masters.* New York: Simon and Schuster.

———. 1977. *Men and Women of the Corporation.* New York: Basic Books.

Lawrence, Paul R., and Jay Lorsch. 1967. *Organization and Environment.* Boston: Harvard Business School.

Lodge, George C. 1989. "Roles and Relationships of Business and Government." *Business in a Contemporary World* 1 (Winter):93–108.

Lozano, Beverly. 1989. *The Invisible Work Force.* New York: Free Press.

Meyer, Marshall W., and Lynne G. Zucker. 1989. *Permanently Failing Organizations.* Newbury Park, CA: Sage.

Miles, Raymond E., and Charles C. Snow. 1984. "Fit, Failure, and the Hall of Fame." *California Management Review* 26 (Spring):10–28.

———. 1986. "Organizations: A New Concept for New Forms." *California Management Review* 28 (Spring):62–73.

Montgomery, Cynthia A. 1985. "Product–Market Diversification and Market Power." *Academy of Management Journal* 28:789–798.

Montgomery, Cynthia A., and Ann R. Thomas. 1988. "Divestment: Motives and Gains." *Strategic Management Journal* 9:93–97.

Newman, Katherine S. 1988. *Falling from Grace: The Experience of Downward Mobility in the American Middle Class.* New York: Free Press.

Pfeffer, Jeffery, and James N. Baron. 1988. "Taking the Workers Back Out: Recent Trends in the Structuring of Employment," in B. Staw and L. Cummings, eds., *Research in Organizational Behavior.* Greenwich, CT: JAI Press.

Piore, Michael J., and Charles F. Sabel. 1984. *The Second Industrial Divide.* New York: Basic Books.

Porter, Michael. 1987. "From Competitive Advantage to Corporate Strategy." *Harvard Business Review* 65 (May–June):43–59.

Schumpeter, Joseph. 1942. *Capitalism, Socialism, and Democracy.* New York: Harper & Row.

Thompson, James D. 1967. *Organizations in Action.* New York: McGraw-Hill.

Tschetter, John. 1987. "Producer Service Industries: Why Are They Growing So Rapidly?" *Monthly Labor Review* (December):31–40.

Wiggins, Philip R. 1988. "Temporary Help in Great Demand." *New York Times*, March 4.

Williamson, Oliver E. 1975. *Market and Hierarchies.* New York: Free Press.

Comments

Peter Hedström

It is a great pleasure to comment on this chapter by Rosabeth Moss Kanter. Her work is always characterized by considerable insights and a sensitivity to important developments in economic life. This chapter is no exception, and it identifies some potentially important current developments in corporate America. As I have been asked to be a commentator on the paper, I will not highlight its many virtues, however. Rather I will assume the role of the skeptic and the critic and will exclusively focus on the parts of the chapter that I believe can be further strengthened and developed.

In this chapter, Kanter describes some provocative findings that seem to suggest that U.S. industries are presently undergoing far-reaching changes in the organization of work and production. She describes this as a change from a bureaucratic to a post-bureaucratic, post-entrepreneurial form of organization that affects not only the organization of the work place per se but also has dramatic consequences for the content of work, the patterns of careers, the security of jobs, and the extent of ties between formally independent business units.

Most sociological and historical research suggests that career patterns, social mobility rates, the size of workplaces, and the ratio of administrative to production personnel have changed only marginally during the second half of the twentieth century and are quite uniform across Western nations. Given these results, the findings presented in this chapter appear even more remarkable. If the structural changes described by Kanter are indeed generalizable to a large number of U.S. corporations, we might well be witnessing the beginning of an era of restructuring unprecedented in recent history.

However, I am somewhat skeptical about the validity and generalizability of the results presented in this chapter. When reading much of the business literature, I cannot help thinking of Fernand Braudel's distinction between the *longue durée* and *l'histoire événementielle*, between studies of the long-term trends and studies of the short-term fluctuations around these trends. I believe one should be highly skeptical about proclamations of new important business trends and upheavals in economic life; more often than not, they seem to be short-term fluctuations that tell us little or nothing about the important long-term social trends in society at large.

Whether the changes identified in this chapter describe more significant long-term changes or not is difficult to tell; we are not given sufficient information about the firms upon which these inferences are based. Given the lack of basic information such as how these firms were selected and whether their inclusion in the study was in any way related to the organizational problems they were experiencing, it is impossible to judge whether or not these results are generalizable.

Another problem with the chapter is a lack of clear distinctions between descriptive and prescriptive statements. I often found it difficult to tell when statements were intended as descriptions of patterns found within these specific firms and when they were intended as recommendations for proper actions in a changing business environment. For example, the chapter contains several references to "synergies," and we are told that "[t]he first major component of post-entrepreneurial strategy is to seek that combination of businesses, array of internal services, and the structure of organizing them that promotes synergies—a whole that multiplies the value of the parts." But how are we to understand statements such as these; are they descriptive or prescriptive? Have these firms already achieved "synergies," or is the above statement meant rather to be a business strategy recommended by the author?

In addition to the lack of clear distinction between "is" and "ought," there is a problem of "now" and "then." Throughout the chapter, descriptions of the present and descriptions of ideal types or future "post-bureaucratic" states that we might be moving toward are difficult to distinguish. Let me take one example. We are told that bureaucracies are position-, rules-, and repetition-oriented, while post-bureaucratic organizations are person-centered, creation-, and results-oriented. I assume that these characterizations are not intended as descriptions of actually existing firms, but I am not quite sure. Perhaps they are intended rather as analytical tools, but if so, then the analytical leverage that we can derive from them must be spelled out in much more detail.

Given these problems with the data and their presentation, I am far from convinced that the structural changes described herein are of the extent and magnitude suggested by the author. But if we nevertheless *assume* that these changes actually are occurring, I am still not quite sure how the author wishes to explain these developments. From reading the chapter, one sometimes gets the impression that a major explanation is that corporations have finally *realized* the considerable efficiency gains they can reap from lean organizational structures with few hierarchical levels and from creative corporate cultures.

But these ideas or insights, of course, have been around for a long time. Herbert Simon wrote about the topic of "fat" organizational hierarchies some thirty-five to forty years ago, and Oliver Williamson formalized the problem some twenty years ago and showed how organizational efficiency is likely to be influenced by the length of the chains of command. So the basic idea that the efficiency of an organization can be hampered by too many hierarchical levels has been common knowledge for some time. An explanation based only on the diffusion of these ideas into the business community seems insufficient unless it is supplemented by some additional mechanisms explaining the apparent rapid diffusion and adaptation during the last few years.

An alternative way of interpreting the arguments presented is that U.S. firms now face such intense foreign competition that they are forced to abandon the inefficient bureaucratic form of organization to which they have been so attached. My problem with this line of argument is that *if* the bureaucratic form of organization is so inefficient and *if* middle managers to a large extent add costs without contributing much value, as is suggested in the chapter, why did these changes not take place much earlier? If, indeed, the efficiency gains of the "post-bureaucratic" mode of organization are of the magnitude described by Kanter, one would have expected profit maximizing firms to try to improve their market positions by reaping the benefits from these organizational reforms a long time ago. Why did the firms need to be *forced* by intense foreign competition to adopt a strategy so obviously in their own interests? It seems as though crucial links in the argument are missing; many of the post-bureaucratic organizational reforms should have also been efficient in less turbulent environments.

How, then, can we explain the inertia in implementing these organizational forms? Was the delay related to internal organizational politics and to a powerful position of middle managers that allowed them to obstruct organizational reforms not in their own interests? Or was it perhaps related to a lack of influence of stockholders over corporations that made it possible for managers to escape the "whip" of the market and allowed them to adopt low-ambition satisficing strategies?

It is difficult to understand the processes that might have produced the situations described in the chapter unless these types of intervening mechanisms are spelled out in more detail. One would particularly like more detailed descriptions of changes in incentive and opportunity structures facing decision makers within these firms. If mechanisms of this kind were to be included in the analysis, I believe this chapter has the potential for making an important and lasting contribution to the literature on organizational and social change in the late twentieth century.

Comments

Edward O. Laumann

Rosabeth Kanter has been devoting a lot of attention in recent years to the structural, collective, and social conditions for innovation in organizations. Through her consulting and more academically oriented research efforts, she has accumulated a rich and variegated set of fieldwork experiences in over eighty companies from which she has drawn a fascinating set of speculative suggestions and conclusions that should provide useful grist for a more disciplined theoretical formulation. This chapter is drawn from her 1989 book, *When Giants Learn to Dance: Mastering the Challenges of Strategy, Management, and Careers in the 1990s.* The book is clearly addressed to a much broader lay audience than to a group of organizational theorists and researchers. As a result, there is a certain looseness in the formulation and definition of key terms and propositions. The prose also suggests a degree of immediacy or recency to the changes in economic life of, say, the past five or eight years that clearly have been in progress for a much longer time.

The central empirical claim of the chapter runs roughly as follows: In confronting the new economic realities of global competition, U.S. corporations have converged upon similar management strategies that constitute "a core of post-bureaucratic, post-entrepreneurial management." The dominant business paradigm is changing from the old "bureaucratic" corporation ideal that is position-centered, repetition-oriented, rules-oriented, and pay for status to the new "post-bureaucratic" style that is person-centered, creation-oriented, results-oriented, and pay for contributions.

At a conference Kanter and I attended in March 1989, a case study was presented by Bruce Gissing, senior vice president of Boeing Commerical Airplanes, that described a massive reorganization of a 2,400-person workplace that assembles the skeleton of the Boeing commercial airliner. Under the advice and guidance of an organizational design consultant trained at the University of Michigan in the mid-1960s, Boeing was installing a reconfigured participative management system in which the advice and consent of line workers, organized into interlocking work-groups and delegated responsibility to collaborate in developing the technical design and layout for the entire work process, were eagerly solicited. If this experiment in worker (and union) participation (with corresponding reductions in managerial supervising layers) were successful, the plan was to generalize the scheme where feasible to the rest of the 150,000-person company. I experienced déjà vu—almost feeling I had stepped into a time warp; it was just the sort of thing Rensis Likert, a major organizational theorist and researcher at the University of Michigan during the 1950s and 1960s, described as System IV in his 1961 book, *New Patterns of Management*.

The point is that these ideas on organization design have been discussed and indeed implemented in a limited number of cases for some thirty or forty years. According to Kanter's account, they now seem to be taken somewhat more seriously by certain corporate giants than formerly; but the issue, for our purposes, is answering more accurately the empirical question about the timing and extensiveness of the transformation of managerial thought and, more important, practice. The diffusion of these ideas over the past four decades has certainly been highly selective and uneven and, to be sure, was much more extensive in certain types of work enterprises and industries than in others (it was notably more extensive in those providing various sorts of customized work services or products that are inherently one of a kind or small batch in character). We should ponder these issues more precisely because we may come up with quite a different causal account of the shift from tall to flat hierarchies. The one implicit in Kanter's account of the shift would point to the goad of contemporary pressures of global competition and the re-diffusion of successful Japanese management practices to the United States. Another, to which I am somewhat more inclined, would point to the massive growth of the service sector over the past several decades, partially at the expense of the heavy manufacturing sector but more at the expense of agriculture and extractive industry. This growing sector seems to employ organizational forms much more congenial with horizontal, or more cooperative and egalitarian rather than command-oriented, work organizations.

In fact, I entertain some serious doubts about the actual extent and dominance of bureaucratic forms of organization in U.S. economic enterprises at any time in our history. Here we are plagued with two problems—the first having to do with how we define bureaucracy in economic organizations and the second having to do with the absence of any compelling time series data over a sufficient time span. (Proxy variables having to do with the changing percentage of white-collar workers simply will not do.) I suspect that only a very negligible percentage of persons in economic organizations ever confronted or experienced at any time in our history a bureaucratic career ladder of the sort idealized by Weber's model. There has been far too much job and occupational mobility in and outside of given economic organizations of even the largest sort to find many individuals who fit the hypothesized pattern. I know of no studies of economic organizations that have good time series data on internal promotion able to track those who leave the organization or jump career tracks within the organization.

It is here that the common-sense way in which Kanter uses the term *bureaucracy* may lead us astray. On the one hand, Kanter clearly intends to mean by bureaucracy the idea of a monolithic pyramid in which each position in the hierarchy reports to only one superior and exercises supervisory authority over a specified set of subordinates. Yet she also speaks of the bloated corporate staff as being somehow associated with tall bureaucracies. But staffs were always an anomalous set of personnel in Weber's original formulation of the ideal type. They, by definition, lack line authority and tend to be professionals of one stripe or another—a group Kanter discusses in quite a different and more favorable context, predicting a "waxing" of their significance in organizations. Certainly, corporate staffs do not have any clear articulation or placement with respect to a notion of bureaucratic career (see Melville Dalton's classic, *Men Who Manage*).

In connection with Kanter's discussion of the three principal career types (bureaucratic, professional, and entrepreneurial), I agree with her contention that the pursuers of such careers face great unpredictability and uncertainty with respect to career advancement. I am not so sure, however, that I would agree with her notion that there have been *increasing* uncertainty and contingency with respect to the career patterns when compared to some former period, unspecified, but presumably within the past twenty or thirty years. Mariah Evans and I (1983) conducted a 1970 census-based study of retention and exit rates in twenty-three professional and technical occupations, including engineering and scientific specialties, medicine, and the law. Our most impressive result was the substantial movement in and out of such occupations. Most professionals, including that of college teaching, displayed a pattern of exits that implied more than half of those studied had left their profession within ten years of entry. Only the professions of medicine, law, and dentistry approximated the myth of a life-long commitment to the profession.

Given my own interests in network analysis, I noted with gratification Kanter's recurring discussion of the growing importance of networks of organizations becoming involved in close working relationships. To quote her, "Strategic alliances and partnerships are seen as a potent way to do more with less. They permit the company to remain lean, controlling costs while gaining access to more capacity than what is owned or employed directly. The traditional corporation was stuck with the limitations of do-it-yourself-or-don't-do-it-at-all mentalities." While I do not entirely disagree with this and related observations, I do note that Kanter tends to set up a contrast between a bureaucratic versus a networking mode of operation. The technical literature on networks would treat network as the more general term that refers to a set of nodes and how they are connected in particular sets of relationships. A bureaucracy conceived as a hierarchy of positions connected by authoritative relations of command and subordination is merely a particular type of network. The interesting theoretical problem then becomes one of specifying the different kinds of networks, including those I have called elsewhere *modes of antagonistic cooperation* and Kanter appears to be calling *networking* as opposed to bureaucratic modes of organization, in order to learn the conditions that facilitate or hinder their formation and transformation. Oliver Williamson's speculations about markets and hierarchies, among others, are relevant to such a discussion.

More generally, my quarrels—such as they are—with Kanter's formulations fall into two general comments. First, I fear there is a degree of imprecision and shifting reference in the use of key terms in her argument that makes it difficult at critical points to evaluate the empirical validity of her claims, particularly with respect to the recency of some of these changes. Second, to the extent that we are both talking about roughly the same things, I would contend that the major features of career uncertainty—whether bureaucratic, professional, or entrepreneurial—have "always" been features of such career patterns—certainly since World War II, if not before. Admittedly, we lack compelling historical evidence on the overall trend line, but I seriously doubt that there has been a major inflection point toward greater uncertainty in career lines over the past decade.

REFERENCES

Mariah D. Evans and Edward O. Laumann. 1983. "Professional Commitment: Myth or Reality?" Pp. 3–40 in Donald J. Treiman and Robert V. Robinson, eds., *Research in Stratification and Mobility*. Greenwich, CT: JAI Press.

3

Indirect Relationships and Imagined Communities: Large-Scale Social Integration and the Transformation of Everyday Life

Craig Calhoun

Talk about the end of an era is once again widespread, perhaps a sign of another *fin de siècle* generation. Yet for all the variety of "postmodernisms" proposed, the modern era remains sociologically undertheorized. This means that most accounts of its transcendence do a poor job of specifying just what counts as an epochal transformation.

In this chapter, I will put forward an argument about two general features of modernity that social theory has pointed to but inadequately thematized and that help to provide a much stronger sociological foundation for grasping some of the phenomena to which postmodern thought calls our attention. The two features both reflect the modern production of an increasing split between the world of direct interpersonal relationships and that of large-scale collective organization. Conceptualizing the first in essentially social structural or network terms, we can call it the proliferation of indirect relationships—those mediated by information technology, bureaucratic organizations, and more or less self-regulating systems such as markets. Conversely, the second can be conceptualized in basically cultural terms as the production of imagined communities (borrowing the phrase from Benedict Anderson 1983). That is, people have come increasingly to conceive of themselves as members of very large collectivities linked primarily by common identities but minimally by networks of directly interpersonal

Earlier versions of this chapter were presented to the Conference on Social Theory and Emerging Issues in a Changing Society, held in Chicago, April 5–8, 1989, and circulated as Working Paper #2 of the Program in Social Theory and Cross-Cultural Studies of the University of North Carolina. I am grateful for discussion and criticism from both groups.

relationships—nations, races, classes, genders, Republicans, Muslims, and "civilized people."

Recognizing the role of indirect relations and imagined communities provides a way to understand the increasing split between everyday life and large-scale systemic integration, thus potentially informing and improving Jürgen Habermas's account of social versus system integration. This split is behind a good deal of the apparent fragmentation of meaning that is a long-standing modern motif and a special theme of postmodernism. It informs a variety of sociopolitical movements (and modes of understanding) in the modern world, from nationalism to populism to the various "new social movements" focused on legitimating the identities of previously repressed or marginalized groups. It is also a reason why theoretical understanding cannot be done away with in favor of a simple proliferation of practical attitudes and a relativism of different relations to the world. If we are to grasp the workings of large-scale social integration (rather than simply lament them), we require theory; they are uniquely different to grasp adequately through practical, nondiscursive knowledge.

INDIRECT RELATIONSHIPS

Perhaps the most important transformation of everyday life in the modern era has been the sharpening and deepening of a split between the world of direct interpersonal relationships and the mode of organization and integration of large-scale social systems. Indeed, this split partially constitutes the contemporary notion of everyday life. We contrast the quotidian no longer with the extraordinary days of feasts and festivals so much as with the systemically remote, with that which "counts" on a large scale. Movie stars, corporate presidents, and famous politicians are thus distinguished from "everyday people."

Certainly, large-scale social organizations have always worked in distinctive ways. The medieval Roman Catholic church and the Imperial Chinese court and bureaucracy worked differently from local peasant villages. But during the modern era, such splits between the systemic and the face-to-face have deepened and taken on new significance, even while new media and changed structures of power have made the modern heirs of pope and emperor more visible and apparently more like everyone else. The capacity of large-scale collective actors and organizational systems has grown dramatically, largely on the basis of improvements in infrastructural (notably transportation and communication) technology. States have become able to administer remote territories far more effectively, businesses to organize dispersed activities, and armies to fight around the world.[1] At the same time, it is increasingly difficult for people to make sense of the organization of large-scale social systems and collective actors on the basis of extensions or analogies from the understanding of everyday, local life. This is not to say that people do not try to make sense of the affairs of nation-states and international markets by forms of reasoning developed in the context of the family or the local community; they certainly do, and populist politicians make playing on this tendency a key part of their rhetorical stock-in-trade (Calhoun 1988). Rather, the point is that understandings derived from the world of everyday, direct social interaction are likely to be increasingly distorting when applied to the world of large-scale social integration and action.

Human society depends on the capacity to coordinate action. Beyond the level of a small-band form of organization, and indeed even to some extent within it, this requires various techniques for mediating distance in time and space. Internalized cultural norms, the fear of specific reprisals, oral traditions, communications technologies from print on, bureaucracies, and markets are all among the ways in which this is done, although this is not necessarily how we usually think of them. The modern world is constituted in part by the radical expansion and transformation of such capacity to coordinate action across time and space. And as Michel Foucault has shown, extension of systems of power was often paralleled by a transformation of interpersonal power. Direct coercion was partially replaced by normalizing discipline, and the workings of power actually intensified in the process.[2]

This concern with the coordination of action can be situated within the general issue of competing forms of societal integration. I propose to revise but appropriate the argument that modernity is characterized by a basic split between distinct "worlds" of experience or spheres of activity and organization—as, for example, between what Habermas (1984, 1988) calls the system and the lifeworld. I will suggest, however, that there are at least four "worlds" to be considered: the world of directly interpersonal relations typified by actual or potential face-to-face interaction, the world of imagined personal connection (through some medium such as television, but also tradition), the one-directional world of active relationships (such as surveillance) known only or primarily to one of the parties, and the world of systemic integration or coordination by impersonal and delinguistified steering media, which give the illusion of not involving human action or interpersonal power. These "worlds" are based on different sorts of social relationships, different forms of mediation, for even directly interpersonal relationships are not simply given materially but are constituted in communication and intersubjective understanding. But I will also suggest that the phenomenological language of "worlds" Habermas appropriates is misleading here, as the very interpenetration of these "different" modes of relationship is of crucial importance. That we should see something such as system and lifeworld as distinct worlds or spheres of life is a structure of modern consciousness that needs to be examined, not simply accepted.

Social Versus System Integration

Habermas's (1984, 1988) division of lifeworld and system is among the latest in the long series of binary oppositions used to characterize modern social life: *gemeinschaft* and *gesellschaft*, mechanical and organic, folk and urban, status and contract, traditional and modern, and so on. There are limits to any binary conceptualization of modes of social organization, but Habermas's offers an important advantage over its predecessors. It does not suggest that one mode of organization has simply supplanted the other, dividing history into two neat phases. Rather, it proposes that modernity is characterized by a division between the world of lived experience and the increasing role of large-scale, systemic integration. The lifeworld does not vanish, but (1) it is able to organize only a constricted and shrinking subset of social activities; (2) it is not able to accomplish integration on a scale approaching that of system integration; (3) it is constructively rationalized by the growing differentiation of subjects and their reliance on communicative achievement of mutual understanding; and (4) it is colonized by the instrumental modes of rationality and the reified, typically cybernetic way of understanding the products of human action characteristic of the system world. Systemic integration does not organize all of life, but it does organize its most important political and economic infrastructure and its largest-scale units of integration.

The general theoretical problem behind this set of concerns is one that has occupied both functionalism and Marxism and a good deal of the rest of modern social theory. It is the question of how to relate understandings of social life and the cohesion of social relationships based on actors and action to those based on notions of self-regulating systems, unintended functioning, or structure. This is the age-old problem Giddens (1985a) has newly posed in his attempt to overcome such dualities with a language (perhaps a theory) of structuration.[3]

David Lockwood put forward a terse account of the distinction between social and system integration in 1964: "Whereas the problem of social integration focuses attention upon the orderly or conflictual relationships between the *actors*, the problem of system integration focuses on the orderly or conflictual relationships between the *parts*, of a social system" (p. 371; emphasis in original). Lockwood was particularly concerned with clarifying this distinction in order to address criticisms of functionalism that, in the 1950s and 1960s—largely because of the prominence of normative functionalism (particularly in Parsons)—were in his view overinvolved with disputes over the role of action and power and somewhat neglectful of more basically systemic issues. In particular, so-called "conflict theory" so completely absorbed the one-sided emphasis on actors that it tended to remove from its purview the basic issue of systemic contradictions:

> Yet it is precisely Marx who clearly differentiates social and system integration. The propensity to class antagonism (social integration aspect) is generally a function of the character of production relationships (e.g. possibilities of intra-class identification and communication). But the dynamics of class antagonisms are clearly related to the progressively growing "contradictions" of the economic system. One might almost say that the "conflict" which in Marxian theory is decisive for change is not the *power* conflict arising from the relationships in the productive system, but the *system* conflict arising from "contradictions" between "property institutions" and the "forces of production." . . . Thus it

is perfectly possible, according to this theory, to say that at any particular point of time a society has a high degree of social integration (e.g. relative absence of class conflict) and yet has a low degree of system integration (mounting excess productive capacity). (Lockwood 1964, pp. 375–376)

Lockwood's argument is part of an apt attempt to show both that societal integration needs to be seen as differentiated as to kind or domain and that it needs to be seen as an empirical variable, not simply a theoretical postulate.

A decade after Lockwood's essay, Habermas (1978) introduced an identically labeled version of the same distinction. A reading of Emile Durkheim's early work provides his basis for drawing "our attention to empirical connections between stages of system differentiation and forms of social integration. It is only possible to analyze these connections by distinguishing mechanisms of coordinating action that harmonize the *action orientations* of participants from mechanisms that stabilize nonintended interconnections of actions by way of functionally intermeshing *action consequences*" (1988, p. 117). It is important that Habermas tries to maintain a nonreified notion of systems as still deriving from action, although working through more or less self-regulating feedback mechanisms based on action consequences rather than international governance or cooperation. This distinction, according to Habermas, calls for "a corresponding differentiation in the concept of society itself" (1988, p. 117). It is this differentiation that Habermas introduces as the distinction between lifeworld and system and pursues in his analysis of their decoupling in the process of modernization.

The contrast is at one level between the phenomena to which functionalist systems theories such as Parsons's (especially 1951) and Luhmann's (e.g., 1982) are well suited and those to which more phenomenological accounts (for example, Schutz 1967; Schutz and Luckmann 1973) are oriented. Our experience in modern society leads to divergent ways of trying to understand the social world and to an experiential and intellectual split between lifeworld and system world (or such common-sense analogs as "the people" and "the system," "everyday life" and "the big picture," and the like).

Habermas focuses little attention on social structural factors influencing such distinctions.[4] I want to claim that our tendency to posit such ad hoc analytic divisions in the course of everyday life derives from the contrast between directly interpersonal social relationships and the indirect relationships that are formed when social action affects others only through the mediation of complex organizations, impersonal markets, or communications technology. Indirect relationships permit a societal scale unimaginable on the basis of direct relationships and simultaneously encourage objectification and reification of their origin in human actions.[5]

Habermas begins with a qualitative distinction in forms of rational action: instrumental (oriented to success in relation to objectified goals) and communicative (oriented to reflective understanding and the constitution of social relations).[6] In his view, both of these develop naturally in the course of human history. They come into conflict when they give rise to competing forms of societal integration: systemic and social (lifeworld). The latter is integrated through communicative action in which people seek mutual understanding.[7] The former is integrated through the feedback mechanisms of "delinguistified steering media," without any actors necessarily understanding the whole system or without such understanding playing a central role. Money is the paradigmatic example of the delinguistified steering media to which Habermas (following Parsons) refers, but a wide range of statistical indicators (of productivity, public opinion, and the like) share many relevant features. These media allow social systems to be "steered" as though they were independent of human action. Through systems theory, they may be understood in the same way. Indeed, the complexity of very large-scale social processes may dictate that they can be grasped better in cybernetic and other relatively abstract academic terms than in terms of the ordinary discourse of the lifeworld. Accordingly, Habermas uses systems theory in his analysis of system integration even while he attacks the reifying (and anti-democratic) tendencies of systems theory (see especially 1988). It is unclear, however, whether or how he maintains in his theory the ability to show that such large-scale indirect phenomona remain nonetheless human social activity and relationships.

What is needed, it seems to me, is a more explicit argument that a systems–theoretic account of very large-scale social organization is an intellectual convenience, a tool for understanding that is genuinely powerful but that must be counterbalanced by continuous reminders that it is a provisional view based on a bracketing of the "real" origins of these large-scale systems in concrete human activity. The existence of such large-scale organizational systems thus predisposes us to think of them in systemic terms; they incline us toward reification, but whatever sense in which they are systems is not one entirely divorced from human action. In other words, when relationships are directly interpersonal we are unlikely to fail to recognize the extent to which they are human social creations. But when they are highly indirect, mediated by technology and complex organizations, we are likely to need to approach their operation through aggregate statistics and cybernetic conceptions. These will tend to make it look as though the large-scale systems were somehow autonomously functioning entities rather than creations of human social action.

This is not the place to address Habermas's conceptualization in any detail. Rather, I want to take up the issue of how the distinction of direct from indirect social relationships might provide us with more of a social structural basis for a theory of contrasting modes of societal integration.

The Dimension
of Concrete Social Relationships

Trying to explain patterns of societal integration primarily by changing orientations to action can obscure the foundation of these patterns on concrete social relationships of different sorts. These concrete relationships form a sort of scaffolding for social integration, a scaffolding highly dependent on infrastructural technology. Habermas's failure to develop this sort of foundation for his argument contributes to several problematic aspects of his generally stimulating and powerful theory: its difficulties in achieving cultural and historical specificity; its too-uncritical acceptance of the systems–theoretical description of systemic integration; its tendency to idealize life-world relationships; and its underdeveloped account of practical, situated activity that cannot readily be reduced to purely communicative, strategic, or rational action.[8]

The world of direct interaction, especially primary relationships, remains emotionally central to people in the most advanced modern societies and at the heart of most people's evaluative frameworks.[9] We have direct relationships with family, friends, neighbors, associates at work, and even people with whom we interact only briefly and in ways essentially defined by role performance—bank tellers, our children's school teachers, and similar groups. Within direct interaction, Cooley's (1909) distinction of primary from secondary relationships suggests a continuum of decreasing closeness, multiplexity, and completeness of grasp of the other. Nonetheless, even secondary relationships are marked by the potential for expansion direct interaction provides. In Schutz's words, "In the face-to-face situation the partners are constantly revising and enlarging their knowledge of each other" (1967, p. 230).

Schutz, indeed, had as much to say about directness and indirectness of social relations as any social theorist, although his account was always strongly phenomenological in that it focused exclusively on the consciousness of the experiencing individual.[10]

> In the face-to-face situation, directness of experience is essential, regardless of whether our apprehension of the Other is central or peripheral and regardless of how adequate our grasp of him is. . . . We make the transition from direct to indirect social experience simple by following this spectrum of decreasing vividness. The first steps beyond the realm of immediacy are marked by a decrease in the number of perceptions I have of the other person and a narrowing of the perspectives within which I view him. (1967, p. 219)

The world of mere contemporaries, those with whom we are not at the present time in contact, is nonetheless itself defined by the face-to-face situation that remains a possibility. Schutz suggests understanding the world of contemporaries in terms of regions of increasing anonymity. In the outlying, particularly anonymous regions lie contemporaries of whose existence as concrete individuals one has no specific knowledge, although one knows that a certain position is occupied or that a certain functional role is being fulfilled by someone; collective entites; and ultimately residuals of human activity such as the grammar of a language or physical artifacts.

The primacy of face-to-face situations is an important but surprisingly often overlooked feature of direct relationships. Webber (1967), for example, introduced the notion of community without propinquity to describe the increasing importance of relationships formed within special purpose associations, encouraged by access to transport, and often mediated by space-transcending communications technology. The descriptive insight was sound; such relationships have indeed grown more important. But the conceptualization was flawed. In particular, it obscured attention to the special features of locally compact communities, notably the much greater likelihood that relationships would be multiplex, linking people in several different spheres of activity or dimensions of their lives (Bell and Newby 1976; Calhoun 1980a). That contemporary neighborhoods may rarely do this is not proof against the argument that locality is important to such multiplexity but is only evidence that, for a mix of reasons, such multiplexity has declined. Following the Simmelian line of thought of Peter Blau's recent structural sociology (Blau 1977; Blau and Schwartz 1984), there is a tradeoff between the expansion of cross-cutting relations linking people widely in a population and the density and intensity of in-group relations within specific sub-populations, including local communities. There is an important sense in which the expansion of supra-local special purpose associations *has*, as the classical sociologists expected, contributed to the decline of community as a form of social organization, if not as a value.

Almost all major premodern forms of social organization depended primarily on direct interpersonal relationships. Kinship, community life, and even most stable, recurrent relationships of economic exchange all took place within the conscious awareness and usually the face-to-face co-presence of human individuals. Not only the immediate parties to any particular transaction but their implicit or explicit monitoring by a field of others directly linked to the main participants brought order to such arrangements. Such relationships could be more or less systematic and complex: Webs of kinship linked hundreds of thousands of members of traditional African societies. The actualization of each relationship as opposed to its latent potential, however, was normally directly interpersonal.[11] While state apparatuses certainly predate the modern era and occurred historically throughout the world, Giddens (1985b, p. 63) is surely right to argue that few if any were able to govern in the modern sense of the word; their capacity for regularized administration of a territory and its residents was very limited.[12] This was largely because power relations could not be extended effectively over large distances.[13] Although cultural variation was enormous and variation in specific patterns of social organization considerable, only rarely were premodern peoples able to produce the physical infrastructure and administrative practices necessary to large-scale social organization of much intensity. China probably went furthest, followed perhaps by Imperial Rome.

Modern political and economic affairs are distinguished by the increasing frequency, scale, and importance of indirect social relationships. Large-scale markets, closely administered organizations, and information technology have produced many more opportunities for such relationships than existed in any premodern society. This does not mean that direct relationships have been reduced in number or that they are less meaningful or attractive to individuals. Rather, it means that direct relationships tend to be compartmentalized. They persist as part of the immediate lifeworld of individuals, both as the nexus of certain kinds of instrumental activities (such as the many personal relationships that smooth or enable business transactions [cf. Granovetter, 1985]) and especially as the realm of private life (family, friends, neighbors). Direct relationships help to make complex organizations work, even while such organizations mediate indirect relations. Direct interpersonal relationships organize less and less of public life, however—less and less of the crucially determinant institutions controlling material resources and exercising social power. Indirect relationships do not eliminate direct ones, but they change both their meaning and their sociological significance (Meyrowitz 1985; Calhoun 1988). As sociopsychologically and culturally powerful as ever, direct relationships are no longer constitutive of society at its widest reaches.[14]

The reproduction of embodied but social sensibilities, habituses (in Bourdieu's 1976, 1980 sense), is altered as social life comes more and more to be coordinated through indirect relationships. Thus, tradition as the passing on of culture remains alive and important in the modern world, but the social organization of indirect relationships undermines its effectiveness in reproducing preexisting patterns of social life. We are led to an apparently more rationalistic orientation to action (in Weber's sense), not just by a change in values or orientation but by transformations in basic aspects of social structure, notably those developed as part of the rise of capitalism and the modern state.

This growing importance of indirect relationships was recognized by both Marx and Weber. Capitalism, for Marx, was not established on the basis of direct interpersonal relationships. It existed only through the mediation of commodities produced and exchanged in the pursuit of capital accumulation. Indeed, Marx defined capitalism as an arena of totalizing relations based on abstract labor largely in opposition to direct interpersonal relationships: "their own exchange and their own production confront individuals as an *objective* relation which is *independent* of them. In the case of the *world market*, the *connection of the individual* with all, but at the same time also the *independence of this connection from the individual*, have developed to such a high level that the formation of the world market already at the same time contains the conditions for going beyond it" (1939, p. 161, emphases in original).[15] Capitalism means the creation of an abstract totality— the whole system of capital accumulation—through the mediation of human activity (in relation to nature, self, and others) by commodities. Marx and especially Engels were fond of borrowing Carlyle's phrase that capitalism left no other nexus between man and man than "callous cash payment" (see Marx and Engels, p. 487; Engels, p. 608). Just as capitalism must disregard or even attack the irreducibly qualitative nature of commodities, so it must disregard or attack the qualitative content of human relationships (Marx 1867, Chapter 1; Lukacs 1922, pp. 83–148). Not so a post-capitalist society. Where Marx envisages a communist future, he does not oppose quantitatively interchangeable individuals to an abstract totality. Rather, he takes pains to stress that "above all we must avoid postulating 'society' again as an abstraction *vis-à-vis* the individual. The individual *is the social being*" (1844, p. 299; emphasis in original). But such a condition is a possible future to be historically created, not a timeless feature of human nature (other than in potential): "Universally developed individuals, whose social relations, as their own communal [*gemeinschaftlich*] relations, are hence also subordinated to their own communal control, are not product of nature, but of history" (1939, p. 162). Natural law and social contract theorists, Marx says at the same point in the *Grundrisse*, focus their attention on "merely objective" bonds among people and mistake them for the spontaneous relationships that are not possible in the existing state of society. So long as the abstract relationships of capitalism remain determinant, the analysis of concrete relationships will be the analysis of more or less arbitrary epiphenomena. When capitalism and the human self-estrangement of private property are transcended, there will still be a difference between activities carried out in direct communality with others and those (such as science) that depend less on the immediate co-presence of the group but that are nonetheless self-consciously social. But each of these will be self-determining in a way impossible under the domination of capitalism:

> Social activity and social enjoyment exist by no means *only* in the form of some *directly* communal activity and directly *communal* enjoyment, although *communal* activity and *communal* enjoyment—i.e. activity and enjoyment which are manifested and affirmed in *actual* direct *association* with other men—will occur wherever such a *direct* expression of sociability stems from the true character of the activity's content and is appropriate to the nature of the enjoyment. (Marx and Engels 1848, p. 298, emphases in the original)

For Weber, the commodity form was also key, but, characteristically, market rather than production relations were central; the "indirect exchange of money" was prototypical:

> Within the market community every act of exchange, expecially monetary exchange, is not directed, in isolation, by the action of the individual partner to the particular transaction, but the more rationally it is considered, the more it is directed by the actions of all parties potentially interested in the exchange. The market community as such is the most impersonal form of practical life into which humans can enter with one another. This is not due to that potentiality of struggle among the interested parties which is inherent in the market relationship. Any human relationship, even the most intimate, and even though it be marked by the most unqualified personal devotion, is in some sense relative and may involve a struggle with the partner. . . . The reason for the impersonality of the market is its matter-of-factness, its orientation to the commodity and only to that. When the market is allowed to follow its own autonomous tendencies, its participants do not look toward the persons of each other but only toward the commodity; there are no obligations of

brotherliness or reverence, and none of those spontaneous human relations that are sustained by personal unions. (1922, p. 636)

Weber's ideal-typical market does not correspond to any actuality, of course, any more than Marx's pure model of capitalism does. But each expresses a distinctly modern tendency.

A convenient way to think about the issue is to borrow Cooley's (1909) language of primary and secondary relations. This conceptualized the idea—not unique to Cooley—that modern, especially urban, life was characterized by an increasing predominance of relatively attenuated, special-purpose relationships over richer, more deeply committed and many-stranded ones. Cooley was developing an implicitly Rousseauian critique of the inauthenticity of secondary relations. But he failed to see something that might have disturbed him further—the increasing role of indirect relationships in which the individual parties are not engaged in even the limited sort of face-to-face or personal interaction characteristic of secondary relations. I have elsewhere (Calhoun 1986 and forthcoming a) proposed extending Cooley's language with notions of tertiary and quaternary relations.[16]

Tertiary relations are those individual parties might in principle bring to full awareness and direct interaction, although in practice this might be impossible. When we write to an identifiable person whom we have never met—say, our congressperson, an official of the National Science Foundation, or the president of an airline that has treated us poorly—we are engaging in a tertiary relationship. How difficult it would be to make this relatively formal and abstract link direct varies. In some cases, a telephone conversation might make it somewhat more direct and might be followed by a face-to-face meeting. In most cases, however, such potential will remain unrealized; as a simple matter of scale, congresspersons cannot develop face-to-face relationships—even secondary ones—with all their constituents. Even more basically, modern large-scale markets introduce tertiary relationships in which there is no reasonable expectation that the abstract possibility of rendering them direct could be acted on. The innumerable steps between workers creating a consumer good—say, shoes in Italy—and the ultimate users of that good may preclude bringing the two face-to-face. Even if only through reified understanding, however, we do recognize that behind the impersonal patterns of the market and the mediation of bureaucratic organizations (wholesalers, department stores, and the like) a chain of concrete interactions exists.

This is more difficult for quaternary relations, those in which at least one of the parties to a relationship is kept systematically unaware of the existence of the relationship. Phone tapping or other instances of surveillance form a paradigm case of this, but, aided by modern information technology, the range of quaternary relationships seems to be multiplying. Credit card records can be analyzed for purposes far beyond any the user had in mind in performing the transaction or is ever likely to be aware of; so can census data and a variety of indirect indicators used in government, marketing, and other monitoring activities of modern life.

What is meant by indirect relationships in this context is, thus, relationships that depend upon the mediation of some combination of information-processing technologies and complex organizations, which may be either bureaucratically administered or self-regulating in the fashion of markets. In relation to Habermas's conception of system and lifeworld, we need to mark an important distinction among the kinds of indirect relationships that form the basis of systemic integration. Those quaternary relationships of surveillance, for example, are clear exercises of power hardly to be grasped by a notion of self-regulating systems, although that may fit markets reasonably well. And there is still another important sort of connection, a particularly illusory one but none the less powerful for that. I refer to the bonds felt among people who take as an important part of their personal identity their membership in categories of persons linked minimally by direct interpersonal bonds but established culturally by tradition, the media, or the slogans of political protest.

IMAGINED COMMUNITIES

I feel a oneness with other Americans, a sense of common membership with people I have never met or heard of as individuals, with people who in direct interaction might repell or anger me. In some settings, such nationalistic sentiments motivate people to die in wars for independence or freedom, or become martyrs in the struggle against colonial powers, to shed the blood of neighbors whose ethnic or religious identity challenges some sense of the purity of nationhood. And yet, the nationalist sentiments that have been important enough to die for in a struggle for liberation seem often to offer little defense against ethnic and other sectionalist divisions after independence. Such phenomena have puzzled social scientists throughout the modern era. From Marx to the present day, theorists of modernity have expected them to die out as part of the process of rationalization. Such phenomena are as difficult to fit into orthodox Marxism as to make sense of in terms of rational choice theory; it is often hard for us to see what "real" interests are being maximized.

Letters flow by the thousands to fictional characters in soap operas; viewers write to offer them advice on the fictional dilemmas and to ask their help in solving their own real ones. Americans felt that Ronald Reagan cared personally about each of them because he seemed so effortlessly and genially to come into their living rooms on television. In the early 1980s, Chinese scholars who had just returned to urban life from years of working with the peasants on a rural commune said they owed their rescue to the personal interview of Deng Xiaoping. Some told stories suggesting that the universities were told to accept deserving students on more academic bases than the "four goods" of party orthodoxy because someone wrote Deng a letter and he was moved by their plight, which newly revealed to him the abuses of the cultural revolution. By 1989, protesting students were equally apt to vilify Deng or Premier Li Peng, seeing them as personally responsible for the absence of democracy in China. Although ostensibly seeking democracy, many of the protesters (especially outside the core student ranks) seemed so eager to find a new hero at the top of the official leadership that one wondered whether they would simply have traded malevolent dictatorship for a more benevolent one (Calhoun 1989b) and gone on assuming that the individual at the top mattered more than the system.

The fantasies of soap opera fans and the delusions of those who think the politics of modern large-scale states are essentially personal matters are more banal than nationalism, but they share a good deal with it. Here I want to explore those commonalties, not in empirically descriptive terms— that is, not by looking at television audiences and patriotic wars as such— but in terms of analytic developments that can help to overcome our puzzlement by both. The proliferation of indirect relationships I have just described is central among these.

Alongside the proliferation of indirect social relationships, we have developed a variety of cultural ways for identifying similarity and difference with other people. This has been necessary, not least of all, because we are drawn by large-scale organization of social interaction into contact with a wide range of people both like and unlike ourselves and because we are obliged to recognize our interdependence—happy or otherwise—with people distant from ourselves. Thus, we develop categorical identities like those of nations or within them those we ascribe to or claim as members of different ethnic groups, religions, classes, or even genders. Some of the time, at least, we imagine these categorical identities on analogy to the local communities in which we live. Even in social theory, when we identify community not as a variable structure of social relationships but as a form of common feeling, we encourage the notion that the community among neighbors and the community among citizens of the same nation are essentially similar.[17] I want to argue, however, that there is a great deal of difference between the social *groups* formed out of direct relationships among their members, although often sharing an imaginatively constructed cultural identity, and social *categories* defined by common cultural or other external attributes of their members and not necessarily linked by any dense, multiplex, or systematic web of interpersonal relationships.[18]

In his account of the structural transformation of the public sphere, Habermas (1962) describes a degeneration of publicity in which public discourse gives way to plebiscitary acclamation for leaders or policies. Bourgeois society (especially of the late nineteenth and early twentieth centuries) had, according to his account, provided for a public sphere— admittedly small and framed by its implicit class character—that had brought men of property into a more or less egalitarian discourse in which arguments, rather than simple power, swayed opinion. A crucial condition for this public discourse was a private sphere that nurtured a strong sense of personal identity. In the late twentieth century, by contrast, Habermas argues that the public sphere has been undermined by a collapse of the public-private distinction and an expansion of its membership without the necessary reconstruction of its basis. Among the results of this is a politics of identification. The public sphere does not exist as a set of discursive relationships but rather is created (or at least simulated) by political actors who put forth images they hope will garner the identification of large numbers of people who may have no discursive relationships with each other or with the political actors. Thus, the National Rifle Association calls for gun owners to identify as a community of interest, and the National Organization of Women calls for a "communification" of women. A key condition for this is that people do not enter the public sphere with well-formed identities, prepared to engage in argument, but rather in some need of identity and seeking not just rational discourse, cooperative social arrangements, or even instrumental ends but in one large part affirmation of their personal identity.[19] Even arguments themselves are no longer attempts to reach an understanding (as in the classical notion of parliamentary debate) but are staged displays, such as debates of presidential candidates—presentations of "symbols to which again one can not respond by arguing, but only by identifying with them" (Habermas 1962, p. 206). The reliance of modern large-scale democratic politics on mass media only accentuates this diversion of publicity away from real public discourse and, indeed, the paradox underlying Habermas's entire book—that the extension of democratic rights to the whole adult population should have resulted in a collapse of the public sphere rather than a more unambiguous progress of democracy.

The politics of identification Habermas describes point to a process of imagining communities; indeed, at one point he borrows R. Altmann's term "communification" to describe it. People without direct interpersonal relations with each other are led by the mediation of the world of political symbols to imagine themselves as members of communities defined by common ascriptive characteristics, personal tastes, habits, or concerns. These are understood at least sometimes as communities because of the strong sense of fellow-feeling, common interest, and shared identity. But at the same time, they are crucially imagined because of their differences from local communities and others based on direct interpersonal relationships. Imagined communities are essentially categorical identities. But although these imagined communities do not reflect dense or multiplex networks of direct interpersonal relationships, they still do reflect social relations. Imagined communities of even large scale are not simply arbitrary creatures of the imagination but depend upon indirect social relationships both to link their members and to define the fields of power within which their identities are relevant.

Benedict Anderson's 1983 account of the origins and spread of nationalism has already provided us with the term *imagined communities*. Nations, he suggests, are "*imagined* because the members of even the smallest nation will never know most of their fellow-members, meet them, or even hear of them, yet in the minds of each lives the image of their communion. . . . [A]ll communities larger than primordial villages of face-to-face contact (and perhaps even these) are imagined" (p. 15). Anderson describes a long history of imagined communities—for example, of co-religionists. But these communities were—at least earlier in history—imagined primarily through visual and aural means—that is, through a concrete iconography and participation in ritual reenactments. This sort of imagined community has a powerful historical importance, but certain developments associated with modernity not only produced nationalism but gave added reach and resonance to the process of constructing imagined communities generally. First and foremost among these was the development of *print capitalism*. By this term, Anderson suggests the importance of printing as a means of communication able both to send complex messages quickly across long distances and to store cultural traditions across generations without reproduction in constant retelling.[20] He emphasizes also the importance of capitalism to spreading the printed word far beyond the control of states or churches. He quotes Elizabeth Eisenstein (1968), saying "printed materials encouraged silent adherence to causes whose advocates could not be located in any one parish and who addressed an invisible public from afar" (Anderson 1983, p. 39) and follows up Georg Hegel's observation that newspapers (perhaps we should now say the "Today" show or NPR's "Morning Edition") serve modern man as a substitute for morning prayers: "The mass ceremony . . . is performed in silent privacy. . . . Yet each communicant is well aware that the ceremony he performs is being replicated simultaneously by thousands (or millions) of others of whose existence he is confident, yet of whose identity he has not the slightest notion" (Anderson 1983, p. 29).

The nation in particular became imaginable, according to Anderson, because the new communications technology of print interacted with capitalism and with "the fatality of human linguistic diversity" (1983, p. 46). One might object that his account gives insufficient weight to certain features of the history of power and the division of the world into states—rather than empires or other political forms. My concern here is not, however, with the specifics of his account of nationalism but with his more general contributions to what I think ought to be a developing theory of imagined communities in general. And in fact, Anderson suggests one further major social support to developing nationalism that links up with my account of indirect relations above and is helpful for the more general notion of imagined communities. This comes in his account of the relationship of colonial bureaucratic careers to the emergence of nationalist ideology.

Colonial regimes, Anderson remarks, created a novel sort of modern pilgrimage: "In a pre-print age, the reality of the imagined religious community depended profoundly on countless, ceaseless travels" (1983, p. 56). Colonial administration called forth a class of pilgrims who journeyed from remote dominions to imperial centers and back again. Their careers were blocked above a certain level; moreover, in most administrations, they could not make lateral moves to other colonies. The Indian rising in the British Raj could not aspire to help govern Hong Kong. At the same time, colonial governance drew people from different provinces (or previously independent groupings) into a common administration and put them on career paths that might station them in several districts of the colony. This both shaped these individuals' consciousness of the colony as a unity (and, therefore, potentially a nation) and gave them interests at odds with the governmental regime for which they worked. Equally important, from our present concern, it made them into mediators of the notion of nationhood for a much broader range of people. First in their capacity as agents of colonial regimes—for example, in propagating languages of state—and then in their capacity as "intellectuals," creating and distributing literatures of national leadership (and sometimes nationalist significance), these "new men" provided as a class a sort of mediation for the emerging imagined national community. Last but not least, this class of people (expanded beyond those specifically employed by colonial regimes to their cousins editing newspapers and teaching in secondary schools) provided a further mediation: They read of and imported the modular image of nationalism (and sometimes of revolution, war of independence, and various techniques for prosecuting these) from abroad. Nationalism was not simply invented anew in every setting (still less inherited from the primeval past); it was in part developed in accord with a model.[21]

Anderson does not pursue his account much beyond print media or much farther afield than his main concern with nationalism. But I would suggest that the building of imagined communities is dramatically accelerated by broadcast media[22] and applies well beyond the range of religions and nationalisms. Classes, he notes in passing, may be thought of as imagined communities—particularly large subaltern classes.[23] As I suggested earlier, so may genders, races, a wide variety of political groupings, and groupings constituted by their contrast to dominant sexual mores or identifications, musical cultures, and even tastes in consumer goods.

Contemporary communications media play an especially important role in constituting these imagined communities. Not only do both broadcast media and more specialized channels such as computer networks facilitate powerful mechanisms of coordination of action through indirect relationships, at the same time, some of these media—television especially—simulate directness of relationship. Television offers visual and aural information at the same time, something closer to the physical embodiment of experiential learning. Research suggests that people tend to trust television more than the written word because they believe they could tell better if someone on screen were lying or concealing something (Meyrowitz 1985). At the same time, television tends to introduce strong biases in the selection of what is shown—biases not as apparent as those that may shape *how* a story is reported in an ideologically oriented newspaper.[24] Not least, television dramas offer powerful images of categorical identities; they present over and over again several basic types—rich and poor, male and female, black and white, the rich, the devious and somewhat uncivilized Arab, and the fastidious, overmannered, upper-class Englishman. As these types recur, viewers are led to believe that they have observed them first-hand. This is not the place to review the literature on the ways in which mass media produce illusions of transcending space and achieving personal relationships between people who have never met.[25] Here I want simply to posit that television and other mass media offer extraordinary potential for furthering the creation of imagined communities, both as objects of identification and as objects of antagonism.

The key issue to which media point in the present context is a need to distinguish the kinds of settings—principally in direct and recurrent interpersonal relations, especially communities—where the practical reason embodied intersubjectively in the regulated improvisation of the *habitus* forms a primary basis of social integration from those in which it cannot. Those in which it cannot are those organizations of indirect relations that accomplish large-scale societal and international integration today. This goes beyond the role of media to those of markets and administered organizations from multinational corporations to governments. Communications media, however, are paradigmatic bases for the passage of information to large audiences without depending on traditional transmission through the mouths and deeds of innumerable people engaged in practical activities of various sorts.

Tradition is often understood as simply the "hard cake of custom" (in Bagehot's phrase), as a static respect for that which has always been (Weber 1922). Shils (1981) suggests the error of such understanding by stressing the etymology of the term, the root sense of *traditio* as continually passing on or handing down. Tradition, in other words, is a form of social practice, an activity. It is akin to and overlaps with communication and should be understood in the same active sense. The stress must be on the passing on itself; it is not simply the length of time for which a practice has existed, it is the communication of the practice within a population that makes it a tradition. If the practice is dictated by external necessity, so that it continues as a response to the environment rather than as a learning from the other members of a society, it is not tradition. Conversely, a traditional practice of relatively recent provenance is no less traditional once established than an ancient one (contrary to the implications of Hobsbawm and Ranger [1983]). To show that a tradition has been created by identifiable actors may impugn its authenticity from the point of view of some internal to it—if, for example, it claims to stretch from primeval history—but this need not make us as analysts doubt that it is truly a tradition.[26]

We tend to associate tradition with authoritative transmissions monitored by specialists. But at a more primary level, much tradition—and more generally the reproduction of highly stable forms of life through tradition—depends on direct interpersonal relationships. In a nutshell, tradition requires a constant process of slight readjustment, of contained and regulated improvisation and adaptation. This is part of what is suggested by Bourdieu's notion of the *habitus*—a socially constructed principle of regulated improvisation (Bourdieu 1976, 1980). When the transmission of tradition takes place through direct interpersonal relations, the practical situations, concerns, orientations, and skills of those involved accomplish this continual readjustment. The tradition is never a substance separated from the practical activity of concrete persons engaged not only in its transmission but in the accomplishment of a variety of personal projects. The demands of these projects call on people to make subtle revisions in the stereotypes they carry, to absorb information conducive to the success of their actions.[27]

Various forms of mediation limit or remove this process of practical adjustment of tradition. Temple art, for example, once produced continues to inform generations of worshippers. Written texts make perhaps history's sharpest break, surviving their creators by millennia yet communicating complex, abstract, and often very precise information.[28] With television and related media, this break is furthered yet disguised by an especially compelling illusion of co-presence. The new media have a paradoxical effect on tradition. They can introduce a far wider range of information than word of mouth, thus allowing challenges to the received biases of various oral communities. Any sense that things must be as they appear locally is thus apt to be fatally undermined.[29] At the same time, these media tend to remove tradition from continual adjustment and somewhat from discourse—at least in everyday life as distinct from specialized centers of learning or cultural production. The reception is more passive and in many cases less likely to be shaped by application in concrete projects—after all, what Americans learn about Arabs, say, has its main practical effects through indirect relations such as government policies toward Israel or Libya, say, and not very often through concrete interactions. Changes in or challenges to received tradition are more likely to depend upon a self-conscious attempt to introduce change and less on nonexplicit adjustments in practice.[30]

Tradition, thus, is a different process when transmission takes place primarily through direct relationships or primarily through indirect ones.[31] A society such as classical China involved simultaneously a long flow of tradition through direct interpersonal relations, at local village levels and within central institutions such as the court, *and* a set of more authoritative institutions for passing on approved traditions, validating their transmission from generation to generation and attempting (albeit very imperfectly) to ensure their constancy. It is a distinctive feature of the great nonmodern civilizations to have accomplished these two forms of tradition simultaneously, in an assortment of improvisationally adjusted local traditions and in largely text-based efforts to convey authoritative statements with as little room as possible for adjustment to practical concerns or situational demands. Thus, we can understand the relationship between Vedic literature and local Hindu traditions, between the lore of Sudanese saints and the carefully protected and codified realms of Sharia and Koran. Medieval Europe showed some similarity to this, with its monastic scriptoria preserving manuscripts (albeit imperfectly, as errors of transcription crept in) and providing for one sort of tradition, while popular practices wove together pagan and Christian culture, festivals of the winter solstice and Christmas. In the modern West, capitalism and state formation—and eventually widespread literary and broadcast media—have pitted the directly interpersonal and the textual-indirect transmission of tradition against each other and enabled the latter to gain a decisive upper hand.

As postmodernist authors have argued, the rationalist Enlightenment account misunderstands this, implying that tradition has vanished in the face of reason.[32] But tradition has not vanished, it has merely changed its form. Television purveys information as dubious and untested as medieval myth, with far more effective reach. It also purveys modern knowledge derived from science, and this, too, is a tradition in many senses of the word. Thus, the legitimation of science, the sense of nationhood, and most people's understanding of the contemporary problem of homelessness all depend on the same sort of mass-mediated tradition. Such tradition may appear more rational and may even offer a seemingly democratic sort of equal access. But it also enhances the oligopolistic character of the elite of message senders and removes most people from direct participation in— and therefore shaping of—the passing on of such traditions. At the same time, face-to-face tradition continues, but it is unable to organize much of large-scale social integration and even on the local scale is undermined by the open-endedness of communication networks and the low level of the density and multiplexity needed to reinforce and reproduce such patterns of traditional organization of action. We appear, thus, to be on our own as individual actors—to depend on rational decisions, not conditioned practices.

The transformation of tradition did not, however, render everyone perfect rational actors. It could not do so for several reasons (many of them familiar limits to rationality within modern rational choice theory). People could not address a world of perfect heterodoxy because it implied that they would choose their beliefs and actions from a range of possibilities far beyond the horizons of potential human attention. The systemic world provided a variety of filters and condensations, giving a manageable order to the range of information but imposing biases in doing so (such as the inevitable and necessary, but generally invisible, selection biases of any television news program). The disruption of tradition thrust people into situations where they had to make more new sorts of decisions for themselves; by doing so, it set in motion a sort of vicious (or virtuous) circle: Each new decision represented uncertainty in the environment of other decision makers, leading them to shorten their own planning horizons, making them less predictable to those in their environment (including the first decision maker), and so on. Individual choice of actions (rational or otherwise) thus helped to undermine the foundations for individual rationality by making the world more complex and less predictable. At the same time, calling on people to act on their own decisions did not guarantee that they would be procedurally rational—that they would, for example, adopt transitive preference orderings. Last but not least, the very project of being a rational individual is one shaped by cultural foundations that were not chosen by individuals. And this self-understanding is only one of the most basic of the many "prejudices" (in Gadamer's [1975] term) that are necessary but unchosen premises for human choices.

To be a rational, individualistic actor in modern society did not mean that one was no longer constituted by the intersubjective, social patterns of a habitus. What it meant was (1) that this habitus called on one to understand oneself as autonomous,[33] and (2) that the habitus had to provide for action with regard to large-scale organizations and systems, and not just other people. The very notion of being an autonomous individual consists substantially of freedom from the bonds of determination by direct relationships and certain ascribed statuses of traditional culture and the suppression from consciousness of the equally strong determinations of indirect relationships and disciplinary patterns of culture. This is why the market can be understood as a realm of freedom at the same time that people's actions with it are explained perfectly deterministically.

CONCLUSION

A world knit together by indirect relationships poses three challenges in the realm of everyday personal existence: to make sense through abstract concepts of forms of social organization for which everyday experience gives us misleading preparation, to establish a sense of personal rootedness and continuity of existence where connections across time are mainly impersonal, and to establish a sense of place and social context when the coordination of action—and the action of our own lives—constantly transcends locality. The small-town main street and rolling Kentucky hills of my youth still move me a little by nostalgia, but my sense of who I am now depends relatively little on those natural and built environments or even on my own current local community; it takes an effort to establish a sense of continuity. I know more of the lives of Martin Luther, Karl Marx, and Thomas Jefferson than I do of either of my own grandfathers. And although I think I have some understanding of the great systems of social organization, it is hard to apply in everyday life.

Both Habermas's distinction of system and lifeworld and modernist and postmodernist accounts of the fragmentation of meaning point to this disconnection. Postmodernists would often go further, asserting that the difficulties of meaning are insurmountable, that true understanding across lines of basic difference is impossible. At least implicitly, some also suggest that the notions of knitting together a human life to achieve a satisfactory continuity of existence or a human community to provide social roots that are more than mere repression are chimerical. Neither Habermas nor postmodernists, however, offer a satisfactory account of the divergent forms of concrete social relationships that underpin the disconnection of the everyday realm of more or less successful practical action from the "larger picture" of self-regulating systems, bureaucracies, fragmentation, repression, and the like. I have tried to sketch some first steps in such an account.

We need to address sociologically the coordination of action through indirect relationships and the formation of identity as members of imagined communities. Although not unique to the modern era, these are distinctively predominant features of it. The practical projects of achieving community and a personal sense of continuity of existence may have become much more difficult, but this does not mean either that they should be abandoned or that social theory can dispense with notions of subjects or of solidarity (as some postmodernists imply). At the same time, the prevalence of large-scale structures of indirect relations and imagined communities poses stiff challenges for any movement aimed at increasing democracy or furthering the project of liberation. The various limits recent critics have shown in the Enlightenment project of simply advancing reason reduce hope for one path to a better future. But these difficulties do not seem to remove the need for social theory, for some way of trying to make sense of the world in order to act within it. On the contrary, they show why theory is needed and practical knowledge is subject to manipulation and radical limits without it.

NOTES

1. The general narrative of increasing capacity of states and other large-scale organizations has been retold and theorized several times in the last few years, notably by Giddens (1985b), Mann (1986), and Tilly (1990). But the stress here is not just on this increasing capacity but on the discontinuity in modes of coordinating—and understanding—activity, the theme of Habermas's (1984, 1988) distinction of system and lifeworld.

2. One might question whether Foucault (1977) does not exaggerate the transformation. Normalizing power does not seem altogether new nor coercive power altogether missing in modern societies. But the point that in the modern era, expansion of scope of power does not mean diminution in its intensity or effectiveness is an important one. And so is Foucault's emphasis on power as an impersonal force productive of social relations—although to refuse attention to distributive power is to deprive such an account of much of its potential critical edge.

3. The language of structuration was used earlier by Bourdieu, from whom Giddens has borrowed a great deal; Bourdieu, however, has avoided the claim that he constructed a "structuration theory."

4. This is partly because, as McCarthy (1985) suggests, Habermas accepts systems theory as offering an adequate account of this dimension.

5. This discussion follows the lines of Calhoun (1988 and forthcoming a). The notion of a contrast between direct and indirect social relations has been raised implicitly by a number of social theorists but not thematized. Parsons and Platt (1973) wrote of "delinguistified steering mechanisms." Something of the idea is present in the very notion of market as a supra-local, self-regulating system as distinct from a spatially bounded setting from directly interpersonal exchanges. It figures in Durkheim's (1893) conception of organic solidarity, society held together by the mutual interdependence and interactions among groups characterized by their differences. Schutz (1967) built a somewhat related distinction out of the contrast between direct and indirect social experience. Building on these bases, I want to try to distinguish the dimension of connection as such, more or less in network terms, from the variety of other aspects of mediation. In Parsonian language, I want to address patterns of interaction (even beyond the direct), as distinct from (although closely related to) patterns of integration. I want to keep the concrete social relations more clearly in mind, partly in order to consider them as part of the *basis* for societal integration, to be able to show the dimension of interaction that helps to make up the systemic, and thus potentially to dereify the latter notion.

Habermas follows the basic Weberian account of modernization as a move away from tradition and toward a rational orientation to action. He placed the *gemeinschaft-gesellschaft* sort of opposition on a new foundation by suggesting a further split within the realm of rational action into "action oriented to reaching understanding and action oriented to success" (1984, p. 341). It is on this basis that he attempts to rescue the Enlightenment project of rationalization as progress from the Weberian iron cage of domination through rational, bureaucratic, systemic means.

6. Actually, this is the dominant distinction among several Habermas makes. At other points, he distinguishes also a four-type scheme of communicative, dramaturgical, normatively regulated, and teleological action (1984, pp. 75–96). Between purely communicative and purely instrumental action, there is also apparently an intermediate form of strategic social action by which, among other things, people try to determine the contexts, frames of reference, and modes of understanding for communicative action in situations where there is not already a preexisting basis for such communication. See Habermas (1988) and McCarthy (1978).

7. It is not the lifeworld in general Habermas wishes to defend but an idealized, purified form of communicative action aimed at interpersonal understanding. He conceptualizes this through the notion of an idealized speech situation in which certain validity claims (to comprehensibility, truth, appropriateness, and sincerity) that are always implicit in speech are universalized. All real historical societies fall short of this ideal, but they may be compared to it and evaluated in terms of an evolutionary scale of undistorted communication (Habermas 1978). Thus, something closer to the ideal emerges from the lifeworld through a process of rationalization: "Correspondingly, a lifeworld can be regarded as rationalized to the extent that it permits interactions that are not guided by normatively *ascribed* agreement but—directly or indirectly—by communicative *achieved* understanding" (Habermas 1984, p. 340). In this way, Habermas tries to processualize Kantian universalistic morality.

8. See McCarthy (1985), Fraser (1985), Young (1987), Benhabib (1986), Frankenberg (1989), Bernstein, ed. (1982), and my critical discussion in Calhoun (1988 and 1989b).

9. A radical loss of importance, even of reality, for this world of direct interaction and immediate social relationships is posited centrally by many postmodernists—especially Baudrillard (e.g., 1983) and his followers. This is part of what they mean by "the death of the social." I see little evidence for this even within the popular media on which they focus (television shows both about and oriented to families are as popular as ever). That is one reason why I think the issue is not a derealization of direct relationships per se but an increasing split between them and indirect relations of various sorts, combined with very problematic means for shifting understanding from one mode of relationship to the other.

10. Habermas (1988) has noted how Schutz remained caught within the philosophy of consciousness even while he, following Husserl, attempted to grasp intersubjectivity. Habermas does not really take up the notions of direct and indirect relations as Schutz suggested them, however; his focus is entirely on the concept of the lifeworld.

11. And the passing on of tradition was through such relationships, not by means of texts or other means dissociated from them. In this connection, we need to see tradition as more of an active verb than a static noun (see Shils 1981; Calhoun 1983). Note, however, the version of indirectness involved in marriage exchanges within a complex system of clanship, such as that of aboriginal Australians (see, e.g., Levi-Strauss 1949).

12. Such "administrative power can only become established if the coding of information is actually applied in a direct way to the supervision of human activities, so as to detach them in some part from their involvement with tradition and with local community life" (Giddens 1985b, p. 47).

13. This is a point recognized some time ago by Innis (1950) in his arguments as to the centrality of certain space-transcending communications media to the building of empires. See also Deutsch (1953, 1963).

14. This is one source of modern "populist" politics—the politics of local communities and traditional cultural values. This is a potent kind of politics, and it offers potentially radical and important visions of alternative modes of social organization. Many of its variants, however, are based on some combination of (1) systematic misrecognition of the opportunities for local autonomy available in a world structured largely by large-scale organizations of indirect social relationships, and (2) systematically biased analogies between the world of direct, personal relationships and that of large-scale organizations of indirect ones (e.g., "balancing the U.S. budget is just like balancing your family checkbook"). See Calhoun (1988).

15. "Comparison," Marx went on, takes the "place of real communality and generality." "It has been said and may be said that this is precisely the beauty and the greatness of it: this spontaneous interconnection, this material and mental metabolism which is independent of the knowing and willing of individuals, and which presupposes their reciprocal independence and indifference. And, certainly, this objective connection is preferable to the lack of any connection, or to a merely local connection resting on blood ties, or on primeval, natural or master-servant relations" (1939, p. 161). See the similar discussion by Engels (1880, pp. 627–628) and in the *Manifesto* (1848, pp. 486–487). It is, however, above all in *Capital*, especially in the relationship between Volumes I and III, that we see Marx creating precisely a theory of a mode of totalization that will make social life appear systematically as other than it is, make capital seem the cause and not the product of human action. If we can identify capitalism with systemic integration, it does not just "colonize" the lifeworld, as Habermas would have it, but constitutes the very severance of each from the other, the compartmentalization of the lifeworld and the reification of mediated action.

16. Abu-Lughod (1969) introduced the notion of tertiary interactions in a similar connection to note the prominence of mediated relationships in the modern city and particularly to supplement Park's classic definition of urbanness in terms of scale, density, and heterogeneity.

17. I have argued elsewhere both for the importance of the concept of community in the face of individualist reductions (Calhoun 1978) and for a social relational conception of community as a complex variable composed of density, multiplexity, and systematicity of interpersonal relationships (Calhoun 1980a).

18. Tilly (1978) has drawn attention to Harrison White's unpublished conceptualization of CATNETS as groupings that are simultaneously categories and networks, the issue being addressed here.

19. This account prefigures those Habermas (1965), Touraine (1971), Melucci (1989), and others developed of "new social movements" in which a politics of identity was central.

20. Habermas (1962) offers a very similar account of the importance of printing, both as a capitalist enterprise and in response to capitalist demand, in describing the role of newspapers and books in the creation of the bourgeois public sphere. The point is worth stressing because it is often overlooked in both accounts of printing that take a too narrowly technologically determinist line and accounts of capitalism that ignore books as insufficiently material. As Anderson comments, "In a rather special sense, the book was the first modern-style mass-produced industrial commodity" (1983, p. 38).

21. Anderson suggests that this model got its birth in Spain's Latin American colonies and its greatest burst of publicity in the European revolutions of the eighteenth and early nineteenth centuries.

22. Anderson does mention, in a footnote, the importance of radio to the Vietnamese and Indonesian revolutions (1983, p. 46), but it is a point that deserves more stress.

23. "The relatively small size of traditional aristocracies, their fixed political bases, and the personalization of political relations implied by sexual intercourse and inheritance, meant that their cohesions as classes were as much concrete as imagined" (1983, p. 74). In my terms, direct relations sufficed for the most part to knit such aristocracies together.

24. Of course, this is only an extension of the notion of journalistic objectivity pioneered in newspapers as editorializing came to be confined to a special page and removed from news reportage as such (cf., Schudson 1979; Hallin 1986).

25. See Meyrowitz 1985 for the best account of this subject (although see also Calhoun 1988, both for other related points and for an argument that Meyrowitz somewhat underestimates the illusoriness of this mediated transcendence of space).

26. Our image of a high level of traditionality should not be drawn from European feudalism or even classical Chinese or Indian civilizations. Rather, we might look at kin-based societies in which there is no sharp break between the ordering of relations in immediate personal life (through the family and kinship) and in the most encompassing order of society (through kinship at higher lineage levels and sometimes clanship and age sets). I have in mind particularly Meyer Fortes's studies of the Tallensi of Northern Ghana (especially Fortes 1942, 1945; see also Calhoun 1980b); such African "acephalous" societies are particularly apt examples, although the same sort of phenomena figure in a variety of settings. A variety of features provides for such traditionality: internal homogeneity of a population, multiplex relations linking people in many different aspects of their lives, limits on the accumulation of personal wealth, and the like.

27. One should not conclude that prior historical periods thus produced any wonderful model of sound knowledge or openness; they generally did not (although it should also be noted that in many cases history has brought regress on this dimension—for example, in the once very cosmopolitan parts of the Middle East). The flexibility of tradition applied only within the relatively constrained limits of substantial personal contact and was not perfect even then (partly because people's interested adjustments might reflect the need for maintaining biases more than correcting them).

28. Note the variation this suggests on Derrida's (1967) theme of the contest between views of speech as originary truth-telling and writing as a source of tension, aporias, and rational-critical thought. Oral traditions necessarily embed tradition more substantially in practical projects that call for its continual readjustment. History also deconstructs written texts, of course, and interpretations vary. But oral tradition is supple and effective in providing for stable social reproduction precisely because it is so continually readjusted (without anyone necessarily assuming the role of self-conscious shaper of it). Whether their statements are more or less true, there is a new sort of fixity to written texts. These do encourage a kind of rational-critical thought missing from speech, as Derrida suggests, but the mechanism is partly the social one of their detachment from practical projects and the corresponding occasions for their continual invisible reformulation. This detachment, it should be stressed, does not mean that written texts are not created and interpreted as part of practical projects, often selfishly motivated ones. The detachment comes, rather, from their capacity to endure and disseminate beyond their producers' reach and capacity for

adjustment, to reach new audiences without the mediation of any new reproducer (and his or her practical concerns, talents, and projects).

29. Thus, Bourdieu (1976) resurrects classical language to describe the movement from *doxa* (the unquestioned self-evidence of how things are within a cultural view) to orthodoxy (an imposed authoritative view) and heterodoxy (the recognition of multiple competing opinions).

30. Although it should be said that television audiences are not just passive recipients of messages, they must interpret them and may make something different of them from what senders intended. Nonetheless, this fact is often overestimated by the "new audience studies" (cf., Fiske 1986). Television audiences can neither interrogate the senders of messages nor respond practically in ways that lead senders to adjust their views—except by mounting an organized movement or appealing to some powerful systemic actor.

31. All relationships are mediated to some extent—we communicate, for example, through speech—but the notion of indirectness suggests a sliding scale of increasing apparent removal of the communicator from the process of communication.

32. See, e.g., Baudrillard (1981, 1983); Lyotard (1984); and discussion in Calhoun (forthcoming b).

33. The notion of systematic misrecognition as a central feature of habituses is presented at length by Bourdieu (1976).

REFERENCES

Abu-Lughod, J. 1969. *The City Is Dead—Long Live the City: Some Thoughts on Urbanity.* Berkeley: Center for Planning and Development Research Monograph No. 12.

Anderson, B. 1983. *Imagined Communities: Reflections of the Origin and Spread of Nationalism.* London: New Left Books.

Baudrillard, J. 1981. *For a Critique of the Political Economy of the Sign.* St. Louis: Telos Press.

———. 1983. *In the Shadow of the Silent Majorities.* New York: Semiotext(e).

Bell, H., and C. Newby. 1976. *Communities in Britain.* London: Allen and Unwin.

Benhabib, S. 1986. *Critique, Norm and Utopia.* New York: Columbia University Press.

Bernstein, R., ed. 1982. *Habermas and Modernity.* Cambridge, MA: MIT Press.

Blau, P. M. 1977. *Inequality and Heterogeneity.* New York: Free Press.

Blau, P. M., and J. Schwartz. 1984. *Cross-Cutting Social Circles.* New York: Academic Press.

Bourdieu, P. 1976. *Outline of a Theory of Practice.* Cambridge: Cambridge University Press.

———. 1980. *Le Sens Pratique.* Paris: Editions de Minuit.

Calhoun, C. 1978. "History, Anthropology and the Study of Communities: Some Problems in MacFarlane's Proposal." *Social History* 3(3):363–373.

———. 1980a. "Community: Toward a Variable Conceptualization for Comparative Research." *Social History* 5(1):105–129.

———. 1980b. "The Authority of Ancestors: A Sociological Reconsideration of Fortes's Tallensi in Response to Fortes's Critics." *Man, The Journal of the Royal Anthropological Institute,* new series, 15(2):304–319.

———. 1983. "The Radicalism of Tradition: Community Strength or Venerable Disguise and Borrowed Language." *American Journal of Sociology* 88:886–914.

———. 1986. "Computer Technology, Large Scale Social Integration and the Local Community." *Urban Affairs Quarterly* 22(2):329–349.

———. 1988. "Populist Politics, Communications Media, and Large Scale Social Integration." *Sociological Theory* 6(2):219–241.

———. 1989a. "Social Theory and the Law: Systems Theory, Normative Justification and Postmodernism." *Northwestern University Law Review* 83:1,701–1,763.

———. 1989b. "Democracy and Science, 1989: A Report from Beijing." *Society* 26(6):21–38.

———. Forthcoming a. "The Infrastructure of Modernity: Indirect Relationships, Information Technology, and Social Integration." In Neil Smelser and Hans Haferkamp, eds., *Social Change and Modernity*. Berkeley: University of California Press.

———. Forthcoming b. "Culture, History and the Problem of Specificity in Social Theory." In S. Seidman and D. Wagner, eds., *Postmodernism and General Social Theory*. New York and Oxford: Basil Blackwell.

Cooley, C. H. 1909. *Social Organization*. New York: Shocken.

Derrida, J. 1967. *Of Grammatology*. Baltimore: Johns Hopkins University Press.

Deutsch, K. 1953. *Nationalism and Social Communication*. New York: John Wiley and Sons.

———. 1963. *The Nerves of Government*. Glencoe, IL: Free Press.

Durkheim, E. 1893. *The Division of Labor in Society*. New York: Free Press.

Eisenstein, E. 1968. "Some Conjectures About the Impact of Printing on Western Society and Thought." *Journal of Modern Social History* 40:416–438.

Engels, F. 1880. "Socialism: Utopian and Scientific." pp. 605–639 in R. Tucker, *The Marx-Engels Reader*. New York: Norton.

Fiske, J. 1986. *Television Culture*. New York: St. Martins.

Fortes, M. 1942. *The Web of Kinship Among the Tallensi*. Oxford: Oxford University Press.

———. 1945. *The Dynamics of Clanship Among the Tallensi*. Oxford: Oxford University Press.

Foucault, M. 1977. *Discipline and Punish: The Birth of the Prison*. New York: Pantheon.

Frankenberg, G. 1989. "Down by Law: Irony, Seriousness, and Reason." *Northwestern University Law Review* 83:360–397.

Fraser, N. 1985. "What's Critical About Critical Theory? The Case of Habermas and Gender." *New German Critique* 35:97–132.

Gadamer, H.-G. 1975. *Truth and Method*. New York: Seabury.

Giddens, A. 1985a. *The Constitution of Society*. Berkeley, CA: University of California Press.

———. 1985b. *The Nation-State and Violence*. Berkeley, CA: University of California Press.

Granovetter, M. 1985. "Economic Action and the Problem of Embeddedness." *American Journal of Sociology* 91(3):481–510.

Habermas, J. 1962. *The Structural Transformation of the Public Sphere* (English translation of *Strukturwandel der Offentlichkeit*, 1989). Cambridge, MA: MIT Press.

———. 1965. *Legitimation Crisis*. Boston: Beacon.

———. 1978. *Communication and the Evolution of Society*. Boston: Beacon.

———. 1984. *The Theory of Communicative Action, Vol. I: Reason and the Rationalization of Society*. Boston: Beacon.

———. 1988. *The Theory of Communicative Action, Vol. II: Lifeworld and System: A Critique of Functionalist Reason*. Boston: Beacon.

Hallin, D. C. 1986. "We Keep America on Top of the World." Pp. 9–41 in T. Gitlin, ed., *Watching Television*. New York: Pantheon.

Hobsbawm, E., and T. Ranger. 1983. *The Invention of Tradition*. Cambridge: Cambridge University Press.

Innis, H. A. 1950. *Empire and Communication*. Toronto: University of Toronto Press.
Levi-Strauss, C. 1949. *The Elementary Structures of Kinship*. Boston: Beacon.
Lockwood, D. 1964. "Social Integration and System Integration." Pp. 370–383 in G. K. Zollschan and W. Hirsch, eds., *Social Change: Explorations, Diagnoses and Conjectures*. New York: John Wiley and Sons.
Luhmann, N. 1982. *The Differentiation of Society*. New York: Columbia University Press.
Lukacs, G. 1922. *History and Class Consciousness*. London: Merlin.
Lyotard, J.-F. 1984. *The Postmodern Condition*. Minneapolis: University of Minnesota Press.
Mann, M. 1986. *The Sources of Social Power*. Cambridge: Cambridge University Press.
Marx, K. 1844. *The Economic and Philosophical Manuscripts of 1844*. Pp. 229–348 in *Karl Marx/Frederick Engels: Collected Works*, Vol. 3. London: Lawrence and Wishart.
———. 1867. *Capital*, Vol. I. London: Lawrence and Wishart.
———. 1939. *Grundrisse*. Harmondsworth: Pelican.
Marx, K., and F. Engels. 1848. *Manifesto of the Communist Party*. Pp. 477–519 in *Karl Marx/Frederick Engels: Collected Works*, Vol. 6. London: Lawrence and Wishart.
McCarthy, T. 1978. *The Critical Theory of Jürgen Habermas*. Cambridge, MA: MIT Press.
———. 1985. "Complexity and Democracy, or The Seducements of Systems Theory." *New German Critique* 35:27–54.
Melucci, A. 1989. *Nomads of the Present: Social Movements and Individual Needs in Contemporary Society*. Philadelphia: Temple University Press.
Meyrowitz, J. 1985. *No Sense of Place: The Impact of Electronic Media on Social Behavior*. New York: Oxford.
Parsons, T. 1951. *The Social System*. Glencoe, IL: Free Press.
Parsons, T., and G. Platt. 1973. *The American University*. New York: Free Press.
Schudson, M. 1979. *Discovering the News*. New York: Harper and Row.
Schutz, A. 1967. *The Phenomenology of the Social World*. Evanston, IL: Northwestern University Press.
Schutz, A., and T. Luckmann. 1973. *The Structures of the Lifeworld*. London: Heinemann Educational Books.
Shils, E. 1981. *Tradition*. Chicago: University of Chicago Press.
Tilly, C. 1978. *From Mobilization to Revolution*. Reading, MA: Addison-Wesley.
———. 1990. *Coercion, Capital and European States, A.D. 990–1990*. New York: Blackwell.
Touraine, A. 1971. *Post-Industrial Society*. London: Wildwood House.
Webber, M. W. 1967. "Order in Diversity: Community Without Propinquity." Pp. 29–54 in L. Wirigo, ed., *Cities and Space*. Baltimore: Johns Hopkins University Press.
Weber, M. 1922. *Economy and Society*. Berkeley: University of California Press.
Young, Iris. 1987. "Impartiality and Civic Virtue." Pp. 56–76 in S. Benhabib and D. Cornell, eds., *Feminism as Critique*. Minneapolis: University of Minnesota Press.

Comments

Gudmund Hernes

There are two basic problems with concepts such as *postmodernism*. It is hard to define what it *is*, what delimits it as a state from, for example, modernism. Hence, it is also hard to say *when* it began. Postmodernism is not a clearly demarcated phenomenon, nor is it a *theory*—it does not answer a *why*. These are criticisms Calhoun would be the first to make.

	Post-	Neo-	Late-	De-	Quasi-
modernism	X				
structuralism					
industrialism	X				
capitalism			X		
mercantilism		X			
constructivism				X	

Figure 3.1

Perhaps the term *postmodernism* is more the expression of the craving for a new tag for the times. Such tags are often the products of a kind of conceptual combinatorics found in cultural criticism. The logic consists of establishing some kind of property space where along one axis you enter terms such as *post-, neo-, late-, de-,* and *quasi-* and along the other axis enter terms such as *modernism, structuralism, industrialism, capitalism, mercantilism, constructivism,* and so on. The result is something like Figure 3.1. You then get labels such as *post-industrialism* (Bell) or *neomercantilism* (Schmitter), and the like. These may feed many arguments among intellectuals—indeed, identify "schools" both in the sociological sense of a group under the same influence and in the biological sense of a number swimming together—but they do no constitute theories.

There are, however, two themes in the postmodernist literature that Calhoun tries to rescue. They are, as I read it, (1) the increasing split between *direct interpersonal relationships* and the *indirect* relationships mediated by (2) the theme of *imagined communities.*

THE SPLIT BETWEEN DIRECT
AND INDIRECT RELATIONSHIPS

It is a professional penchant of sociologists to use fourfold tables as an analytical tool. If they are too far between, we all betray symptoms of abstinence. So, to soothe the sense, for comfort and consideration, here is such a table (Figure 3.2). Along the historical axis, there is a structural change in social relations from direct to indirect ties. Along the vertical axis, there is a cultural change toward imagined communities.

In terms of this fourfold table, Calhoun's argument seems to be that modern society has moved from the lower left to the upper right box and that there is a causal relation between the changes on these variables. In other words, a theory is suggested: *The more indirect relations you have in society, the greater the potential for imagined communities.* Or, more generally, the *relations between positions* shape *perceptions.*

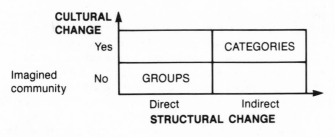

Figure 3.2

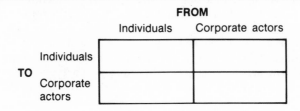

Figure 3.3

But I find several problems with the specific claims Calhoun makes. My first problem is with his argument that "understandings derived from the world of everyday life, direct social interaction, are likely to be increasingly distorting when applied to the world of large-scale social integration and action." He also has a statement to the same effect: "to make sense through abstract concepts of forms of social organization for which everyday experience gives us misleading preparation."

My objections would be: (1) Do people really think that states, political parties, firms, or other corporate actors behave like actual persons in face-to-face interactions, and (2) does not everyone from early childhood on gain experience in all of the types of interactions shown in Figure 3.3? Clearly, children interact with other children as individuals in friendships and fights. But do they not also as individuals face a corporate actor (or organization) at their school or act as a member of one corporate actor interacting with another when their basketball team confronts another team?

In other words, I doubt that this distortion exists based on the extrapolation of interpersonal experiences, as even children from early on gain experiences about impersonal interaction. Hence, if there is no direct application from face-to-face relations, there is no distortion.

Furthermore, one can ask whether corporate actors are not *more* predictable, *more* rational, and hence easier to understand and anticipate than individual persons. And are we not as individuals *more rational* in our corporate or organizational roles than in our personal relations? I suspect I am more rational in the execution of my professorial duties than in my love life and hence easier to understand as a member of a university organization than in private encounters.

There also seems to be a problem in that Calhoun builds on Habermas's distinction between "the world of lived experience" (Lebenswelt) and the role of large-scale, systemic integration. But *is* there really this opposition? Is it not more correct to say that people increasingly have their world of lived experience *within* corporate actors? Does not an expanding share of face-to-face relations arise, unfold, and develop *within* organizations? To take a simple example, is it not within organizations that we find both friends and marriage partners?

In sum, I believe both Calhoun and Habermas are on shaky ground here. For example, it is hard for me to believe a historical argument that the Kaiser's Germany was one of strong personal identities and rational discourse, whereas Kohl's Germany is one of weak identities and a public discourse based on images.

Calhoun proposes "to revise but appropriate the argument that modernity is characterized by a basic split between four worlds or experiences." But then a problem arises because he introduces two types of classifications, both in four points, while the connection between them is unclear:

Classification 1	Classification 2
1. Face-to-face	1. Primary
2. Imagined connections (e.g., television)	2. Secondary
3. One-directional (e.g., surveillance)	3. Tertiary (can in principle be brought to awareness)
4. Systemic integration	4. Quaternary (one of the parties systematically unaware)

These two classifications are partly alike yet are not the same. Why? What is the relationship between them? To what uses should they be put? Should they be considered stages in transitions to modernity or be used to identify changes in the distribution of the types of relation?

I must also mention the problem of dating in Calhoun's chapter. For example, when he states "Almost all major premodern forms of social organization depended primarily on interpersonal relationships," I wonder: When did modernity start? Before the Roman Empire? What about the mandarins and organization of ancient China? Or when the statement is made that "direct relationships are no longer constitutive of society at its widest reaches," I wonder: When and where were they?

IMAGINED COMMUNITIES

The second major theme Calhoun rescues is that of *imagined communities:* a group that develops a sense of common membership without those constituting it meeting or hearing of each other as individuals.

After having first read the chapter, I found this a very intriguing concept. For example, I ran across a journal I had never seen called *Tattoo.* It is the journal connecting the imagined community of those tattooed. They even have a national tattoo convention. So Calhoun seems to be right that there is a proliferation of all sorts of imagined communities, and this illustrates his second point: that these communities are tied to mass media.

But Calhoun also claims that the media "remove from practical adjustment and somewhat from interpersonal discourse the way we are integrating practices from everyday experiences in contrast to traditions transmitted through the mouths and deeds of innumerable people." He also declares that the media enhance "the oligopolistic character of elite messages and remove most people from direct participation in—and therefore the shaping of—the passing on of such traditions." And finally, "We appear, thus, to be on our own as individual actors to depend on rational decisions, not conditional practices."

In reading this, I was first surprised that no reference was made to reference group theory or to the process by which such imagined communities develop. Second, a kind of media determinism seems to underly these propositions. When I arrived in this country recently, I read in the *New York Times* about the increasing role of black talk radio. The *Times* story suggests that the media function differently and in a much less one-directional way than Calhoun asserts.

It also seems that Calhoun has an individualistic bias in his interpretation of the media. Individuals do not just listen and watch in isolation from each other. The media create conversation and make people react to each other. Hence, if we are to figure out how new identities and imagined communities develop, we have to bring small groups back in.

Media enhance the oligopolistic character of elite messages. On the other hand, at least in this country, media function within a pluralistic society. I am sure that after the Alaskan oil spill, Exxon deplored the fact that the control of the media was not more oligopolistic. In short, corporate actors and elites fight each other through the media.

THE PHANTOM PAINS
OF SOCIAL CHANGE

Finally, there is a pessimistic undertone running through Calhoun's chapter, an undertone also found in some of the other chapters, such as James Coleman's. Moreover, it is a tone and a theme found in much of the sociological literature. It could be called the phantom pains of social science. "Phantom pains" are those felt after an amputation: even after a limb is lost, one may experience pain in it.

The social science version of this pain is the lament of loss: the "loss of community," the "loss of meaning," the "loss of *gemeinschaft*," the "loss of identity," the "loss of kinship," and so on. Man lived and belonged in a folk society, with mechanical solidarity, in touch with nature, spontaneously expressing creativity in soft interpersonal relations. Then this world was cut off from man, and he was left with routinization, bureaucracy, atomization, isolation, anonymity, impersonal roles, mechanical regulation, and estrangement from nature. But the pain is still felt in lost social limbs, and there is a longing for the world irrevocably gone.

But then, the loss may just be a bad dream. Milking cows was not just a direct—even tactile—contact with nature; it was also a fatiguing chore. Scything the grass or grain smelled good, but it made backs ache and was different from singing *Oklahoma* on Broadway. Net migration has been *to*, not *from*, urban areas, with their impersonal markets and bureaucracies. Indeed, one could say to those who long most for the tight, close ties of small communities in rural settings, unstained by modernity, "I sentence you to a week in the Middle Ages!"

It may be a bad dream because interpersonal relations and intimacy are *not* lost. At least, my limbs are all here. I have face-to-face relationships. I have long-lasting interpersonal ties, and they are not oppressive. Most of them I have developed *within* organizations or corporate actors. Bureaucracies are marvelous for making friends—or for adding zest to life by making enemies or outwitting rivals. I do not have the sense of loss or the phantom pain. The only pain I have had in my legs is the real pain from tendonitis, a result of belonging to the imagined community of joggers.

Comments

Edward Shils

Professor Calhoun's erudite and perceptive chapter is evidence of what I once called, in a discussion about modern sociological thought, the *tyranny of tradition*. The particular tyrant to which I referred was the sociological tradition that saw all social institutions and societies in terms of *gemeinschaft* and *gesellschaft*.

Ferdinand Tönnies, as we know, was the heir of Thomas Hobbes and Henry Sumner Maine, of Adam Smith and David Ricardo, of Hegel and Karl Marx. Professor Calhoun presents us with a modified version of this dichotomous classification of types of society. He has tried to go further than Tönnies and than his U.S. counterpart Charles H. Cooley by differentiating the analysis and by trying to enrich the category of *gesellschaft* that purports to describe the nature of modern Western societies. I feel that he does not go quite far enough in that part of his chapter and that he neglects to analyze with a sufficiently fresh eye the phenomenon of *gemeinschaft*. He remains fixed at Cooley's definition of "primary group," although he designates it as "direct relationship."

Calhoun's main interest is in the nature of modern Western societies, which, in the fashionable lingo of the day, is called "modernity." There he goes further than Tönnies and Cooley, but not far enough. The absence of further analysis of direct relationships impedes his understanding of the most inclusive collectivity—society. These are substantial charges, and I will try to make clear my grounds for criticizing Calhoun's admirable achievement.

I will begin by pointing out that he has not paid any attention to one particular feature of the major type of collectivity formed from direct, or face-to-face, relationships. He does not take into account the general significance of real or imputed biological relationships in the collective consciousness of the family. Calhoun does not reach into the constitution of a direct face-to-face relationship with the acumen he displays when he deals with coordinated indirect relations and with "imagined communities," although in his treatment of the latter, I find omissions of fundamental significance.

Let me deal first with the direct relationships. Calhoun does not seem to appreciate that little or nothing is given by the simple fact of spatial propinquity and even real biological relatedness. Presumed biological relatedness and spatial propinquity are significant only because they become referents in the collective self-consciousness. This aspect, which is fundamental to the understanding of the family, the lineage, and the locality—which are at the center of Tönnies's analysis of *gemeinschaft*—was not sufficiently taken into account by Tönnies, Cooley, or Calhoun. The result is a gap in Calhoun's analysis not only of direct relations but of imagined communities as well.

I think Calhoun's analysis would be improved by taking into account quite explicitly the primordial phenomena of biological connectedness and territoriality and their role as referents in collective self-consciousness. Calhoun does not attribute any significance to collective self-consciousness. Yet, without reference to primordiality and collective self-consciousness, Calhoun's analysis of modern societies is forced to remain at a superficial level.

Durkheim has been much criticized for his notion of "conscience collective," but for the wrong reasons. The important criticism to be made of Durkheim in this regard is that he did not elaborate on what he meant by the term. It is, if it can be properly formulated, one of the most crucial variables of realistic sociological analysis. Tönnies, by failing to see its function in the constitution of *gemeinschaft*, also failed to see its persistence in *gesellschaft*. Cooley had a glimpse of what was involved when he used the term *larger mind* in the subtitle of *Social Organization;* the subtitle read *A Study of the Larger Mind*. But his analysis of the larger mind did not live up to the suggestiveness of the subtitle. Calhoun avoids the matter entirely; yet, the imagined communities would not be communities—or societies— without it. Calhoun is perhaps imprisoned by "methodological individualism," which is evident in his statement on collective actions or movements; their individual participants seek "in some large part affirmation of their personal identities." He does not consider that they might be seeking to transcend their personal identities. He does not adhere consistently to this individualistic conception; he knows that society is more than a market. It is indeed that insight that leads him to distinguish quite sensibly between imagined communities and the indirect relationships that include the market and what Coleman has in mind when he speaks of purposeful "corporate actors."

There is a fruitful suggestion in the notion of imagined communities. Its fruitfulness lies in its suggestion that the mind has a place in the constitution of society. But as Calhoun uses the term, the mind is not accorded that place.

It may appear strange to lay a charge of neglect of the mind against a chapter of which a large part is devoted to the existence of communities that are said to be "imagined," that are not directly experienced in the relationships of their members with each other but depend on the imagination of distant persons and classes of persons. Now, these are real collectivities— they are capable of giving rise to purposeful structures of coordinated indirect relationships; churches, sects, political parties, trade unions, ethnic associations, and government itself are formed and maintained out of the matrix of these imagined communities. These imagined communities are realities because they possess a collective self-consciousness; otherwise they would be only imagined by separate individuals.

Each of these imagined communities incorporates not only living persons who have the properties referred to in the collective consciousness; they also incorporate no longer living persons who possessed those properties. The living and the dead are linked through the possession by the living of beliefs, images, and physical properties once possessed by the dead. The members of those collectivities receive—and in many cases know that they have received—use, and reenact significant works and patterns of practices from the past. In all these imagined collectivities, vital values such as biological features, territorial (telluric) location, hierarchical status, knowledge of vital empirical and sacred things, and centrality and the link with centrality as civil quality are referents of the collective self-consciousnesses. That is why and how nationalities; ethnic groups; social classes (or strata); scientific, scholarly, and religious communities; and societies as such—above all—can exist. Calhoun misses the point about the significance of the referents of collective self-consciousness. He correctly says, "Imagined communities are essentially categorical identities," but he does not ask himself why those particular categories are significant to the individuals who so categorize themselves. He says that they are "not simply arbitrary creatures of the imagination." But if they are not arbitrary, what are the criteria by which the categories are selected? There is much matter here for further reflection. Meanwhile, I recommend that Calhoun give more thought to the question of how "categorical identities" are transformed into communities; he should break down the word "identity" into its components. As the word "identity" is used by him, it is an obstacle to deeper penetration.

I will now discuss the presence of knowledge, as contained in collective self-consciousness, in what Calhoun calls direct relationships. The knowledge we have of our partners in direct relationships is not gained simply through the process of the interaction that makes up that relationship. We learn about our pastness from knowledge not given in the process of interaction itself. For example, the knowledge that we were born to a particular woman, that she is our mother, is not simply a product of the direct interaction between ourselves and our parents. It is provided by our mother and father from events prior to our interaction with them and our acceptance of the reality of those events outside our own interaction.

Calhoun is rare among sociologists in his appreciation of the significance of tradition, but when he speaks of direct relationships, he does not mention it. Although he does point out that traditions pass from generation to generation in the family, which is one of the main sites of direct relationships, he does not attend to the role of that traditional knowledge in the constitution of the family. In passing, I note that in his discussion of the sources of the knowledge that enters into the formation of imagined community, he refers to printed works and, of course, to television, but he does not mention the family or the schools as sources of knowledge of things that are remote in the past and remote in space. Had he paid more attention to this, he might not place so much weight on his view that, although direct relationships continue to exist in modern societies—even in their latest phases—they are "compartmentalized" or cut off from the rest of society and have little or no influence over it. Direct relationships are extremely important in the constitution of imagined communities.

I think that even the most hard-headed empiricist will agree that knowledge plays a vital role in society. I will go a bit further and emphasize that this is not just knowledge possessed by many individuals about things they have learned from experience or study. It is knowledge that is collectively possessed, not just identically possessed by many separated individuals. It is, of course, possessed by individuals, but it is also possessed by them in awareness that it is possessed by others. The knowledge is a common possession—I emphasize that I do not mean identical possession. This might be called collective knowledge or collective consciousness; when an individual knows some of this collective knowledge or shares or participates in it, he or she is a participant in an objective phenomenon—a set or body of symbolic objectivations. (These symbolic objectivations possess reality, which Karl Popper—modernizing the old idea of "objective spirit"—has called "World 3"; he tended to confine it to scientific or other studied knowledge— that is, to knowledge of things outside our collective selves.) Objective knowledge also exists with respect to any other kind of knowledge as soon as it is possessed by more than one member of a collectivity. It exists for our knowledge of the collectivities of which we are members or in which we participate.

The existence of World 3 is obvious if we speak of printed or written symbolic objectivations, but it exists for our unwritten knowledge of our fellows in ethnic, religious, scientific, national, economic, political, and familial collectivities. Our knowledge of our own collectivities—our studied or common knowledge of our own collectivity—is our knowledge or con-sciousness of our collective self. That is why I have used the term *collective self-consciousness*. I recognize that there are obscurities in this term. Its tenability depends on our clarification of the term *collective self*.

By collective self, I do not mean something outside individual minds; it is in the minds of individuals, but it is different from the individual's self. When an individual says "we," he or she does not mean "I." That is a fundamental datum. Without paying heed to it, the phenomenon of solidarity, the phenomenon of collective action, would be impossible. Yet, if solidarity did not exist, if collective action did not exist, society would not exist. When Calhoun speaks about imagined communities, he opens up an intellectual Pandora's box. He should look carefully at its contents. I will go no further in my comment on Calhoun's chapter. It is obviously a rich one, full of possibilities for further and deeper analysis of very fundamental problems.

PART TWO

Changes in Cultural Institutions and Cultural Transmission

4

Social Structure, Institutions, and Cultural Goods: The Case of the United States

Paul DiMaggio

Research in anthropology, sociology, and other fields unanimously reports that people's choices of expressive goods are profoundly cultural and social. They are cultural in the sense that people respond less to intrinsic attributes of symbolic goods than to particularized meanings instilled in them. They are social, first, because these meanings emerge in social interaction and, second, because the desirability of a cultural good to a consumer depends on the number and identities of its other consumers (Douglas and Isherwood 1979; Granovetter and Soong 1988). Except for economists, who usually apply a utilitarian paradigm of independent choice to people's tastes for art, music, cuisine, and fashion, most scholars agree that cultural goods derive utility from social processes and not from the creature or aesthetic needs of isolated individuals; that different people's decisions about symbolic goods are both interdependent and (insofar as the *social* significance of a good—who else consumes it—fluctuates) unstable; and that demand for cultural goods responds to their socially constructed unit character: Such goods cannot be viewed as bundles of utility-bearing characteristics. In other words, they are consumed for what they say about their consumers to themselves and to others, as inputs into the production of social relations and identities.

Despite this agreement on micro-principles, scholars have found it difficult to characterize change in expressive culture at the societal level. Sociologists and lay people alike customarily discuss change in symbolic economies with reference to broad labels ("mass culture," "the culture of capitalism," "postmodernism") that are flawed in three respects. First, they conflate a

I am grateful to Wendy Griswold, Richard A. Peterson, and the conference's organizers and participants for helpful critical reactions and editorial assistance.

variety of dimensions that are empirically and analytically distinct: the orientations and modes of action of actors; the social classification of expressive goods; and dimensions of social structure. Second, the failure to "unpack" such labels systematically renders each interpretation of "cultural change" incomplete; debate revolves around different *dimensions*, rather than comparing distinctive views of the same phenomena. Third, conventional labels are heavily laden with resonant evaluative overtones.

We need to equip ourselves with a less familiar analytic apparatus. Briefly, societies vary with respect to four dimensions of symbolic classification: *differentiation* (the extent to which cultural goods are grouped into a few or many types or genres); *hierarchy* (the extent to which such types or genres are viewed as vertically arrayed or of equal value); *universality* (the extent to which genre distinctions and hierarchies are commonly recognized); and *symbolic potency* (the extent to which transgressions of boundaries and hierarchies elicit strong negative reactions). Systems of classification are shaped by changes in the organization of cultural authority and in the mode of allocation of cultural goods. Social structure affects the dimensions of symbolic classification by influencing the capacity of actors to organize and the uses to which individuals may put cultural resources (DiMaggio 1987a).

Concretely, I shall argue that changes in social structure and the rise of an open market for cultural goods have weakened institutionalized cultural authority, set off spirals of cultural inflation, and created more differentiated, less hierarchical, less universal, and less symbolically potent systems of cultural classification than those in place during the first part of this century.

Pierre Bourdieu's notion of *cultural capital* (1984) is indispensable for comprehending sociological aspects of the symbolic economy. The importance of the *capital* metaphor lies in the fact that it directs us to both the uses that actors make of cultural competencies in their daily efforts to improve their lot and to institutions that mint, guarantee, and sacralize certain kinds of culture as signs of distinction—that is, to the problem of institutionalized cultural authority. Consequently, analysis of change in the cultural economy requires attention both to individual and collective action *and* to institutions of cultural production and consecration.

I distinguish between *cultural capital*, by which I refer to proficiency in the consumption of and discourse about generally prestigious—that is, institutionally screened and validated—cultural goods, and *cultural resources* (Collins 1979), by which I refer to any form of symbolic mastery that is useful in a specific relational context. Within certain milieus, the ability to speak intelligently about the wheat futures or funny-car racing may be a cultural resource, but neither is a form of cultural capital because neither is generally valorized by a nationally authoritative institutional system.

The difference is not intrinsic to particular expressive goods: Cultural capital and cultural resources must be distinguished empirically. At the micro-level, cultural capital includes those cultural resources that positively affect measures of life chances (educational attainment, marital selection, occupational attainment) within a national population (as opposed to only within local subgroups). At the macro-level, cultural capital can be distinguished from other cultural resources on the basis of collective investments in formal organizations devoted to its maintenance and consecration.

As Bourdieu and Jean-Claude Passeron (1977) have argued, in most modern industrial societies the university is the specialized institution with the greatest power of consecration. Mass parties or established churches may also play such a role. (I use the term *role* rather than *function* because societies vary not simply in the locus of cultural authority but in the extent to which the cultural authority of *any* institution can be said to extend to the society as a whole—that is, in the extent to which the cultural economy revolves around a centrally valorized currency as opposed to a multiplicity of local bartering arrangements.)

For a society to have cultural capital—sets of cultural goods and capacities that are widely recognized as prestigious—there must be institutions capable of valorizing certain symbolic goods and social groups capable of appropriating them. A society with cultural capital must have a common focus of public life; its culture must be differentiated to some degree, universal enough to admit a common currency of interactional exchange, and hierarchically organized into genres with some ritual potency. In other words, it must be a society with a state, a relatively high level of political incorporation, and substantial institutional differentiation. Thus, the symbolic economy associated with cultural capital comes into being with industrial capitalism.

THE EMERGENCE OF HIGH CULTURE: DIFFERENTIATION AND HIERARCHY

The constitution of certain cultural goods as "cultural capital" was by no means automatic, but rather required collective action on the part of elites. The particulars differed from place to place, but the process occurred from the late eighteenth to early twentieth centuries throughout the industrializing West. In Europe, "high culture" emerged out of court culture as aristocracies were overthrown by or made their peace with rising commercial classes (see, for example, White and White 1965; W. Weber 1976; Tuchman and Fortin 1988; DeNora 1989). In the United States, institutions of high culture emerged as part of a larger process of upper-class formation by urban elites familiar with recent European precedents.

This process was marked by the increasingly public character of cultural consumption. The rise of consumer markets for cultural objects emerged centuries earlier (Altick 1978; Burke 1978; Mukerji 1983), of course, but the extension of the market to new forms of expression and new publics represented a disjunctive step. This was especially the case in the United States, where before 1850, the arts were ordinarily produced and consumed in the home or in public venues characterized by a mixing of genres and classes. Increasingly, after 1870, the arts became the business of organizations that, like the art they purveyed, were segmented into two fields: the "high" and the "popular." In the United States, within fifty years each of the fields was institutionalized on the national level, and the classifications high and popular (and the contents of each side of this dichotomy) were largely taken for granted. Once these systems were in place and tied, on the one hand, to systems of near-universal secondary and mass higher education and, on the other, to the apparatus of consumer capitalism and mass communications, the stage was set for an enlargement of the role of taste and style in the construction of selves, not just in art but in other domains.

The emergence in the United States of organizations segmenting high and popular culture has been described elsewhere (DiMaggio 1982a and 1982b; Levine 1988). In Boston, representatives of a commercial and industrial upper class established an art museum and a symphony orchestra at the same time they were creating private schools, social clubs, and other institutions that enabled them to maintain a bounded collective life and a distinctive cultural style. Both the museum and the orchestra began as ostensibly civic institutions providing a range of offerings. As they became more secure, they retained cultural experts who—supported by wealthy patrons—defined canons of "serious" works, expelling others from the collections and repertoire, respectively. In the course of doing so, they established conventions of public demeanor emphasizing restraint and respect, and restricted the public that had access to high culture to the upper and upper-middle classes.

Other cities reached the same end point by trajectories that varied with differences in local social structure. By contrast to Boston, New York possessed both a middle class that was large enough to ensure the viability of commercial orchestras and an elite that was too large and too poorly integrated to monopolize cultural authority. Shifting coalitions within this fragmented elite created numerous orchestras, none of them sufficiently successful to define a single canon of fine-arts music. Competing orchestras sought public favor through product differentiation, light programming, novelties, and extravaganzas long after Boston's symphonic repertoire had become limited and austere. Competition among elites prevented any from wresting control from the orchestra's commercial entrepreneurs (Shanet 1975; Jaher 1982; Martin 1983). Nearly fifty years after the founding of Boston's symphony, financial pressures caused a series of mergers that created the New York Philharmonic Symphony, which adopted a repertoire similar to Boston's. By this time, the increasingly national institutional basis of high and popular cultures had already eroded regional differences.

THE NATIONALIZATION
OF HIGH CULTURE:
FROM RESOURCE TO CAPITAL

The emergence of the high-popular culture dichotomy as a hierarchical, universal, and symbolically potent system of symbolic classification was more than an aggregate outcome of separate events in scattered cities.

Equally important was the institutionalization of cultural capital at the national level, which entailed both near-universal apprehension (and acknowledgment as legitimate) of the scheme of classification of symbolic goods and the emergence of institutions with the cultural authority to sustain and regulate the currency. Rather than provide a narrative account of this process, I shall simply emphasize three aspects: the systematic construction of national organizational fields; the incorporation by universities of the arts; and the role of commercial culture industries.

The Construction of Organizational Fields

The first step in the vesting of cultural authority over the arts in organizations rather than persons was the creation of U.S. art museums and symphony orchestras. Until the 1920s, however, the "formal" quality of these organizations was more apparent than real; in effect, they were corporate charters draped over the ongoing collective life of the wealthy men and women who organized and controlled them. Little by little, the patrons came to share control with professional experts; and these professionals were quick to organize national associations that sought to shape the development of the institutions over which they exercised nominal authority.

This process was most visible in the museum world, where such organizations as the American Association of Museums, the College Art Association, and the American Federation of Arts were active by the 1920s. Such organizations established national standards for the exhibition and care of objects, the responsibilities of trustees, the design of exhibitions, and the teaching of art in university courses. They also created a national network of museum professionals who shared a common understanding of the artistic culture to which their institutions were devoted.

Equally important were the national foundations—especially the Carnegie Corporation and the Rockefeller philanthropies—that supported this organizational infrastructure (DiMaggio 1988 forthcoming; Lagemann 1990). Whereas before 1920 such foundations were primarily extensions of their founders, afterward they boasted professional staff who took substantial initiative (albeit under their trustees' watchful eyes). Their ideology was "progressive"; that is, they sought to use experts to rationalize the organizations their foundations supported (and thereby to increase their contribution to the public good) (Lagemann 1983). Taken together, the foundations' programs and those of the national associations they supported tended to institutionalize and diffuse elite definitions of high culture and models of high-culture organizations (DiMaggio 1988; Keppel and Duffus 1933; Lagemann 1990).

The Universities

Equally important in the constitution of high culture as cultural capital were the universities. As Bourdieu has argued, the expansion of higher education and the pivotal role of certification for the careers of children of both the upper and upper-middle classes in contemporary society have given universities substantial influence over the definition of "official" culture. As keepers of the canons, universities and liberal arts colleges play the key role in disseminating cultural hierarchies in the fields in which they provide instruction.

Although instruction in art, music, and even drama antedates the turn of the century, the arts attained a solid place in university curricula only during the 1920s, in part through the efforts of private philanthropies. In 1876, just seven institutions offered courses in art history or appreciation; in 1916, fewer than one-quarter of U.S. colleges and universities did so; by 1930, such courses were offered by nearly every institution, and faculty who had been strewn among several departments were consolidated in departments of art history. University art history departments, in turn, trained a cadre of art historians whose business it was to make aesthetic judgments according to standard criteria and to develop lists of artists worthy of study. Because these art historians often worked as curators or museum directors and as consultants to art dealers or collectors, they contributed to a nationalization of elite culture. The same was true, to a lesser extent, in music. Courses in art and music made strides in U.S. high schools as well; moreover, the period witnessed a partial shift from courses that emphasized the "doing" of art (for example, training in shape-note singing) to courses in "appreciation" that disseminated the high-culture canon to the increasing proportion of adolescents who attended high school (Hiss and Fansler 1934; Levy 1938).

Commercial Culture Producers

The rise of an institutionalized high culture was inseparable from the emergence of popular culture industries, which provided a profane contrast to the sacred offerings of the former. Such industries arose alongside U.S. museums and orchestras during the same period: first the national vaudeville chains, then the oligopolistic theatre touring operations, the film industry, sound recording, and—by the 1920s—radio broadcasting. The unfortunate emphasis of the Frankfurt School on the "massifying" effects of commercial culture has distracted attention from the role that its producers played in extending popular understanding of and exposure to high culture during the first part of this century. Newspapers publicized the exhibitions of art museums and served as bases for music critics schooled in European traditions. Commercial presses published volumes with titles such as *Standard Symphonies* and *Pictures Every Child Should Know*. Phonograph record companies offered classical lines. The RCA Victor Company's Educational Department distributed *Music Appreciation with the Victrola for Children* (1923), a guide that provided music teachers with lesson plans keyed to items in the Victor catalogue.

Radio gave a special impetus to the nationalization of the fine-arts music canon, in part because radio depended on live music to fill its program hours during its first decades. (Music accounted for 74 percent of New York

City broadcast time in 1927 and 62 percent of Minneapolis–St. Paul radio broadcasts in 1932 [Lundberg et al. 1934].) The National Broadcasting Company even retained famed conductor Walter Damrosch, host of an educational symphony hour, as its "musical counsel."

Popular media extended to small towns and rural areas the heterogeneity that had long existed in U.S. cities. To grasp the interdependence of the popular and elite, consider the origins of the "Grand Ole Opry," the long-running country music program that epitomizes much of what highbrow media critics detest. The "Grand Ole Opry" began as a standard variety show (the "WSM Barn Dance") on Nashville's NBC affiliate, where it followed the network feed of Damrosch's "Music Appreciation Hour." One night in 1927, Damrosch offhandedly criticized musical "realism." The "Barn Dance" host opened his show with a humorous rebuttal. "For the past hour," he added, "we have been listening to music taken largely from Grand Opera, but from now on we will present the Grand Ole Opry!" (Moore 1969). Thus, popular culture defined itself in contrast to an increasingly powerful high-culture model, and radio created a national audience for both (Horowitz 1987).

THE INSTITUTIONALIZATION OF CULTURAL CAPITAL

Thus, it happened that by 1930 a particular selection of European artworks and styles was constituted as cultural capital in the United States—that is, it became hierarchically differentiated from other kinds of culture, symbolically potent, and universally acknowledged. Locally, high culture was anchored in new kinds of formal organizations: art museums, symphony orchestras, opera companies, and, eventually, dance and theatre companies organized according to the nonprofit model. This infrastructure was embedded in a national interorganizational network of professional associations, service organizations, private foundations, and proprietary corporations equipped to profit from the diffusion of art. At the apex of this system were the universities, authorized to validate, inculcate, and—within limits—expand the high-culture artistic, musical, and literary canons. Virtually none of this organized activity existed in 1870; before 1910, the high arts operated almost entirely at the local level. Only later did the arts shift from an urban cultural resource to a national cultural capital.

Much more might be said of this period, especially about the tensions implicit in both local variations in the adoption of institutional models and in the distinctive interests of nationally organized actors, which would often clash with the desire of urban elite status groups for a relatively exclusive and stable high culture. For now, however, it is more important to address three other issues.

First, what were the effects of the institutionalization of high culture as cultural capital? The 1920s witnessed a sharp increase in several indicators of middle- and upper-class interest in the arts: a dramatic rise, for example, in the value of imported artworks; a 75 percent increase in the census count of artists, sculptors, and art teachers between 1920 and 1930; and similar trends in other cultural indicators (Keppel and Duffus 1933). Moreover, scattered surveys from the 1930s point to high levels of radio listenership, piano and phonograph ownership, childhood music lessons, avocational instrument playing, and—to a lesser extent—attendance at live high-culture performing arts events among the middle and upper-middle classes (Lundberg et al. 1934; Allard 1939).

At the organizational level, we see the spread of orchestras and art museums to large and mid-sized cities and the widely held assumption that, as the Ogburn Commission report put it, "It is generally agreed that every city of 250,000 population or more can support an art museum" (Keppel 1934). Judith R. Blau's study (1988) of the diffusion of art museums points to the taken-for-granted nature of museums as part of the furniture of large urban places. Whereas before 1900, museum founding was more characteristic of slowly than of rapidly expanding cities (presumably because of the greater stability of upper classes in the former), after 1930, population expansion was positively rather than negatively associated with museum foundings. Moreover, whereas before 1930, change in a city's median level of educational attainment was unrelated to museum foundings, after 1930, increases in educational attainment became a strong predictor, reflecting the incorporation of the fine arts into legitimate school knowledge.

Second, what was the impact on the process of technological change and mass consumption? Certain inventions—the automobile, the telephone, cinema, and radio—were critical in their own right. Telephones and automobiles lowered the cost of interaction among people living substantial distances apart and increased the zone of privacy, permitting persons to segregate audiences and segment social networks to a greater degree than in the past. As Lewis Erensberg (1981) has shown, middle-class and elite night clubs emerged about the same time that automobiles and telephones came into widespread use, expanding opportunities for social interaction outside the home. Presumably, the separation of social relations from the home (and from emblems of status the home contained) increased the utility of what Bourdieu (1986) calls "embodied cultural capital," including the display of the self and its achievements through conversation. Cinema and radio vastly increased the range of social experience, providing an array of imitatable styles and selves with which persons could experiment in the enlarged social space created by the automobile and the telephone.

More generally, as Daniel Bell (1976) has noted, mechanization and advertising rendered style an inescapable force in the lives of the middle class. Mechanization entailed mass production and merchandising of goods that previously had been available only to the rich, but it also meant small-batch production of designer items for the public that shopped in urban department stores. Such stores, often in alliance with museums of art, sought to cultivate the public's aesthetic sensibilities, to enable consumers to distinguish the beautiful and well made from the coarse and insubstantial.

Although the effusions of the 1930s—"the granddaughter who buys a new rug discriminatingly is quite as clearly an artist as was her grandmother who, with spinning wheel and loom, made her colorful carpet"—now appear quaint, what is clear is that mechanization and advertising increased the number of distinctions the middle-class American had to make and the number of things there were to know about style (Haggerty 1935, p. 21). Command of such knowledge became a basis for evaluation at the time that such traditional markers of identity as family and place became less reliable.

Finally, my interpretation of this period is at odds with one of two parts of received wisdom about the advent of the mass media. Mass-culture critics correctly alleged that the rise of corporate culture producers turned the arts from producer to consumer goods. This was certainly the case for music: Survey data indicate that the percentage of middle-class Americans taking music lessons and playing instruments was far higher in the 1930s than it is today. (Levels of participation in visual arts and crafts activities appear to be roughly similar, however.)

But mass-culture critics erred in their preoccupation with "brow levels," which owed more to elite ideology than to social research. What was important about the arts that record companies, department stores (sometimes working with art museums), and radio stations brought to the U.S. public was not that they were a "dilute" form of a high culture that had existed in the past in pristine purity. Rather, the very process of definition of a dominant high culture in the arts relied upon the assistance of commercial enterprises in packaging for middle-class consumption an institutionally authorized mix of prestigious cultural goods, much of which had been part of a general popular culture less than a century earlier. Although "middlebrow" products were not to the liking of critics with the greatest stake in maintaining an unwatered cultural currency, they were essential in constituting as cultural capital a public version of the culture that the critics valued.

THE EROSION OF HIGH CULTURE
IN THE LATE TWENTIETH CENTURY

The United States entered the post-war era with a strongly classified high culture organized around university training of artists and consumers and nonprofit producing and exhibiting organizations commanded by trustees drawn from their communities' wealthiest and often oldest families. Despite rhetorical salutes to the value of education, these institutions were largely in the business of defending three kinds of related symbolic boundaries. One boundary was between fine art and good music—canonized works defined as unique, timeless, and nonutilitarian—and the "degenerate" products of commercial popular culture. Another was social, between people of taste who were capable of the disinterested appreciation of true art (largely the upper and upper-middle classes) and the vulgar "mass public." A third was organizational, between governance by trustees and aesthetic specialists on behalf of art for its own sake and the kinds of bureaucratic and market-oriented administrative systems characteristic of commercial enterprises—systems that, it was asserted, would compromise both the freedom of artistic personnel and the integrity of art.

During the last thirty years, the high-culture system has been eroding, and with it the strong classification between a sacred high culture and its profane popular counterpart. This erosion is visible at the level of production in the annexation of advertising and commercial art styles and even objects into fine-arts compositions; in the emergence of performance art out of dramatic, circus, and vaudeville traditions; in the ever-thinning boundary between ballet and modern dance; in the production by opera companies of musical comedy; in the repertoires of chamber ensembles that, like Kronos, mix fine-arts compositions with songs by Jimi Hendrix and Argentinian tango masters; in shifts of composers and performers from rock to orchestral music (Frank Zappa), from jazz to fine arts (Ornette Coleman), from performance art to rock (Laurie Anderson) and country music (K. D. Lang), and from porn to performance art (Annie Sprinkle); and in the increasing prominence of what Bourdieu (1965) has called *les arts moyennes*—for example, photography, jazz, new age music, and craft art. Such developments, which are far more numerous than earlier transgressions of genre boundaries and which have lost their predecessors' capacity to shock, are often remarked upon by critics and journalists. But they are poorly understood because of the habit of attributing them either to internal change in specific art worlds or to a postmodern *zeitgeist*, rather than to change in social structure and organization.

I shall argue below that the system of classification of artistic goods is becoming more finely, but also less clearly, differentiated, less universal, and less symbolically potent. The social structure continues to generate high levels of demand for the cultural goods with which social identities can be fashioned. But structural changes that weaken the institutional bases of cultural authority transform this demand into an inflationary spiral, undermining the cultural capital on which the symbolic economy has rested while proliferating weaker currencies.

The engine behind declassification is the market economy. High culture emerged as a status culture of a class in formation; as Max Weber (1968) noted, dynamic markets are inherently antagonistic to status cultures. Markets for cultural goods enable consumers to convert financial wealth into symbols of status and drive producers to efface genre boundaries in search of larger audiences. Yet men and women who understood this fact designed the high-culture system in both structure and ideology to buffer a high culture from market forces. So these observations about markets do not by themselves explain why the system now fails to do so.

The answer lies, I believe, in three interacting sources of change. The first is change in social structure, of which two aspects are crucial: a transformation of the U.S. elite from a confederation of cohesive urban upper classes knit together by kinship, place, and culture to a national elite defined by positions of authority in large organizations; and the rise of a massive, college-educated, mobile upper-middle class for whom taste and cultural style are important emblems of identity and sources of interpersonal information. The second change is the eclipse of private patronage and the rise of institutional patronage from private foundations, corporations, and an expanding state. A third change, following from the first two, has occurred at the organizational level and can best be characterized as a managerial revolution in the arts. I shall consider each of these developments in turn.

The Changing Basis of Elite Authority

In *Philadelphia Gentlemen*, E. Digby Baltzell noted the "democratization of plutocracy," the decline of the inner-directed upper classes with the destruction of family capitalism and their replacement by a national elite, detached from loyalty of place, whose authority rests on bureaucratic command rather than on kinship, club life, or culture. These fading urban upper classes, at once elites and status groups, formed the principle constituency for and organizers of a bounded high culture. Not only did they create the U.S. high-culture institutions; for many years, they maintained their exclusivity, resisting pressures for expansion. Such resistance was exemplified by the Metropolitan Museum of Art's rejection in the 1930s of a Carnegie Corporation grant that would have supported a branch museum for immigrants on the lower East Side; by the Philadelphia Orchestra's arm's-length relationship to the popular Robin Hood Dell concerts (Arian 1971); by the opposition in 1953 of 91 percent of the board chairmen of the nation's five hundred symphony orchestras to public subsidy for the arts (Hart 1973); and by the ambivalence of museums to educational programs and their tendency, for many years, to schedule them at times of the day when most adults were at work (Zolberg 1986).

With the passing of self-reproducing urban upper classes, the most influential constituency for a strongly bounded high culture vanished. Arts trustees, now more numerous with the vast expansion in the numbers of arts organizations and more likely to be recruited from the corporate middle class, are increasingly open to an expansionist dynamic that pushes their institutions closer to the market and threatens conventional forms of insulation of high-culture audiences and artists alike.

The Social Bases of Increased Demand

Declines in the solidarity and functional importance of traditional urban upper classes explain a decline in resistance to growth by nonprofit arts organizations. They do not, however, explain why consumers demanded more of the exhibitions and performances that these organizations offer. Although much expansion of artistic output during the 1960s and 1970s was fueled by increasing numbers of artists and new sources of subsidy, this output would not have been sustained had it not been for a genuine increase in consumer demand (Heilbron 1984).

If economists were right in viewing demand for symbolic goods as driven by individual utility maximization, we would expect increases in income and leisure time to be the best predictors of artistic consumption; economists often point to aggregate increases in each to explain expansion of demand (Lindner 1970; Scitovsky 1976). Fortunately, we can now test these assumptions at the individual level with high-quality national sample data collected by the U.S. Census Bureau—the Surveys of Public Participation in the Arts of 1982 and 1985. Our analyses of these data demonstrate that the availability of leisure has virtually no influence on whether or not persons attend high-culture arts events and that the influence of income is decidedly secondary (DiMaggio and Ostrower 1990).

The major predictor of arts consumption, of course, is educational attainment. Indeed, it seems reasonable to assume that most of the increase in cultural demand stems from the vast expansion of educational attainment of the 1960s, which resulted in the mass production of art consumers. The familiar imagery of "brow-levels," by which distinct patterns of aesthetic taste are said to map isomorphically onto social strata, is nowhere visible, however. Rather, the Census Bureau data reveal a pattern of *stratification without segmentation*. Highly educated people are more likely to report going to movies and enjoying rock, folk, and rhythm-and-blues music. John P. Robinson, et al. (1985) called this "the more-more principle": People who attend or like presentations of any kind of art are more likely to attend or like any other.

What we have, then, is a large, well-educated, geographically mobile upper-middle class, with attenuated ties to place and complex role structures that facilitate and reward participation in multiple cultural traditions. Whereas the nineteenth-century urban logic of cohesive status groups militated toward the exclusive allegiance of the members to tightly bounded status cultures, the rapid growth in numbers of the college educated engenders pressures toward cultural inflation (Collins 1977).

The role of formal education in such a social structure is, as Bourdieu has argued, to inculcate not tastes per se but a capacity for aesthetic adaptation: The self and its tastes become a project upon which the middle-class consumer constantly works. In the 1982 U.S. Census Bureau survey, with controls for family background, we found that cultural socialization has been distanced from family socialization—taking place less in the home and more in classes and workshops, both at school and in later life. The product is an eclectic disposition inimicable to a strongly bounded high culture and open to the proliferation of weakly insulated *arts moyennes*, with attributes of both traditionally high and popular cultural forms. This is consistent as well with Judith Blau's finding that the number of arts organizations of selected kinds in U.S. cities (which I interpret as a proxy for the degree of differentiation in styles available to consumers) is a positive function of the size of the educated upper-middle class (Blau 1986).

The Eclipse of the Private Patron
and the Rise of Institutional Support

If changes in social structure account for reduced opposition by arts trustees to expansionary growth and the rise in demand for differentiated forms of aesthetic experience, neither by itself explains the large-scale growth of the nonprofit arts. Had arts organizations merely followed existing routines, they would not have captured much of this increased demand, for nonprofits typically respond less quickly to market forces than do their proprietary competitors (Weisbrod 1988).

The rise of institutional sponsorship made a nonprofit response possible, altering the structures, programs, and objectives of the arts organizations that have been their beneficiaries. Increases in institutional funding have been substantial. Support from independent foundations grew from about $12.6 million in 1955 to approximately $350 million in 1984. Corporate assistance, negligible through the early 1960s, rose to nearly $400 million by the mid-1980s. By 1988, federal assistance—virtually nonexistent before 1965—stood at more than $160 million, while state government subsidies amounted to about $300 million.

What explains this massive rise in institutional subsidy? The conventional story is that it was necessary for the arts' survival. As deficits outran the ability of private patrons to cover them, foundations and government stepped in to make up the difference. The most sophisticated and influential version of this argument (Baumol and Bowen 1966) emphasizes increasing deficits due to the inability of arts suppliers (like other labor-intensive service industries) to keep pace with technologically induced productivity growth in the manufacturing sector.

Without doubting that this dynamic exists, we may question its centrality to the abrupt growth of institutional patronage in the 1960s and 1970s. First, productivity disparities between the service and manufacturing sectors have always existed; why these disparities should have made institutional support shoot up so rapidly over a particular twenty-year span is not apparent. Indeed, as productivity growth in the economy has slowed with the transition from an industrial to a service economy, the discrepancy between service-sector and overall growth rates has narrowed. Second, it has become apparent that arts organizations can exploit administrative rationalization and marketing techniques to increase revenues significantly. Third, and most important, the economic trials of the arts have been crises of growth, attributable to dramatic expansion both in the size of existing organizations and in the number of arts organizations (DiMaggio 1987b).

The rapid increase in foundation support for the arts, led by the Ford Foundation programs of the 1960s, represented a concerted effort to expand the artistic resources available to Americans, not simply to maintain the status quo. The emergence of the first major government program, the New York State Council on the Arts, reflected both the strong ties of Governor Rockefeller to the arts and philanthropic communities and the unique economic significance of the arts industry in that state. The creation of a federal arts agency, the National Endowment for the Arts, in 1965 was a natural concomitant to the expansion of the central state (the United States was the only major power without a cultural agency at the national level) and might have occurred far earlier but for the peculiar political legacy of the New Deal arts programs and the reluctance of traditional performing arts patrons to accept government aid.

Once in place, institutional funding entailed three parallel logics that, in tandem, have tended to erode the power of traditional trustees, expand the definition of art and its public, and—paradoxically—push the nonprofit arts toward dependence on the marketplace. The first of these is the *logic of access.* Almost all institutional patrons encourage grant recipients to increase the size of the publics they serve and, to some extent, take audience expansion as evidence of organizational success. The preoccupation with numbers pushes organizations toward the market and toward marketing, whether through blockbuster exhibitions, performances of works that appeal to large publics, or—in experimental forms—to post-performance cocktail parties that break down barriers between artists and audience.

A second logic shared by nearly all institutional funders, especially government, is the *logic of accountability.* Accountability is defined, in practice, as the capacity to generate grant proposals and reports containing detailed financial and audience data and in terms of the creation of administrative structures consistent with the expectations of institutional patrons. Many such patrons have linked support to nonartistic warrants of organizational virtue, such as marketing schemes, endowment policies, and strategic plans.

One effect of the logic of accountability is to minimize the viability of nonbureaucratically managed organizations, whether performers' collectives or elite institutions with patrimonial, club-like administrative systems. A second is to create new forms of expertise, the possession of which represents a source of power for administrators in their conflicts with trustees and artistic staff. A third is to increase the sheer administrative intensity of arts organizations. In analyses of data from the National Center for Educational Statistics' 1980 Museum Program Survey, we found that both the proportion of revenues received from government and the heterogeneity of funding sources (expressed as a Herfindahl index) significantly increased the proportion of staff and budget that art museums devoted to administration (DiMaggio and Powell 1984).

A final logic of institutional patronage, largely restricted to governmental funders, is the *logic of constituency formation.* From its creation, the National Endowment for the Arts worked to build a national constituency to support its efforts to garner larger appropriations from Congress. Lured by the availability of federal grants, by 1972 every U.S. state had created an arts agency; in turn, many states encouraged the proliferation of local arts agencies, of which there are now roughly three thousand. (Many local agencies now define themselves as "chambers of commerce for the arts," further legitimating the notion of culture as a public service linked to economic growth. California requires the state's three hundred-odd local arts agencies to engage in "community cultural planning and evaluation" as a condition of state support.)

A Managerial Revolution in the Arts

Most nonprofit organizations have ambiguous goals, numerous missions, and multiple constituencies; the internal politics of nonprofits are often characterized by tension between trustees, administrators, and professional staff. In the high-culture organizational model of the first part of the century, trustees and aesthetic professionals shared power. In recent years, institutional funding and organizational growth have altered the balance of influence, rendering administrative staff more numerous and more powerful.

The last two decades have witnessed the emergence of a new cadre of professional arts managers, especially in the performing arts, trained in university arts administration programs or management schools (Peterson 1986). These administrators are accomplishing what might be called, after Burnham and Berle and Means, a managerial revolution in the arts.

The managerialists contended that the profit-making corporation had succumbed to a managerial revolution that altered the operating objectives of the firm. This view has been called into question by an unlikely combination of neo-Marxist sociologists and agency-theory economists, both of whom point to powerful mechanisms that create identity of interest between top executives and major shareholders. It may well be that it is in nonprofit sectors such as the arts—where goals are ambiguous, evaluation difficult, and financial mechanisms that control agency relationships weak—that Berle and Means's ideas are most apt.

The new managers' training and interests make them receptive to calls for growth and administrative reform and frequently hostile both to social exclusionary pressures and aesthetic boundary-drawing. Because administrative hierarchies in the arts are flat, they usually attain executive positions while still in their thirties; further opportunities for upward mobility by job-changing are limited. Moreover, in the performing arts, managerial salaries are tightly tethered to organizational budgets. The managers' best hope for mobility is through rapid and dramatic organizational expansion, accompanied by high levels of grant support and even higher levels of earned income. These goals are consistent both with the orientation of administrative training toward efficiency and rationalization and with the agendas of many of the new institutional patrons that have been the managers' most constant allies.

As with other professional movements, the managerial revolution in the arts is promoted by collective efforts of arts administrators to enhance their status, authority, and career opportunities. Their project has included the establishment of an academic base in university arts administration degree programs, of which more than thirty have formed since the advent of federal arts funding; the systematization of specialized knowledge not easily accessible to trustees; the building of personal ties between managers and corporate and government grantmakers, rendering trustees more dependent; and, in some cases, the elaboration by service organizations of fieldwide standards.

The new administrators participate actively in professional activities in a manner that is both rational and consequential. We created indices of professional participation for art museum directors, orchestra managers, and managing directors of resident theatres surveyed in the early 1980s, tapping involvement in activities sponsored by the major service organizations as well as service on federal state advisory panels. In all three fields, participation was a significant predictor of managers' salaries, net organization size, gender, and several measures of educational attainment, family background, and professional experience (DiMaggio 1986).

Such participation also appears to have organizational consequences. Melissa Middleton (1989), who studied strategic planning by performing arts organizations in two Connecticut SMSAs, reported that managers' participation in fieldwide networks was a significant predictor of whether their organizations had undertaken formal efforts resulting in multi-year planning documents.

Fieldwise participation also shapes administrators' orientations to their roles. In our study of arts managers, factor analyses of attitude measures yielded indices of managerialism, reflecting an orientation toward rationalization, administrative efficiency, and the market. With appropriate controls, professional participation significantly predicted managerialism among administrators of theatres, art museums, and orchestras. It was also a strong predictor of art museum directors' orientation toward social and educational values (an endemic issue in the museum world). In other words, participation in fieldwide activities appeared to engender and reinforce orientations toward administrative efficiency and (for art museum directors) social missions, as opposed to the orientations toward social and aesthetic exclusivity characteristic of traditional high-culture institutions.

THE FUTURE
OF THE CULTURAL ECONOMY

The high-culture system rested on three pillars: local status groups committed to the elaboration and maintenance of a relatively stable status culture based on the high-culture arts; nonprofit arts organizations, insulated from market forces and politics by upper-class patronage and governance; and the system of higher education, which trained specialists in high culture, established and renewed canons in the several art forms, and inculcated in students awareness of and respect for the products of high-culture art worlds.

At least two of these three pillars—the dominance of local status groups and the insulation of nonprofit arts organizations from market forces—are crumbling, and the fate of the third—higher education—is contested. We must not discount the hold that the classification high versus popular still exercises over U.S. culture: Taste remains highly stratified, theatre and dance (and, to a lesser extent, craft art, jazz, and literary publishing) have been annexed to the high-culture nonprofit system, and the traditional high arts—classical music, the visual and plastic arts, opera—thrive by historical standards. Yet, in the long run, it is not obvious that the institutional prerequisites for the preservation of centralized cultural authority—and thus for the persistence of a generalized cultural capital—will long remain in place.

At the same time, however, the social structure bases of demand for symbolic goods—wide social range, diffuse social networks, weak corporate primary groups, segmented role structures, and mass higher education—are well established. Even if the arts were to stop functioning as cultural capital tomorrow, demand for symbolic goods would remain high. Intimations of the effects of an extreme decentralization of cultural authority may be gained by observing other cultural spheres where, even more than in the arts, one finds an adumbration and blurring of genres, an increase in things to know and opportunities to make distinctions, and the persistent use by middle-class Americans of symbolic props for the definition of cosmopolitan selves.

Take, for example, the fashion revolution of the past two decades and the emergence of small-scale producers selling varied subpublics a wide variety of styles (Crane 1988). The familiar fashion cycle of the first two-thirds of the century seems to have succumbed to a more or less chronic state of syncretic pluralism. The production regime is based entirely in the market; institutionalized cultural authority is weak; and, although huge enterprises are influential, vacant niches are available to small producers with relatively little capital. In fashion (as in cuisine), the system of classification is highly differentiated, but boundaries are weak, relatively nonhierarchical, and far from universal.

Is this to be the future of the arts? Will the culture of the twenty-first century represent, as Henry Adams predicted in his *Autobiography*, "not a unity, but a multiple"? Certainly the trends in the United States suggest that this may be the case. Although I have said little about technology and popular culture, the segmentation of audiences—first, for magazines and radio in the late 1950s (Peterson and Berger 1975), then for television (with the penetration of cable systems above 60 percent by the late 1980s)—cannot but reinforce centrifugal tendencies.

Yet it would be rash to suggest the demise of cultural authority, high culture, and the current place of cultural capital in the symbolic economy. Although demand for cultural goods emerges more or less directly out of social structure, the organization of supply has become to some extent a matter of public choice, embedded in an extensive, albeit highly decentralized, policy apparatus. Four axes of choice (which, to be sure, is more frequently taken by oversight than by decision) are especially important in the short run.

Policy Toward Cultural Pluralism

A current byword in arts policy circles is *cultural pluralism* (or *cultural diversity*), which ordinarily refers to a commitment to the value of (and, by implication, subsidies to artists working in) a variety of cultural traditions, especially those of Americans of Asian, African, and Latin American descent. At their most pragmatic, advocates of cultural pluralism seek a reallocation of public funds to "minority" arts organizations, including those working in European high-culture traditions. At their most idealistic, cultural pluralists embrace cultural democracy, a communitarian view of art as a collectively created force for community change. Although much talk about cultural pluralism is lip service for the benefit of liberal legislators and minority constituencies, some of it is more than this. And African-American, Hispanic, and Asian political activism, fueled by demographic change (which is occurring most swiftly in the two arts centers of the United States—New York and California), will secure a permanent place for cultural pluralism on the policy agenda.

Cultural pluralism makes problematic the dominance of Euro-American high culture; that is, its advocates ask why artists working in certain traditions—which, more or less by historical accident, have been buffered to some extent from the market—should receive public funds, whereas artists working in traditions that have not been so favored should not. In so doing, they seek to enlist the arts policy enterprise in an effort to reassess, perhaps quite radically, the definition of serious art. If they succeed, the allocational problem—which was solved efficiently, if not equitably, by restricting the focus of most institutional funders to a relatively narrow slice of the artistic spectrum—will be formidable and—barring a dramatic rise in public support that seems unlikely in the short run—the debates will be highly contentious. Such reforms would dilute the cultural authority of universities and most conventional art museums and nonprofit performing arts firms.

Policy Toward Arts Organizations

The general thrust of arts policy in the United States has been toward what is referred to in policy circles as *institutionalization*: nurturing arts organizations, preventing existing organizations from failing, encouraging small organizations to become larger and large organizations to seek immortality. The reasons for this policy are clear enough: The constituency-building imperative leads arts agencies to try to keep their constituents healthy and alive and to respond more quickly to organized constituencies than to unorganized supplicants. Policies of institutionalization and expansion encourage arts organizations to become larger, more bureaucratic, and more dependent on both institutional subsidy and earned income. Although many institutional patrons try to support innovative programming, dependence on earned income (especially in the performing arts, where audiences are organized by subscription) tends to overwhelm such efforts and drive presenting organizations toward safe or commercially rewarding repertoire. Moreover, the emphasis on expansion through earned income has been self-defeating, insofar as larger organizations require more institutional patronage (in absolute terms) even if a larger proportion of their income is earned through the sale of services.

An alternative policy, which would probably be more effective in stimulating innovation (although less effective in maintaining constituencies and providing artistic services to large publics), would be to lower barriers to entry rather than attempting to ensure institutional immortality. To an extent, this would involve doing the opposite of what public agencies now do: focusing grants on new, unproven enterprises, discouraging expansion, investing in organizations with the expectation that many of them would expire. A full embrace of such a policy would be politically suicidal for public agencies. Nonetheless, some pressures are building for a modest reorientation of this kind, which—like cultural pluralism—would tend further to decentralize cultural authority.

Policy Toward Higher Education

Because demand for culture is fueled by higher education, the shape of the university system—the site of the most vigorous debates over the status of high culture (e.g., Bloom 1987, and Bloom's critics)—will also have important implications for the direction in which the cultural economy evolves. Universal higher education would further stimulate demand for and production of symbolic goods; sharp cutbacks in enrollments or an even more massive redirection of students into vocational commuter programs than has already occurred (Brint and Karabel 1989) would restrict demand. By contrast, the stronger the level of support for the traditional humanities disciplines, the better the life chances of the conventional cultural hierarchies.

Policy Toward Mass Communications

A final question with which public policy must come to grips is the extent to which access to information and cultural goods should be allocated by the market. In the nineteenth century, it was believed that cities and philanthropists had a responsibility to make artistic experiences available to the poor, and, indeed, the civic uses of art and music tended to render culture a form of public good. These impulses lessened with the consolidation of a cultural hierarchy in the late nineteenth century, although they were renewed in the New Deal arts projects of the 1930s. As they flagged, however, the problem of a common culture was largely solved when the mass media of radio and television were established as public goods, supported by the sale of audiences to advertisers rather than by the sale of programs to the public.

The rise of cable and other forms of pay television (as well as the instrumental data services being offered to computer users) is converting a much larger portion of culture to a private good and portends both a sharp increase in cultural inequality and an end to the mass media's role as purveyors of a shared symbolic universe in which most Americans participate. The deregulatory policies of the Reagan administration encouraged the fragmentation of the audience, at the same time facilitating the centralization of economic control over programming. Moreover, the fate of public broadcasting, rendered redundant by the availability of cable to its core audience, becomes ever more clouded. To the extent that the current drift of policy continues, it will reinforce tendencies against universality and toward greater differentiation in U.S. culture.

CONCLUSION

Such policy choices will shape the resolution of two more broadly significant questions affecting our cultural well-being. If the current system of classifying art and sponsoring artistic production and distribution is creaking under the weight of social and political change, can we devise alternative institutions to preserve the autonomy of some artistic practice from the dictates of the economic marketplace? I do not mean to imply that the market is constraining whereas other forms of patronage are benign, any more than I would agree with the often-echoed, nineteenth-century view of the market as a free and neutral means of releasing artists from the yoke of patronage. Rather, I believe that artists are likely to be most productive and creative if they are collectively subject to a variety of constraints rather than just one.

The virtue of the high-culture system is that it succeeded in cordoning off a sector of cultural production from the demands of the marketplace. Its great disadvantage is that it assisted only some kinds of artists in a way that responded to the status interests of the wealthy rather than to the functional needs of either the arts or society. To the extent that the high-culture system erodes, we face the challenge and opportunity of constructing a reclassification of symbolic goods that does not map neatly onto the structure of social inequality—in other words, systems of patronage and cultural authority consistent with a democratic art.

Second, we should anticipate the effects of cultural inflation on the capacity of persons to navigate the relational waters of a complex and highly differentiated organizational society. An advantage of highly bounded and ritually potent cultural classifications is that they possess much communication value, enabling people to connect with others on brief exposure. An advantage of universal classifications is that they provide a common field of discourse. I shall not jump on the bandwagon of the cultural literacy movement, which has failed to grapple seriously with the exercise of domination implicit in any effort to codify significant cultural knowledge (Hirsch 1988). I do, however, believe that Daniel Bell's observation that "the system of social relations is so complex and differentiated, and experiences are so specialized, complicated, or incomprehensible, that it is difficult to find common symbols" (1976, p. 95) warrants our attention. If the dominant form of cultural capital (which provides a set of common symbols) is devolving into a diffuse set of disparate cultural resources—that is, if authority were to become as decentralized in the arts and literature as in fashion and cuisine—then we should be able to predict what, if any, effect this might have upon social integration and patterns of inequality in cultural property.

The received terminology of lay and academic cultural criticism—phrases such as mass society, highbrow/lowbrow, postmodernism—will not get us very far in addressing such issues. Terms that have entered the sociological vocabulary during the past two decades—cultural capital, cultural industry systems, and others developed by Pierre Bourdieu and his associates in France and Richard Peterson and students of production systems in the United States—will provide more leverage. What such recent progress promises is an analytic sociology of culture, distinct from criticism and textual interpretation, sensitive to the structural and pragmatic aspects of the symbolic economy, rigorously empirical in method and temperament, and thus capable of a comprehension of contemporary cultural change that is independent of the categories of the nineteenth century.

REFERENCES

Allard, Lucille Edna. 1939. *A Study of the Leisure Activities of Certain Elementary School Teachers of Long Island.* New York: Bureau of Publications, Teachers College, Columbia University.

Altick, Richard D. 1978. *The Shows of London.* Cambridge, MA: Harvard University Press.

Arian, Edward. 1971. *Brahms, Beethoven and Bureaucracy.* University: University of Alabama Press.

Baumol, William J., and William G. Bowen. 1966. *The Performing Arts: The Economic Dilemma.* Cambridge, MA: MIT Press.

Bell, Daniel. 1976. *The Cultural Contradictions of Capitalism.* New York: Basic Books.

Blau, Judith R. 1986. "The Elite Arts, More or Less *De Rigueur*: A Comparative Analysis of Metropolitan Culture." *Social Forces* 64: 875–905.

_____ . 1988. "Historical Conditions of Museum Development." Paper presented at the annual meetings of the American Sociological Association, August 1988.

Bloom, Allan. 1987. *The Closing of the American Mind.* New York: Simon and Schuster.

Bourdieu, Pierre. 1965. *Un Art Moyen: Essai sur les Usages Sociaux de la Photographie.* Paris: Editions de Minuit.

_____ . 1984. *Distinction: A Social Critique of the Judgment of Taste.* Translated by Richard Nice. Cambridge, MA: Harvard University Press.

_____ . 1986. "The Forms of Capital." Pp. 241–258 in John G. Richardson, ed., *Handbook of Theory and Research for the Sociology of Education.* Westport, CT: Greenwood Press.

Bourdieu, Pierre, and Jean-Claude Passeron. 1977. *Reproduction: In Education, Society, Culture.* Translated by Richard Nice. Beverly Hills: Sage Publications.

Brint, Steven, and Jerome Karabel. 1989. *The Diverted Dream: Community Colleges and the Promise of Educational Opportunity in America, 1900–1985.* New York: Oxford University Press.

Burke, Peter. 1978. *Popular Culture in Early Modern Europe.* London: Temple Smith.

Collins, Randall. 1977. "Some Comparative Principles of Educational Stratification." *Harvard Educational Review* 47:1–27.

_____ . 1979. *The Credential Society: An Historical Sociology of Education and Stratification.* New York: Academic Press.

Crane, Diana. 1988. "Fashion Worlds: An Anatomy of Avant-Garde Fashion Tradition." Paper presented at the fourteenth annual Conference on Social Theory, Politics, and the Arts, American University, Washington, DC, October 1988.

DeNora, Tia. 1989. "Musical Patronage and Social Change at the Time of Beethoven's Arrival in Vienna: A Case for Interpretive Sociology." Manuscript, Department of Sociology, University of California at San Diego.

DiMaggio, Paul. 1982a. "Cultural Entrepreneurship in Nineteenth-Century Boston: I. The Organization of a High Culture in the United States." *Media, Culture and Society* 4:33–50, 303–320.

_____. 1982b. "Cultural Entrepreneurship in Nineteenth-Century Boston: II. The Classification and Framing of American Art." *Media, Culture and Society* 4:303–322.

_____. 1986. *Managers of the Arts: Careers and Opinions of Executives of U.S. Art Museums, Resident Theaters, Symphony Orchestras and Community Arts Agencies.* Washington, DC: Seven Locks Press.

_____. 1987a. "Classification in Art." *American Sociological Review* 52:440–455.

_____. 1987b. "Nonprofit Organizations in the Production and Distribution of Culture." Pp. 195–220 in Walter W. Powell, ed., *The Nonprofit Sector: A Research Handbook.* New Haven, CT: Yale University Press.

_____. 1988. "Progressivism in the Arts." *Society* 25:70–75.

_____. Forthcoming. "Constructing an Organizational Field as a Professional Project: The Case of Art Museums, 1920–1940." In Walter W. Powell and Paul DiMaggio, eds., *The New Institutionalism in Organizational Analysis.* Chicago: University of Chicago Press.

DiMaggio, Paul, and Francie Ostrower. 1990. "Participation in the Arts by Black and White Americans." *Social Forces* 68 (March).

DiMaggio, Paul, and Walter W. Powell. 1984. "Institutional Isomorphism and Structural Conformity." Manuscript, Sociology Department, Yale University.

Douglas, Mary, and Baron Isherwood. 1979. *The World of Goods: Towards an Anthropology of Consumption.* New York: Norton.

Erensberg, Lewis. 1981. *Steppin' Out: New York Night Life and the Transformation of American Culture, 1890–1930.* Chicago: University of Chicago Press.

Granovetter, Mark, and Roland Soong. 1988. "Threshold Models of Diversity: Chinese Restaurants, Residential Segregation, and the Spiral of Silence," in Clifford Clogg, ed., *Sociological Methodology.* Washington, DC: American Sociological Association.

Haggerty, Melvin E. 1935. *Art as a Way of Life.* Minneapolis: University of Minnesota Press.

Hart, Philip. 1973. *Orpheus in the New World: The Symphony Orchestra as an American Cultural Institution.* New York: W. W. Norton.

Heilbron, James. 1984. "Once More, with Feeling: The Arts Boom Revisited," in William S. Hendon, ed., *The Economics of Cultural Industries.* Akron, OH: Association for Cultural Economics.

Hirsch, E. D. 1988. *Cultural Literacy* (2nd ed.). New York: Vintage.

Hiss, Priscilla, and Roberta Fansler. 1934. *Research in Fine Arts in the Colleges and Universities of the United States.* New York: The Carnegie Corporation.

Horowitz, Joseph. 1987. *Understanding Toscanini: How He Became an American Culture-God and Helped Create a New Audience for Old Music.* Minneapolis: University of Minnesota Press.

Jaher, Frederic Cople. 1982. *The Urban Establishment: Upper Strata in Boston, New York, Charleston, Chicago and Los Angeles.* Urbana: University of Illinois Press.

Keppel, Frederick P. 1934. "The Arts," in William F. Ogburn, ed., *Recent Social Trends in the United States.* New York: Whittlesey House–McGraw-Hill.

Keppel, Frederick P. and R. L. Duffus. 1933. *The Arts in American Life*. New York: McGraw-Hill.

Lagemann, Ellen Condliffe. 1983. *Private Power for the Public Good: A History of the Carnegie Foundation for the Advancement of Teaching*. Middletown, CT: Wesleyan University Press.

————. 1990. *The Politics of Knowledge: A History of the Carnegie Corporation of New York*. Middletown, CT: Wesleyan University Press.

Levine, Lawrence. 1988. *Highbrow/Lowbrow: The Emergence of Cultural Hierarchy in America*. Cambridge, MA: Harvard University Press.

Levy, Florence N. 1938. *Art Education in the City of New York: A Guidance Study*. New York: School Art League of New York.

Lindner, Staffan B. 1970. *The Harried Leisure Class*. New York: Columbia University Press.

Lundberg, George A., Mirra Komarovsky, and Mary A. McInerny. 1934. *Leisure: A Suburban Study*. New York: Columbia University Press.

Martin, George. 1983. *The Damrosch Dynasty: America's First Family of Music*. Boston: Houghton Mifflin.

Middleton, Melissa. 1989. *Planning as Strategy: The Logic, Symbolism and Politics of Planning in Nonprofit Organizations*. Ph.D. dissertation, Organizational Behavior Program, Yale University.

Moore, Thurston, ed. *Pictorial History of Country Music*, Vol. 1. Denver: Heather Enterprises, 1969.

Mukerji, Chandra. 1983. *From Graven Images: Patterns of Modern Materialism*. Berkeley: University of California Press.

Peterson, Richard A. 1986. "From Impresario to Art Administrator: Formal Accountability in Nonprofit Cultural Organizations." Pp. 161–183 in Paul DiMaggio, ed., *Nonprofit Enterprise in the Arts: Studies in Mission and Constraint*. New York: Oxford University Press.

Peterson, Richard A., and David Berger. 1975. "Cycles in Symbol Production: The Case of Popular Music." *American Sociological Review* 40:158–173.

Robinson, John P., Carol A. Keegan, Terry Hanford, and Timothy Triplett. 1985. *Public Participation in the Arts: Final Report on the 1982 Survey*. Washington, DC: Report to the National Endowment for the Arts, Research Division.

Scitovsky, Tibor. 1976. *The Joyless Economy: An Inquiry into Human Satisfaction and Consumer Dissatisfaction*. New York: Oxford University Press.

Shanet, Howard. 1975. *Philharmonic: A History of New York's Orchestra*. Garden City, NY: Doubleday.

Weber, Max. 1968. *Economy and Society*, ed. by Guenther Roth and Claus Wittich. New York: Bedminster Press.

Weber, William M. 1976. *Music and the Middle Class in Nineteenth-Century Europe*. New York: Holmes and Meier.

Weisbrod, Burton. 1988. *The Nonprofit Economy*. Cambridge, MA: Harvard University Press.

White, Harrison C., and Cynthia White. 1965. *Canvasses and Careers: Institutional Change in the French Painting World*. New York: John Wiley and Sons.

Zolberg, Vera. 1986. "Tensions of Mission in American Art Museums." Pp. 184–198 in Paul DiMaggio, ed., *Nonprofit Enterprise in the Arts: Studies in Mission and Constraint*. New York: Oxford University Press.

Comments

Wendy Griswold

Paul DiMaggio's chapter analyzes a social change in the organization and use of culture within a theoretical framework. The change: In the early nineteenth century, the cultural field in the United States consisted of mixed genres and broad, unstratified participation. By the late nineteenth century, local urban elites had managed, with greater or less success (Boston versus New York), to achieve a high-popular culture separation rooted in institutions for the former that were patronized by these elites. The early twentieth century saw the nationalization and institutionalization of what had been local high-culture enterprises, this taking the form of the development of national organizational fields for arts professionals and administrators, the incorporation of the arts as part of the mandate of growing universities, and the increase in commercial cultural production facilitated by technological changes such as cinema and radio. The 1920s through the 1950s represented the heyday of cultural capital in the United States. Institutional changes undermined the system in the postwar period, accelerating in the 1960s; these included reorganization of the elite from kinship to organizational positions, increased consumer demand for cultural goods based on rising education, the shift from private to state and corporate patronage, and the managerial revolution among arts administrators that rewarded innovation and expansion. The result was cultural inflation, leading to an erosion of the social value of cultural capital.

The theoretical framework: The organization of cultural authority influences dimensions of cultural classification, and it is these dimensions with which people interact as they use cultural goods. In the case at hand, the allocation of cultural goods moved from a traditional to a market system, while the structure of elites moved from status group and class to networks, characterized by dispersion and role segmentation. This led to an overall weakening of the elite cultural authority, as such authority moved from being centralized to being diffuse. A weakening of cultural authority has a number of specific effects on systems of cultural classification: an increased differentiation of genres, a reduced hierarchy among such genres, a reduced universality of knowledge about them, and a reduced ritual potency to symbolic classifications. Such an exploded classification system reduces the value of participation in and knowledge of any particular genre—one's cultural capital no longer buys very much. Cultural goods go from being potential advantages in social competitions to being constitutive of individual differences that do not matter much to anyone outside the individual. *Postmodern* is simply a description of the cultural state of things when a magazine called *Self* can give advice on shaping one's pectorals, relationships, musical taste, and spirituality and can give ideas on fashion and cuisine, with the goal set by the title; if postmodern is the description of the prevalence of this type of constitutive cultural object, the erosion of cultural authority is the explanation.

Since DiMaggio has so beautifully set up this relationship of the cultural consequences of a changing society and the theoretical basis for these consequences, I will raise some points for discussion at these two levels as well. First, the changing society: I wonder if the cultural authority of elites was ever quite as great as represented at the starting point of DiMaggio's account (and as suggested in Pierre Bourdieu's theory of cultural capital). DiMaggio refers to the work of Peter Burke, who argues that in early modern Europe there was a courtly culture in which only the elite participated and a popular culture in which everyone participated. The former did not have much ritual potency, in DiMaggio's terms, because it lacked universality. Now, of course, cultural capital is not needed in a system where everyone more or less understands their social positions—lords do not need to impress peasants with their knowledge of the arts. It was only in the late eighteenth century in Europe, according to Burke, and about a century later in the United States, according to DiMaggio, that cultural hierarchies came to have social significance in terms of competition among social groups. But even in the nineteenth century, plenty of questions were raised about the relationship between cultural authority and elite social position. Matthew Arnold wrote off the aristocracy as "barbarians" and saw the potential for true culture coming only from the yet-unawakened philistines of the middle class. Henry James based his literary career on the distinction between social position (kinship-based—the old elites of both Europe and the United States) and moral worth, a worth that was often signaled by a capacity for cultural sensitivity; in DiMaggio's terms, the relationship between social reputation and character was highly problematic. Mark Twain and late nineteenth-century U.S. humorists made the same point: It was the common, ill-educated person of innate common sense, honest character, and a high regard for his or her own dignity that pricked the pretensions of the elite. The Boston elite in particular was subject to withering scorn, as when T. S. Eliot mocked the desiccated readers of Brahmin genealogy in the *Boston Evening Transcript*.[1] People such as Eliot, James, and the other writers I have mentioned represent—very self-consciously represent—a distinction between money, family, and social prestige on the one hand and true culture, character, and what Eliot called "the appetites of life" on the other. The pervasiveness of these themes in the late nineteenth-century and early twentieth-century U.S. writers at least raises the empirical question of whether or not the claims of the social elite were plausible in the eyes of others, even others such as Eliot (from a St. Louis business background) who were most interested in cultural participation, and of how successful this social elite was in using cultural goods to bolster its claim to status. It may be that its cultural capital, financial and personal participation in a limited set of artistic institutions, was a coin of currency only among its members: The dedicated culture students such as Eliot wanted a deeper participation in the life of the mind and spirit than attendance at the Thursday matinee of the Boston Symphony Orchestra could represent, while the common man was not impressed. (A gender distinction, not remarked upon in DiMaggio's work, may also be at work here.)

This question of the empirical status of the elite's cultural authority in DiMaggio's starting period raises the more theoretical questions of who uses cultural capital and why. In Bourdieu's analyses, it seems to be mostly those members of the educated middle classes who do not have much of the other kind of capital. Among the dominant classes, Bourdieu has found the structure of the distribution of economic capital to be largely "symmetric and opposite" the structure of the distribution of cultural capital. Thus, teachers both labor to pass on their educational advantages and benefit from having these increasingly esteemed. Barbarians do not bother. (Of course, the low regard with which teachers are held in U.S. society should be a warning here.) A second group would be those having new money, who want to take on the attributes of old money and do so through symbolic representation such as wearing Ralph Lauren fashions. T. S. Eliot came from this group, although he did not act as the theory would predict. The first group can be identified as class fraction, the second as a status group.

DiMaggio seems to blur, or overlap, the difference between class fractions and status groups, and I think this ambiguity matters to his theory. (Weber himself vacillated on this.) If cultural authority is only another property of dominant classes, then one wonders if cultural capital is necessary—the old-fashioned kind seems sufficient. (Garry Trudeau can get all the laughs he wants among the educated readers by poking fun at the utter tastelessness of Donald Trump—Trump may be a barbarian, but his class position is threatened not when someone calls attention to his lack of cultural capital but when he runs short of money.) Bourdieu suggests this when he points out that schools serve to legitimate the value of the cultural capital that non-elites, lacking the equipment to crack the symbolic codes, will never really be able to appropriate. If, on the other hand, cultural authority is the property of status groups, then I suspect that the human capacity for making meaningful distinctions is a constant; specific genres and systems of genres may well change in their degrees of differentiation, hierarchy, universality, and potency, but status groups sharing lifestyles always figure out ways to recognize one another and to recognize those who do not really belong. In other words, such authority may only be legitimate for the status groups in question; teachers or readers of Garry Trudeau share a set of symbolic representations that allows them to locate one another, but other status groups trade in different symbolic and material goods. There is no good reason why members of one status group should be dazzled by the cultural goods of another (to assume such is to assume what Jon Elster has called *asymmetrical rationality* between groups), and there is considerable empirical evidence indicating that non-elite groups are quite able to resist buying that which elites—institutionalized in systems of education—try to sell.

DiMaggio argues that the high-culture system rests on three pillars—(1) local status groups committed to elaborating and maintaining a stable culture based on high-culture arts; (2) nonprofit arts organizations insulated from market forces by these status groups; and (3) a system of higher education that trains high-culture specialists, establishes canons, and inculcates respect for high culture in students—and that at least the first two of these pillars are crumbling and the third is contested. While the social changes and the specific changes in arts organization he describes have undoubtedly taken place, I wonder if he has not identified the wrong pillars (or, as in the postmodernist architecture of William James Hall, identified support pillars that do not really support anything). It seems to me that a high culture is perpetuated as long as there are institutions—the court, the church, the academy, and others—that produce men and women such as Eliot who will defend key cultural distinctions as they currently understand them. The relationship between these people and social elites is never an easy one, even though there may be periods of considerable overlap of personnel, and often involves considerable mutual contempt. Such people produce a discourse—whether it involves an appreciation of Old Masters or a post-modernist celebration of banality in terms of an abstract theoretical irony—that enhances direct and indirect ties within the group while justifying the barbarians, high and low, outside. Although, of course, the barbarians who read *Self* magazine with a serene absence of Derridean irony could not care less.

NOTES

1. T. S. Eliot, "The Boston Evening Transcript," p. 16 in *The Complete Poems and Plays 1909–1950* (New York: Harcourt, Brace & Co., 1952).

Comments

Richard A. Peterson

Paul DiMaggio's chapter, "Social Structure, Institutions, and Cultural Goods: The Case of the United States," serves as an excellent introduction to the purposively constructed nature of culture and provides the basis for conjecturing about the nature of cultural goods a few decades into the twenty-first century. My comments thus consider the topic of cultural capital or cultural entrepreneurship in an age of multinational corporations. In his provocative and carefully researched study, DiMaggio shows how the consolidating late-nineteenth-century commercial-industrial elite used the fine arts as a cultural resource to buttress its claim to prominence in U.S. society. In his equally well-researched study of the role of art as a group marker in the first half of the twentieth century, DiMaggio argues—less convincingly—that art was no longer just a cultural resource signaling class status but had become a form of cultural capital for the society at large. He then shows that just as art was being codified as cultural capital in the middle third of the twentieth century, fine art's value as cultural capital rapidly collapsed. A la Daniel Bell (1976), DiMaggio uses a "cultural contradictions of capitalism" argument to explain this paradox. I would like to resolve the paradox that art's value as cultural capital was so quickly squandered by the same people who had labored so long to establish it. I begin by considering several key concepts.

WHY THE FOCUS ON GOODS THAT ARE "PREDOMINANTLY" CULTURAL?

DiMaggio identifies cultural goods as "goods and services that are predominantly symbolic or aesthetic in character." Restricting attention to those goods that are *predominantly* symbolic is a useful simplification in that it sidesteps the complex empirical problem of how to distill the symbolic component of predominantly utilitarian goods (Peterson 1983).

Eliminated by DiMaggio from the inventory of cultural goods, however, are the nuances of language, dress, and grooming by which individuals and groups make their identities known. Nonetheless, these and other utilitarian elements that carry strong cultural meanings have been crucial for scholars of culture otherwise as diverse as Pierre Bourdieu, Edward Shils, Irving Goffman, Herbert Gans, Clifford Geertz, Daniel Bell, and Raymond Boudon. In focusing narrowly on predominantly symbolic goods, DiMaggio is making the untested assumption that what he finds for these will apply as well to symbol-laden utilitarian goods. That this is often not warranted is illustrated in the classic clash between the new rich and the old. Although the former may acquire prestigious cultural goods, they may still be frozen out of the circles of the latter for not knowing how to talk and walk and what to say (Baltzell 1964).

WHY SHOULD ART BECOME CULTURAL CAPITAL?

Cultural goods are used both to signal shared group membership in a system composed of like-structured groups (a la Emile Durkheim) and also to distinguish between groups within a hierarchial system (a la Max Weber). For this purpose, any readily identified sign—such as blue for Union and grey for Confederate troops in the U.S. Civil War—will do. If, however, cultural goods simply serve as exclusive or inclusive markers of group membership, why have they been the focus of such great polemical attention? I think it is because cultural goods are presumed to play a vital role quite apart from signaling boundaries—they connote moral value. This seems clear in the world of symbolic affairs where one finds that the meaning and propagation of cultural goods are hotly contested. Whether debating issues of media censorship (Reisman 1983), public art (Jordan 1987), or the state of civil knowledge (Bloom, 1987), protagonists presume that the most important role of cultural goods is to display and to teach morals, values, beliefs, and the like.[1]

This need for a moral component helps to explain why art, in particular, was useful as a marker of high-class position. It was a costly form of display, but so were pearl necklaces and elegantly prepared meals. Arts connoisseurship was relatively difficult to obtain, but the same could be said of knowing how to dress properly or how to ride to the hounds. As distinct from these symbolic goods, however, arts connoisseurship was believed to connote and to foster high moral stature. Thus, for bourgeois individuals and for the class as a whole, patronage of the arts served to signal their moral superiority over contending individuals and classes (Bourdieu 1984, 1985). This moral component helps to explain the extreme reaction that Theodor Adorno and other members of the Frankfort School had to jazz. In their eyes, it was not only aesthetically inferior but morally decadent and polluting of fine art music.

The need for cultural goods to be vested with moral worth helps to explain why symphonic music and painting in particular, among all the arts, were first adopted as cultural goods in the United States and suggests the particular meaning with which they were invested. Sculpture and painting were associated with the antiquities, and following their sanitized interpretation through the work of the French Academy, they connoted noble and patriotic thoughts. Symphonic music, being abstract—that is, without words or pictures—could be vested with high moral meaning. Operas in the United States, unlike the tradition in other countries, were sung in their language of composition. This allowed audiences to focus on the beautiful voices and grand gestures without attending to the often-sordid dialogue. U.S. Victorians did not place theatre and dance as cultural goods on the same high moral ground. The former was associated with bawdy entertainments, and the latter was generally defined as being too sexually charged to be considered an art form (Williams 1960; Harris 1966).

CULTURAL RESOURCES
AND CULTURAL CAPITAL

DiMaggio distinguished between *cultural resources*, which include any form of symbolic mastery useful in facilitating interaction, and a special form of resource, *cultural capital*, which is "proficiency in the consumption of and discourse about generally prestigious—that is, institutionally screened and validated—cultural goods and services" whose high value has been created by an institutionalized elite in the name of the entire community, nation, or civilization at large. It follows that a country can have but one coinage of cultural capital and—as has been the case for most of U.S. history—may have none at all. This distinction between cultural resources and capital, I think, will prove useful in future research.[2]

At various times in history, an established church, an academic community, or a mass political party has been able to consecrate particular cultural resources as capital. In his own research on the United States, however, DiMaggio suggests a more complex pattern of consecration—one that took half a century, went through two distinct stages, and ultimately failed.

DiMaggio shows that in the late nineteenth century, the commercial, industrial, and banking elites of Boston, New York, and Chicago began to use
cultural goods—particularly the patronage of symphonic music, opera, and
the visual arts—as indicators of class membership. Up through World War I,
following DiMaggio's usage of the term, art was not cultural capital in the
United States because it was not "generally valorized by a nationally authoritative institutional system." He shows, however, how by 1930, the fine arts
had become systematically elevated to the status of cultural capital. He points
to the development of national associations of fine-arts organizations, arts
education at universities, and the more clear-cut differentiation of the fine arts
from "lowbrow" culture in the movies, theater, radio, and commercial advertising, and on phonograph records. Together these factors served, according
to DiMaggio, to valorize the fine arts as the cultural capital of U.S. society.
DiMaggio also shows that a number of people had a professional stake in
promoting the sanctity of the arts. He does not, however, show the sanctioning
of art as cultural capital by state, church, or party.

Compare this with the early establishment of the arts in France. The
French Royal Academies established by King Louis XIII in the early sev-
enteenth century continued to hold sway through the revolution right up
through the middle of the nineteenth century (White and White 1965). For
two centuries they did form the backbone of a system in France that
established and protected art and literature as cultural capital in DiMaggio's
special sense of the term.

Even granting that the network of museums, foundations, orchestras,
universities, and associations of arts professionals existing in the 1930s
functioned to establish art as cultural capital, DiMaggio does not show that
the national elite actually used the arts as *cultural* capital. Insofar as he
provides evidence, it brings the assertion into question. This is the rapid
decay of the fine-art distinction following World War II. If culture indeed
is a form of capital, why would its holders allow its value to be dissipated
so rapidly? Thus, in practice, art did not then become established as anything
other than *economic* capital in the United States.

WHY MUST CULTURAL CAPITAL
BE NONUTILITARIAN GOODS
AND SERVICES?

Does this mean that there is no cultural capital in the United States?
DiMaggio uniquely restricts the designation *cultural capital* to predominantly
nonutilitarian goods and services such as art. I see no reason for this
limitation. While art never became cultural capital in DiMaggio's strict sense
of the term in this country, this does not mean that there is no such thing
as cultural capital here in Bourdieu's (1984, 1987) sense of the term. If one
examines the symbolic component of primarily *utilitarian* goods and services,
there is clear evidence of an established cultural capital by the 1930s.

Consider, for example, the regularization of pronunciation, vocabulary, and grammar that was enforced by the State through the public school system. Immigrants, blacks, Southerners, and working-class people were all taught to devalue their own speech patterns and to value those called "standard English" (Cookson and Persell 1985). This standard English gained further value as cultural capital as informal and standardized ability and achievement tests became widely used by organizations of all sorts to screen job applicants and candidates for promotion.

CULTURAL CAPITAL
OR CULTURAL ENTREPRENEURSHIP?

DiMaggio does not have a single designation for those who over the past century have actively reshaped the symbolic value and meaning of cultural goods. Following Schumpeter's (1934) basic definition of the term *entrepreneur* and Peterson's (1981) extensions of the term, however, the neologism *cultural entrepreneur* used earlier by DiMaggio (1982) seems to be appropriate. Cultural entrepreneurship involves the purposeful restructuring of symbolic elements to shape them as resources and potentially as capital.

This focus on entrepreneurship suggests a different reading of the evidence DiMaggio offers. Rather than seeing a period of cultural resources formation followed by a period of cultural capital consolidation, it suggests two periods in which art was used by emerging elites to lend moral rectitude to their assertions of hegemony. Recall DiMaggio's evidence. Each of the individuals and organizations he discusses, from the nineteenth-century creators of fine arts in Boston to the consolidators of the national fine-arts field in the 1920s and 1930s, worked to systematically restructure symbolic cultural elements, shaping them to fit the symbolic needs of the newly emerging power elite of the time. In the late nineteenth century, this was the emerging bourgeois industrial class; in the early twentieth century, it was the national corporation.[3]

The idea that new (or at least newly interpreted) forms of art are championed by emerging centers of power would seem to receive a great deal of support from the historical record. Think of the link between emerging power and the flowering of art in the French courts of both Louis XIII and Louis XIV and in the Italian city-states of the Renaissance. There have also been periods of newly consolidated power without new art. Think of the Roman Empire and Victorian England, for example. But cases of new art without new power are more difficult to find. I would, therefore, like to propose for further testing the following proposition: The emergence of new art forms requires the patronage of an emerging center of socioeconomic power. A correlate of this proposition particularly useful for research is that as the center of socioeconomic power attains predominance, it will reduce its patronage of new art forms.

CULTURAL ENTREPRENEURSHIP
IN AN AGE OF MULTINATIONALS

I will conclude by briefly sketching the outlines of a possible emerging power center—the multinational corporation—and pointing to the sorts of art its contending for legitimacy might call forth by making what Weber called a mental experiment.

The multinationals I contemplate do not simply produce in, and sell products to, a number of different nations. They assert that the corporation commands not simply the labor of its employees but also comprises their master identity and the focus of loyalty for them and their families. In exchange for this loyal work, the corporation sees to all the life-needs of its employees and their dependents. In many ways, the corporation seeks to displace the nation-state and instill in each of its members the pledge: "My company, right or wrong."

Art would be used to show the power and the virtue of the corporation and to foster a world view compatible with the needs of the corporation in an environment of corporate entities. To this end, the arts could be used in a number of ways: (1) the acquisition and display in corporate collections of famous works of art of past eras; (2) the preservation or recreation of famous or holy edifices, objects, and environments; (3) support of the performing arts; (4) the patronage of new works of art; and (5) aesthetic education monitored to ensure that moral values are attached to the appropriate objects. In all these ways, the people see the power, permanence, moral rectitude, and legitimacy of the corporation as reflected in the art.

What would likely be distinctive of the new art patronized by twenty-first century multinationals? First, as sophisticated electronic communication is essential to the multinational, most art would be presented through the media. Media presentation allows for the manipulation and editing of images and sounds so that all are rendered synthetic. At the same time, the media rendering rather than the live performance will be identified as the authentic artwork, making it difficult for groups without access to advanced media technologies to compete on an equal footing. Second, as the corporation would want to break the power of class associations, distinctions between high art and popular culture would not be perpetuated. Instead, elements from diverse sources and traditions would be transvalued as worthy of appreciation. Third, as the corporation would want to break the loyalties to nation, religious affiliation, and ethnic group, elements of diverse traditions would be collaged together.[4] Fourth, as the multinational would want to break the loyalty to the particular geographic locale, the arts could not emphasize distinctive places.[5] Such artwork might not fit your aesthetic or mine, but it is hardly more shocking than a walk through today's New York Museum of Modern Art would be for a cultivated Victorian of 1851.

NOTES

1. Within sociology, this focus on the moral and didactic role of cultural goods was articulated by Jaeger and Selznick (1964), but the position has not been taken up by other main-line American sociologists.

2. As Lamont and Lareau (1988) have shown in their useful review of the concept, there has been a remarkable variation in the operational meaning given to the term *cultural capital* since the concept was introduced by Bourdieu and Passeron (1977).

3. To be sure, DiMaggio more clearly shows the link between the emergence of the industrial elite and the differentiation of the fine arts in the late nineteenth century than he does the link between the emerging power of national corporations and the consolidation of the arts fields in the early decades of the twentieth century, but I think the case for this association can be made.

4. Elsewhere, I discuss the processes of *transvaluation* and *collaging* as they apply to the aesthetic revolution taking place in contemporary art music, particularly as presented on public radio (Peterson 1990).

5. There are several means of deemphasizing such particulars. One is abstraction, another is to use animation, and yet another is to set dramatic action in an imagined past or future time. Language, of course, presents a particular problem for the performing arts. One solution is dubbing. Another is to accent dance and word-free music. A third is the development of a universal vocabulary of gestures such as once existed in a number of art traditions before the modernist era of naturalism or as developed more recently in European animation films.

REFERENCES

Baltzell, E. Digby. 1964. *The Protestant Establishment.* Glencoe, IL: Free Press.

Bell, Daniel. 1976. *The Cultural Contradictions of Capitalism.* New York: Basic Books.

Bloom, Allan. 1987. *The Closing of the American Mind.* New York: Simon and Schuster.

Bourdieu, Pierre. 1984. *Distinction: A Social Critique of the Judgment of Taste.* Cambridge, MA: Harvard University Press.

———. 1985. "The Market of Symbolic Goods." *Poetics* 14:13–44.

———. 1986. "The Forms of Capital." Pp. 241–258 in John G. Richardson, ed., *Handbook of Theory and Research for the Sociology of Education.* Westport, CT: Greenwood.

Bourdieu, Pierre, and Jean-Claude Passeron. 1977. *Reproduction in Education, Society and Culture.* Beverly Hills: Sage Publications.

Cookson, Peter W., Jr., and Caroline Persell. 1985. *Preparing for Power: America's Elite Boarding Schools.* New York: Basic.

DiMaggio, Paul. 1982. "Cultural Entrepreneurship in Nineteenth-Century Boston: I: The Organization of a High Culture in the United States." *Media, Culture, and Society* 4:33–50, 303–320.

Harris, Neil. 1966. *The Artist in American Society.* New York: Simon and Schuster.

Jaeger, Gertrude, and Philip Selznick. 1964. "A Normative Theory of Culture." *American Sociological Review* 29: 653–669.

Jordan, Sherrill. 1987. *Public Art, Public Controversy.* New York: ACA Books.

Lamont, Michele, and Annette Lareau. 1988. "Cultural Capital: Allusions, Gaps and Glissandos in Recent Theoretical Developments." *Sociological Theory* 6:153–168.

Peterson, Richard A. 1981. "Entrepreneurship in Organizations." Pp. 65–83 in Paul C. Nystrom and William H. Starbuck, eds., *Handbook of Organizations, Volume 1.* New York: Oxford University Press.

———. 1983. "Patterns of Cultural Choice: A Prolegomenon." *American Behavioral Scientist* 26:422–438.

———. 1990. "Audience and Industry Origins of the Crisis in Classical Music Programming: Toward World Music." Pp. 207–223, in David B. Pankratz and Valerie Morris, eds., *The Future of the Arts: Public Policy and Arts Research.* New York: Praeger.

Reisman, Joseph M. 1983. "The Legal Obsession with Obscenity: Why Are the Courts Still Being Challenged?" *Journal of Arts Management and Law* 13(3):54–79.

Schumpeter, Joseph A. 1934. *The Theory of Economic Development.* Cambridge, MA: Harvard University Press.

White, Harrison C., and Cynthia White. 1965. *Canvasses and Careers: Institutional Change in the French Painting World.* New York: John Wiley and Sons.

Williams, Raymond. 1960. *Culture and Society: 1780–1959.* Garden City, NY: Doubleday.

5

The New and the Old in Religion

Thomas Luckmann

SOCIAL THEORY AND RELIGION

Religion, stubbornly refusing to disappear as a moving force in the conduct of human affairs, continued to pose a seemingly intractable problem for modern social theory. As the heir to eighteenth-century social philosophy, modern social theory was singularly ill-equipped to approach religion without rationalist prejudice. The immediate precursors of nineteenth-century social theory, the philosophers of the Enlightenment, were as one in assuming that the influence of religion would shrink in direct proportion to the ascendancy of reason. They were convinced that the ultimate victory of reason over superstition was inevitable as soon as the fetters imposed upon the minds of men by the unholy alliance of the church with the absolutist state were thrown off.[1]

As their successors in the first half of the nineteenth century learned to view religion as a complex, although deficient, social phenomenon rather than as a simple pathology of thought and emotion, some of them invested considerable effort in searching for a *rational* and *scientific* substitute. This Comtean motif continued to inspire Durkheim half a century later. After a pioneering analysis of the social roots of religion and of the function of religion in maintaining the bonds of solidarity under different structural conditions, he still seemed to hope that a universal morality might eventually replace the narrower values operative under the conditions of a mechanical division of labor, which were apparently weakening under the anomic conditions of modern life.

Compared to the attitudes toward religion set by the philosophers of the Enlightenment, the post-Hegelian critique of religion may be said to have had a better—and an astonishingly "modern"—grasp of the universal human basis of religion. Formulated successively by Anselm Feuerbach and Karl Marx, its premise is that *"man makes religion,* not religion man."[2] But Marx was far from abandoning the then-already traditional, not to say conventional, assumption of religion as an essentially deficient mode of human existence in the world or, more precisely, as a deficient mode of orientation in an as-yet deficient world. For Marx, this deficiency was rooted in an alienation caused fundamentally by the division of labor and historically by the capitalist mode of production.[3]

At the beginning of the present century, this range of positions regarding religion had not undergone substantial changes in the different camps of social theory. The Marxists, otherwise inclined to ignore the writings of the early "pre-scientific" Marx, kept repeating his characterization of religion as the opium of the people. They expected religion to disappear automatically after the revolutionary overthrow of the *objective* conditions of misery, which were assumed to produce the *subjective* illusions of religion. Their prognostic formula "no capitalism, no religion" was reversed in bourgeois social theory by a quasi-empirical formula: "modern capitalism, no religion." The blindness and deafness in social theory regarding religious matters remained remarkable. Although the Spencerian account of the evolution of functional differentiation in society became the dominant model for the interpretation of global social change, its implications for corresponding changes in institutional forms of religion were not pursued. It was ideologically more convenient to cling to both camps of the etiological myth of modernity as the age of the final decline of religion and the ultimate ascendancy of reason—now understood as science. In social theory, the myth was eventually transformed into a "theory" of secularization.[4]

Max Weber alone kept an open mind, although it was he who provided a detailed and convincing account of the process of *Entzauberung* of modern life and was convinced that functional differentiation was leading to a rational-bureaucratic social order—the "iron cage" of modern society. His account of the various factors encouraging rationalization—a process that, according to him, was ironically ushered in by religion as a systematizing and disciplining force—contributed to an understanding of the freeing of the economy and polity from overarching religious norms. But Weber saw no reason to assume that human nature was radically changed in this historical process, and thus he anticipated the advent of new and terrifyingly irrational gods in the minds of those who were to live in the rational cage of modern society.

Still another school of thought, which regarded religion in another perspective but did not exert much lasting influence on social theory, was instituted by the postrevolutionary traditionalists (Louis G. de Bonald, Joseph de Maistre) and found representatives in the first half of the twentieth century in thinkers such as Max Scheler (perhaps, one should say, one of the several "Schelers") as well as in various, more marginal proponents of an "organic" theory of the corporate state and society in which (traditional) religion was to play an essential role. A tenuous thread connects their intellectual positions with those held in contemporary neoconservatism.

These views on religion persisted in simplified versions, if anything. They were current well past the middle of the present century. They formed a rather loose paradigm that influences the social theory of religion to this day. The attitudes associated with these views were, of course, anything but identical. The decline of religion was regarded with smug satisfaction by enlightened progressives and with profound despair by traditional conservatives. The perception of facts as well as the imputation of specific causes also varied significantly. But whether structural differentiation, modern capitalism, industrial society, technology, or science were taken to have already dealt the deathblow to religion, or whether the communist *Aufhebung* of the social conditions responsible for alienation—and thus the religious illusion—was expected to do so shortly, the common denominator of these views is obvious. It is the assumption that the social structure and the culture of the modern world are intrinsically hostile to religion. A second common premise underlying these views was that religion and its traditional (Western) institutional forms could be considered identical for all practical purposes. Thus, the decline of doctrinal and ritual adherence to these forms that was registered at least in Europe during the nineteenth and twentieth centuries was naively generalized, extrapolated to the future, and taken as evidence for a global "theory" of secularization.

Yet, religion refused to behave as expected. Instead of fading away, it continues to show remarkable signs of life.[5] It must be admitted, however, that "religion" put on various disguises—disguises from the point of view, prevalent in the social sciences well into the 1960s, equating religion with its institutionally specialized Western Christian forms. This made it possible for general sociologists (with a few notable exceptions) no longer interested in such an outdated phenomenon as religion and for the somewhat marginalized sociologists of religion to cling to their preconceptions about the secular and rational character of modern society. Although Christianity (in Parsonian terms: the Judaeo-Christian tradition) was seen as the most important cultural factor in the motivation of social change and, eventually, modernization, few sociologists took note of Weber's prediction of the "new gods" to come, and most persisted in ignoring the continued presence of the old gods. In social theory, this state of affairs concerning religion began to change only in recent years, at least in part because of the visibly political consequences of Islamic anti-modernist fundamentalism. Even in the sociology of religion, however, where there were signs of a less superficially motivated theoretical reorientation somewhat earlier, the rate of change is slow. The reason—I alluded to it with the "disguise" metaphor—is simple.

In most archaic and many traditional societies, only one social form of religion either existed or was dominant to the near exclusion of others.[6] In the West, this situation prevailed from the Middle Ages—with its Universal church, sects, and heresies—well into the early modern period. However, since the late nineteenth century, and at an accelerated pace after World War I (with the emergence of powerful political religions) and World War II (with the spread of privatization and subjective syncretism in religious matters), religious functions were incorporated into many different, apparently nonreligious institutions or were diffused into new semi-institutional and even noninstitutional (invisible) forms. With the exception of the formerly prevalent social form of religion for which the church-sect or the expanded church-denomination-sect-cult typology had proven adequate, religious phenomena fell through the conceptual meshes in use in the sociology of religion.

Political religions were therefore not considered to be "genuine" religions, even if their avowed goals were the Walhalla of the Third Reich or the Parousia of the classless society. And the most modern subinstitutional subjectivisms escaped attention until a supporting commercial and mass-media apparatus developed on such an order of magnitude that it simply could no longer be overlooked. Thus, only the "downs" and occasionally the "ups" of the traditional social form of religion to which the church-sect typology applied were registered.[7] Even from this limited point of view, the difference in the vitality of this social form of religion between traditional Europe and the modern United States, being the reverse of what one might expect, needed considerable explaining. But these forms, which appeared anachronistic to most social scientists steeped in the lore of rationalism, continued to do much better everywhere than could be expected on the basis of simple extrapolations from the statistics from the second half of the nineteenth and the first half of the twentieth centuries on church membership and various indicators of religious participation.

Religion in the modern world represents an extraordinary amalgam of old and new social forms of religion; the incorporation of religious functions by political movements; civil religions of modern states; fervent socialisms and nationalisms in modernizing states and similar self-declared secular entities; the involutions of modernism and fundamentalism in the established churches and denominations; and the spread of one version after another of romantic subjectivism, hedonism, and occultism and their subinstitutional coalescence around commercial and mass-medial support structures. It is not an overstatement to call this a challenge to social theory.

THE RELIGIOUS FUNCTION:
COPING WITH TRANSCENDENCE

Social realities are the immediate and proximate results of human actions. Having become established as historical realities, they constitute the condition for further human actions. In other words, social realities are constructed, maintained, and changed in intersubjectively meaningful sequences of behavior. Therefore, they present a fundamental difficulty to the *social* sciences: How are interactionally *pre*constructed historical realities to be *re*constructed as data with such parsimony as to allow comparison (and more complex generalizing treatments) and yet with sufficient richness as to keep its intrinsically human historical quality?[8] Evidently another, equally fundamental methodological problem—that of adequate *explanations*—is shared by the social sciences with those sciences whose data are not preconstructed as human realities in ordinary human activities but are only constructed in scientific procedures of theoretically simple, if technologically complex, observation.

None of the social sciences can avoid the descriptive problem of adequate reconstruction of intersubjectively meaningful historical social realities. However, this problem must be faced in its most acute form by the social theory of religion. The reason is obvious: Religiously motivated actions, their anticipated and unanticipated results, the interpretations attached to them, and their historical institutionalizations are part of the ordinary, observable[9] social realities. To this extent, their sociological reconstruction as data is neither more nor less difficult than that of other kinds of social reality. But according to the *pre*constructions of the actors, the typical meanings of these actions refer to a reality that is not normally accessible through direct observation. The descriptive task of the sociology of religion, therefore, consists of a careful reconstruction of the structures of action that are part of observable reality and of the accounts given of their intrinsic meaning by the actors.

It is primarily through a systematic interpretation of the latter that a social theory of the *functions* of religion may be attempted. In my view, such a theory must be part of a general theory of religion. More specifically, it will help in identifying that which is common to the great variety of structures constituting the heterogeneous social forms of religion that so confusingly coexist in modern societies. A consideration of functions should play an important role in meeting the challenge religion today poses to contemporary social theory.[10]

Religion is commonly taken to refer to a particular part of human existence—the part that is concerned with the supernatural, with the ultimate meanings of life, with transcendence. Of course, in human life the supernatural is bound up with the natural; ultimate meanings only make sense in the context of the ordinary significance of everyday affairs; and the transcendent is only transcendent with respect to something that is immanent. Wherever these poles of human existence are kept apart with reasonable distinctness, one has little difficulty in applying the term *religion* to activities in which experiences pertaining to one of these poles are objectified and localized in symbols, sacred places, times, dates, persons, and the like. The familiar forms of tribal religions, ancestor cults, and the classical universal religions (especially when they are institutionalized in the form of church and sect) are obvious examples. Such historical institutionalizations of the symbolic (sacred) core of a world view are specific instances of a universal human social process. In this process, world views are constructed in long historical chains of communicative acts whereupon they serve as objective models of socialization.

The basic function of religion is to transform members of the natural species *homo sapiens* into actors in a historical social order—in a "cosmion illuminated from within."[11] Components of social reality that are essential to this function may legitimately be called religious, whether or not they explicitly refer to the supernatural. Religion is to be found wherever the behavior of the members of the species becomes morally accountable action—where a self finds itself in a world shared with other selves, interacting with them on the basis of the elementary principle of the reciprocity of perspectives.[12] The ethnographic and historical record of mankind shows a great variety of social phenomena that have served this basic religious function. However, all are products of two closely related elementary social processes in which the ordinary human reality of everyday life is linked to something that is taken to transcend that reality, to "another" reality.

The first of these processes—the intersubjective reconstruction of experiences of transcendence—consists of communicative acts in which subjective experiences of various kinds of this- and other-worldly transcendences are given an elementary social form as mythical narratives, as invocatory or commemorative rituals, as symbolic reminders and references. In the second of these processes—the social construction of "another" reality—the primary intersubjective reconstructions are interpreted, systematized, reformulated, and canonized—a process that may involve censoring deviant accounts. The reality to which these accounts refer is given firm and usually preeminent ontological status. The relation between ordinary and extraordinary reality is explained, and the norms that guide conduct in everyday life are systematically linked to the ultimate significance of the other reality.

The distinction between these two processes is rather artificial. Talking of universal human experiences of transcendence makes sense only in the context of phenomenological reduction. Concrete experiences of transcendence are necessarily historical, however, and are therefore determined to a large extent—in form and in content—by antecedent social constructions of reality, including those of the "other" reality. Nonetheless, there could be no social construction of transcendent realities without a logically antecedent intersubjective reconstruction of universal aspects of human experience. The historical selection, codification, and institutionalization involved in the second process presupposes the processes of the first. On the other hand, the concrete subjective experiences of transcendence are always molded to a greater or lesser extent by historical socially constructed models of such experiences.

What do I mean when I speak of experiences of *transcendence*? What are constructions of another, an *extraordinary* reality? Every normal human being knows the limits of his or her experience and the boundaries of his or her existence. There is a before, after, and behind one's ongoing, actual experience and a before and after one's own life. Nobody seriously doubts that the world into which he or she was born existed long before he or she became aware of its existence, and nobody expects the world to end when his or her consciousness of it ends. Furthermore, we take it for granted that many things happen that we do not want to happen and that many things occur that we do not want to occur. Sooner or later, every child discovers that the world is independent of its fears and hopes. In the naive realism of everyday life, we *know* the boundaries of our existence, even if we do not constantly *think* about them. Every normal human being knows about the transcendence of the world and knows that this knowledge is an essential part of the common sense—the practical theory of everyday life—of all societies.

In addition, all persons also know of things that transcend them *within* the world. We meet other beings and notice that some of them are remarkably like ourselves. We discover that we are not alone in the world—and this is another component of human awareness that is constitutive of normality. We see that other people are born and that other people die, and, given our knowledge that we are like other people in respect to birth, we are forced into the conclusion of an elementary syllogism. Even the experience of transcendence within the world, the experience of other selves, serves to remind us of the ultimate boundaries of our existence. Finally, we are constantly confronted with certain additional transcendences within the world of everyday life—but, as it were, on a smaller scale. We must turn around to see what is behind us; sounds, pleasures, pains that are overwhelming in their actuality recede into the past, become memories. Not even the simplest perceptual experience is enclosed in itself. It contains some of the immediate past; it anticipates some of the immediate future. In other words, human experience is a continuous flow of transcendence.

A detailed and precise analysis of the experience of transcendence may not be necessary here, but a summary of its results may be helpful. First, whenever anything that transcends that which at the moment is concretely given in actual, direct experience can itself be experienced in the same manner as that which it now transcends, we may speak of the "little" (spatial and temporal) transcendences of everyday life. Second, when that which is actually experienced—such as the body of another self—is taken to refer to something that cannot be experienced directly—such as the consciousness, the inner life of the other self—we may speak of the intermediate transcendences of everyday life, *provided* that that which cannot itself be experienced directly is taken to belong to the same *everyday* reality as the self and its experiences. Third, when an experience presents itself as pointing to something that not only cannot be experienced directly but in addition is definitively not part of an ordinary reality (in which things can be seen, touched, handled), we may speak of the "great" transcendences.

There is more than one path in which everyday reality can be left behind: in dreams, ecstasy, meditation. These paths have one thing in common: They are departures from ordinary life, and they suspend its practical theory—common sense. In dreams, ecstasies, and meditation, everyday life loses its status as the preeminent reality for the human being, at least for the duration of these experiences. After one returns to everyday life, only recollections of such experiences remain.

Human societies differ significantly in the ways in which they organize subjective experiences of the little transcendences of time and space in ordinary life. Societies differ still more in the way in which they deal with the intermediate and the great transcendences. The importance for social structure of the ways in which the intermediate—the social—transcendences are interpreted and systematized is obvious. And the experiences of the great transcendences are by their very nature always close to disorder. Their organization and control represent a serious problem for all societies. Whether

dreams are taken as other-worldly symbolic pointers, as this-worldly psy-
chodynamic signs, or as symptoms of a heavy dinner the night before is
not a trivial issue. Whether the realities we remember from ecstatic experiences
are defined as illusions or as ultimate reality, and, if the latter, whether the
ultimate is seen as radically different or as closely intertwined with everyday
affairs constitutes an essential part of world views. *How* people interpret
their experiences of transcendence on its different levels is neither a matter
of a natural religiosity of the species nor of some archetypal religion. It *is*
a matter of a variety of historical social processes and their products: of
the ways in which subjective experiences of transcendence are being com-
municatively reconstructed, of the ways in which such reconstructions are
being built into overarching social constructions of everyday and other
realities, and of the ways in which such social constructions—in their turn—
serve as models for subjective experiences of transcendence.

THE SOCIAL FORMS OF RELIGION

After these brief functional considerations, it is necessary to look at the
structural foundations for the social constructions of "other" realities.[13] Until
the late modern period in the industrial societies of the West, there were
three basic kinds of arrangements. The first is characterized by the diffusion
of religious functions throughout the entire social structure. In the second,
there is a certain differentiation of religious functions; they tend to coalesce
in institutions in close proximity to, or partial identity with, political
institutions. In the third, religious functions are monopolized by a specialized
institutional domain.

The first social form of religion was universal in the sense that all archaic
societies (hunting and gathering, early nomadic, and horticultural) seem to
have been characterized by one of the variants of this arrangement. The
second developed after the agricultural revolution in the civilizations of the
city-states and early empires. The third emerged from medieval beginnings
in the early modern societies of the West and spread, to a certain extent,
to the Americas and elsewhere in the footsteps of colonization. Although
these forms succeeded one another in historical sequences, they are not
stages in an evolutionary pattern. Furthermore, at least two of these forms
may have coexisted in any given society for long periods.

In archaic societies, the maintenance and transmission of the sacred
universe are based on the social structure in its entirety. To what extent
transcendent realities are segregated from ordinary ones—to what extent
sacredness is accented and isolated—varies from society to society, otherwise
conforming to this basic arrangement. Nevertheless, in all such societies,
religion is diffused among the various institutions of society, with minimal
crystallizations at certain points in the kinship system (ancestors) and among
the first transcendence specialists (shamans). Transcendence-oriented collective representations legitimize the norms of kinship (the dominant dimension of social organization), of the simple division of labor, and of the

kinship-based exercise of authority. The meaning of all ordinary action, insofar as it is defined and sanctioned by institutions, is linked either directly—in symbols and rituals—or indirectly—in etiological narratives, proverbs, and the like—to transcendent realities. These motivate and legitimate social action in a great variety of situations and bestow ultimate significance on all relevant stages of an individual's course of life.[14]

The second social form of religion is much younger. Its development is best documented in Pharaohic Egypt and the hydraulic societies of the Near East nearly five thousand years ago.[15] Although the entire social structure still supported a sacred universe, just as transcendent realities legitimated the entire social structure, important religious functions were institutionalized separately and gained strong and highly visible ties with the differentiated institutions of power as, for example, in divine kingship. Increasing complexity in the division of labor, the production of a surplus over the subsistence minimum, central control over storage and distribution (as in the temple-based economy of Old Egypt), growth of supra-communal and supra-tribal political organizations, emergence of distinct occupational roles, and the formation of social classes are processes connected with functional differentiation of social institutions. Yet the logic of the sacred universe continued to dominate all other institutions. The supreme sense ascribed to transcendent realities joined together the meanings of the most diverse everyday actions. It endowed these actions with a certain coherence within the life of the individual, both in its routines and its crises, and linked them to the transcendent life of the family, the community. In any case, the rural majority of the population continued to live in archaic folk communities.

The third of these basic arrangements of religion in society is characterized by a radical change in the relationship between the sacred universe and social structure. Institution specialization of religion means that one particular set of institutions came exclusively to maintain and transmit the social constructions of transcendent reality, in ever-increasing separation from the transmission of the other parts of the social stock of knowledge. Religion acquired a visibly separate location in a special set of social institutions. This social form of religion emerged in societies that were already marked by a relatively high degree of structural complexity. The general differentiation of the social structure into functionally specialized institutional domains, far from being the result of unilinear evolution, was limited to one particular line of historical development. And within that general process of social differentiation of *some* societies, the institutional specialization of religion in the form of the Christian churches again represents a particular Western—although fateful—historical development.

The institutional specialization of religion in the historical form of the Christian churches in *conjunction* with a state of affairs that superficially approximated the social universality of religion in archaic and, partly, traditional societies—although structurally unlikely—was the result of a historically unique constellation of circumstances. Societies that have reached a certain level of complexity and achieved a high degree of functional differentiation cannot easily maintain the social universality of an essentially religious world view. In such societies, norms and orientations (including those that refer to transcendent realities) cannot be transmitted to everyone in basic socialization processes as generally and as successfully as mythical world views were transmitted to the entire community in archaic societies. Nor can functionally differentiated social institutions reinforce and support such a world view in the course of an individual's life in a manner analogous to social interaction in the face-to-face communities of archaic societies. As is well known, and as I indicated earlier, the long-range consequences of institutional specialization of religion have been customarily interpreted as a process of secularization.[16] However, in my view, the structural instability of the institutional specialization of religion leads to its partial replacement by an emerging fourth social form of religion. This form is linked to another profound change in the location of religion in society, a process best described as *privatization* of religion.

A NEW SOCIAL FORM OF RELIGION: PRIVATIZATION, INDIVIDUAL SYNCRETISM, AND MASS CULTURE

Privatization of religion is part of the general privatization of individual life in modern societies. The social condition most directly connected with privatization is, of course, the high degree of functional differentiation in the social structure.[17] The "big" institutions exert considerable control over individual conduct by their functionally rational norms and by the mixture of rewards and punishments characteristic of the political economy of modern capitalistic nation-states. But the institutional segmentation of the meaning of actions left large spheres of life without institutionally predefined meaning-structures and without obligatory models of biographical coherence.[18] The life-space that is not directly touched by institutional control may be called "the private sphere." As individual consciousness—not individual conduct— is liberated from social structural constraints, a process typically accompanied by legal provisions for freedom of opinion, people gain a sense of individual autonomy. Totalitarian reactions having been unsuccessful, the individual is given the freedom of choice from a variety of sacred universes. These sprang up as the cultural correlate of structural privatization.

Modern social constructions designed to cope with various levels of transcendence are extremely heterogeneous. For several generations, the traditional Christian sacred universe was no longer the only transcendent reality mediated in social processes of specialized churches and sects did not even retain their monopoly on specifically religious themes without challenge from secular ideologies. Collective representations originating in social constructions of the intermediate transcendences of nation, race, classlessness, and the like successfully shaped important aspects of modern consciousness. In recent decades, concern with minimal transcendences symbolized by notions such as self-fulfillment and the like has become widespread, if not dominant. The derivation of such notions from romanticism, certain branches of philosophic idealism, and the more recent depth-psychologies is obvious. But what were marginal bohemian, avant garde, and intellectualist phenomena at one time now seem to have become characteristic of the orientations of broad strata of *embourgeoisé* populations.

The shift of intersubjective reconstructions and social constructions away from the great other-worldly transcendences to the intermediate and, more and more, the minimal transcendences of modern solipsism cannot be said to have been directly determined by structural privatization of individual life in modern society. However, an elective affinity does seem to obtain between the latter and the sacralization of subjectivity that is celebrated in much of modern mass culture. Evidently, the traditional religious orientations (at whose center are social constructions of the great transcendences) have not disappeared. But their social distribution has become narrower, and the institutionally specialized basis of these orientations (the churches, sects, and denominations) no longer represents the socially dominant form of religion.

The ascendant privatized social form of religion is characterized by a wider range of different actors on the social scene being involved in the social construction of various kinds of transcendence.[19] The basic structure of the process is that of a demonopolized market supplied by (1) the mass media, (2) churches and sects that are trying to reinsert themselves into the processes of modern social constructions of transcendence, (3) the residual carriers of nineteenth-century secular ideologies, and (4) subinstitutional, new religious communities formed around minor charismatics, commercialized enterprises in astrology, the consciousness-expanding line, and the like. This social form of religion is thus characterized by immediate mass-cultural accessibility of the supply of representations referring to varied levels of transcendence.

However, this does not mean that no form of mediation exists between the market and potential consumers. Much of modern (Byronian or Baudelairean) consciousness is rooted in the cultivation of immediate sensations and emotions—which are notoriously unstable and offer considerable resistance to clear articulation in myths, symbols, and dogmas. Nonetheless, a variety of secondary institutions—typically arising in subinstitutional movements around charismatics, entrepreneurs, and small-group revival attempts of older occult, spiritualist, and similar movements—have taken the challenge and turned it into a profitable business. These institutions address the problem of the verbalization of topics arising in the private sphere, of packaging the results in easily digestible portions, and of distributing the results to potential consumers. Inner-worldly analogies to traditional devotional literature range from treatises on positive thinking to *Playboy* articles on the expansion of consciousness by various (for example, sexual) techniques, pocketbooks on popular psychology—especially psychoanalysis—Eastern mystical literature, astrological advice columns, offerings on bioenergetics and meditation, and the like. The products convey a more or less systematically arranged set of meanings (and, occasionally, techniques) referring to from minimal to intermediate and, rarely, great transcendences. The set can be bought and kept for a short or longer period. It can be individually combined with elements from other sets. The sets are, of course, not obligatory models characteristic of the older social forms of religion. They *can* be taken up by groups—typically on the periphery of modern society—and converted into a sectarian model, but the chances of success for such firm institutionalizations are not great.

This social form of religion can best be illustrated by recent syncretistic developments[20] such as the New Age movement and the new occultism and its predecessors, such as spiritism. The New Age movement lays stress on the spiritual development of each individual. Sometimes it revives elements of older religious traditions that had not been canonized and that it interprets in unorthodox (often far-fetched) ways. It collects abundant psychological, therapeutic, magic, marginally scientific, and older esoteric materials,[21] repackages them, and offers them for individual consumption and further private syncretism. The New Age movement programmatically refuses organization in terms of big institutions; instead, it cultivates the notion of networks. This allows the formation of commercially exploitable cultic milieus, which are characterized by varied—generally weak—forms of institutionalization.[22] The New Age movement illustrates the social form of the invisible religion. It has no stable organization, canonized dogmas, recruitment system, or disciplining apparatus. This may be a structural precondition for the successful maintenance of its vague holistic approach, which meets—among other things—the rising demand for an overall hierarchy of meaning that overcomes the specialization of those cultural domains, such as science, religion, art, and the like that had found reasonably firm institutional bases. Instead of segmentation, it offers integration—no matter how superficial this may seem to the outside observer. Thus, the New Age and similar representatives of a holistic, magical world view supply individual searchers with the bricks and some straw for further individual bricolage.[23]

The structural conditions leading to various privatized forms of religion characterized by the search for a new wholeness—intended to overcome the segmentation of meaning into specialized institutional spheres and cultural regions—also give rise to another holistic option that is diametrically opposed to bricolage, that is to fundamentalism. One must distinguish between the sociostructural conditions (the specialization of institutional domains, the pluralism of mass culture, and the development of a market of world views— all of which are prevalent in modern industrial societies) and the strains similar conditions produce upon their emergence in modernizing societies. The relatively sudden loss of religious legitimations for everyday life seems to lead to anti-modernist reactions among substantial segments of the populations of modernizing countries.[24] But even in modern Western societies, Protestant and Catholic versions of fundamentalism have chosen traditional models of wholeness in reaction to modernity (institutional specialization, immorality of economic and political life, lack of obligatory controls for private life and pluralism and a lack of cognitive support for one's own world view, disorientation, and mass availability of immoral products and behavior).[25] It seems unlikely, however, that these reactions, which range from the Catholic *opus dei* to Protestant moral majorities, will prove successful in the long run. The fit between this kind of world view and the social structural determinants of modern life is rather poor. It can be improved, however, in closed communities of various kinds. On the whole privatized syncretism seems to have a better chance to become established as a (minimally) social form of religion.

NOTES

1. It might be optimistically supposed that those philosophers of progress who lived to observe the pathetic symbolism of the revolutionary Cult of Reason were disabused of their illusions.

2. To quote the well-known passage written in 1843–1844 by Karl Marx in "Zur Kritik der Hegelschen Rechtphilosophie" (published in Siegfried Landsbut, ed., *Die Frühschriften* [Stuttgart: Kroener, 1955], p. 207).

3. "This means that religion is the consciousness of self and the sentiment of self on the part of human beings who have not yet attained to themselves or have already lost themselves again." (Ibid., p. 208, my translation.)

4. See Hermann Lübbe, *Säkularisierung. Geschichte Eines Ideenpolitischen Begriffs* (München: Alber, 1965), and my "Secularization—A Contemporary Myth," in Thomas Luckmann, *Life-World and Social Realities* (London: Heinemann, 1983), pp. 124–132 (first published in Italian in *Cultura e Politica* 14 [1969]:175–182). For an excellent review of various theories on the origins of modernity from Max Weber to Michel Foucault and Alan McFarlane, see Alois Hahn, "Theorien zur Entstehung der Europäischen Moderne." *Philosophische Rundschau* 31 (1984):178–202. A different view is presented by Franz-Xaver Kaufmann, "Religion und Modernität," in Johannes Berger, ed., *Die Moderne—Kontinuitäten und Zäsuren* (Sonderband 4 der "Sozialen Welt") (Göttingen: Schwartz, 1986), pp. 283–307. It is regrettable that those essays are not available in English.

5. I do not think that this indicates anything like an unexpected revival of religion, a New Age of spirituality, a return of repressed irrational forces, a breakdown of rationalism and science, or anything of the sort. I rather think, and thought a quarter of a century ago when I wrote *The Invisible Religion* (New York: Macmillan, 1967), that despite certain cyclical movements that had occurred at least in the most publicly visible forms of religion during the last two hundred years as well as in other epochs of human history, religion as a part of human life had never weakened substantially and that, in fact, it remained embedded in the lives of ordinary people, even in modern industrial societies.

6. By "social form" of religion, I refer to the basic model for the institutionalization of religious functions. For a detailed discussion of this concept and the sketch of a historical typology, refer to my *The Invisible Religion*.

7. The typology had served well in the sociological study of Western Christianity, which was for obvious reasons a central topic of interest in the sociology of religion since its professional inception roughly one hundred years ago. But even after interest extended to other cultural regions and historical epochs, the limited applicability of the typology was not readily recognized. The sense of epochal change was satisfied by the myth of secularization. Therefore, the notion that a *transformation* in the social

forms of religion, rather than its final decline, might be occurring did not find easy acceptance.

8. I need not document here the successes and failures of the various attempts to solve the problem of the "subjective" adequacy (as Max Weber called it in the earliest clear articulation of this basic methodological issue) of scientific reconstructions of the social world.

9. I am not using this concept in a simple-minded behaviorist sense.

10. I shall not take up here the problem of functionalism in the abstract. It will be obvious that some of my elementary assumptions are Durkheimian but that I do not accept the notion that religion is a representation of society. Starting from Alfred Schutz's phenomenological analysis of the experience of various levels of transcendence (Alfred Schutz and Thomas Luckmann, *The Structures of the Life-World II* [Evanston, IL: Northwestern University Press, 1989]), I tried in several recent papers to add the outline of a specific theory of the functions of religion to the more generally functionalist assumptions made in *The Invisible Religion*. The last of these is "Religion and Modern Consciousness," in *Zen Buddhism Today* (Annual Report of the Kyoto Zen Symposium) 6 (1988):11–22.

11. To use a term coined by Eric Voegelin in *The New Science of Politics: An Introduction* (Chicago: University of Chicago Press, 1952).

12. Alfred Schutz, *Collected Papers I* (The Hague: Nijhoff, 1962), pp. 11 ff.

13. In order to stay closer to the terms and concepts commonly used in the social theory of religion, I shall refer to such constructions as "sacred universes."

14. A society with a single—and an essentially religious—world view presupposes a pattern of life based almost exclusively on face-to-face social relations and homogeneous socialization procedures.

15. See James H. Breasted, *The Dawn of Conscience* (New York and London: Russell, 1933); Jan Assmann, *Aegypten—Theologie und Frömmigkeit Einer Frühen Hochkultur* (Stuttgart: Vohlhammer, 1984); Henri Frankfort, *Kingship and the Gods: A Study of Ancient Near Eastern Religion as the Integration of Society and Nature* (Chicago: University of Chicago Press, 1978); Karl A. Wittfogel, *Oriental Despotism: A Comparative Study of Total Power* (New Haven: Yale University Press, 1963).

16. As I also indicated, this notion is an etiological myth of modernity that usurped the status of social theory.

17. Previously multifunctional institutions, which regulated social interaction in archaic and also in traditional societies, slowly accented *one* function and lost most of the other functional components that originally constituted them. At the same time, institutions with similar functions coalesced into large specialized domains, such as the state and the economy. In contemporary industrial societies, institutions have become highly interdependent elements of social subsystems. These subsystems, however, are rather autonomous parts of the social structure. The norms of each subsystem are *comparatively* independent of the rules that govern action in other subsystems. Depending on the domain in which it is performed, institutionalized social interaction obeys rather heterogeneous norms. The connection of these norms— which have been described by Max Weber as functionally rational ones—to the "logic" of a transcendent reality is severed.

18. In this connection, Parsons spoke of "institutional interstices."

19. See Jacob Needleman and George Baker, eds., *Understanding the New Religions* (New York: Seabury Press, 1981) (especially Robert Wuthnow, "Religious Movements and the Transition in the World Order," pp. 63–79 and Joseph P. Chinnici, "New Religious Movements and the Structure of Religious Sensibility," pp. 26–33); James A. Beckford, ed., *New Religious Movements and Rapid Social Change* (London: Sage,

1986); and James A Beckford and Thomas Luckmann, eds., *The Changing Face of Religion* (London, Newbury Park, and New Delhi: Sage, 1989).

20. See Colin Campbell and Shirley McIver, "Cultural Sources of Support for Contemporary Occultism." *Social Compass* 34 (1987):41–60.

21. For an early study, see Andrew Rigby and Bryan S. Turner, "Findhorn Community, Centre of Light: A Sociological Study of New Forms of Religion," in M. Hill, ed., *A Sociological Yearbook of Religion in Britain*, Vol. 5 (London: SCM Press, 1972), pp. 72–86.

22. Not unlike what Troeltsch rather misleadingly called "mysticism." For "cultic milieus," see Danny L. Jorgensen, "The Esoteric Community: An Ethnographic Investigation of the Cultic Milieu." *Urban Life* 4 (1982):383–407; Rodney Stark and William S. Bainbridge, *The Future of Religion: Secularization, Revival and Cult Formation* (Berkeley: University of California Press, 1986).

23. Colin Campbell, "The Cult, the Cultic Milieu, and Secularization," in M. Hill, *A Sociological Yearbook of Religion in Britain*, Vol. 5 (London: SCM Press, 1972), pp. 119–136.

24. See, for example, Bassam Tibi, *Der Islam und das Problem der Kulturellen Bewältigung Sozialen Wandels* (Frankfurt: Suhrkamp, 1985).

25. See Frank J. Lechner, "Fundamentalism and Sociocultural Revitalization in America: A Sociological Interpretation." *Sociological Analysis* 46 (1985):243–259; Donald Heinz, "Clashing Symbols: The New Christian Right as Countermythology." *Archives de Sciences Sociales des Religions* 59 (1985):153–173.

REFERENCES

Assmann, Jan. 1984. *Aegypten—Theologie und Frömmigkeit Einer Frühen Hochkultur.* Stuttgart: Vohlhammer.

Beckford, James A., ed. 1986. *New Religious Movements and Rapid Social Change.* London: Sage.

Beckford, James A., and Thomas Luckmann, eds. 1989. *The Changing Face of Religion.* London, Newbury Park, New Delhi: Sage.

Breasted, James H. 1933. *The Dawn of Conscience.* New York and London: Russell.

Campbell, Colin. 1972. "The Cult, the Cultic Milieu, and Secularization." Pp. 119–136 in M. Hill, ed., *A Sociological Yearbook of Religion in Britain*, Vol. 5. London: SCM Press.

Campbell, Colin, and Shirley McIver. 1987. "Cultural Sources of Support for Contemporary Occultism." *Social Compass* 34(1):41–60.

Chinnici, Joseph P. 1981. "New Religious Movements and the Structure of Religious Sensibility." Pp. 26–33 in Jacob Needleman and George Baker, eds., *Understanding the New Religions.* New York: Seabury Press.

Frankfort, Henri. 1978. *Kingship and the Gods: A Study of Ancient Near Eastern Religion as the Integration of Society and Nature.* Chicago: University of Chicago Press.

Hahn, Alois. 1984. "Theorien zur Entstehung der Europäischen Moderne." *Philosophische Rundschau* 31:178–202.

Heinz, Donald. 1985. "Clashing Symbols: The New Christian Right as Countermythology." *Archives de Sciences Sociales des Religions* 59(1):153–173.

Jorgensen, Danny L. 1982. "The Esoteric Community: An Ethnographic Investigation of the Cultic Milieu." *Urban Life* 4:383–407.

Kaufmann, Franz-Xaver. 1986. "Religion and Modernität." Pp. 283–307 in Johannes Berger, ed., *Die Moderne—Kontinuitäten und Zäsuren* (Sonderband 4 der "Sozialen Welt"). Göttingen: Schwartz.

Lechner, Frank J. 1985. "Fundamentalism and Sociocultural Revitalization in America: A Sociological Interpretation." *Sociological Analysis* 46(3):243–259.

Lübbe, Hermann. 1965. *Säkularisierung. Geschichte Eines Ideenpolitischen Begriffs.* München: Alber.

Luckmann, Thomas. 1967. *The Invisible Religion.* New York: Macmillan.

———. 1983. *Life-World and Social Realities.* London: Heinemann.

———. 1988. "Religion and Modern Consciousness." *Zen Buddhism Today* (Annual Report of the Kyoto Zen Symposium) 6:11–22.

Marx, Karl. 1955. "Zur Kritik der Hegelschen Rechtsphilosophie." P. 207 in Siegfried Landshut, ed., *Die Frühschriften.* Stuttgart: Kroener.

Rigby, Andrew, and Bryan S. Turner. 1972. "Findhorn Community, Centre of Light: A Sociological Study of New Forms of Religion." Pp. 72–86 in M. Hill, ed., *A Sociological Yearbook of Religion in Britain,* Vol. 5. London: SCM Press.

Schutz, Alfred. 1962. *Collected Papers I.* The Hague: Nijhoff.

Schutz, Alfred, and Thomas Luckmann. 1989. *The Structures of the Life-World II.* Evanston, IL: Northwestern University Press.

Stark, Rodney, and William S. Bainbridge. 1986. *The Future of Religion: Secularization, Revival and Cult Formation.* Berkeley: University of California Press.

Tibi, Bassam. 1985. *Der Islam und das Problem der Kulturellen Bewältigung Sozialen Wandels.* Frankfurt: Suhrkamp.

Voegelin, Eric. 1952. *The New Science of Politics: An Introduction.* Chicago: University of Chicago Press.

Wittfogel, Karl A. 1963. *Oriental Despotism: A Comparative Study of Total Power.* New Haven: Yale University Press.

Wuthnow, Robert. 1981. "Religious Movements and the Transition in the World Order." Pp. 63–79 in Jacob Needleman and George Baker, eds., *Understanding the New Religions.* New York: Seabury Press.

Comments

Andrew Greeley

First, this commentary allows me to express my gratitude to Professor Luckmann for the important contribution his work on the invisible religion made to my thinking at a critical time.

Second, my main dissent from his theory focuses on his use of the word "privatized" to describe religion in a complex multi-institutional society. The word can easily be interpreted to mean trivialized. I prefer the word "personalized." Instead of religion having a diffuse cultural impact on society, it now has an indirect effect through the image systems of individual persons and groups. Is that impact greater or less than it was in the past? I am not sure the question can be answered. I am content with the different adjective.

Does Mario Cuomo's Catholicism have more or less impact on how he governs the state of New York than, say, did the Catholicism of Richard the Lion-Hearted on the latter's governance of England? (I have little doubt which is the better Catholic.) I do not think the impact of Cuomo's religious vision on his behavior is any less great because he does not permit the cardinal rear admiral of New York to dictate his policy stands any more than I think Rich Daley lacks a Catholic vision because the local cardinal cannot dictate his stand on gay rights.

It is usually difficult, even in a group of U.S. sociologists, to challenge the myth of secularization, no matter how much data one has. It is even more difficult to suggest that the myth is a classic example of the fallacy of misplaced concreteness when sociologists from other countries are present. Everyone knows that religion is less important than it used to be. Thus, attempts at verification and falsification are unnecessary and impossible; no one sees any need to operationalize either "important" or "used to be."

Gentlepersons, I know a dogma when I hear one.

In the present context, I would suggest that the proper way to state the question is: Under what sets of circumstances do which kinds of religions have what kind of effects in which sorts of societies? Usually one emerges from exercises that strive to answer such modest questions with very modest answers—significant correlations under, say, .15, if one is lucky. I must note for the theorists that such is the fate of almost every hypothesis in our discipline that is taken out of the sheltered protection of the cloistered monastery of theory and exposed to temptation in the mundane world of verification and falsification.

I understand that in the present context, Luckmann is asserting that in modern Western societies religious "fundamentalism cannot be organized into substantial politico-religious movements." He does concede that in modernizing societies, such movements can be transformed into powerful politico-religious movements, "at least temporarily."

I will leave aside the question of the modernizing countries and discuss Western society. I will also leave aside Ireland because social scientists are never made to take Ireland seriously. Patently the Irish do not count. Nonetheless, I will assert that when social theory leads one to conclude that religious movements have only occasional and marginal importance in developed nations, there is something profoundly wrong with the theory, and it ought to be either refined or jettisoned.

In my work on falsification, I will cite two cases—the United States and Poland. In the former, I will not discuss such issues as abortion or prohibition in which religious movements played and still play an important part. I will rather point at the black (or, if you wish, African-American) civil rights movement. Not to perceive that this movement is profoundly religious in its origins, organization, style, leadership, symbols, and goals is not to understand it at all. I have the impression that many white secularist social scientists do not take the religious aspects of the civil rights movement seriously. The religious symbols, they seem to imply, are a scam—albeit a legitimate one—used for political purpose and are not something that the leaders and followers, both in great part, take very seriously. Let me ask those who live in a major city how many nights in the last three months political rallies in black churches appeared on television. Surely that would suggest that the movement is both political and religious and that the two components cannot be separated, not even by the most convinced believer in secularization.

I would add that the black civil rights movement is fundamentalist, an assertion that will offend many secular sociologists. The blacks are a good cause, the fundamentalists are bad. How dare I link the two? Such a response only demonstrates ignorance of U.S. religion. The goals of the television evangelists and the Reverend Jesse Jackson may be quite different, but how can anyone who has watched both doubt the similarity of style? Both white fundamentalism and black civil rights are essentially Southern Baptist movements.

It is worth noting, incidentally, that true to their fundamentalist heritage, blacks are the group in the United States most likely to oppose abortion, even more than white Catholics: You will not read that fact in the *New York Times*.

I do not see how anyone can argue that the civil rights movement is either marginal or occasional. The New Age religion Luckmann cites is a trivial epiphenomenon in the contemporary United States. The religious nature of the civil rights movement is both durable and enormously important. How can it be missed?

My second case for the falsification of Luckmann's proposition is, if anything, even more powerful. While the black movement is Baptist and fundamentalist, Polish Catholicism is conservative, perhaps, but not fundamentalist. Again I do not comprehend how anyone with even a basic familiarity with the events in Poland can fail to see the profoundly religious nature of this unusual revolution.

There have probably been two authentic people's revolutions in the last forty years—the Iranian and the Polish. The first is surely a reaction to modernity, as Luckmann has suggested, and a bloody one at that. The second is an authentic liberal revolution—maybe the only one since 1776— with no loss of life, save for an occasional priest murdered by a zealous police force. It has been a very sophisticated, patient revolution whose final achievements are still in doubt. However, there is little question now as to which side has gained the advantage. It may also be the first case that disproves Max Weber's theory that all revolutions produce more centralized power than the regimes they replace.

I confess that I do not understand why the Polish revolution does not draw more sociological attention. Perhaps the reason is that the Poles, like the Irish, really do not count.

In Solidarity, as in the case of the civil rights movement in the United States, religion—both as a personalized faith of individuals and groups and as an ecclesiastical institution—is deeply and inextricably bound up with the political movement. Where does Lech Walesa have his meetings? At the same place Martin Luther King had his—in the local church. The simple-minded secularist observer may write off Solidarity as mere politics with a religious veneer, but this would be as unperceptive as to write off Martin Luther King as a politician with a ministerial veneer.

In both cases, there is a mutual and reciprocal causality in which religion and politics influence one another. Only the convinced dogmatist could fail to grasp this point. The dispassionate scholar should be interested not in dogmatically dismissing the religious factor but in understanding and analyzing the interaction of both religious and political factors.

I will surely be told that these two phenomena do not falsify the theory because they are exceptions. This is doubtless the case. Doubtless, too, is the fact that General-Secretary Gorbachev's almost unseemly haste in drawing the Orthodox church into his glasnost cause is only "marginal and occasional."

Thus, if I am asked what I feel will be the impact of religion on social structures in the next millennium, I would say that it may not be that different from what it has been in the past two or three millennia. In some societies, it will have only a slight impact on the functioning of other social structures. In other societies (such as the local one), it will have considerable impact. And yet, in other societies—east or west, north or south, modernizing or not—under certain circumstances it will have a powerful and even revolutionary impact. A social theory that does not consider the set of possibilities involved in such a prediction, I submit, is blinded by its own dogmatism.

Comments

Seymour Martin Lipset

Luckmann's comprehensive chapter still leaves me with the feeling that I do not fully comprehend the subject. What is religion? Can its persistence and adherents be explained in the terms outlined by Luckmann? The phenomena we call religions become even harder to analyze if we extend them to include—as he does—political religions, socialisms, and nationalisms.

Luckmann seeks to define religion by its functions, particularly "the transformation of *homo sapiens* into actors in a historical social order." "Religion is to be found wherever the behavior of the members of the species becomes morally accountable action," where people interact "on the basis of the elementary principle of the reciprocity of perspective."

How do we specify the great variety of phenomena that have served this function? Luckmann suggests that there are two processes to be found in religion: (1) the reconstruction of experiences of transcendence through narratives or rituals; and (2) the construction of these accounts so they become an existential reality, as in sacred writings. Societies vary in how they do these between "intermediate" and "great" transcendences.

Religion, as Luckmann notes, has taken on different forms: (1) universal in small tribal societies; (2) some differentiation in the ancient states; (3) a more complete separate institutional domain with a high degree of structural complexity, from medieval times on. This leads in the modern world to secularization and (4) privatization—individual secretism in the personal sphere—as in the new religions concerned with expansion of consciousness such as New Age movements, which emphasize the spiritual development of each individual. I agree with Andrew Greeley that this development is not important, even if the phenomena are newsworthy.

Luckmann's analysis is useful for a historical evolutionary account of religion. It links changes in structure, organization, and belief to shifts in the larger society—from primitive, tribal cultures to complex, highly differentiated, pluralistic, cosmopolitan cultures. Religious differentiation and secularization are functionally related to macro-societal complexity. But this kind of evolutionary analytic scheme is not what Luckmann is interested in. Rather, the chapter seeks to update Durkheimian functionalist analysis.

As I see the phenomenon, it is linked to other major sources of personal identity, nationalism, and, to a lesser extent—depending on the level of intensity—politics, a point stressed by Luckmann. Religious affiliation and national citizenship are largely, although not exclusively, birth-right statuses. Each links us to our ancestors through a family chain. The family is the core transmission agent, the key to socialization. It uses religion and nationalism to legitimate, externalize, and provide sources for values. And clearly it is necessary to do so. Families used to be closely linked everywhere; they still are in a few developed countries whose identity or independence is tenuous—such as Ireland, Poland, and Israel—but are more generally closely linked in many less developed nations.

Religion is unique in often helping us to deal with the transitory character of human life—with birth, illness, and death. In many, although not all, societies, it assumes continuity beyond physical earthly life; it may justify moral actions and hierarchical status in terms related to the afterlife.

To say this still leaves us to account for the vast variety of religious behaviors, structures, and beliefs. Sociological reductionist efforts to do this, from Karl Marx through Durkheim to various modern students, remain problematic. The Marxist "opiate of the people" interpretation, as Robert Merton has noted, is similar to the Durkheimian societal integration one. They fail in the face of the numerous cases of religion serving as the justification—the ideology—for revolt, civil war, class struggle, and efforts to overthrow the social order. Liberation theology is the most recent example.

Religion has frequently been dysfunctional for societal unity. India, Ireland, Lebanon, and Nigeria are a few extreme examples of this point. Religion has also challenged the organizing principles, the hegemonic beliefs, not only of communist societies but of capitalist orders as well. We often forget that Catholicism is inherently anti-bourgeois; it has institutionalized medieval values and structures. Pre–World War II right-wing Catholicism, including clerical fascism, was anti-capitalist. Emotionally, it favored a return to medieval corporatism.

Liberation theology is the other side of the anti-capitalist coin. It emerged in Latin America and Europe after clerical fascism and other ultra-right-wing doctrines were delegitimated by the outcome of World War II. Liberation ideology and clerical fascism dislike the same elements in the modern world. The former simply shifted the solution from corporatism to socialism.

If I may particularize my thoughts on the subject, I am a Jew, or rather—as far as I know—my ancestors have been Jewish. My skin color and my looks link me to people who lived in the Judean desert, and every Passover I celebrate God's having led them out of Egypt close to four millennia ago. Why do I still identify? Why do I occasionally go to synagogue and try to fast on Yom Kippur? I cannot answer these questions except to say: Who am I to give up a commitment, an identification, my ancestors maintained for over three thousand years, resisting—I assume—violent efforts to get them to change or convert or more subtle pressures to assimilate? Such feelings are particularly strong for those, like myself, who are of the Holocaust generation. While my intellectualizing in this fashion may not be a theologically acceptable basis for religious identification, I do not think it is too different from the intellectualizing of most people in the world. Religion is their tie to family, to tradition, to community, and to being part of the human race.

Those assumptions help to account for the persistence of Japanese Shintoism, which is essentially animism, as among tribal societies. I have been fascinated watching gray flannel-suited businessmen in Tokyo entering Shinto shrines, clapping to gain the attention of the local god in residence, then saying a prayer and leaving a written request. Do they really believe a god is there? In Japan, of course, Shinto is linked to the family and nationalism, to the endless chain identified with the emperor.

This still leaves us with the problem of accounting for variations from country to country and for change, conversions, the rise of new religions, the range from fundamentalism to highly secular and undisciplined creeds, the existence of atheistic religions such as Buddhism, and those who believe in an afterlife and those who do not. If the hypothesis that secularization stems from differentiation, science, modernization, and urbanization makes sense, how can we account for the fact—as Andrew Greeley has documented—that the United States has been the most God-believing and religion-adhering, fundamentalist, and religiously traditional country in Christendom, except perhaps for a few agrarian Catholic states such as Ireland and Poland where religion and nationalist resistance to a foreign imperialist have been closely linked? The United States is also the most religiously fecund country. More new religions have been born here than in any other society—Mormon, Christian Science, Jehovah's Witness, the Churches of Christ, Conservative Judaism, and many others.

De Tocqueville, Engels, and Weber stressed the modernity of the United States, but if religion and fundamentalism are traditional, then this country is the most traditional society in the Western world. Clearly, the United States is not that different from Japan. Both are economically modern and religiously traditional.

There are basic problems with reductionist treatments of religion, much like those involved in explanations of high culture. The sociology of religion does best in reporting intrasocietal correlations, not in explaining macrosocietal phenomena. New religions and conversions can be correlated with existential variables. For example, many of the Moslem and Christian areas of the Indian subcontinent were heavily inhabited by Untouchables, who seemingly chose universalistic religions to escape their pariah status within Hinduism. In Japan, many of the country's Untouchables—the Eta—have become Christians. Fundamentalist strength in the United States correlates with rural and small-town environments.

There is some evidence that extremist secular political movements do well in areas that have abandoned religion. In Europe, Communists and anarchists had their greatest strength in Catholic countries—such as France, Italy, and Spain—where church adherence had declined. France has been defined by the Catholic church as a missionary region, a dechristianized area. Some obvious functionalist hypotheses are suggested by this. But the cross-national evidence is not consistent with the assumption that the irreligious and the secularized are attracted to extremist total political solutions and to functional alternatives for religion. Highly irreligious Scandinavia, which is largely de-christianized, seemingly does not have any substitute for religion.

I regret ending on this note of confusion. I find it impossible to do justice to the complexity of Tom Luckmann's thought. He did not try and could not be expected to present a theory that accounts for all the variations that fall under the heading of religion. But he attempts to do too much by subsuming under the phenomenon political and other forms of deep commitment. Still, if we define religion by its functions, there is the obvious need to explain its nonappearance as well, to suggest functional alternatives, and this is what Luckmann is trying to do.

6

Families, Childrearing, and Education

Opening Remarks

Charles E. Bidwell

How the institutions of family and education are related is not well understood, either historically or in contemporary societies. This statement holds for the various levels of social aggregation—for example, the interaction of families, schools, and educators in processes of socialization and, as well, the participation of family-based social groups in the formation of educational policy. Nevertheless, the family-education relationship has become a key element of present-day societies. Therefore, it is our purpose to outline promising lines of analysis that may expand our understanding of the evolution and present character of this relationship.

To say that family-education relations are not well understood is not to say that the topic has been unnoticed by social theorists. For example, in his pedagogical lectures delivered at the close of the 1800s, Emile Durkheim (1961) dealt with the role of the school in socialization and touched on the place of the family in the process, although primarily to show that by comparison with the school, it was unfit to prepare children for modern life. Like Willard Waller (1932), who some forty years later wrote with great insight about the small society of the school, Durkheim's principal interest was in the internal social life of the school itself.

Max Weber (1947, pp. 341–358) and Pitirim Sorokin (1959, pp. 182–211), considering whole societies, had important things to say about the family and education in relation to social stratification and mobility. Sorokin, for example, provided a provocative analysis of the conditions under which schools, gaining institutional autonomy, teach students and judge their accomplishments in ways that weaken the transmission of social standing across generations.

None of these works led to a truly systematic analysis of family and education in either historical or contemporary societies. To date, the one systematic theoretical treatment of school and family has derived substantially from Talcott Parsons's (1959) depiction of the structural and normative development of "modern" societies and from complementary studies of the development of citizenship in the nation-state (Marshall 1981). There is much to be learned from this interpretation, but in important respects, it is limiting. I shall briefly summarize this line of analysis, draw out a few of its more interesting implications, and touch on a few new analytical directions for work on family and school.

The Parsonian interpretation begins at the level of structural and normative change in societies but almost at once turns to the Durkheimian question of the place of family and school in processes of socialization. At the macrosocial level, the very fact of a family-school relationship arises as an aspect of the secular trends toward differentiation and bureaucratization that have been hallmarks of the emergence and development of industrial societies. As social differentiation has progressed, families have lost functions to specialist organizations. Consequently, families must enter into relationships with these organizations through which they can be supplied with goods or services that they themselves no longer produce.

This story of differentiation begins with the movement of economic production out of the household, away from the control of kin-based groups and into markets. Then, in large part as a result of the economic disablement of the family, one functional activity after another is stripped from the household, moving from the primary control of the family to the control of formal organizations and their increasingly professionalized staffs.

This process is very clear in the case of education. The classic account is by the social historian Lawrence Stone (1964) in his work on the "educational revolution" in sixteenth- and seventeenth-century England. Although Stone's work is not self-consciously Parsonian, it is fully consistent with the Parsonian interpretation. According to Stone, the key event in England was the growth of an independent middle class. Middle-class families wanted their children to be educated, but they lacked the land and large inheritances that could support an enclosed, multifunctional household in which a child's education could be accomplished. Thus, the rise of the middle class created a market in which charitable schools were turned into grammar schools, beginning a sustained, market-driven process in which formal education became a normal, lengthening life-course stage for the bulk of the English male population.

However, market growth is only part of the story. The rise of the national state and, with it, the expansion of citizenship are, in this account, intrinsic to the development of the differentiated industrial society. As functional differentiation proceeds, there is a strong tendency for each of its emerging institutional sectors to define citizenship rights or entitlements, which the state defines and regulates. Education is among these sectors.

Everywhere in the West (and now in the Third World), efforts at centralized governmental control of the schools through formal organization and procedure are evident, driven variously by egalitarian and stratifying impulses (Archer 1984). Even in the United States, where there is a less ministerial structure of common education than is found in most other places, the nation was not very old when efforts at state intervention began. By the middle of the nineteenth century, such school reformers as Horace Mann in Massachusetts and Henry Barnard in Connecticut made vigorous, re- markably successful efforts to rationalize the provision of education through state boards of education. These boards approved or recommended texts, certified teachers, sponsored normal schools, and collected information about the condition of education.

In sum, within what has been the dominant interpretation, the family- school relationship is one in which nuclear families individually send their offspring to be educated in schools that are bureaucratically rationalized, that are conducted by a staff of disinterested professionals, and that are regulated by the state. This interpretation has interesting implications for research into the political economy of education (including the negotiation of school-family exchanges), the social organization of the educational process, and the way families make decisions about their offsprings' education. With respect to each of these topics, the very fact of an institutional boundary between family and education and of the often-disjoint interests of family welfare and social welfare (whether interpreted by professionals or political bodies) suggests that the differentiation of family and education may be as much a source as a result of social change; that the family-education boundary is likely to be the location of sharp and persistent conflict, both locally and more broadly in society; and that family and school may often act at cross- purposes in the upbringing of the young.

However, the work that has followed from the starting point of institutional differentiation has for the most part bypassed issues of political economy and power, conflict or contradiction, and has not dealt with the more macro- social aspects of the family-education relationship. Instead, it has focused on the ways in which school and family are related in the socialization of children and youth, especially their preparation for life in a bureaucratic society. Here, pride of place is given to equilibrium, sequence, and com- plementarity. Family and school take part in socialization in a way that provides a productive sequence of steps in the child's cognitive and moral development.

Take, for example, Robert Dreeben's thoughtful book, *On What Is Learned in School* (1968). Dreeben asks how the distinctive social organizations of family and school respectively provide contexts in which children learn the norms that will regulate their conduct in adult society. In the family, with rare exceptions, each child occupies a unique age grade. Consequently, it is possible for the child to develop close, warm, nurturing bonds with the parents in which he or she builds a capacity for intimacy that is in itself an important part of socialization and that, once the school years begin, will permit the child to identify with teachers in a way that generates powerful motives to behave and achieve.

The social organization of the school class, by contrast, places the child as one among a number of pupils of the same age, confronting the same tasks and rules and similarly related to the same teacher. Here is where the child learns the norms of achievement, of independence, and of bureaucratically appropriate conduct that will be required in the formal, instrumentally oriented settings of adulthood. The child is likely to encounter strains entailed by the move from the warmth and particularism of the family to the school's organization around effective neutrality, achievement, and universalism (school attributes that become stronger and clearer as the child moves up the school grades). However, these strains are moderated initially by the family's provision of social support and tension management.

Now, the question is whether this account is sufficient or whether we can do better. It is hard to argue against the core proposition that the appearance of schools and schooling means the appearance of formal instructional procedure, and the professionalization of teaching. But what are the consequences? The notion of a triad of actors—family, the rationalized and professionalized school, and the state—provides a useful starting point. I should like to suggest three new directions to travel. Consider further the question of socialization. The Parsonian interpretation shortchanges the family as a participant in the process. Doing so, it loses sight of significant contradictions in the relationship of family and school within socialization and cannot show how this relationship structures the educational life chances of children and youth. By advancing the concept of family social capital, James Coleman (1988) has taken a significant step in this direction. From the idea of social capital, it follows that what the child learns—in both moral and cognitive terms—is the outcome of continuing, rather than discrete and sequential, family and school influences. It also follows that when either contribution is deficient and when these deficiencies are systematically distributed across the social classes, the stage is set for the creation and perpetuation of class-based imparities in preparation for adult life. Needed now is theory that specifies the continuous action of family and school in socialization, accompanied by evidence adequate to evaluate the theory.

A further shortcoming of the Parsonian interpretation is its representation of the student as a passive recipient of professionally administered education and, by implication, of the student's parents as passive bystanders during the process. This representation cannot be justified. In fact, as schools or systems of schools gain institutional autonomy, decisions about such matters as the length and direction of students' educational trajectories do not become the exclusive domain of educators, as Sorokin argued. Rather, they are open to influence by a triad of actors—educators, parents, and the students themselves. The relative strength of the influence of each, the degree to which conflicting interests come into play, and the means by which such conflicts are resolved probably vary with the stage of the student's schooling, the social standing of the family, the sector of the educational system, and the degree to which student careers are fixed or open (Bidwell and Friedkin 1988). Again, we require theory that specifies the decision processes and the conditions under which they may vary as well as the findings that would let us evaluate these arguments.

Finally, from the postulates of institutional differentiation and state regulation, it is easy to derive a large number of questions that draw one into the study of the political economy of education in national societies. For example, in whose interest is state regulation conducted, and with what effect on the criteria and procedures through which regulation occurs? Independently acting families, for the most part, have severely limited power to affect the conduct of professions or of organizations and state systems. To what extent is this imbalance characteristic of the school-family relationship? Under what conditions has it been possible for families or other kinship units to act in concert—for example, through hierarchies of voluntary associations—to alter this distribution of power? Work on such questions should help us understand how the interests of family groupings, educational occupations and organizations, and state agencies are aggregated and expressed in the formation of policies that will condition the action of families and schools in socialization and in decisions about the educational futures of individual students.

REFERENCES

Archer, Margaret S. 1984. *The Social Origins of Educational Systems*. Beverly Hills, CA: Sage.

Bidwell, Charles E., and Noah E. Friedkin. 1988. "The Sociology of Education." Pp. 449–471 in Neil J. Smelser, ed., *Handbook of Sociology*. Beverly Hills, CA: Sage.

Coleman, James S. 1988. "Social Capital in the Creation of Human Capital." *American Journal of Sociology* 94 (suppl.):S95–S120.

Dreeben, Robert. 1968. *On What Is Learned in School*. Reading, MA: Addison-Wesley.

Durkheim, Emile. 1961. *Moral Education*. Glencoe, IL: The Free Press.

Marshall, T. H. 1981. *The Right to Welfare and Other Essays*. New York: The Free Press.

Parsons, Talcott. 1959. "The School Class as a Social System." *Harvard Educational Review* 29(4):297–318.

Sorokin, Pitirim. 1959. *Social and Cultural Mobility*. Glencoe, IL: The Free Press.

Stone, Lawrence. 1964. "The Educational Revolution in England, 1560–1640." *Past and Present* 28:41–80.

Waller, Willard. 1932. *The Sociology of Teaching*. New York: John Wiley and Sons.

Weber, Max. 1947. *The Theory of Social and Economic Organization*. Glencoe, IL: The Free Press.

Institutions and Human Capital Development

Mary C. Brinton

This panel has been assigned the task of looking at the question of how the process of bringing a new generation into society changes with the increasing rationalization of society. We are taking as our dual task the delineation of universal changes in the distribution of responsibilities for the socialization and education of children and young adults as well as the delineation of cultural *differences* in the distribution of responsibilities.

Although I am a sociologist, I am going to rephrase our task in terms of human capital. First, how are the processes and the agents involved in human capital development changing as we approach the end of the twentieth century? (Here, we can think about the distribution of responsibilities for human capital development across the institutions of the family, the educational system, and even the workplace.) Second, what are our criteria for determining whether our means of raising and educating youth—of investing in human capital at young ages—are efficient, rational, fair, humane, and— simply put—the optimal social arrangements? Third, how can we explain cross-cultural variation in the processes and agents of human capital development? Can institutions that are rational in one industrial (or post-industrial) society or cultural context be irrational in another? I pose these questions not because I intend to answer them in the time alloted to me but because I hope they will provoke some discussion.

Jim Stigler points out a number of efficiencies and benefits of the Japanese system of human capital development, especially elementary schools. He suggests some of the reasons for differences between Japanese and American schools. He asserts—and I agree—that Japan demonstrates a case where the family has turned over its educational function nearly entirely to educational authorities. I am reminded of a popular film that came out in 1983 when I was living in Japan, a film that won the Japanese equivalent of an academy award. In this film, the Japanese director satirized the way that the life of an urban Japanese family with two sons was dominated by the tutor they had hired to help the younger son pass the high school entrance exam. It was black humor at its best, mocking the power and control Japanese families have given over to *katei kyoshi* (private tutors) in the race to get their children (especially their sons) into good universities.

So in Japan we are confronted with an image of the stable, cohesive family—witness the low Japanese divorce rate—which is also in many cases a family in which people spend very little time together and in which parents are not specifically helping their children study. Nevertheless, the family is providing the material and the psychological infrastructure or base from which children develop high aspirations and learn.

It is a common feature of advanced industrial societies that women with higher education have higher rates of labor force participation than their less-educated counterparts. This is not true in Japan. Highly educated Japanese women are *more* likely than less-educated women to withdraw from the labor force when their children are young. This signifies that highly educated Japanese women are making significant "home investments," as labor economists would say. But they are not helping children study. If I may move to the everyday for a moment, from personal observation I can attest that many mothers get up at dawn to make school lunches and stay up late at night to welcome children home and fix a meal and talk after their after-school lessons or tutoring. Psychological support—and accompanying pressures on children to prosper from this support by passing school entrance exams—is intense.

One question we can ask is whether this is a wise use of highly educated women's human capital. We can debate that. Some will say yes because of the "quality of children" being produced. Some will say no, arguing that the human capital of these women is not being put to its most productive use. Almost all Japanese families now have one or two children. Although marriage age is late for an industrial society, the first child is typically born within three years of marriage, and the second child arrives soon thereafter. Japanese women currently have greater longevity than anyone in the world. Thus, by the time the typical woman's second child has entered school, she still has over forty years of life left. That is a lot of time to develop and use human capital, but the jobs open to highly educated women at this point in life are extremely limited. So, many women choose to stay out of the labor force permanently.

Whether we think that the significant home investments of highly educated Japanese women are good or bad investments, we are assuming a causal relationship between children's school performance and mothers' non-labor force participation. And this is something we could test empirically. Indeed, there are two other institutional "layers" involved in human capital development in Japan that we should consider as well: extra-school or after-school schools and tutoring outside the formal system (*juku* and *katei kyoshi*), and on-the-job training. So, in addition to thinking about the roles played by the formal educational system and by the family in educating and socializing the young, in creating and enhancing human capital, we need to think about these other institutional layers because they are social creations and are important parts of the system of bringing the young fully into society.

The most recent figures from the Japanese government indicate that in cities of over 100,000 population, more than one-third of all sixth graders attend after-school schools (*juku*). This shoots up to over 50 percent for ninth graders. Of these, one-quarter are spending between two and three hours a day in such schools. Thus, a whole extra layer of differentiation exists in Japanese schooling. With the mushrooming of these schools in the past fifteen years and the recognition that they are indeed big business, greater differentiation has occurred within this class of schools. Some are remedial to help children catch up with their classmates, and some are accelerated to help children cram harder for the impending high school and university entrance exams. The educational competition has become so intense in Japan that some other Asian countries have made such after-school schools illegal or have attempted to do so.

Thus, while the *formal* educational system in Japan does not cater to special and diversified clienteles, the informal system does. And I wonder whether the informal system is not complementing or supplementing the formal system in this respect. In other words, we need to think about what it is about the formal educational system that makes the informal system necessary—What are its origins, and why is it thriving? We also need to try to assess its consequences. After-school schools cost money, and the possible contribution of these schools to greater social stratification is a worry to many Japanese. That is, given that cram schools cost money, *if* they help students perform better on entrance exams they may be exerting a dampening effect on intergenerational social mobility. The verdict on this is not yet in, but this issue is debated in Japan.

I have discussed briefly the role of the family and the system of after-school schooling in educating the young. On-the-job training is also important. I think of Rosabeth Moss Kanter's comments (see Chapter 2) comparing European school graduates as generalists and U.S. graduates as specialists. This is a rather apt way of comparing Japan and the United States as well. That is to say, professional and technical educations have not yet had much of a role in Japanese society. I do not have time to discuss the transformations occurring in Japanese employment practices with the burgeoning of the service sector (particularly the information- and knowledge-intensive industries). But I will say that while changes are occurring, and while there may be the beginnings of a trend toward greater educational specialization prior to leaving school and entering the labor market, the stereotype of the graduate with a general education being hired into a large firm that will train him or her is still quite accurate for the large-firm sector of the Japanese economy. Large Japanese firms expect to train their new recruits. And small firms do, too, if they can afford it.

James Rosenbaum and Takehiko Kariya of Northwestern University have discovered that some Japanese high schools have implicit contracts with local employers to refer their top graduates year after year to those employers. This is a demonstration of a mutually beneficial institutional relationship— we will invest in training these people if we can take your word that they are trainable and will be good workers. This is an example of the institutional division of the labor involved in educating and socializing young people as workers. And I stress that it is an *institutional* arrangement that does not conform to a strict open labor market. Is it efficient? I am inclined to think there are efficiencies in it. Is it fair? I am inclined to think that women may suffer in such a system if they are tracked by school counselors into highly sex-segregated, low-paying jobs.

These issues of efficiency and fairness bring me full circle. How far have I come in answering the questions I laid out at the beginning? I hope I have succeeded in fleshing out the idea of differentiation in the types of institutions for socializing and educating the young. And I hope that in doing this, I have implicitly suggested that there are many models. I agree with Seymour Martin Lipset (Chapter 5) that we should not rush too quickly into proclaiming that the Japanese have models we should emulate *in toto*. I hope I have sketched some of the possible deficits and advantages, efficiencies and inefficiencies in such models. But I do not agree with Lipset's suggestion that everything we like about Japan was originally exported from the United States. I think that, in particular, there is much to be studied in the functional differentiation among organizations in Japan—hierarchically arranged or not—and the exchange linkages between institutions.

In closing, I suggest that we can inform social theory by studying the layers of institutions involved in human capital development and tracing their implications for efficiency, stratification, and health in both its physical and psychological dimensions. And in so doing, we can hopefully develop wise policy decisions about how we can improve our social institutions in the coming decades.

Individuals, Institutions, and Academic Achievement

James W. Stigler

Sociological theories about the relationship of individuals to institutions address an important set of issues that are generally ignored by psychologists interested in explaining the course of individual human development. At the same time, however, sociologists may not have paid enough attention to the role that culturally constructed and individually held social theories may play in mediating the relationships of individuals to institutions. In this brief subchapter I will argue first, that there are cultural differences in conceptions of the proper relationships between institutions (such as schools) and their clienteles (such as children and families). Second, I will try to convince you that such differences in conceptualization can make a difference in the way a culture designs its institutions and in the effectiveness of institutions in promoting the goals of individuals and families. I will rely, particularly, on work comparing educational institutions and academic achievement in Japan and the United States.

INDIVIDUALS AND INSTITUTIONS: AN ANALOGY FROM BILINGUALISM

Before discussing schools and families, let me introduce an analogy from the research literature of bilingualism that will help me to distinguish two alternative views of the relationship between individuals and institutions.

Lambert (1978) was the first to distinguish between two types of bilingualism, which he called additive and subtractive. With additive bilingualism, learning a second language is considered in positive terms. An individual who learns a second language increases his or her knowledge and life chances by becoming skilled at a second language, and fluency in the second language is seen as opening up opportunities that would have been unavailable without competence in the additional language. Subtractive bilingualism, on the other hand, emphasizes the costs of second language acquisition. In this view, there is direct competition between the two languages so that learning the new language will lead to negative results, such as loss of the native tongue, loss of the native culture, and—consequently— loss of personal identity.

Both types of bilingualism can be shown to exist. For example, native English speakers who reside in Quebec and learn French as a second language clearly fit the model of additive bilingualism. They do not lose their English but rather gain French, which gives them valuable access to social, political, and economic opportunities that would otherwise be unavailable to them in French Quebec society. Puerto Ricans who move to the mainland United States, on the other hand, could be said to fit the model of subtractive bilingualism. As they learn English in school, children of Puerto Rican immigrants rapidly lose their Spanish and consequently risk losing their cultural identity as well.

Different bilingual populations will tend to follow one pattern or the other, for reasons that are beyond the scope of this discussion. The point I wish to make, however, is that the relationships of individuals to institutions can be conceived in a similar way as being either additive or subtractive. An additive conception of individual-institutional relationships would obtain when the differentiation of functions resulting from the rationalization process is seen as increasing the power of individuals, much like learning a new language does in the case of additive bilingualism. In this view, what is gained by the development of institutions supplements and extends the power of individuals rather than taking away from individual power. A subtractive conception of individual-institutional relationships, on the other hand, implies that there is a zero-sum game—a struggle between individuals and institutions such that functions taken over by institutions are necessarily *taken away from* individuals.

As in the case of bilingualism, it is clear that both types of individual–institutional relationships can be found to exist, varying according to the individuals, functions, and institutions involved. What I want to suggest here is that as a society and as social scientists, we tend to have shared normative conceptions of how individuals and institutions interrelate, and these normative conceptions influence the way we design our institutions and the way we think about their effects. In particular, I would argue that, in the domain of education, Americans tend to have a subtractive conception of how schools and families interrelate and, further, that this subtractive conception may be partly responsible for the declining excellence of U.S. schools.

THE "MATCH" THEORY

There is a long tradition of research by social scientists that focuses on how families socialize their children for success in school. Theories that have emerged to explain the family correlates of school success and failure tend to coalesce around a general notion that I refer to as the "match" theory. According to this theory, children who do well in school do so at least partly because of a match between the values, attitudes, expectations, and knowledge existing in the home with those existing in the school. Conversely, children who fail in school fail partly because they come from home environments that are not academically oriented and in which the culture of the home contrasts with, rather than complements, the culture of the school.

As an explanation for empirical results, the match theory has not fared particularly well. As expected, one can find studies of subgroups of children who do well in school and whose homes appear to be highly academically oriented (Bempechat et al. 1989). Yet, one also finds children who fail in school despite an emphasis in the home on academic achievement (Ogbu 1989), as well as children who do well in school in a family environment that does not stress socialization for achievement (Peak 1989). What is more intriguing to me than the empirical findings, however, is what I perceive as a normative belief, widely held by U.S. social scientists and citizens alike, that there *ought* to be a match between families and schools.

This normative belief is, I suggest, a consequence of viewing school–family relationships as subtractive rather than additive. Sociologists (for example, James Coleman, Charles Bidwell) speak of schools and other institutions as "taking over" functions previously performed by the family, as compensating for a loss of functionality in the family. Rather than conceiving the functions of schools and families to be inherently different, this kind of rhetoric implies that the basic goals of schools and families are similar, so that functions taken over by one no longer have to be performed by the other. In other words, the rhetoric implies a subtractive view of school-family relationships, and the match theory follows from this view: Because of the high degree of overlap between the functions of family and school, each might be expected to resemble the other to the extent that they are performing their tasks efficiently. Further, there is, perhaps, a fear that if the school becomes too successful, there will be a corresponding loss of meaning for the family, a feeling that the family has become almost extraneous.

Consequences of the widespread cultural belief that individuals and institutions, children and schools, should reflect each other can be seen both in the ways we design schools and in the expectations we have for family life. I will briefly discuss each of these arenas.

The School

Schools in the United States, perhaps more than anywhere else in the world, are expected to reflect the particular clienteles they serve. This is evidenced in a number of ways. Historically, for example, the principle of local control of the schools has been a powerful force in the shaping of U.S. educational policy and has prevented us from developing even the rudiments of a national curriculum for our schools. The message is clear: Each locale is different, and so the institutions that serve the people must in some sense be unique. A similar principle has been applied to issues of minority education. Although much has been made of the fact that schools often fail to be sensitive to ethnic and cultural characteristics of the children they educate, such sensitivity is nevertheless seen as a legitimate goal in the design of schools. And so, a great deal of effort is put into the design and implementation of special programs that are seen as more suitable for children of various minority groups.

In fact, the idea that school curricula should be specially tailored to meet the needs of particular subpopulations of children goes far beyond the domain of minority education. We have special programs for the gifted, retarded, and learning disabled; for those planning on entering vocations and those deemed headed for college. In the United States, a great deal of money is spent on the diagnosis and documentation of individual and group differences among children and then on the provision of special educational experiences to meet the unique needs of individuals and subgroups.

Aside from matters of curriculum, the belief that schools must respond to individual differences also has a great influence on the way classroom instruction is organized in U.S. schools. In contrast to classrooms in most other societies, those in the United States place a heavy emphasis on individualized instruction—that is, the teacher spending class time working with individual students. The norm elsewhere is whole class instruction, with the teacher working with the class as a unified group. U.S. classrooms are organized this way, I would argue, because educators and parents believe that it is the most efficient way to teach children who differ from each other in important and basically immutable ways. My purpose here is not to argue that we are wrong but only to point out that the individualized instruction is not universally seen as the ideal way to organize education, and thus it is important to understand the cultural beliefs that underlie our decision to organize education in this way. Individualized instruction and the special programs alluded to above are all very expensive. It is worth asking whether scarce funds might be better spent in some other way.

Finally, it is interesting to note that a goal for schooling often emphasized by both teachers and parents in the United States is one that traditionally was almost exclusively ascribed to the family: the development of children's self-esteem and general emotional well-being. This, again, appears to reflect the zero-sum tug-of-war between the home and the school: not an additive differentiation of function but the supplanting of what was once the family's by the institution of schooling.

The Home

Just as U.S. schools are expected to reflect the variability in their clienteles and to serve at least some of the functions previously assigned to families, the U.S. home is expected to socialize children for academic achievement and to duplicate and support functions of the school in some fundamental ways. When U.S. teachers and school principals are interviewed and asked to explain the causes of poor school achievement, as I have done in my own research, the model response is to blame the family: broken homes, parents not teaching their children academic-related skills or helping with homework, and the like. This, to me, is fascinating. What educators are assuming is that the home ought to share responsibility for academic performance with the school—that is, "match" in some sense. Because the functions of the school and the family are conceived to overlap to a high degree, there will always be some doubt as to where the blame should be assigned when a function is not adequately performed. Indeed, one phenomenon familiar to most researchers who study U.S. education is the finger pointing that occurs between home and school when it comes time to assign responsibility for low academic standards. Again, the perception of home–school relations is not additive, with each allowed to perfect its own functions, but subtractive, with home and school struggling for control of the educational process.

THE CASE OF JAPAN

Much has been made of the high levels of academic achievement produced by Japanese schools, particularly when compared to U.S. schools (Stevenson et al. 1986; Stigler and Perry 1988). I would like to suggest in this section that Japanese educational excellence occurs within the context of a quite different conception of individual-institutional relations than that which I have argued to be widespread in U.S. society. In contrast with the prevalent U.S. view, the Japanese appear to have a truly additive conception of the relation of home to school and thus expect a high differentiation of function between home and school. Consequently, one does not find the Japanese striving for a match between home and school: Schools have their own goals and ways of working, and they do not need to reflect the particular characteristics of their clienteles. Homes, on the other hand, serve functions distinct from schools and do not tend to be concerned with academic objectives.

The primary goal of schools in Japan is to teach academic skills and knowledge and the values and attitudes that support the acquisition of knowledge. Missing from the interviews with Japanese teachers and parents is any mention of self-esteem as a concern of the school. Self-esteem and the emotional well-being of children are generally relegated to the family in Japan and are not seen as appropriate functions for the schools. Schools in Japan tend to make little or no adjustment to the individual differences that exist within the classroom, even though the variability within Japanese classrooms, in terms of achievement levels, is as great as it is in the United States (Stigler et al. 1990). Elementary school classrooms, unlike those in the United States, are taught exclusively by the teacher working with the class as a whole. In addition, special educational programs of all kinds are practically nonexistent: The experience of school does not vary across individuals and groups as it does in the United States. The school in Japan is not *supposed* to conform to individual differences among students.

Let me turn now to a discussion of the Japanese family and present some findings that I think many Americans will find surprising. Our stereotype of the Japanese family casts the mother as a surrogate teacher—pressuring children to study, working with them on their homework, teaching them academic skills, and the like. But recent research from a variety of investigators reveals that this is not the case. Lois Peak (1987), for example, impressed with the superior academic performance of Japanese children, set out to study the ways in which Japanese families socialize children for achievement. She spent a great deal of time with families of Japanese preschool children but, try as she did, was unable to find any evidence that Japanese parents were socializing their children to do well in school. Several of the parents in her study expressed amazement that she would be studying families if her ultimate goal were to understand school achievement. Their inevitable advice was: If you want to see what makes Japanese children good students, study the school, not the home.

The results of qualitive investigations such as Peak's are supported by survey research with larger, more representative samples. Stevenson et al. (1990) conducted interviews with 288 Japanese mothers and 288 U.S. mothers of kindergarten children (children in the year of preschool directly preceding entry into first grade). The Japanese mothers were from Sendai, the U.S. mothers from Minneapolis. Mothers were sampled from a total of 24 preschools in each city, chosen to represent the total population of preschools. A number of questions were asked to assess the degree to which the mothers were consciously socializing their children for high academic achievement.

For example, mothers were asked a series of questions about the kinds of skills they had attempted to teach their children at home before first grade. They were asked whether they taught their children the alphabet (or *hiragana*), how to read some words, how to read some sentences, something about numbers, how to do simple addition, and how to write their names. Out of a maximum score of six "yes" answers, the average Minneapolis mother scored 3.7, the average mother from Sendai only 1.7. Mothers also were asked why they decided to send their child to preschool. Ninety-two percent of the Japanese mothers cited the opportunity for their child to learn social skills, while only 0.7 percent mentioned learning academic skills. (By contrast, 8.3 percent of the Minneapolis mothers mentioned learning academic skills.) When asked "Should a kindergarten teacher assign academic homework?" 35.4 percent of Minneapolis mothers said yes, as opposed to only 7.5 percent of the Sendai mothers. The point is not that U.S. mothers are strongly academically oriented. They are not, as evidenced by the low percentage of U.S. mothers (8.3 percent) who cited academic learning as the primary reason for sending their child to preschool. However, the Japanese mothers are even *less* concerned with academic learning than are the U.S. mothers, a finding clearly contrary to the stereotypical view.

If Japanese mothers are not teaching academic skills, what is their role vis-à-vis their child's experiences in school? In general, a picture emerges of the Japanese mother as commiserator: The school is a tough, demanding place, and there is no time in the Japanese school to attend to the child's emotional well-being. So, when the child comes home from school, he or she is not met with more pressure ("Do your homework") but with sympathy: "School is really tough, I feel so sorry for you. Let me take your shoes off, get you a snack. How about watching television?" Japanese children feel the academic pressure, but not from their parents as much as from their teachers.

Japanese families and schools are not supposed to match in ways outlined above in the discussion of U.S. schools. Families and schools in Japan are functionally quite distinct, each institution pursuing its own goals in the most effective ways it knows. And the relationship of family to school is seen as additive, not subtractive, in Japan. The school as an institution adds a unique dimension to children's lives that is not duplicated within the domain of the Japanese family.

CONCLUSION

Societies construct their institutions, and hence the lives of individuals, by using the cultural resources that are available, including beliefs, goals, values, ways of representing information, and the like. What I have proposed in this brief discussion is that conceptions of how individuals and institutions ought to interrelate vary cross-culturally, and in particular I have suggested that U.S. society tends to conceive of the family-school relationship as subtractive while Japanese society perceives it as additive. Furthermore, I have argued that which conception one holds, or which is most easily available in the culture, makes a difference in how we design our families and our schools.

As long as we continue to see schools and families in a subtractive relationship, it will be difficult psychologically to allow the true differentiation of function that is required if schools are to be able to perfect themselves as schools, rather than as institutions expected both to educate and provide the secure emotional base that has traditionally been provided by the family. As long as schools are required to match their clienteles, then we will continue to hear the excuse that schools cannot educate well because of *who* they are required to educate. Just as it is difficult for the family to compensate for the academic shortcomings of a poor school, it may also be impossible to design an excellent school that, in addition to academic goals, must respond as well to the nonacademic goals of its clientele. Perhaps the best way to enable the U.S. school to achieve more in terms of academic excellence is to expect less from it (in terms of restricted functions).

REFERENCES

Bempechat, J., E. Mordkowitz, J. T. Wu, M. A. Morison, and H. P. Ginsburg. 1989. "Achievement Motivation in Cambodian Refugee Children: A Comparative Study." Paper presented at the Biennial Meetings of the Society for Research in Child Development, Kansas City, April 1989.

Lambert, W. E. 1978. "Some Cognitive and Sociocultural Consequences of Being Bilingual." In J. E. Alatis, ed., *International Dimensions of Bilingual Education*. Washington, DC: Georgetown University Press.

Ogbu, J. U. 1989. "Academic Socialization of Black Children: An Inoculation Against Future Failure?" Paper presented at the Biennial Meetings of the Society for Research in Child Development, Kansas City, April 1989.

Peak, L. 1987. *Learning to Go to School in Japan: The Transition from Home to Preschool Life*. Ph.D. dissertation, Harvard Graduate School of Education, Harvard University.

_____ . 1989. "Who Teaches Taro to Behave at School?: Training Classroom Conduct in Japanese Preschools and Elementary Schools." Paper presented at the Biennial

Meetings of the Society for Research in Child Development, Kansas City, April 1989.

Stevenson, H. W., S. Y. Lee, C. Chen, J. W. Stigler, C. C. Hsu, and S. Kitamura. 1990. "Contexts of Achievement: A Study of American, Chinese, and Japanese Children." *Monographs of the Society for Research in Child Development* 55:221.

Stigler, J. W., S. Y. Lee, and H. W. Stevenson. 1990. "Mathematical Knowledge of Japanese, Chinese, and American Children." *Monographs of the National Council of Teachers of Mathematics*. Reston, VA: National Council of Teachers of Mathematics.

Stigler, J. W., and M. Perry. 1988. "Mathematics Learning in Japanese, Chinese, and American Classrooms." Pp. 27–54 in G. Saxe and M. Gearhart, eds., *Children's Mathematics*. San Francisco: Jossey-Bass.

PART THREE

Changes in Systems
of Social Control

7

On the Individualistic Theory of Social Order

Alessandro Pizzorno

CONSIDERING THE THEORY OF SOCIAL ORDER

In 1936, a very ambitious sociological work was published—Talcott Parsons's *The Structure of Social Action*—which aimed to reconstruct a *sociological tradition*. At that time, there was much ambiguity concerning whether or not one could speak of a sociological tradition at all, whether there had been founding fathers, and even whether an agreement could be reached about the central problems around which the reflection and the research hypothesis of the discipline should turn. Determining a sociological tradition would have made possible the recognition of precise boundaries and given strength and consistency to the internally generated theoretical discourse. Specific research puzzles would have derived from it. Suggestions and borrowings from public discourse would have been reduced and rigorously translated into systematically generated terminology. From his theoretical reconstruction, Parsons established that the central question for the discipline was to be the question of social order, which had found expression for the

---

Alessandro Pizzorno presented in the conference a paper that represented an earlier stage in his search for a solution to the Hobbesian problem. Chapter 7 evolved from that earlier paper and, as a later stage in intellectual evolution, is published here. It represents, in a way, the explication of the first of the four theories of order introduced in the original paper. This development, obviously, makes the typology in Figure 1 represent only an introductory device. The unfolding of the analysis is meant to show its limitations.

As biological evolution sometimes casts aside developments that in other circumstances would provide productive, the evolution of a person's ideas may do so as well. For this reason, a summary of the original paper is presented on p. 232, followed by comments of the two discussants of the paper, Rogers Brubaker and Donald N. Levine. [Editors' note]

first time in "secularized" terminology in the work of Thomas Hobbes. But the solution given by the Hobbesian tradition, which Parsons called "utilitarian," was seen as inadequate. An alternative had to be proposed, and sociology would busy itself in elaborating it and forming, out of this task, its research programme.[1]

But not much later, in total independence from, and indifference to (and probably ignorance of), the enterprise aimed at reconstructing a theoretical field for the discipline of sociology, political philosophers rediscovered the contractarian tradition. They fully accepted the radically individualistic premises of this tradition and only revised or developed the old solutions in order to make them meet the concerns of the modern public discourse. At the same time, game theory proposed new formalized ways of probing the coherence and limits of the traditional argument and cleared the way for alternative ones. Couched either in the terms of a solution to the prisoner dilemma or in terms of coordination games, the Hobbesian problem of order came again to occupy the central stage. The radically individualistic premises were thus taken for granted. A whole new corpus developed that one may call the Hobbes Game Theory approach to the problem of social cooperation.[2] This I shall examine here.

CONSIDERING HOBBES
IN TERMS OF GAME THEORY

The game theoretical reconstruction of the Hobbesian problem of order analyzes the state of nature in terms of the prisoner dilemma (PD). As in a PD, people in a state of nature have a strong interest in breaking out of the situation in which they find themselves. To do that, they would need to reach a covenant with each other. But each is prevented from doing so by the fear that the other will defect from the covenant, leaving him as a lone peacekeeper. He would thus encounter death, while the defector would receive the rewards of victory. The matrix for two participants in the state of war would correspond to a PD matrix, in which: victory $>$ peace $>$ war $>$ defeat. The two options are either entering the covenant (E) or violating it (V); then:

	E	V
E	3,3	1,4
V	4,1	2,2

(On the left of each cell is the outcome for the row-chooser; on the right that for the column-chooser).

The two players have a common interest in achieving peace (upper left cell) by choosing to enter the covenant. But each fears that if he does so, the other will choose to violate and defeat him (upper right and lower left cells). Therefore, they both avoid entering the covenant and consider remaining in a state of war as a rational option (lower right cell).

Hobbes solves the problem by imagining that the players agree to institute a sovereign, charging him with the task of keeping peace by threatening the violators of the covenant with punishment—that is, with losses greater than the gains they could expect from their breach of faith. The sovereign alters the matrix in the following way:

	E	V
E	4,4	2,1
V	1,2	3,3

in which peace > war > defeat > penal sanctions.

When a player violates the covenant, he is punished. Instead of gaining from the violation, he will suffer from it and, indeed, can be sentenced to death. The choice of the upper right or lower left cell being therefore irrational, each player will be confident that the other will not violate the covenant. Thanks to the sovereign, therefore, both will choose to enter and keep the pact.

The obvious difficulty here is to explain how any agreement can be reached when the leviathan is not yet in operation and nobody is in awe of a punishing authority. But I think it is important to discuss this traditionally mentioned difficulty after having delineated two different, if related, problems. The first leads one to ask with what resources a leviathan (a state with a penal system) is set up. Given that the leviathan is to be seen as an apparatus producing norms, how are its costs paid? Where do the resources come from? The second question leads one to ask how the rationality of the activity of producing norms can be established so that somebody is led to engage in this activity. I will deal with these last two difficulties in the next two sections and will tackle the traditional one following these.

THE RESOURCES NEEDED
TO PRODUCE NORMS

Let us suppose, first, that the original agreement has been reached. A sovereign, a third agent—an authority of sorts—has been chosen to punish the violators of the covenant and, thus to alter the original matrix. More generally, this authority is asked to distribute selective incentives (either negative, such as punishments, or positive) so that the positive tradeoffs included in the upper right and lower left cells become negative. In the usual examples of the production of public goods, some authority is present. Thus, the administration punishes those who fail to perform the fiscal contract. The trade union distributes benefits to its members so that they observe the duties of membership and engage in the collective action on which the leadership decides. The army distributes decorations to those who do not defect in hard circumstances. The resources needed to intervene with penal sanctions, to mobilize help, or to invest a symbolic act with values have already been produced. All these resources are assumed to be external to the game.

Do we know how they have been produced? We can only assume that they are public goods themselves. This means that their production engenders the same problem that is present in the dilemmas the intervention of the authority is considered to solve. In other words, public goods seem necessary to create the conditions for the production of public goods.

The question can be stated as follows. When two or more actors who enter a pact do not trust each other, they need to be guaranteed that breaches of faith will not occur. This can happen in two ways. They can set up a third person empowered to use incentives, negative or positive, so that breaching faith will be considered too costly; this we may call the *leviathan* model. Or they can both transform their original definition of interest so that they come to consider it rational not to defect; this we may call the *conversion* model.

The leviathan model encounters the difficulty mentioned above. It has to explain the origin of the resources needed for setting up a penal apparatus. In other words, it has to determine who will pay the costs of the leviathan. Hobbes's answer is deceptively simple: The leviathan incurs no costs at all. The conditions stipulated in the covenant imply that the subjects will not resist the commands of the sovereign. All but one of the parties to the covenant have divested themselves of their rights, hence of their powers, to disregard the norms of the sovereign. Their natural right to use whatever means are necessary to secure self-preservation is absolute but inachievable. The convenant leaves only one party with the absolute right to use any means necessary to secure the preservation of the collectivity: This is the sovereign (a person or an assembly). It would be irrational for the subjects not to comply with his (its) commands. No repressive apparatus is therefore needed.

If this is Hobbes's position, why is there any talk of the sword at all? To clarify this point, we need to introduce a distinction, which Hobbes himself neglects to spell out explicitly, between two kinds of rationalities. One is *public* rationality, which prescribes public peace and hence loyalty to the commonwealth. The other is *private* rationality, which prescribes the use of whatever means are advantageous for self-preservation—hence, if necessary, private conflict and breach of faith. In other words, rationality prescribes public trust and private mistrust. To prevent breaches of faith, the sovereign will intervene with his sword of justice. But no repressive apparatus is needed because it is rational for subjects to obey the sovereign's commands when they are commanded to help him prevent private disputes or punish transgressors.

If this interpretation is correct, the leviathan model—intended to explain the possibility of trust—comes very close to its opposite, the conversion model. A reading of the process of authorization seems to confirm this convergence. This is the process by which the parties to the pact empower the sovereign by transferring to a new collective entity the resources that are essential to them as persons—*words* and *actions*. "A person is he, whose words or actions are considered, either as his own, or as representing the words or actions of another man. When they are considered as his own, then, he is called a natural person" (Hobbes 1960, p. 105). Also, "of persons artificial, some have their words and actions *owned* by those whom they represent. And then the person is the actor, and he that owns his words and actions is the *author*" (Hobbes 1960, p. 105). It is as if each person naturally owns his words and actions, and these could be transferred to another agent "to the end he may use this strength and means of them all" (Hobbes 1960, p. 112). Preservation and duration are achieved only by transferring this individually defined but impermanent and never fully achieved identity to some collective entity. Identification in a collective person provides the essential context for norm production.[3]

Difficulties do not cease here, however. If we consider the process of norm production as made possible by bestowing trust on a third party, and if we consider it as a form of collective conversion, we are left with something unexplained. Consider the first. We are required to explain how the trustworthy third party is chosen. But trust can only be the fruit of past experience, and this is not conceivable in the state of nature, where duration and recognition of individual identities are excluded. Their presence would imply the very civil society the covenant is called to constitute.

Second, we are required to determine the population whose conversion empowers a sovereign. Definite boundaries are needed to establish who must obey and who is entitled to be protected. But how are such boundaries set, and by whom? If we assume that the process of authorization takes place within *natural* boundaries, which set distinctions between one population and another, and that these distinctions are recognizable, then we again assume that identifiable societies are already at work.

THE RATIONALITY
OF PROVIDING NORMS

The reasons for the producer and enforcer of norms to engage in such an activity seem mysterious. Why should one make the effort (and possibly pay the costs) of engaging in it? Of course, any single specialized producer of norms can draw wages from the activity, and therefore, for him, the rationality of these actions can involve some maximizing of utilities. (This cannot be said, however, of nonspecialized producers of norms, such as parents who produce and enforce norms for their children, possibly at great cost.) But if there is rationality in that specific activity, it should be such that it causes *higher* wages to be drawn for *better* norms. Is it possible, then, to establish the rationality of bestowing higher rewards for better norms? This would imply that somebody is capable of evaluating the degree of good of the norms and would retribute its procedures accordingly. And it would require determining some equivalence of amounts of goodness with amounts of usefulness, a rather difficult task.

The reconstruction of the process of authorization just sketched seems to provide the reason for the activity of producing norms. Authorization has been described as a process through which a person, the author, makes his own identity that of another person, the actor. The latter represents the words and actions of the former and becomes his *mask* or *persona* (Hobbes 1960, p. 111). When the rights of a multitude of authors have been transferred to the actor, the actor is made capable of acting. Moreover, since the actor wears a mask, as it were, he can be recognized as a durable and identifiable unity. The wills of the multitude of authors have been reduced to one will, the will of the collective actor. It is not simply that this multitude of individuals *consents* to the will of the collective artificial actor; they *coincide, identify,* with his (Hobbes 1960, p. 112).

It will be clear now that the rationality of the activity of producing and enforcing norms follows the circumstances in which the producer of norms and the receivers of norms are not to be conceived as separate entities. Each author within this multitude of subjects *authorizes* "all the actions and judgements of that man or assembly of men, in the same manner, as if they were his own" (Hobbes 1960, p. 113). The multitude of men, by the process of authorization, is made one person (Hobbes 1960, p. 107). The process of law-giving, therefore, is to be thought of as a process by which one person (artificial or natural) is giving norms to himself "because every subject is by this institution author of all the actions and judgements of the sovereign instituted."[4] But because norms, by definition, regulate future action, *giving norms to oneself* simply defines the best use of means to reach the natural aim of the natural person—self-preservation. This should be seen as being achieved (1) through identification with the durable collective person artificially created and (2) in the observance of the norms that regulate its life. The rationality of the activity of norm-making consists, therefore, of producing those norms that promote the duration of the collective persons thanks to which the single individual human being is able to pursue his singular self-preservation.

THE DIFFICULTY OF CONCEIVING
THE ORIGINAL AGREEMENT

It is time to deal with our third question: How is the original agreement possible so that self-regarding individuals can institute social order? This is the traditional question all contractarian theorists must solve.

The PD matrix has the merit of having illuminated the interactive structure of this contractual situation so as to show that no endogenous solution is logically possible unless certain conditions are relaxed. Several solutions have consequently been suggested. I shall briefly examine the two most typical solutions and point to what they imply.

The first solution is usually referred to as the "prisoner's dilemma supergame." It considers the game of the two prisoners as not played just once, but iteratively. It shows that if it is rational for a player to defect when the game is played only once, it can become rational to cooperate if the players are instead faced with the possibility of an indefinite number of games. By cooperating, a player induces the other player to respond by also cooperating, thus opening the possibility of stabilizing a better Pareto optimum equilibrium.[5]

This solution implies logically that the number of games be strictly indeterminate. If a player knows which is the final game, he will find it rational to defect. But this makes the outcome of the last game a foregone conclusion so that the penultimate game effectively becomes the last, and the previous argument will apply to it. By backward induction, it will then become rational to defect at the very first game.

In practice, one could observe that more than one real-life situation comes close to an iterated game in the sense of the last transaction remaining indeterminate. The idea of "being in business together" and avoiding cheating in order not to lose the advantages of future cooperation is a feeling that one can consider habitual in economic and social life. One could even define institutions just by saying that their function is to make mutual expectations of iteration normal. The notion of social roles, or positions, as patterns of interaction that last independently from the physical continuity of the incumbents induces and stabilizes the idea that to defect would deprive one of the future advantages of cooperation. The possibility of counting on future cooperation between agents is indeed what social life is made of. But the mental experiment of imagining a state of nature has a meaning only if one uses it to investigate a situation in which the condition of continuity and, hence, of recognition of an individual as being the same throughout different interactions does not operate.

It is true that in his answer to the "fool," Hobbes implies that a sort of iterated game is possible in the state of nature. This would explain why the fool is wrong in thinking that reneging on a covenant when the other party has already performed his part is rational. Hobbes strongly maintains that to do that would be foolish because defecting would deprive the defector of the advantages of future cooperation. It would also give him a bad reputation and make it difficult for him to enter into future covenants. Clearly here, for Hobbes, the conditions of the state of nature are radically relaxed. Both time and identification of the participants are introduced.[6]

Imagining iterated games does not, therefore, offer a solution to the problem of the emergence of cooperation. It assumes what is to be demonstrated—that is to say, the possibility of a durable identity of the parties and of the repetition of the circumstances of a game. To consider the nature of iteration, however, can be of help. It reminds one that behind the question of how cooperation emerges, one finds the questions of how social institutions operate to assume conditions of relative permanence for human transactions and of what can ground the capacity for achieving that task.

It has also been suggested that the original context of the contract be conceived not as a PD but as a type of *coordination game*.[7] These games occur where two or more persons face the problem of coordinating their actions in the pursuit of common ends. Their interests in cooperating coincide, hence no contract is needed. "The benefits of the bargain are sufficient to motivate the parties to perform the actions agreed on" (Hampton 1986, p. 142). Because each party exploits "suitably concordant mutual expectations" (Lewis 1969), the pursuit of ends is successful for all or for none. When a solution to the game is envisaged such that it appears convenient to each party, each party will know that the other will adhere if he himself adheres, and this will be sufficient for him to conform. Whereas it was impossible, as Emile Durkheim has shown, to think of a contract without first conceiving of an institution that made the contract possible, the same logical presupposition does not seem to be needed for the kind of (implicit) agreements that give the solution to coordination games.

The agreement that institutes this state could therefore be conceived as a solution to a coordination game. Each party to the game knows that all the other parties share the same interest in escaping the status quo. None, however, can attempt to pursue this aim alone, and together they have to find a way to coordinate their actions toward a common solution. They need a clue, a focal point (Schelling 1960, pp. 57–58). The idea of the state provides such a focal point and thus provides a solution to the game. Once the solution is introduced, if an individual would refuse it—hence, hold out of, or defect from, the collective action—he would behave irrationally. The individual would become a lone warrior; he would have the organized force of the collectivity against him and would therefore incur much higher costs than would be met by adhering to the convention. To take a simple view of a similar state of affairs, imagine a population of car drivers using the convention of driving on the right-hand side of the road: No driver would be judged to be in his right mind if he defected from that convention. Or imagine a community of speakers using a certain language: No imaginable self-interest would lead any of the speakers to defect and use a different language. Communication, which is the very end of language, would be frustrated. The same reasoning is applied to the state. As the adherence to the rule of driving on the right-hand side of the street is the best means to avoid accidents, and the adherence to the rules of a certain language is the best means to succeed in communicating with other members of a certain community, by analogy abiding by the rules of the state is conceived as the best means to achieve the fundamental need of human beings—self-preservation.

But considering the state as merely the prominent solution to a coordination problem leads one to the same dilemma I formulated above. The state is a clearly bounded collectivity. The set of the individuals entering a convention or, in general, participating in a coordination game should be distinguished from the set of the excluded ones. How, then, are the boundaries established? On the other side, if the state is the outcome of a process of coordination, why is coercion needed? Moreover, if breaking away from the state of nature is seen as the solution of a PD brought about by the intervention of the state, then the question of how the state is formed finds no answer, as its formation can only be the outcome of a game to which the very intervention of an already existing third party (the state) is the only solution. If, on the other hand, breaking away from the state of nature is seen as the solution to a coordination game in which all participants have common interests, then it is a mystery as to why the state is armed with instruments of force.

A partial way out of this dilemma may be found by distinguishing the good of self-preservation from other types of good. Indeed, one can suggest that all the goods human beings desire are of two kinds. The first kind is made of the good of *self-preservation*. All the other desirable goods are of the second kind: *appropriation*. Securing the former is the aim of a coordination game, and, hence, cheating and holding out are self-defeating. We are in the domain of public rationality. To trust is rational. Securing the goods of appropriation gives rise either to coordination games (driving on the same side of the road, for example) or to PD games. Here, mistrust is rational. Defecting and cheating have to be prevented by the threat of sanctions. The state as a penal institution becomes necessary. There, social coordination seems to be sufficient.

To set the scene in this way helps, but much is still unexplained. There should be a difference between coordination games that ensure self-preservation and games that take place in civil society, where a penal system is at work. The difference should hang on the nature of the first type of good, or value—self-preservation—which therefore needs to be explicated.

FROM SELF-PRESERVATION
TO MUTUAL RECOGNITION

At first, the concept of self-preservation could be read merely as supplying a biological metaphor for the modern, more abstract concept of utility. Thus, establishing the value of a good for self-preservation would be equivalent, in today's terminology, to establishing the utility of that good. This equivalence, however, does not hold. Whereas the concept of utility expresses a certain relationship of the individual with the object of his desires, the notion of self-preservation expresses a relationship between persons. Remember that what makes self-preservation arduous, or impossible, is the state of war. This is defined in relational terms. It is a certain *type of interaction* among parties—one of enmity, force, and fraud. Hobbes makes it clear that the use of force and fraud as such is not rational, is forbidden by the second law of nature, and is therefore not the consequence of some "natural" disposition of human beings to attack each other. Rather, it is due to a relationship of mistrust. The disposition of human beings would be to entertain peaceful relationships with each other, only they cannot trust the other to act with the same end in mind. Not knowing what the others will do, they think they have reason not to trust them. Mistrust is rational in ignorance, as use of force is rational in self-defense. It follows that peace must be seen as occurring not when violence is made impossible but when *trust is made possible*. Were the aggression or just the presence of others the only cause of fear and distress in the state of nature, such fears could be avoided by individuals insulating themselves from others. But solitude is not a solution Hobbes envisages to the anxieties and fears of the individual. He deems "solitary" to be an undesirable attribute of the life men are leading in the state of nature. And in any case, it would be difficult to see how from such a solution one could then explain the emergence of society. If people, therefore, think that they can break out of the state of nature by forming a civil society among them, they must think that they have something in common "naturally" that they do not have with the rest of nature. And one cannot perversely suggest that this common attribute can be found in the capacity to entertain mutually harmful relationships. Human beings can also harm and be harmed by animals. If human beings harm each other, it is out of mistrust. When mistrust ceases, self-preservation is made possible, and the other person is recognized, for some reason, as *worth preserving*. Everything hangs, therefore, on the reasons one can find for such a recognition.

One would think that there are reasons grounded in self-interest. I can imagine myself planning to use another human being to my ends. I, the master, may recognize the slave as worth preserving. I need him. But I cannot imagine myself planning this strategy in the state of nature. Remember that the state of nature is a state of war because of the circumstances that no one can long muster more power than another. Individuals are more or less equal, and no machinery can be set up to exploit others or reduce them to slavery. Moreover, if a machinery of power were built, some confederacy of individuals would join together to subjugate others. To do so they must trust each other, and there must be some ground in order for this trust to be formed. We are back to the argument above. Equality among people makes cooperation (among some) a premise for exploitation (of others). But the cooperation of the first group still must be predicated upon some trust. This implies an original relationship where the worth of the other to be preserved is recognized, which is what we need explained. There is no way, therefore, to prove that human beings originally consider other human beings as worth preserving only with the view of using them. There should be some other reason.

The following seems more compelling. My fundamental aim that I be preserved in time cannot be achieved when I insulate myself from other human beings. I need other human beings to judge that I am worth preserving. Do they have grounds for doing so? They certainly have. Consider: They themselves need to be recognized by me as worth preserving. Needing the same recognition, I will act as a mirror. Preservation of self, real *formation of self*, is the outcome of this interaction. One's being in awe of some authority coercing or inducing human beings to refrain from harming each other is, therefore, not—as such—what leads to the preservation of individual selves, nor is the gain one individual could receive by using the resources another could produce. The original resource a human being can offer to another is the capacity to recognize the worth of the other to exist—a resource that cannot be produced if it is not shared.

An interesting point of morals should be seen in this account of the original phase of socialization. Recognizing the other human being as an end in itself, and recognizing the same human being as a means to the end of preserving oneself are as being united. The contradiction between a morality, which requires the former attitude, and an instrumental rationality, which requires the latter, is eliminated. The good of self-preservation is achieved when mutual recognition between human beings is also achieved. The fact that recognizing the other brings about the reciprocal recognition oneself needs does not make this attitude merely instrumental. Oneself is *constituted* by the recognition the other bestows upon him. The very relationship's means-to-ends is inconceivable in this account. The capacity for oneself to calculate the means needed to reach some end is predicated on the achievement of the relationship of reciprocal recognition. To calculate, one needs to measure, and without one's measures being recognized, one cannot measure. No "private measuring" makes sense.

One can now say that the concept of the coordination game can be a good way of describing a precontractual mode of agreement in first approximation. But one has to assume that the parties enter into these types of agreements with preconstituted interests. How the interests have emerged—or, more precisely, how the identities of the persons bearing those interests have been constituted—is not explained. Referring to a previous process by which each party recognizes that the others are entitled to participate in the game seems inescapable. This is what I have called (with Hobbesian terminology) the mutual recognition that the other is worth preserving.

Once mutual recognition is assured, individuals pursue their singular projects of self-preservation through processes of appropriation. In the endeavor to pursue individually defined ends, each agent can find it rational to cheat. Enforceable norms are, therefore, needed to regulate the agents action. However, human beings do not merely find themselves back to a state of nature with a sovereign added. Unlike the state of nature, now they have received an identity, and they may count on being recognized by some circles of others. These circles make recognition durable and, hence, trust rational. Individual interests grow out of different positions in the networks and circles of recognition.

FROM MUTUAL RECOGNITION TO
SOCIAL CONTINUITY AND INDIVIDUATION

To sum up, what Hobbes defined as a *right of nature*—that is, "the liberty each man hath, to use his own power . . . for the preservation of his own nature"—has been construed as being grounded on the achievement of a state of mutual recognition between individuals (1960, p. 84). Therefore, for a social order to be possible, the individuals who will be part of this order must first recognize each other's worth of being preserved, or—in a different terminology—of entering the game. They do this through forming identities and conceiving of their recognized selves as being identical in time. The recognized others will be conceived of similarly. It is as if a sort of "conspiracy of identities" were at work. Individuals threatened by nature to impermanence get together to simulate reciprocal recognition and thus lend each other (relatively) stable identities. The momentariness of their acts is thus cancelled, concealed, or merely controlled. They can now live as if they will last. If these are the circumstances of self-preservation, defecting, cheating, or riding free are of no use. All this would simply amount to depriving oneself of duration.

Self-preservation is thus used as a *relational* concept. And such it has to be, if—as it was originally intended—it is used to overcome the uncertainty that exists due to the relativity of moral values. What is common to all human beings, irrespective of the culture in which each lives, should therefore be seen as consisting of the fact that they all need to see the worth of their preservation recognized by other human beings. The interpersonal reality thus achieved will then allow the specific endeavor of each *now-socialized* individual toward self-preservation to be cast in the form of some socially defined appropriation (contract, role, ownership, and the like). Here, the identification of each individual becomes specific. Individuals receive names as members of families, incumbents of roles, parties in contracts, owners of property, and so on. A legal system with enforceable norms will define what is allowed and what is expected by these name-bearing individuals. Recognizing is followed by name-giving, which is sanctioned by norm-giving.

Hobbes has long been seen as inaugurating a totally new tradition in social thought, one defined as symmetrically opposed to the tradition derived from Aristotle.[8] The latter considered man as a *social* being. And social beings were—first of all—fathers or sons, husbands or wives, workers or owners, citizens or foreigners. They were defined by the roles society assigned them. The new view (from Hobbes on) was described as assuming as a unit of analysis the individual as such, before—as it were—his entry into society. Hence, the need to solve the problem of how individuals can join together and agree to form a society. The contractarian tradition from Hobbes to the present has considered this as its central problem. It cannot be otherwise if the view of some unsocialized, unidentifiable individual is the premise for reasoning about social reality.

By engaging in an explication of the concept of self-preservation, and by showing how the apparent "naturality" of the desire to conserve oneself has deceived its users into misunderstanding the logically inescapable grounding of self-preservation in mutual recognition, I have meant to draw a different picture from that of the contractarian tradition. The fiction of individuals not yet involved in social relations but originally knowing what their interests are and what the consequences of their choices can be is discarded in favor of a view in which the interaction between persons mutually recognizing their right to exist is the only originally conceivable reality. No preestablished interests are imagined. The individual human agent is constituted as such when he is recognized and named by other human agents. No original agreement is presupposed, only the acknowledgment that the presence of other people is necessary for acting. Before becoming a possible means for individual ends, the interaction with others appears as an end in itself. The very individual ends emerge on the premise that such an interaction, or webs of interaction, is possible. But there is more. "Recognizing" must be completed by giving names. One cannot avoid it if one wants recognition to last. Thus, one receives an *identity* through time. Hobbes says it well: Names are marks "to remember thereby somewhat past, when the same is objected to his senses again" (Hobbes 1839, IV, p. 20).

It has been observed that "to say of anything that it is identical with itself is trivial, and to say that it is identical with anything else is absurd. What then is the use of identity?" (Quine 1987, p. 90). The use of identity, in the description I am giving, is to designate a state in which the subject is acting on the assumption that when the events that will follow his action occur, the individual will judge them as he is judging them now, in anticipation. But because the subject cannot judge, as we have seen, without some reference criteria that others share, his identity will depend on others recognizing it. In the individual's *foro interno*, one may think he does not hesitate to refer to some future acts as being of the same person acting now. But if he does not find anybody to share this reference, such a confidence would be of no use. Were situations of this kind diffuse and long-lasting, individuals would find themselves in despair, and social order would fail. There is, therefore, an answer to the question about the use of identity. It tells us that social institutions are to be seen as set up to maintain the series of actions that appear intelligible because they are referable to subjects defined as identical in time. By this I mean that to understand the specific working of an institution, one would have to describe the kind of identities it leads individuals to assume. And to understand the differences between societies, and between moments within the same society, one would have to describe the different types of individual identities that are produced and that allow series of actions to be predicted.

I have stressed the process through which reciprocal recognition, giving names, and forming identities produce social stability and continuity. But the same process generates individuation and distinction. Names lend continuity to their bearers and allow identity to be formed through successive recognitions. At the same time, they allow individuals to bear durable marks of distinction and, hence, entertain assurances that their life plans will produce consequences and that these will continue to be imputed to them as the agents they are now. Not only the moral and the legal communities will call these individuals singly *responsible* for their acts, but they themselves will generally see themselves as being so and act accordingly. Instituting responsibility implies instituting continuity of selves.

Such a process will not be a single one for each individual. Multiple processes of recognition will cross and overlap. They are generated by the different circles to which a person is exposed. To paraphrase W. V. Quine

(1987, p. 28), there are multifarious ways of getting at the identities of persons. We can define social order as the state in which these identities all link up across society in a coherent network.

There are times when that coherence weakens or is missed. Some call these times "identity crises." We do not know whether the meanings we intend to give to our life plans anticipate what others will uncover in them. We become insecure. But this is not something happening within each of us. It is the language used around us to define identities that seems to escape our grasp. Not being clear about how others will evaluate the worth of our actions, we have difficulty communicating with others about ourselves—indeed, we have doubts about the meaning our actions could receive. We may express such feelings by saying that we fear others are unable, for some reason, to give precise boundaries to our identity. This generates uncertainty about what belongs to us, what consequences can be ascribed to our action, and what alterations will derive for our identity.

BOUNDARIES OF IDENTITY
AND THE FEUD GAME

Why do I need the notion of boundaries to describe the formation of identities? Consider how this notion is used in defining a convention. Sanctions for transgressing a convention reside in the very circumstance of finding oneself outside the boundary of the population observing that convention. One who *transgresses* a norm is in fact *transgressing* certain boundaries. Now, think of a circle of persons recognizing the worth of another person. For the recognition to be of value, the recognizers have to be conceived as enjoying some recognition themselves. They therefore have to belong to some identifiable collective body, defined by social boundaries of sorts. A social boundary is any sign that allows a social entity to be recognized as distinct. Until the boundary holds, that entity will be conceived as being the same. Social institutions provide for boundaries and distinctions to be recognized and to endure. The institution of property is one such boundary. The institution defining positions (roles, statuses, and the like) in the organization of work is another. So is the nation-state.

For this last, the use of the concept of boundary seems more compelling. It is used to describe not only the state but also the nature of being a member of that state. Indeed, it is held that the duty to defend the boundaries of a state can represent the very essence of being a member of that state. But what makes this so? What exactly is defended when boundaries are defended? For whom is it an advantage that certain boundaries are preserved? We are returning to the core Hobbesian problem: To whom does one owe political allegiance? And the Hobbesian answer that we owe allegiance to the sovereign who is able to protect us only goes halfway. It comprises the situation of civil disorder and the case of the sovereign who is incapable of solving conflicts and protecting citizens from crime. But, strangely, it is inconsistent if applied to external war. Consider: In the case of a *total* war in which all the subjects of a sovereign would be killed, in case of defeat by the enemy army, no problem of political obligation emerges. The subjects would have no alternative. They would have to stay with their sovereign and their fellow subjects and win or be killed with them. But if, on the other hand, the war is *not* total, the nature of the protection the sovereign is meant to provide—and in exchange for which the subjects should owe him allegiance and follow him in defending the boundaries of the state— is left undefined. What is protected and what is defended in such a case?

Surely one would not express oneself by saying that it is *useful* for a person to defend the boundaries of his state. If these fall, if the individual citizens of a state become citizens of another state, their profits and wages and their wealth in general could increase or stay the same. And yet, they often go to war to defend those boundaries. Or, in other cases, people fight and suffer deprivation because they want their territory to become independent and to form a different state. Some of them could die in going to war, or resist and struggle, and their memory is honored because they have done something for the recognition of the boundaries in question. Often, public discourse calls such a recognition "freedom." At times, the object to be defended or achieved is called the "identity" of that population. It seems that by confirming or conquering those boundaries, the individual members of that population want to be recognized as a separate collectivity of persons. Would that attempt fail, their own personal identities would be felt to be at stake.

The argument of utility, I repeat, does not explain those facts. Some stronger link must be at work connecting the processes of macro- and micro-recognition. It is as if those members of the collectivity I have depicted fighting for the recognition of its boundaries and identity acted because they felt that the way they daily recognize each other and appreciate each other's worth would be altered, impaired, or obscurely threatened if these boundaries fell. Only by imagining such a link can one make sense of the Hobbesian view according to which a state, defined by precise boundaries, represents the answer to the original individual need of self-preservation.

STATE AND LOCAL IDENTITIES

Let us now consider the general (and typically Hobbesian) issue of a state attempting to incorporate a local identity (a clan, a tribe, an ethnic or religious minority, or similar group) and encountering resistance of some kind. The state has two main ways to overcome this resistance. One is the use of penal sanctions, which are meted out to individuals who abide by the norms of their group rather than by the norms of the state. The state can apply penal sanctions; the local group cannot (if the local group can apply penal sanctions, the case is mixed and I will not deal with it here). The individual is then confronted with a choice. On the one side are the negative consequences of violating the laws of the state, which can be the loss of liberty or the loss of life. On the other side, one finds the loss of "local" identity. Historically, it has often been the case that people have chosen to incur penal sanctions rather than to lose their local identity. The theory I have been developing suggests the reason. Losing one's identity entails nullifying the circumstances in which one sees oneself recognized by others he can recognize. The standards by which one evaluates what is positive or negative for him are then left without any possible validation. One who would submit to the rules of the state and relinquish his identity would also be made incapable of judging the real import of the consequences of what he does.

It would seem that the import of the loss of liberty is easily gauged and so, even more, the import of the loss of one's life. How can one fail to judge that losing one's life is more serious than losing one's identity? That many make such a choice seems puzzling, but it should not be. Identity, being defined by the recognition by a circle of others, may go beyond life and refer to memory. When circles of recognition are strong (as is the case for religious groups, warrior groups, ideological movements, large families, dynasties, clans, and tribes), they have a well-organized capacity for memory. Penal machineries, even including capital sanctions, are generally weak against local identities with strong memories.

When, then, can the state be stronger than local identities? When it offers a stronger recognition. But when is recognition stronger and when weaker?

The state may bestow identity upon individuals by recognizing them as citizens. Citizenship is a mode of identity, but, as such, it is rarely a strong one. Strong identities are those that allow an individual both to be clearly recognized and to offer recognition in return. The opportunity of offering recognition in return leads to making distinctions. One separates individuals one from the other and uses marks by which one can consider that some of them are "different." The determination of a difference is essential for the maintenance of the identity. The identity of citizenship performs this function in its pure mode only in the situation of war, or in situations similar to war. It is likely that a state in war against other states could easily break, within its territory, the equilibrium a feud has established between local identities. It makes new boundaries become prominent and their protection become constitutive of the individual identity of every single citizen (to the extent that the citizen identifies with the state). By participating in the protection of common boundaries, a sort of mutual recognition emerges between the state and the citizen.

The case of war and of threatened boundaries is not the only case in which the larger identity of the state appears stronger than the local identities it confronts. A larger identity is also strong when it *generates* local identities itself. All centralized states allow for some form of local identity and, of course, federal states even more so. But this is not what I have in mind, even if it is true that the strength of a state—other things being equal— is a function of the local identities that have been allowed or encouraged to take root in its territory. These local identities are grounded on preexisting foundations. The absolute state can be considered to have been supported for a period by the presence of traditional identities that it recognized or tolerated. When the liberal representative state abolished most of these, it seemed at first that the identity of citizenship was the only one it could afford to offer. Since such an offer could appear weak and leave people uninterested in citizenship, war was made a means by which to make the new boundaries prominent and the identification with the state stronger or inescapable. What came to the assistance of the cohesion of the liberal state was what Hobbes would have considered its mortal illness—the right for partial and partisan identities to be represented within the institutions of the state. The process of representation revealed itself to be a mechanism of the production of partisan local identities, or subidentities. In the very electoral act of choice, and—obviously—even more in becoming a member of some political party, association, movement, or other partisan group, the individual citizen accepts an identity that he will bear in common with other citizens and in the name of which he will operate and fight and generally act in a way that is easily recognizable, understandable, and predictable by the other members of the state. The same choice that attributes to the individual identity he will have in common with this group will also separate him from members of other groups. This will make partisanship the basis for a strong identity. Although its nature is "local," it is also somehow organically dependent upon the identity of the state. A sort of mutual recognition is predicated between the state and the partisan identity. Some would say that such is not always the case. It could be that one bears an identity that implies that one does not recognize the state and instead recognizes some higher (universalistic) identity to "complete" the local one. (This was the case of the socialist identities in many European states before World War I and of the Communist identities in liberal-democratic states later.) In turn, these identities were not recognized by the states within which they operated. But very often such a nonrecognition was a sort of fiction. The very practice of participating in the political life of a state made these purportedly anti-state identities a parcel of its fabric and contributed to the strength of the identity the state was capable of transmitting to its citizens.

In other words, the centralized identity of citizenship is, as such, weak and somehow one-sided. It can be strengthened by the presence of partisan local identities, even when they proclaim anti-state ideology, because of the very fact that they operate predictably according to the rules set by the state. These identities are strong because they can continuously set off one group from another and hence determine distinctions and oppositions, not only common ends. The action of the individuals is then shaped by the presence of prominent and immediately perceived distinctions. The same happens, as I said, to the state as a whole in a context of an international conflict.

Hobbes saw the state as the only agent of social order. The state could perform this task because it was the only organizer of a penal system. Were such the only weapon of the state, social order would not obtain, or not for long. If alternative sources of identity formation challenge the state, penal machineries do not suffice. In Hobbes's terms, they would suffice if the meaning of self-preservation were "physical survival." But because solitude as a way of survival is excluded, and the pact to escape the state of nature is among human beings and not with animals, not physical survival but recognition—hence, preservation of one's identity—is the meaning we should give, in the very texture of Hobbesian reasoning, to the fundamental human need of self-preservation.

We have seen that the state can be one source of identity formation, but it is not the only one. It is such when the enemies of the state on the one side cannot be ignored and on the other are felt by its members to be their personal enemies or are seen as so strange that no mutual recognition with them can be conceived. But these situations rarely prevail, at least in their pure descriptions. Within the state, partisan communities can be sources of identification. Outside of the state, innumerable forms also exist where the individual can live in a web of mutual recognitions that practically cover his whole life and assure continuity and boundaries.

It is now time to take up again the idea of authorization as conversion that I mentioned above. Such an interpretation implies that the subject abandon his standards of evaluating his interests and adopt the sovereign's judgment instead. Were such a "complete conversion" true, as Hampton notices, the threat of punishment and, in general, the penal apparatus would be rendered unnecessary. This disappears if one analytically separates the two possible realities of the state. The state regulating appropriations surely cannot be the object of the identification of its subjects and of the conversion of their utility functions. Its administration must use incentives, positive or negative, to produce public goods and to be alert against free riders. The state, however, is *potentially* the direct provider of the identity of its subjects or citizens. It is then made the object of identification and conversion, and its utility function tends to coincide with that of its citizens, and vice versa. When not the state, some other social entity provides the terrain where mutual recognition is possible. Some conversion of the utility function of the individual into a collective utility function then occurs.

CONCLUSIONS

I have gone a long way to answer my initial question. I have chosen to penetrate the territory of the theory of social order as the most abstract of, and apparently most impermeable to, the influences of "recent social changes." Within this territory, I have considered the individualistic theory of order in its more radical expression, as it is to be found in the work of Thomas Hobbes. I have examined its premises. It became clear to me that one could draw from these premises conclusions that turn out to be radically different from the conclusions traditionally attributed to the theory. Some of the clichés generally used to represent Hobbes's doctrine—that people are like wolves to each other and that, as a consequence, a coercive apparatus is needed to keep society in order—thus appear reversed. Those positions are derived from the idea that the rationality of individual action consists of pursuing the goal of self-preservation but that, to achieve this, human beings can neither avoid nor attack other human beings. They have, then, to engage in some pact with them. Such a pact becomes possible if human beings receive recognition from other human beings. The roots of social order are therefore to be found in this process of mutual recognition. The repressive apparatus of the state appears only as one of the many possible sources of social order. When it is needed, it is not to form a civil society out of "natural" individuals but rather to protect certain individuals from the aggressiveness of others who have been socialized in reciprocally incompatible ways.

Some would say that such a reading of Hobbes is anachronistic and ask whether Hobbes could be brought to accept my conclusions as a correct description of what he meant.[9] I must, therefore, justify my procedure. I shall do this by engaging in a sort of (Rortyan?) conversation with Hobbes. Unfortunately, I shall be the only one who speaks. Some other person would enter in the person of Hobbes and judge whether I have been persuasive enough. This is what I would say.

"I realize that the problem that moved me in reanalyzing your theory is very different from that (or those) that moved you in building it. Personally, I was puzzled by the impossibility of explaining certain facts with the tools of an individualistic theory of social action. Traditionally, one would call them, in a word, the facts of social cooperation. But I have stressed that they should include processes such as the formation of identities, collective and individual, setting up boundaries and distinctions between them and struggles for maintaining these distinctions. To understand why these phenomena escaped the understanding of the theory, I went back to its fully fledged formulation, and this was to be found in your work. I encountered a concept that was clearly foundational for the theory, and I discovered that it had not been explicated enough. This is why I dealt at length with the concept of self-preservation. It is through the explication of that concept that I have reached conclusions one would judge as rather distant from those you are considered to have reached. But I would propose that we set aside a confrontation of conclusions. What you have transmitted to centuries of Western political thought is the structure of the arguments you used. Your radical individualistic premises have been transferred from the theory of natural right and political obligation to which they belonged to a general theory of social action.

"This is why one returns to the analysis of your original premises and seeks to understand what they really implied. They implied more than you thought, and you did not care to be aware of that. Why should you have cared, after all? You had different problems in mind. Some would say that your real problem was to overcome the dualism of the personality of the ruler and the personality of the people, a residue of medieval political theory that tormented the school of natural law in your times.[10] You argued that the dualism was untenable and that the state had one single personality.[11] Some others would say that your real problem had to do with political obligation.[12] You argued that political allegiance was due to the sovereign who would be capable of protecting his subjects, not to the one who received their expressed consent. Some others would say that your real problem was to give a response to the moral skepticism that penetrated European culture in the wake of the new awareness of the relativity of all moral values among different populations.[13] And you proposed to consider that preservation of self was the value that could with certainty be considered common to all human beings. For all these questions and others, it was not necessary to decide whether preservation of self should merely mean survival of one's body or whether it referred to the preservation and recognition of one's identity. The idea that *solitude* was not a solution could safely be taken for granted (it was not foreign to the literary production of the epoch, however). No hitch was suspected.

"Your problems, whatever they were, were different from ours. To solve them, however, you set up a certain theoretical machine. The quasi-perfection of that machine is what makes a theorist today read your work rather than the work of other minor authors. That machine has been lent to a general body of theories, which used it independently of the problems they purported to solve. It is part of the working of this machine that I have tried to analyze. Similar interest has also brought the game theorists to your work. The difference is that they intend to streamline the machine, whereas I looked for the faulty piece. I knew it was there because the machine stopped working, or worked badly, when put to explain the phenomena I mentioned.

"I found that this piece lay where you fuse together survival of the body and preservation of the identity of the individual, physical fear and fear of the loss of recognition. This lack of distinction would not disturb your view of the state of nature. There, recognition of identity is in any case impossible, and every single choice seems not to be connected in that string of choices that we call 'person.' But in civil society, or in durable social interactions in general, that string of choices becomes a person. One would like to know how it happens. You call this person 'natural,' but it is obviously an artificial construct of our observational and interactional procedures. It is as artificial as the person you call artificial. And, in your process of authorization, you explain well how this is produced. Of the other, you seem to take the presence for granted. And yet, you are well aware of the constructivist nature of the operation of giving names which is no small matter for you. It is not natural, rather it is an artificial construct of our observational and interactional procedures, exactly as is the case for the person called artificial. Thus, the operation of giving names allows us to see unity in a series of choices of one individual. The possibility of social order proceeds from it. Receiving names goes together with receiving norms.

"Seeing things this way is not much different from how you also saw them. How would you explain otherwise that you should be so concerned with the 'poisonous effects' for the commonwealth of 'seditious doctrines'

(Hobbes 1960, p. 211)? You feared that those doctrines would assign names and norms in contrast to the sovereign and that disorder would ensue. If giving names and norms—constructing identities—is the essence of social order, then human institutions, in order to be valid and to endure, need absolute univocation.

"But now a paradox emerges. Private discourses about the commonwealth, you say, should be forbidden. What, then, is the nature of your own discourse? You assign, after all, names and norms. Surely you do not consider yourself one of those 'public ministers' of whom you say that they 'have authority to teach . . . the people their duty to the sovereign power' (Hobbes 1960, p. 158)? Your message seems to be addressed to a sort of bifurcated audience—the sovereign on the one side, the people on the other. Coherent with your view of the new scientific method, you meant your discourse to be *methodological*. As a consequence of heeding your message, the sovereign should have found the reasons for his own discourse. This would consist of producing norms according to the procedure you had established. The people should have found the reasons for stopping their discourses about norms altogether. In fact, neither the sovereign nor the people much heeded your message. You did not realize that as a very consequence of your discourse about scientific method, a new audience emerged. Political discourses were traditionally mediated by a theological class, which was interested in the substance of the conclusions. These were then transmitted to some popular audience. Some of your contemporaries could still derive prescriptions for action by what you concluded about political obligation. But it was inherent in the very intention of adopting for matters political the same method used in analyzing matters mechanical that the 'methodological audience' should prevail. Here names are used and identities defined, or—better—*redefined*, not as a way of formulating norms or acting upon them but rather as a way of distinguishing and understanding how people live in different moments and different societies. This is why your political message can be neglected, your methodological message received and refined. We do not read your work as sovereign or as subjects.

"Also, meta-name-givers, however, live among name-givers of the first level and speak in their public discourses. This is why our theorizing is affected by recent social changes and other 'contextual' minutiae, as was yours. And if we cast scaffoldings that reach the discourse of authors such as you, it is to try and be above impermanence, if just for a short while."

Thus I spoke to Thomas Hobbes. And no answer was expected.

NOTES

I presented this paper in several seminars and discussed it with several friends. In particular, I want to thank Pasquale Pasquino, Gunther Teubner, Antonio La Spina, Maurice Glasman, and Carlos Forment.

1. The reason I call Hobbes's theory "radically individualistic" will become clear in the following analysis. I know that in his classification of the theories of social

order, Jeffrey Alexander places Hobbes in the section dealing with "the collectivistic presupposition in its rationalist form" (Alexander 1982, pp. 98 ff). But he probably has in mind the *solution* Hobbes gives to the problem of order. The *presupposition*, though, is clearly individualistic. I would find it difficult to give a different name to a theory that assumes that the individual as such is asocial and comes before society is ordered and that the state is the product of individual will and individual calculation. As Leo Strauss says convincingly: "For Hobbes obviously starts not, as the great tradition did, from natural 'law,' i.e. from an objective order, but from natural 'right,' i.e. from an absolutely justified claim which, far from being dependent on any previous law, order, or obligation, is itself the origin of all law, order, or obligation" (Strauss 1952, p. viii).

2. The first clear expression of this corpus is to be found in Gauthier 1969. See then Ullmann-Margalit 1977; McLean 1981; Hampton 1986; Kavka 1986; Gauthier 1987; Sacconi 1986. One of the first definitions of the Hobbesian state of nature is in Rawls 1971, p. 269.

3. A similar solution is proposed by James Coleman (1986). He sees the process that makes a collective decision possible as a process of surrendering individual resources, which are then invested in a collective actor. The interests of this actor are seen as being essentially "interests in the future in contrast to [individual] interest in the present" (p. 316).

4. I am aware that this interpretation of the authorization argument comes close to the one sharply criticized by Jean Hampton (1986, pp. 208–220). But I think her criticism would fall if she makes the distinction between "public" and "private" rationality I suggested above, as well as the distinction between "self-preservation" and "appropriation" I develop below. Her argument cannot account for Chapter 16 of *Leviathan*. In fact, she does not quote it.

5. Cf. Taylor 1987; McLean 1981.

6. The discussion of how to interpret the answer to the fool is conducted in David Gauthier 1969 and Edna Ullmann-Margalit 1977.

7. This is the central argument in Hampton (1986). Implicitly, a large body of literature on the foundations of law is using the same kind of arguments; see, for example, John M. Finnis 1989; Gerald J. Postema 1982; and Noel B. Reynolds 1989. The two texts on which this literature is based are, of course, Thomas C. Schelling 1960 and David Lewis 1969.

8. Otto Gierke 1960; Norberto Bobbio 1965.

9. I use here Quentin Skinner's (1970) terms.

10. Gierke 1960.

11. Amos Funkenstein 1986, pp. 324–338, maintains that Hobbes keeps a dualistic position and that the state represents the teleological tension between nature and convention.

12. Skinner 1970.

13. Richard Tuck 1989; Pasquale Pasquino 1990; Stephen Toulmin 1989.

REFERENCES

Alexander, Jeffrey C. 1982. *Theoretical Logic in Sociology, Vol. 1: Positivism, Presuppositions, and Current Controversies.* London: Routledge and Kegan Paul.

Bobbio, Norberto. 1965. *Da Hobbes a Marx.* Napoli: Morano Editore.

Coleman, James. 1986. *Individual Interests and Collective Actions.* Cambridge: Cambridge University Press.

Finnis, John M. 1989. "Law as Co-ordination." *Ratio Juris* 2:97–103.

Funkenstein, Amos. 1986. *Theology and the Scientific Imagination.* Princeton: Princeton University Press.

Gauthier, David. 1969. *The Logic of Leviathan.* Oxford: Oxford University Press.

_____. 1987. "Taming Leviathan." *Philosophy and Public Affairs* 16:280–298.

Gierke, Otto. 1960. *Natural Law and the Theory of Society.* Boston: Beacon Press.

Hampton, Jean. 1986. *Hobbes and the Social Contract Tradition.* Cambridge: Cambridge University Press.

Hobbes, Thomas. 1960. *Leviathan.* Michael Oakeshott, ed. Oxford: Basil Blackwell.

_____. 1839. *English Works.* Sir William Molesworth, ed. Germany: Scientia Verlag Aalen.

Kavka, Gregory S. 1986. *Hobbesian Moral and Political Theory.* Princeton: Princeton University Press.

Lewis, David. 1969. *Convention—A Philosophical Study.* Cambridge, MA: Harvard University Press.

McLean, Iain. 1981. "The Social Contract in Leviathan and the Prisoner's Dilemma Supergame." *Political Studies* 29:339–351.

Parsons, Talcott. 1936. *The Structure of Social Action,* Vol. 1. Glencoe, IL: The Free Press.

Pasquino, Pasquale. 1990. *Hobbes: Natural Right, Absolutism and Political Obligation.* Unpublished paper.

Postema, Gerald J. 1982. "Coordination and Convention at the Foundations of Law." *Journal of Legal Studies* 11:165–203.

Quine, W. V. 1987. *Quiddities.* Cambridge, MA: Harvard University Press.

Rawls, John. 1972. *A Theory of Justice.* Oxford: Oxford University Press.

Reynolds, Noel B. 1989. "Law as Convention." *Ratio Juris* 2:105–120.

Sacconi, Lorenzo. 1986. *Teoria dei Giochi, Contratto Sociale e Giustizia Distributiva.* Milano: Politeia.

Schelling, Thomas C. 1960. *The Strategy of Conflict.* Oxford: Oxford University Press.

Skinner, Quentin. 1970. "The Context of Hobbes's Theory of Political Obligation." Pp. 109–142 in M. Cranston and R. Peters, eds., *Hobbes and Rousseau.* New York: Doubleday.

Strauss, Leo. 1952. *The Political Philosophy of Hobbes.* Chicago: University of Chicago Press.

Taylor, Michael. 1987. *The Possibility of Cooperation.* Cambridge: Cambridge University Press.

Toulmin, Stephen. 1989. *Cosmopolis: The Hidden Agenda of Modernity.* New York: The Free Press.

Tuck, Richard. 1989. *Hobbes.* Oxford: Oxford University Press.

Ullmann-Margalit, Edna. 1977. *The Emergence of Norms.* Oxford: Clarendon Press.

Social Control and
the Organization of the Self
(A Summary of the Original Paper)

Alessandro Pizzorno

Social control is a term of the sociological trade that seems to be intuitively understandable by ordinary thought. Moreover, the influence of the work of Michel Foucault has opened a new field of inquiry largely overlapping the classical field of social control. The central term used by Foucault is *discipline,* or *social discipline,* or—in some of his writings—*power.* At this point, one cannot deal with the field of processes covered by the terms social control or social discipline without bringing to light its relationship with those social theories that have been advanced for dealing with the Hobbesian problem of order. I shall, therefore, sketch a redefinition of three classical views of the problem of order. First comes the original Hobbesian view, which is the closest to classical political theory; I shall call it the *leviathan* view. Then comes what one could call the *market* view of order. Finally is what has represented, from Emile Durkheim to Talcott Parsons, the mainstream sociological view; I shall call this the *value integration* view.

The *leviathan* view maintains that social order is achieved through external—that is to say, material—coercion on individual action. The *market* view maintains that social order is achieved through a process of automatic coordination of the actions of individuals. The *value integration* view maintains that social order is achieved through the internalization of values.

That is to say, order can be achieved either by *repressing* conducts that can threaten it (this is what the leviathan is supposed to do) or by *inducing* the individual to behave in a way that falls into order (this is what both value integration and market achieve), *internally* to the individual (as does value integration) or *externally* (as does market). Effects are long-term in the case of value integration and short-term in the case of the commands of the leviathan or the incentives of the market.

Can a mode of producing order be conceived that coerces action lastingly? This fourth type of process is defined by saying that its effects become imprinted on the individual self and last long, possibly throughout life. Socialization of the child, military discipline, and sports provide examples of this mode of control. It operates via internalization but in a way that is different from the process of value integration. In disciplining, an original act of coercion is found, which then ceases. From then on, the individual

TABLE 1   Theories of Social Order

| | | MODES OF ACHIEVING ORDER | |
		by coercion	by inducement
DURATION OF EFFECTS	Short-term	(a) LEVIATHAN (Coercion of the body)	(b) MARKET (Specific incentives to action)
	Long-term	(c) DISCIPLINING (Coercion of the will)	(d) VALUE INTEGRATION (General orientations to action)

will regulate his or her own conduct. He or she has become a (self-) disciplined person and can thus be trusted by others.

The typology of the theories explaining how order is produced can be represented as shown in Table 1.

Within a theory of the upper row, one would say that the individual a chooses x instead of y because it is convenient for him or her to do so from the presence of a positive incentive or of a command that would include expectations of sanctions. By contrast, within a theory of the lower row, a is seen choosing x because he or she does not take into consideration the possibility of y. How is such a situation achieved? The answer is that in every society, institutions are at work that constitute persons in a certain way. Social order is simply seen as reproduced by the normal person, whose production is made possible by the working of social order. But the production of normal persons is never fully successful. One would expect that persuasive communication, in different guises, will be addressed to a. Preaching, teaching, and disciplining should be expected. Persuasion, propaganda, seduction, conversion, struggles for allegiance, and schism—innumerable forms for coercion of the will—are motivating and impelling courses of action where mere incentive and commands would be too weak or too costly to be tried. This is what the theories of the lower row make theirs. But theories of the lower row have to explain how an event occurring to some individual in time t still affects the choices of that individual in times $t_1, t_2, \ldots t_n$. Three types of theories can be proposed.

First, in the original molding of the self, some fundamental principle of action is instilled into the personality. Everyday choices of the individual maintain a connection with the fundamental component, assuring some constancy and predictability.

Second, the self is marked at some point in time by one or more "burning" experiences, which form it in a way that will prevent future resistance to the requirements of society.

Third, the self is recognized and received by some collective unit. A process of adjustment causes it to fit the requirements of that unit. The individual comes to feel agreement and recognition as enjoyable. The self, in the form that achieves recognition, will become the durable identity of the individual, contingent upon the duration of the recognizing collectivity.

Imagine now a society in which the following phenomena occur.

1. Discretion for the individual agent in productive tasks as well as expansion of freedom of choice in consumer behavior increase. The individual agent is allowed increasingly relative discretion in the modes of work. On the consumption side, the consumer is spurred to keep his or her demand at a constant and high level, and to that effect mechanisms of easy credit are devised. The single individual is required to care for his or her health according to predictable patterns. Through systems of insurance, he or she is required to distribute disposable income in fair proportions throughout his or her life cycle. The individual is required to choose, but to choose in a responsible way. Institutions are, therefore, devised to produce trustworthy individuals.

2. Credit or disgrace and reputation or blame are decreasingly attributed through direct, face-to-face interaction. Control of individual conduct is no longer assured by the eyes of the other. It is, rather, the outcome on the one side of the mechanisms of the production of disciplined persons and on the other of the surveilling eyes of the institutions systematically collecting information about the individual.

3. Competition among individual economic agents is decreasingly decided by the anonymous evaluations occurring within the market of goods and increasingly by the evaluations of other individuals in positions to judge. The individual bringing goods to the bureaucratic market tends to fashion itself as a complex organization, with recordkeeping, filing, and scheduling. The failures of the bureaucratic market being socially more threatening than the failures of the markets of goods, special institutions emerge. Welfare and therapeutic protection and control tend to care for a well-ordered exit of the unsuccessful.

4. Extension of individual political rights and distribution of political power tend to make the exercise of legitimate coercion more difficult.

Altogether, in our imagined society, several trends point toward an increase on the part of discipline among the mechanisms that produce social order. Coercion is less used. Market incentives work only within the framework of a disciplinary selection. The controlling effects of value identification are weakening. Disciplinary methodologies seem, therefore, to offer the crucial mechanisms for the maintenance of social order. More empirical research should provide us with a better knowledge of those mechanisms and examine whether the imagined society that has been proposed here for analytical consideration resembles the societies in which we live.

Comments

Rogers Brubaker

Professor Pizzorno does four things in this subtle and richly suggestive paper. First, he relates the changing agenda of social control theory to a secular curve of social disorganization and reorganization. Second, he invokes the Hobbesian problem of order, identifying three classical solutions and ordering them on two dimensions, staking out in this way the conceptual space for a fourth solution—a solution suggested by the new literature on social control. Third, Pizzorno contrasts two ways of thinking sociologically about individual persons and their conduct. One view takes individuals as consciously calculating choosers, oriented in their choices by stable sets of preferences. The alternative view takes individuals as developing, socially constructed selves and focuses attention on the social shaping of will and character. Last, Pizzorno sketches four sorts of changes in social structure, as a result of which social order depends increasingly on the production of disciplined, responsible individuals and decreasingly on state coercion, market inducement, and value integration.

Underlying this fourfold analysis is a double argument about social theory. On the one hand, Pizzorno develops a general argument for sociological attention to the social production of persons. On the other hand, he develops a specific argument for a broadly Foucaultian approach to this subject. This double argument can be neatly characterized with the help of Pizzorno's diagram (Table 1). On the one hand, Pizzorno defends theories of the lower row against theories of the upper row. Beyond the historical references to liberal and utilitarian thought, one detects here a defense of the traditional sociological project of accounting for the social production of persons and a critique of rational action theory for neglecting this topic. But having argued with the mainstream sociological tradition against rational action theory, Pizzorno then argues *against* the mainstream sociological tradition in favor of a different view of the social production of persons, based on the internalization of discipline rather than the internalization of values. This argument is both more original and more problematic than his general critique of rational action theory, and I shall focus my comments on it.

Although Michel Foucault is mentioned only twice in the paper, Pizzorno seems centrally concerned to make sociological sense of Foucault, particularly of *Discipline and Punish*. A number of characteristically Foucaultian motifs appear in the paper. The emphasis on the subtle shaping of persons rather than the mechanical control of behavior; the notion that discipline penetrates and permeates the individual; the idea that discipline individualizes, that it literally makes individuals; the concern with surveillance; the deemphasis on the overawing power of leviathan in favor of what Foucault calls the "humble modalities" of power—all of these themes are echoed in Pizzorno's paper.

This concern to make sociological sense of Foucault accounts for Pizzorno's otherwise puzzling concern with the Hobbesian problem of order. Pizzorno turns Foucault to sociological account by locating him in the conceptual space of sociological theory, by suggesting that Foucault provides a new and better solution to the perennial problem of order.

The idea that modern sociology developed with central reference to the Hobbesian problem of order—put forward half a century ago by Talcott

Parsons—has fared better than many other contributions of Parsons. Piz-zorno's paper testifies eloquently to the wide diffusion and staying power of this view. Yet the Hobbesian problem of order is a false problem, an artifact of Parsons's own analysis. As Charles Camic has shown, the problem of order arises only if we make certain rationalistic assumptions about action, assumptions that utilitarian theorists such as David Hume and Adam Smith did not, in fact, make. And Anthony Giddens has shown that the problem of order was not, in fact, a problem for Emile Durkheim. It is misleading, then, to characterize the development of social theory as a perennial struggle to solve the Hobbesian problem of order.

Even if one brackets this historical point and accepts the terms of the Hobbesian problem of order, Pizzorno's two-dimensional classification of solutions is problematic. One dimension is temporal. The processes that produce social order may be conceived as having fleeting or long-term effects. They may be understood, in other words, as shaping behavior from outside, as altering the situation of action but leaving the criteria of choice unchanged; or they may be understood as regulating conduct from within, by producing and transforming what Hume called the "springs and principles of action." Now, this is an important analytical distinction, although concretely even state coercion and market inducement, which Pizzorno treats as paradigmatic of fleeting interventions, are likely to leave long-term traces in the individual—habits of obedience, for example, or habits of calculation. My quarrel is not with this temporal dimension but with the second dimension of Pizzorno's scheme—the distinction between coercion and inducement, which Pizzorno uses to oppose a broadly Foucaultian conception of discipline to a broadly Parsonian conception of value integration.

The coercion-inducement distinction is triply problematic. First, it is logically unsatisfactory, being neither exhaustive nor mutually exclusive. Second, it is not very helpful in characterizing alternative approaches to the social production of persons. It fails even to distinguish Parsons and Foucault. For Parsons, the internalization of values occurs crucially in the family, beginning from earliest infancy, through mechanisms such as positive and negative reinforcement, inhibition, substitution, imitation, and identi-fication. Now this set of mechanisms includes elements of both coercion and inducement, plus others that cannot be classified as either coercion or inducement. A similar point could be made about Foucault. Pizzorno says that discipline begins "with an original act of coercion," which then ceases. Yet the inventory of disciplinary mechanisms in *Discipline and Punish* explicitly includes inducement as well as coercion, and Foucault emphasizes mech-anisms that escape the coercion-inducement distinction entirely—for example, the organization of the spacing and timing of activity.[1] It is artificial and misleading, then, to think of Parsons and Foucault as offering alternative solutions to the problem of order, based respectively on inducement and coercion.[2]

But there is a third and more fundamental problem. The coercion-inducement distinction is a false alternative. A theory of social order—or a theory of the social production of persons, as I prefer to say—need not choose between the two. Pierre Bourdieu's theory of the habitus, for example, bypasses this alternative entirely. And Bourdieu's theory, in my view, provides more powerful and flexible conceptual tools for the analysis of the social production of persons than the theories of either Foucault or Parsons.

Insofar as it is about theories of social order, then, the paper is problematic, both because the problem of order is a false problem and because the inducement-coercion distinction does not help one classify theories of social order or social control. The discussion of theories of social order, in my view, does more to obscure than to clarify the fundamental issues raised by the paper.

What are these issues? Let me try to specify them in conclusion. The central question raised, I think, concerns the match or mismatch between the social production *of* persons and the socially rooted demands *on* persons. These demands, Pizzorno suggests in the last section of his paper, have changed as a result of certain changes in social structure. These social structural changes include (1) the increasing discretion left to individual agents in production, consumption, and other spheres of life; (2) the declining significance of face-to-face interaction at the expense of the indirect relationships analyzed by Craig Calhoun (see Chapter 3); (3) the increasing allocation of economic rewards through the decisions of identifiable performance judges rather than through the impersonal processes of the market; and (4) the increasing legal and political encumbrances to the exercise of legitimate coercion. Under such conditions, Pizzorno suggests, social order depends increasingly on the production of disciplined, responsible individuals and decreasingly on state coercion, market inducement, and value integration.

Now, there is a functionalist tinge in Pizzorno's closing argument that I want to resist. Neither societies nor institutions necessarily get the types of persons that they "need." Nor do individuals necessarily get the types of dispositions that they need. Even if we agree that institutions increasingly "require" disciplined and self-disciplined persons, or that persons require self-discipline to manage their increasingly complicated lives, this does not mean that increasingly disciplined and self-disciplined persons will be produced. The social formation and re-formation of persons and their dispositions in families, schools, imagined communities, and remedial and auxiliary institutions obeys a logic of its own, which is not determined by— or necessarily compatible with—what persons or institutions could be said to need.

With the increasing uncoupling of instances of socialization from one another and from the various fields in which socialized agents must act, mismatches between the social production of persons and the socially rooted demands on persons are likely to become increasingly frequent and increasingly consequential. Perhaps it is such structurally generated mismatches that underlie Pizzorno's penetrating and disturbing observation that the social boundaries appear to be strengthening between responsible and nonresponsible populations, with the latter relegated to what Foucault calls disciplinary careers in a parallel cradle-to-grave world of remedial and custodial institutions.

NOTES

1. There are two further respects in which Foucault does not fit Pizzorno's classificatory scheme. (1) Theories of discipline, according to Pizzorno, differ from theories of leviathan in that the former emphasize the coercion of the will, and the latter the coercion of the body. The implication is that coercion of the will is durable, while coercion of the body is fleeting. Yet Foucault emphasizes the durable shaping and training (*dressage*) of the body, independently of any immediate influence on the will. (2) Theories of discipline, Pizzorno suggests, differ from theories of value integration in that the former emphasize control by specific persons, the latter a diffuse and impersonal mode of social control. In the former case, he says, decisions are made by somebody; in the latter, they are not. Yet Foucault emphasizes the anonymous, diffuse shaping of will and character, not the actions of specific decisionmakers. This emphasis on the diffuse ubiquity of power, this decentered and agentless conception of power, is crucial to Foucault's analysis of discipline.

2. To be sure, Pizzorno does not claim to be contrasting Parsonian and Foucaultian solutions to the problem of order. Yet he does introduce his typology as a typology of theories of order (although it later becomes a typology of mechanisms of the production of order). And if anyone can be said to hold the theories thus distinguished, it seems plausible to treat Parsons as the leading exponent of a theory of order based on value integration and Foucault as the leading exponent of a theory of order based on discipline. It does not seem unreasonable, then, to probe the usefulness of the distinction between the two "theories of the lower row" by seeing how well it would apply to Parsons and Foucault. If Pizzorno does not have Parsons and Foucault in mind in talking about theories of value integration and theories of discipline, whom does he have in mind?

Comments

Donald N. Levine

Chapter 7 differs substantially from the paper presented at the symposium. Although time does not permit me to compose an extended critique of Chapter 7, I shall make two comments on it.

First, I would take issue with Pizzorno's implication that the effort by Talcott Parsons in *The Structure of Social Action* (1937) represented the first attempt to reconstruct a sociological tradition. In particular, I would emphasize that two earlier attempts to reconstruct the sociological tradition were current in the sociological community at the time Parsons was writing his work: Park and Burgess's *Introduction to the Science of Sociology* (1921) and Pitirim Sorokin's *Contemporary Sociological Theories* (1928). Indeed, Parsons's reconstruction in *The Structure of Social Action* must be viewed in part as an attempt to challenge the conception of the sociological tradition offered in those two works.[1] One should note, moreover, that Park and Burgess as well as Sorokin cited Thomas Hobbes as a preeminent early figure in the tradition.

Second, I would support Pizzorno's interpretation, in contrast to that of Jeffrey Alexander, that with respect to his basic presuppositions about action, Hobbes must be viewed as an individualistic rather than a collectivistic theorist.

Professor Pizzorno's earlier paper was entitled "Social Control and the Organization of the Self." This was an extremely interesting piece, which posited three basic types of theories as explaining social control and then went on to inquire how each might be relevant to understanding the post-industrial system. I found that earlier piece enormously suggestive and hope that the following comments on it may both capture some of its insights and present points worth making in their own right.

There is much to respond to in Pizzorno's rich and stimulating paper. I am particularly struck by his concluding identification of four major changes that affect the organization of personal conduct in contemporary modern societies: (1) changes in the technology of work and the availability of easy credit have greatly increased the degrees of personal discretion in the activities of producers and consumers; (2) face-to-face controls in daily life have diminished and to some extent have been replaced by forms of institutional surveillance; (3) the primary arena of occupational competition has shifted from large impersonal markets to smaller-scale bureaucratic settings; and (4) the dispersal of political power has made the exercise of legitimate coercion more difficult.

Rather than address those propositions—discussion of any one of which could easily fill the space alloted to me—I shall confine my substantive comments to the summary proposition with which Pizzorno concludes: *All of these changes conspire to create an order in which society increasingly relies on individuals who have been disciplined to act in a trustworthy manner.* On the way to doing that, however, I wish first to comment on other matters in Pizzorno's paper by way of glossing the more general theme of this conference: how to use social theory more effectively to help us analyze the formations of contemporary society. Let me set forth three maxims.

OPENLY ACKNOWLEDGE AND TAKE ACCOUNT OF THE ESSENTIAL AMBIGUITY OF OUR CONCEPTS[2]

Pizzorno begins by observing that social control is a term we find easy to understand intuitively but that is hard for disciplined thought to define in a clear manner. I agree. However, can we think of any other major concept in sociology about which the same might not be said? It is true that a long line of originative thinkers in our field—including Condorcet, Thomas Malthus, Emile Durkheim, Yilfredo, and Pareto—have argued that salvation in social science depends on the univocal definition of our terms. Yet the fact remains: Concepts such as anomie, anxiety, elite, equality, freedom, modernity, power, rationality, secularization, social class, stranger—indeed, most if not all of the other central concepts of the social sciences—appear intractably ambiguous. Every one of these concepts carries vastly different meanings, polemical overtones, and ideological valences. These properties mark them, to use the apt phrase of W. B. Gallie, as "essentially contested concepts." Precisely because social control is an essentially contested concept, we need to take care not to lose sight of its semantic richness and theoretical complexity. This observation leads directly to my second maxim, which concerns the way we represent the heritage of sociology.

DO NOT OVERLOOK THE COMPLEXITY
OF THE THEORETICAL TRADITIONS
WE HAVE INHERITED

In Pizzorno's brief history of sociological thought about social control, sociologists at the turn of the century used social control in the sense of ways to restore social organization in the wake of large-scale dislocations produced by the processes of urbanization, immigration, occupational mobility, and the like; whereas today, they use it chiefly to signify the processes by which persons are constrained from acting out deviant inclinations.

I read that history differently. As I see it, sociologists have used the notion of social control in at least four significantly different senses, each of which has informed a distinct tradition of social thought throughout this century.

First, social control has been understood to refer to processes that control the animal nature of man. Here one thinks of a number of French theorists, from Montesquieu and Rousseau down to Jacques Lacan. Durkheim explored the institutions of family, religion, education, law, the state, and public festivals as mechanisms that could overcome the excessive egoism of modern man and relieve the modern malady of infinite aspirations. Alexander Mitscherlich presented comparable diagnoses later in the present century. Many observers today direct attention to ways to counteract what some consider an epidemic of unregulated impulsive tendencies, manifested by widespread abuse of chemical substances, sexual hedonism, incivility and social violence, an ethos of "consumerism," and greater fickleness in personal commitments and tastes.

A second tradition thinks of social control in the sense of processes that dispose people to act in a disciplined manner. Max Weber emphasized the need of modern factories and bureaucratic organizations to regulate the conduct of their members according to formally rationalized routines—a development for which military discipline stood as the prototype. This notion of social control came to inform two radically disparate kinds of research programs: that of Reinhard Bendix, with his concern for ideologies of work in industry and of students of the developing economies generally, with their concern for securing a more reliable labor force; and that of Herbert Marcuse, with his critique of surplus repression and one-dimensional living in advanced industrial societies.

Social scientists have long been concerned with processes that counteract tendencies to deviance, delinquency, and criminal behavior. One thinks of the work of U.S. social workers and some Chicago sociologists earlier in this century or that of the Austrian psychoanalyst, August Aichhorn. In the early 1950s, a focus on counteracting deviant tendencies came to dominate the writings on social control by sociologists such as Talcott Parsons, Richard LePiere, and Albert Cohen. Today, the journal *Sociological Abstracts* restricts the rubric of social control to the areas of penology and the sociology of correction problems.

Finally, we have social control in the sense advanced by John Dewey and George Herbert Mead as referring to ways to constitute publics to organize more effective communal action in modern societies. Robert Park took up this theme in his work on "the crowd and the public," while Dewey and Walter Lippman advanced it with their works in the 1920s on the formation of publics in the service of social reconstruction. Karl Mannheim added significant work along these lines in the 1930s and 1940s with his concern for cultivating a democratic consensus behind programs of public planning. More recently, Morris Hanowitz devoted much innovative work to recovering this conception of social control, which he defined as the capacity of a social group or a society to regulate itself according to desired principles and values.

To sustain this more differentiated reading of our traditions of thought about social control (or anything else)—to resist the temptation to fasten on one exclusive meaning of the term and instead attend to its enduring historical multivocality—is to secure a richer inventory of theoretical resources. This leads to my third maxim.

DRAW ON OUR HERITAGE
IN A PROGRESSIVE MANNER
(RECYCLE THE CLASSICS)

Instead of assuming that because times have changed, ideas that were useful for analyzing earlier periods must be scrapped, we would do well to develop those ideas in a more differentiated manner and apply them innovatively to contemporary conditions. For example, if Dan Bell wants to understand the emergence of such twentieth-century figures as Lenin, Mussolini, and Hitler or, for that matter, Gandhi, Nkrumah, and Khomeini, why should he not draw on what Max Weber said about the dynamics of charismatic leadership, including Weber's conjecture that new prophets might arise later in this century? If Jim Coleman wants to contrast spontaneous with constructed organization, why should he not avail himself of William Graham Sumner's arguments about crescive and enacted institutions or Ferdinand Tönnies's distinction between *Wesenswille* and *Kürwille*?

Pizzorno provides an exemplary utilization of classical theories when he turns to consider an array of what he calls theories of social order. My comments at this point are intended to support and extend that part of his argument.

Although Pizzorno presents his schema as a typology of theories of social order and constructs it by juxtaposing the theories of Hobbes, Smith, and Durkheim, I do not think he is really after a classification of different theories. What Pizzorno articulates with that schema, rather, is really a single theory—one that uses the historically distinct conceptions of theorists such as Hobbes, Smith, and Durkheim as resources to generate a systematic typology of *mechanisms of social control*. And when one considers the language he employs when employing the schema—phrases such as "motivating and impelling courses of action" and "control of the individual conduct"—it becomes clear that by social control he is referring to processes of bringing pressure on others so as to secure compliance with certain expectations. (This is a meaning consistent with the second and third meanings of social control I outlined earlier: securing disciplined behavior, and counteracting deviant dispositions and conduct.)

If we reframe Pizzorno's schema as a typology of ways to control the behavior of others, then the horizontal axis would consist of *types of control*—control through modes of coercion on the one hand and through modes of inducement on the other. These can be glossed, in familiar sociological language, as negative and positive sanctions, respectively. Pizzorno presents the vertical axis in two ways. He prefers to consider it in terms of the duration of the effects of interventions that act on the individual, whether these are short-term or long-term. But first he considers it as a distinction about the location of the mechanisms: whether they operate external to the individual or internally. He rejects this distinction on grounds that "the notion of some 'internal' mechanism is not necessarily clear." Well, it may not be necessarily clear, but to this reader at least, it is practicably clear—and particularly helpful. Indeed, this way of constituting the vertical axis is consistent with the way Pizzorno tends to talk about the mechanisms further on (as when he refers to the mechanisms of the lower row as modes of "forming and altering the will of the individual person"). An advantage of sticking to this way of construing the distinction is its connection with a good deal of literature on socialization and moral development: The contrast between whether persons are directed mainly by external incentives or by internalized values and norms figures prominently in the work of social learning theorists, attribution theorists, and personality and culture theorists.

If we revise Pizzorno's schema in this way—cross-classifying mechanisms of social control by type of sanctions and channel of action (whether they act on the external situation of the actor or directly on the actor's will or intentions)—we find he has reinvented a schema Talcott Parsons presented some twenty-five years ago. That a schema virtually identical with that of Parsons has been constructed independently so much later lends considerable support, I think, to its utility. What is more, through progressive incorporation of the Parsonian formulations, we can draw on related analyses that enrich the schema as a theoretical instrument and so extend the substantive insights Pizzorno offers when he applies it.

Modes of Bringing Pressure to Bear on Actors[3]

Types of Sanctions

Channel of Action	Positive	Negative
Control over situation	Inducement	Coercion
Control over other's intentions	Persuasion	Activation of commitments

I will mention two such pieces of the Parsonian theory. First, to each of these modes of control there corresponds a generalized symbolic medium of interaction. For inducement, it is money; for coercion (or deterrence, as Parsons later termed it), power; for persuasion, influence; and for activation of commitments, what Parsons calls the generalization of commitments. Second, all of the symbolic media of interchange are reliably effective only insofar as they have been institutionalized.

Pizzorno's discussion of the two contrasting conceptions of the individual person entailed by the two rows adds to this body of theory the suggestion that the motivation for responding to these different kinds of sanctions comes from disparate psychological dispositions. Responsiveness to the sanctions of inducement and coercion (or deterrence) stems from a disposition to pursue discrete preferences. Responsiveness to the sanctions of persuasion or fear of moral disapproval stems from a disposition to act in a way that actualizes identity.

Let me now complete this revisionist exercise by discussing Pizzorno's historical hypothesis, to which I referred at the outset: that the conditions of late-modern society are such as to entail much greater reliance on the latter disposition, which in turn is ensured especially by the negative intentional sanctions—those that operate to instill discipline, which is equivalent, in the Parsonian schema, to fear of moral disapproval.

1. The media that convey all these modes of social control are institutionalized; therefore, all of them involve some degree of normative compliance. What is more, all of them depend on trust.

2. What is different in the modern world generally, and increasingly so in our time, is the extent to which these media have become generalized. Therefore, what may be different in the development Pizzorno is hinting at may be not a shift from mechanisms of deterrence and inducement to mechanisms of persuasion and moral appellation or discipline, but an expansion of the circumference of the societal circles in which these media operate together with an increase in the abstractness of their operation.

3. Putting the matter this way is altogether consistent with the notion of an increase in trustworthiness as the basis of social expectations and interchanges.

4. This is also entirely consistent with the notion of a shift from short-term to long-term temporal frames of reference.

5. Finally, it is also consistent with a tendency toward greater impersonality in the force of control. Accordingly, I would relocate the personal-impersonal distinction from the horizontal axis to the vertical one.

Let me conclude with three substantive points related to this line of interpretation. First, it directs us to expect new forms of deviant conduct. I think the expanded sphere of trust would lead us to expect an increase in forms of deviance that violate the most generalized norms of trust—embezzlement, insider trading, computer hacking, plagiarism, and international terrorism.

Second, I would pick up and affirm Pizzorno's suggestion that we may be witnessing a widening gap between the responsible and the irresponsible elements of the population.

Finally, greater societal reliance on trustworthiness implies a tendency for the modal person to be guided by a more abstract and demanding internalized ego ideal. To say this is to be reminded of the notions of a number of classical theorists regarding the enhanced moral qualities entailed by the institutions of modern society—for example, the suggestions of Comte and Spencer that modern institutions will create more altruistic kinds of persons; of Durkheim that they will create persons of greater moral autonomy; and of Simmel that they provide the basis for increasingly individuated personalities. All this suggests that the old classics might well be revisited for new kinds of relevance.

NOTES

1. I have spelled out this point in a recent paper, "Simmel and Parsons Reconsidered." *American Journal of Sociology* 96 (March 1991):1097–1116.

2. See Donald N. Levine, *The Flight from Ambiguity* (Chicago: University of Chicago Press, 1985), Chapter 1.

3. See Talcott Parsons, *Politics and Social Structure* (New York: The Free Press, 1969), Chapters 14–16; and Rainer C. Baum, "Introduction: Generalized Media in Action," in *Explorations in General Theory in Social Science*, vol. II, ed. Jan J. Loubser et al. (New York: The Free Press, 1976), pp. 448–469.

8

Discretion, Institutions, and the Problem of Government Commitment

Kenneth A. Shepsle

In their whirlwind tour of Western economic history (eight centuries in 150 pages), Douglass North and Robert Thomas provide a simple premise for the rise of the Western world: getting property rights right.

> Western man . . . has broken loose from the shackles of a world bound by abject poverty and recurring famine and has realized a quality of life which is made possible only by relative abundance. . . . Efficient economic organization is key to [this] growth; the development of an efficient economic organization in Western Europe accounts for the rise of the West. (North and Thomas 1973, p. 1)

The Middle Ages, and even the medieval and early premodern periods, were often anarchic; the absence of order derived from the fact that no one authority possessed more than partial control of force over a limited geographical domain. Natural dangers—famine, drought, pestilence—combined with human dangers—invasion, predation, theft—to threaten the security of life, liberty, and property in many human communities. In the absence of this security, there were only modest incentives to invest in the physical and human capital that would have provided a foundation for economic growth.

North and Thomas trace how the crystallization and concentration of force, beginning locally with the manorial system and eventually maturing into the nation-state, provided the security necessary for economic growth. The threat to liberty and property, however, did not disappear; rather, the random predations of anarchic times were replaced by the prospect (and often the reality) of appropriation and extortion by central authority. Economic growth in Western Europe during this millennium was uneven, principally because some polities got things right regarding the protection of property rights, while others did not. The economies of France and Iberia languished, while those of the Dutch and English flourished, partly at least because political arrangements in the latter favored the development of "those institutions which enable units to realize economies of scale (joint stock companies, corporations), to encourage innovation (prizes, patent law), to improve the efficiency of factor markets (enclosures, bills of exchange, the abolition of serfdom), or to reduce market imperfections (insurance companies)" (North and Thomas 1973, pp. 5–6). In short, the shape of political arrangements was crucial for economic health.

How and why these differential economic performances materialized are things with which the North and Thomas monograph only briefly and suggestively deals. I can certainly not claim, within the confines of a short chapter, to do even that. Instead, I will examine one prominent feature that is embodied in the idea of "getting property rights right" and is directly relevant to contemporary affairs—namely, the notion of *commitment*. Let me hasten to say that this is but one attribute of a complex of issues surrounding the notion of optimal organization or optimal institutional arrangements. Other features—coordination, enforcement, efficiency, and fairness—are alluded to only fleetingly in this chapter.

It seems appropriate, first, to say where in the intellectual galaxy the problems I wish to discuss and the form of analysis I intend to offer fit. In a sentence, it is "Discretion is the enemy of optimality, commitment its ally."[1] By this I mean that the ability to commit often (not always) expands one's opportunity set, whereas the capacity to exercise discretion—which includes the latitude to renege or to behave opportunistically—reduces it. In order to hear the Sirens without being seduced by them, Ulysses needed to be able to make commitments to his current self on which his later self could not renege. He needed to bind himself, both figuratively and literally (Elster 1979).

The commitment problem is an aspect of self-management or "egonomics" (Schelling 1984), of which Ulysses and the Sirens is the exemplar. But it also arises in dealings among distinct individuals or between individuals and organizations (contracts) and between individuals and governments (policy-making). My ultimate concern is with whether and how governments can credibly commit themselves to an intertemporal plan or policy, which, if implemented, would enhance social welfare or some other governmental objective.

The now-classic statement of the potential conflict between discretion and optimality is found in Finn Kydland and Edward Prescott (1977). The ideas contained in that paper have much in common (although they were arrived at independently) with the notion of "subgame perfection" in game theory (Selten 1975).[2] In each, discretion is associated with consistent maximizing behavior by an agent. The paradox is that such behavior may have perverse consequences, a point I elaborate below.

In what follows, I focus on the ways in which discretionary authorities— whether individuals, organizations, or states—seek to *disable that discretion* in order to expand their opportunities. The ability to disable discretion in a convincing fashion is one thing I mean by a credible commitment. If there is a novel feature of this chapter, it lies in the argument that institutional arrangements, often justified on a functional basis or on the grounds that they serve the interests of the currently powerful, may provide—if only as a by-product—the means for making credible commitments.

COMMITMENT

In ordinary language, a *commitment* is a promise, pledge, vow, covenant, guarantee, or bond to perform in a specified fashion. A commitment is *credible* in either of two senses—the motivational and the imperative, respectively.

On commitments, it may be observed that "while parties may have strong incentives to strike a bargain, their incentives ex post are not always compatible with maintaining the agreement" (North and Weingast 1989, p. 4). Should this divergence between *ex ante* and *ex post* incentives not develop, then a commitment is motivationally credible. That is, a commitment is credible in the motivational sense if subsequently (at the time of performance) the committee continues to want to honor that commitment; a commitment is motivationally credible because it is incentive-compatible and hence self-enforcing. It is credible in the imperative sense, on the other hand, if the committee is unable to act otherwise, whether he or she wants to or not; in this sense a commitment is credible, not because it is compatible with contemporaneous preferences but rather because performance is coerced or discretion to do otherwise is disabled.

Consider a commitment over a time horizon [0,T]. At $t = 0$, an agent commits to a plan of action,

$$X_T = (x_1, x_2, \ldots, x_t, \ldots, x_T),$$

in which he or she vows to perform x_t at time $t = 1, 2, \ldots, T$. Suppose at $t = 0$, it may be anticipated that x_t is precisely what the agent will *wish* to do at time t. Then X_T is credible in the incentive-compatibility sense. Alternatively, suppose that at each time period t, x_t is precisely what the agent *must* do, either because he or she will be coerced to do so by some exogenous authority or because doing otherwise is beyond the agent's control. X_T is again credible, but now it is in the imperative sense.

Against this backdrop, consider an agent who *at each period t* optimizes for the rest of the horizon, conditional on what has already transpired. That is, the agent has *discretionary authority*. If X_T is motivationally credible, then the agent will not wish to alter the performances promised at $t = 0$, despite having the discretion to do so.[3] But if X_T is not motivationally credible, and if the existence of discretion now means that the agent cannot be coerced or disabled, then he or she will wish to deviate at t by choosing, say, y_t instead of x_t. The idea of exercising discretionary authority, optimizing a period at a time, is called *consistency* (as in "consistent maximizing behavior") by Kydland and Prescott (1977).

The existence of discretionary authority in those circumstances in which the motivational basis for credibility does not hold poses problems for an agent because the agent cannot deny that he or she will consistently optimize, even if he or she would be better off if this could be denied. A special case of this problem is the one-shot game (T = 1) possessing a unique inefficient Nash equilibrium. The players would all be better off if they could deny themselves the discretion to play their respective optimal strategies, but they have no way of credibly committing themselves to do other than play their best responses. No other outcome, including the one that constitutes a Pareto improvement, is immune to the prospect of defection, which is feasible when discretion may be exercised. Of course, the reader will recognize the one-period prisoners' dilemma (PD) as the classic instance of this problem. But it is more general than this.[4] In the absence of motivational credibility, (1) an optimal plan may be inconsistent (incompatible with period-by-period maximizing) and hence unrealistic for players with discretionary authority, and (2) a consistent plan may be suboptimal.

These are the important conclusions of Kydland and Prescott, which they illustrate with the following example:

> [S]uppose the socially desirable outcome is not to have houses built in a particular flood plain but, given that they are there, to take certain costly flood-control measures. If the government's policy were not to build the dams and levees needed for flood protection and agents knew this was the case, even if houses were built there, rational agents would not live in the flood plains. But the rational agent knows that, if he and others build houses there, the government will take the necessary flood-control measures. Consequently, in the absence of a law prohibiting the construction of houses in the flood plain, houses are built there, and the army corps of engineers subsequently builds the dams and levees. (Kydland and Prescott 1977, p. 477)

The government, in this example, is a discretionary agent who most prefers the "no houses, no flood control" outcome, the "houses, flood control" outcome next, and the "houses, no flood control" outcome least. Let x_t be "no flood-control measures in period t" and y_t be "flood-control measures." If the government could credibly commit itself to (x_1, x_2, . . . x_t), then it could achieve the social optimum in each period. But if it cannot bind itself to this plan, then if in any period, say, the tth houses were built, then at $t + 1$, x_{t+1} would no longer be consistent. A government with discretion would choose y_{t+1} instead. This is the government's optimal response to the presence of houses on the flood plain. A prospective dweller with intelligent foresight can "force" this socially suboptimal result.[5] Or, as Kydland and Prescott (1977, pp. 473–474) put it, "a discretionary policy for which the policymakers select the best action, given the current situation, will not typically result in the social objective function being maximized."[6]

THE PROBLEM
OF INDIVIDUAL COMMITMENT

The conflict between credibility and discretion and its implications for optimality exist at both the individual and the collective levels, as the

Ulysses and the Sirens and flood-control examples illustrate, respectively. Shortly, I concentrate on the problem for collectivities, but first I want to examine the individual-level problem.

Early on, Thomas Schelling recognized the optimality dilemma caused by the conflict between commitment and discretion. Thirty years ago, in a justly famous essay (Schelling 1956) reprinted in *The Strategy of Conflict*, Schelling examined the bargaining tactic of binding oneself, of disabling whatever discretion one might originally have possessed.[7] Once again, Schelling, in a 1974 essay reprinted in his *Choice and Consequence: Perspectives of an Errant Economist* (1984, pp. 33–37) observes that external coercion may be a substitute for commitment. Massachusetts barbers, he writes, "appreciate mandatory closing on Wednesday . . . since it precludes competitors from staying open." Thus, exogenous coercion, like the act of disabling discretion, provides another source of imperative credibility.

There are several problems with imperative credibility, two of which I will briefly elaborate. The first is *verifiability*. Imagine one's discretion being constrained or disabled, but that this condition is not verifiable by interested others. In the United States Congress, a legislator's rule-of-thumb defense for deviating from a party position is that the issue at hand is "a matter of conscience or constituency." The latter may be easily verified—and Speaker Sam Rayburn was known to castigate the Democratic congressman who used that defense disingenuously. The former, however, may be difficult to verify, especially if the matter at hand is a novel legislative issue or the legislator is new at the job.

A second potential pitfall of imperative credibility is *symmetry*. If *both* drivers, in another famous Schelling example, disconnect their steering wheels and tie down their accelerators as they approach a one-lane bridge from opposite directions, no one will deny their credible commitments, but the optimality of the result is surely in question.

We should, therefore, not be too precipitous in our admiration of commitment and our condemnation of discretion. Indeed, many social arrangements recognize tradeoffs. Clubs, organizations, and legislatures, for example, credibly commit themselves to standing rules of procedure, not by making it *impossible* to suspend such rules but only by making it difficult. This arrangement does not destroy the credible commitment of simple majorities to specific rules of procedure, as their discretion is disabled. Discretion, however, is retained by harder to assemble special majorities.

The tension over whether or not to be committed by having one's discretion disabled or behavior coerced is clear. The advantage resides in the salutary effect on *current* behavior induced by *future* expectations. If I know the government is irrevocably committed not to provide future flood protection, then I will not develop real estate on a flood plain. The disadvantage is that expectations may be rational but wrong, incomplete, or vulnerable to unanticipated future developments. The government's irrevocable commitment, for example, might fail to anticipate some costly consequences of a flood to the flood plain's ecology—the destruction of breeding grounds for some rare and valuable species or of access to a newly discovered mineral deposit; the very irrevocability of the commitment may make it impossible or costly to respond to this new information.

In what follows, I ignore this tension. In public choice especially, both the inability of government to commit and its disabled capacity to uncommit (that is, lack of flexibility) are serious problems. But I believe the former is currently the greater challenge. From discretion, the best is the enemy of the good because there is "no mechanism to induce *future* policymakers to take into consideration the effect of their policy, via the expectations mechanism, upon *current* decisions of agents" (Kydland and Prescott 1977, p. 481). The problem as it manifests itself collectively and the consequent social damage done are the focus of the remainder of the chapter.[8]

CREDIBLE COMMITMENT
BY GOVERNMENT[9]

In the Middle Ages, princes often found it difficult to commit to the repayment of loans. Their local authority was insufficient for them to seize property whenever a need for resources arose, but it was often adequate to allow them to honor loan repayments in a discretionary fashion— postponing or stretching out repayment schedules, for example. In many instances, this discretion produced suboptimalities in the capital market: Loans were smaller and more infrequent, possessed higher interest rates, and may have necessitated the inconvenient posting of bonds (such as hunting privileges on royal lands) more often than would have occurred if a credible commitment strategy had been available.[10] In a similar fashion, European monarchs, even into the premodern period, found it formidable to induce private economic agents to invest their wealth domestically in productive capital. They often could not credibly commit to a policy against the selling of economic privileges that would compete with these investments, rendering them less profitable.[11]

The point of this discussion is that institutional arrangements offer the prospect of enabling various agents to make credible commitments. Thus, getting property rights right, as I put it at the beginning of this chapter, involves not only (or even mostly) specifying rights and enforcing them or exercising discretionary authority in a prudent fashion, but it also means arranging political institutions so as to disable or render costly the exercise of discretionary authority. Consider some more contemporary examples.

1. The Fifth Amendment to the United States Constitution states, in part, "Nor shall private property be taken for public use, without just compensation." Known as the takings clause, this imperative allows the government to commit itself against expropriation and uncompensated exercises of the power of eminent domain. This, in turn, functions to assure property owners of security from governmental predations. The credibility of the assurance is enhanced by virtue of its constitutional status. Imagine the consequences, the sobering effect on investment activity, of erosion of this guarantee,

something some fear is well underway as the courts narrow the coverage of the clause (Epstein 1985).

2. Once resources have been devoted to inventive activity and new products and processes have been developed, the efficient policy is to afford no patent protection. Patent protection creates monopoly rents and restricts the diffusion of the fruits of inventive activity. The absence of patent protection, however, would surely diminish the incentives for inventive activity in the first place—there would be fewer fruits to diffuse. A statutory commitment to fixed-life patents encourages investments in research and development (see the quotation attributed to Joan Robinson in note 1). The optimal life, balancing investment incentives against consumer surplus from diffusion, is surely not infinite, but it is not zero either.[12] A statutory commitment is credible if, despite temptations to the contrary to expropriate monopoly rents, a government finds it difficult to revise the statute (Kydland and Prescott 1977, p. 477). Constitutional provisions against *ex post facto* laws provide further protection from official predations of already-existing patent privileges.

3. Legislatures are popularly elected by a current generation of voters who may not give much weight to the welfare of future generations of voters. There is thus an electoral incentive and discretionary authority for a current legislature to finance spending by incurring debt, the repayment of which constitutes a burden on future generations. Since the current generation of voters is itself the future generation for some previous legislature, it, too, will be burdened by excessive debt. If the generations could be assembled *ex ante* in a sort of intertemporal constitutional convention, they might wish to arrange institutions and pass self-denying ordinances (Riker 1980) disabling or delimiting the legislature's capacity to incur excessive debt. But, of course, the various generations cannot be assembled. Should a current generation, then, take it upon itself to remove discretion from its legislature and its successors? This question is at the heart of current debates on a balanced budget amendment to the Constitution (Brennan and Buchanan 1985; Cukierman and Meltzer 1986).[13]

4. The formation of a coalition government in a multiparty parliamentary democracy consists of (1) an agreement by the coalition partners on major policy directions, and (2) the allocation of governmental portfolios to the partners. The latter, however, confer agenda power on their holders. If, for example, a rural party joins the coalition and controls the Agriculture Ministry, it is unlikely that policies inimical to its rural constituents will be implemented, whether they are part of the coalition agreement or not. Thus, only some agreements are credible, and they are made so by appropriate portfolio allocations that police implementation. Many policy compromises may be appealing to potential coalition partners, but they are not implementable by any feasible distribution of portfolios and therefore are not available to them; ministerial discretion cannot be disabled in important respects so that an announced policy agreement inconsistent with portfolio assignments is no more than pie in the sky.[14]

All of these illustrations put discretion at the center of an optimality problem. In some sense, things would be better if discretion could be constrained by coercion, disability, or proper incentives. If governments could be enjoined not to expropriate real property or appropriate the rents derived from inventive activity; if legislators could disengage, from time to time, from the contemporaneous electoral pressures to borrow and spend; if partners to a coalitional agreement could invent cheap means for enforcement; then—in all these instances—by the actors' own lights or according to some broader measure of welfare, social improvements could be achieved.

In both private and public settings, positive theories of political economy based on a rationality hypothesis have been suspicious of approaches that wish the credibility problem away, either assuming some exogenous source of enforcement or the existence of "natural" incentives to exercise discretion in a prudent, other-regarding fashion. Certainly in the modern world, as the grip of primordial sentiments weakens and the authority of religious values erodes, exogenous sources of enforcement and natural incentives have been diluted.[15] Discretionary authority threatens to enfeeble social life unless political arrangements are structured in a manner that enhances credibility. It is therefore appropriate to explore institutional solutions to the prospective failure of credibility. Before doing so, I will briefly take up this same problem in collective settings without government.

CREDIBLE COMMITMENT
WITHOUT GOVERNMENT

In the medieval world of weak governmental authority, there were nevertheless some means for making credible commitments. International trade, for example, involving numerous exchanges among agents across space and time, took place "outside the shadow of the law"; indeed, there was little formal law even to cast a shadow. Village life in many parts of the world, to take another example, embraced a variety of intergenerational transfer schemes, both to smooth intertemporal consumption and to provide catastrophic insurance. In each case, credible commitments—between traders or between generations—existed without the luxury of exogenous enforcement institutions.

While there may have been no shadow of the law in these examples, there was the shadow of the future. Game-theoretic explanations have exploited this latter fact in seeking to understand the emergence of trust and the evolution of cooperation.[16] The core idea here is that in the absence of credible commitments—for a young generation to support members of a predecessor generation in their old age, or for some trader to fulfill quality assurances for the commodity he or she sells in long-distance trade—there will be Pareto-inferior equilibrium outcomes. If traders need fear, in subsequent dealings, no retribution for current cheating, or if a generation can renege on its social security commitment without lamentable consequences to itself, then such commitments are incredible. The result, much in the spirit of Kydland and Prescott, is consistency (that is, period by period maximizing) accompanied by suboptimality.

Suppose, however, that there *were* some way to produce lamentable consequences for such reneging. That is, suppose it were possible for a current agent to exploit the shadow of the future (that is, repeat play), punishing (or arranging to have punished) anyone reneging on a promise. If a punishment regime could itself be made credible, then it would enhance the prospects of making credible commitments in the first place.

I cannot go into the technical details here, so let me simply mention that various "folk theorems" in game theory suggest that, in particular kinds of repeat-play settings, credible punishment regimes do exist that permit trust and cooperation to develop (Abreu 1988; Fudenberg and Maskin 1986). These theorems do not imply that unique forms of trust or cooperation develop; to the contrary, they establish that *multiple* forms of each can hold in equilibrium. What they do demonstrate, however, is that improvements over the consistent but suboptimal outcomes that accompany discretionary behavior are possible *without recourse to exogenous enforcement*.

An example dealing with international traders in the medieval world is elaborated by Paul Milgrom, Douglass North, and Barry Weingast (1988). Their claim is that an unofficial position, known as the *law merchant* and much like the modern credit bureau, had a stabilizing effect on long-distance trade by allowing individual traders to learn about prospective trading partners in an expeditious and unbiased fashion. The law merchant was in the business of holding hearings, collecting data, and rendering judgments on claims of opportunistic trading behavior—information he or she was prepared to share (for a fee) with traders before they entered into arrangements with others. Thus, despite the obstacles of space and time, traders could obtain reputational information on prospective trading partners that would condition their willingness to enter into exchange relationships. The details of this argument are omitted here. Suffice it to say that the endogenous emergence of an institution facilitated the making of credible commitments that would otherwise have been subject to opportunistic behavior.

The fear of future retribution is, I claim, only a partial explanation when considering *governmental* credibility. This is partly the case because governmental agents have shorter time horizons than their counterparts in the private sector, so the efficacy of reputational and punishment mechanisms is more limited in this sphere.[17] As important, however, are the transaction-cost inefficiencies associated with reputational mechanisms, a point suggested by Milgrom, North, and Weingast (1988): Collective commitments, in contrast to bilateral commitments, require more effort to arrange and are vulnerable to free riding. Finally, there is the comparative advantage of an *institutionalized* way of dealing with credibility. This is taken up next.

INSTITUTIONAL ARRANGEMENTS AS GUARANTORS OF GOVERNMENT CREDIBILITY

Relegated to an intellectual backwater during much of the behavioral and rational choice revolutions, there has been a renaissance in political science of the study of institutions. This renewed interest derives from two sources.

First, post-behavioralists, like their pre-behavioralist brethren, maintain that institutional arrangements and practices condition, channel, and constrain individual behavior and rational action; that is, institutions *affect* individual behavior, collective action, and social consequences. The atomistic world of behavioral social science and Arrovian social choice theory abstracted much of this institutional richness away. Second, the tools are now available to understand the choice, emergence, or evolution of institutions. The latter can now be seen not only as a cause of social equilibrium (institutional equilibrium) but also as the product of an equilibrium of forces (equilibrium institutions) (Shepsle 1986).

In this intellectual renaissance, however, little systematic attention has been given to institutions as instruments of collective commitment. Here I want to focus on this property of institutions. I wish to make a case for the proposition that institutional structure and practice have the effect of disabling some forms of collective discretion, therefore making public commitments more credible. I also want to suggest to reformers, eager to get on with transforming the ways we do things collectively, that their reforms may have undesirable implications for public credibility.

This agenda is ambitious, and I cannot hope to give the definitive statement here. Thus, as in the rest of this chapter, I will rely on partial argument and examples. My claim is that the disabling of discretion entails institutionalizing an asymmetry, making it easier to do than to undo. The former allows a promise to be made; the latter places obstacles in the way of reneging. I will focus on two features of institutions—structure and procedure.

Structure

The division of labor is often described and defended in terms of contemporaneous efficiency-enhancing properties. Yet such structural arrangements may also have longer-term impacts. To take a prominent example with which I am familiar, the institutional arrangements of the United States Congress were essentially in place by 1825 and persisted in virtually the same form for 150 years (Gamm and Shepsle 1989). Early generations of legislators were children of the Scottish enlightenment and applied the lessons derived from Adam Smith's pin factory to legislative structure. By 1825, both chambers of the national legislature were decentralized through a division of labor system of standing committees. Each committee had a property right to a policy jurisdiction in which, to oversimplify, its members had near-monopoly agenda powers. They were the exclusive source of proposals to change the status quo in their jurisdictions, on the one hand, and they could block or veto such changes, on the other.

By way of contrast, consider an unstructured majority rule legislature, the sort of collectivity that is the traditional object of study in social choice theory. Suppose some legislators were displeased with the prevailing status quo, x^0, and sought to replace it with an alternative, x. So long as x can prevail over x^0 in a pairwise majority contest, the majority's will can be done. But we now know (as, say, those who believe there is some unique and unitary public interest do not) that there are *many* majorities, that their respective preferences need not be coherent or consistent, and that one majority cannot commit or bind a subsequent majority. Thus, x may be replaced, in turn, by x', x' by x'', and so on. Indeed, perhaps even more perverse, it is entirely possible to cycle back to x^0.[18] So long as majority coalitions are easily mobilized, successive majorities may transform, redo, or undo the work of their predecessors.[19] In short, the polity may lack the ability to commit itself to a course of action, leaving other agents vulnerable to the whims of whichever majority happens to be currently mobilized.

In these circumstances, suppose rural and urban legislators (collectively comprising a majority) agree to an omnibus policy of multi-year spending for both crop subsidies and mass transit. If the legislature could credibly commit to this policy, then presumably both urban and rural economic interests could adapt their plans to this condition. Suppose, however, that this multi-year plan were vulnerable to changes. For example, an intervening election might increase the representation of anti-mass transit legislators. What would prevent them, if they now constituted a majority, from undoing the previous policy? And, if this were a possibility, would not economic agents outside the legislature take this prospect into account *ex ante* in formulating their own plans? In short, because a legislature cannot bind a successor legislature and a majority coalition cannot bind another, public policies are always vulnerable to reneging. The optimal economic adaptation to a policy if it were credible is therefore not available under this institutional arrangement—Kydland and Prescott again. An unstructured legislature has unlimited, and therefore too much, discretion.

Let us now return to the highly structured, division of labor committee system. As in the unstructured case, let us again suppose that a majority of urban and rural legislators is eager to pass a multi-year spending bill on crop subsidies and mass transit. Suppose, as well, that majorities on the relevant committees are prepared to initiate the necessary legislation. Once in place, however, this multi-year plan is vulnerable to the same kinds of changes we saw above. However, the consequence is much different. Even if anti-mass transit representation increases in the next Congress, the will of this new majority might well be frustrated. Unless it is also able to reconstitute the committee controlling the mass transit jurisdiction, its efforts can be blocked. Any effort to rescind the mass transit spending would be vetoed by the mass transit committee, which presumably is dominated by those favorable to mass transit and has exclusive authority over the origination of new legislation in this jurisdiction.[20]

In the United States Congress, it may be difficult to make policy promises. But once made, it is even more difficult to renege on them. This state of affairs has developed because members typically get assigned to committees in which they have a vested interest, and they are able to keep a committee berth once assigned (Shepsle 1978). Many committees, populated in this self-selected fashion, are insulated from electoral shuffles. In the context of even extraordinary turnover at the legislative level—for example, in the modern era the "Watergate election" of 1974 resulted in a 21 percent rate of turnover in the House of Representatives with seventy-five new Democrats and sixteen new Republicans—many committee majorities remain only minimally affected. If, to continue the earlier example, there were a solid majority on the mass transit committee in favor of the multi-year spending bill, this majority may remain virtually intact in all but the most dramatic electoral reversals. Consequently, the commitment implicit in a multi-year spending proposal is insulated from subsequent reneging, *even if a major electoral reshuffle occurs.*

A division of labor committee system is ordinarily justified either on contemporaneous efficiency grounds, much like Adam Smith's primitive theory of the firm, or on the grounds that it entrenches the currently powerful. Both justifications have merit. But there is an additional important consequence: *The arrangement enables credible public commitments because it disables the discretion of momentary majorities.*

Clearly, there are disadvantages to the loss of flexibility entailed in this arrangement (see note 8 and Becker's comments), not the least of which is that public policy is prevented from being responsive to majoritarian wishes. I would only claim that *governance* (the capacity to commit to policies) and *representation* (the capacity to respond to majorities) are sometimes at odds and that institutional shortcomings in the latter respect have gotten much press and attracted the passions of reformers, but that the former constitutes— at least for the purposes of this chapter—a worthy objective, too.[21]

Many other features of our institutional and constitutional landscape, in addition to legislative committee systems, enhance the credibility of public policies. An independent judiciary and independent regulatory commissions, for example, allow agents to adapt to policy pronouncements over longer time horizons than would be possible if the composition and disposition of these bodies were constantly in flux. The increasing use of ad hoc commissions, covering a variety of subjects but most visible recently in reforming social security and raising federal salaries, constitutes another example. And, of course, the unanimity game between House, Senate, and president—each dependent on different electorates and different timings of elections—gives existing policies credibility by empowering multiple veto groups.

Procedures

A parallel argument may be made for procedures. Suppose there were a new public policy that constituted the current status quo, x^0. We have seen that structural arrangements insulate this policy—make it more credible and durable—by creating veto groups. Procedural arrangements undergird these groups. For example, most organizations require various forms of *mandatory delay* before changing the status quo (Schelling 1984, p. 97). In legislatures, bills must go through several deliberations, and often must be held over for a prescribed amount of time to allow for proper consideration.

In the Administrative Procedures Act governing the deliberations of regulatory agencies, there are requirements of proper notice. In my own department, the senior faculty may recommend no senior appointment unless the matter has been discussed in at least two successive meetings.

In each of these cases, procedures place substantial transactions costs in the path of change in order to mitigate the flux that otherwise characterizes collective choice. These transactions costs disable decision-making discretion, thereby enhancing the credibility of existing commitments.

Finally, it should be noted that some procedures have exactly the opposite effect. Sunset provisions in legislation, for example, *force* the reconsideration of existing policy. The credibility of the commitment implicit in a policy is damaged in direct proportion to the distance of the sun from the horizon. Zero-based budgeting and the practice of single-year appropriations cause all kinds of perverse behavior; the ability to plan and act over multi-year horizons is severely attenuated.

THE PROBLEM OF PUBLIC COMMITMENT: WHY IS IT IMPORTANT?

My claim in the latter part of this chapter has been that institutional arrangements—structure and procedure—affect the credibility of public policies and, therefore, the capacity of public institutions to effect social improvements. The implication of this modest claim is two-fold: (1) If the reader agrees that the commitment problem I have been writing about is a serious one, then he or she should not overlook the important role played by institutional arrangements in enhancing or diminishing credibility. (2) If the attention of the reader is drawn—for whatever reason—to the performance of institutions, then he or she should not, in his or her reformist zeal, ignore the unintended effects of "reform" on the ability of government to make credible commitments.

I began the chapter by agreeing in principle with a sweeping claim made by North and Thomas: Political economies that "got property rights right" flourished relative to those that did not. As the twenty-first century approaches, getting property rights right remains a continuing challenge. Recent changes in collectivist and free market economies alike—whether under the rubric of deregulation, privatization, or perestroika—suggest as much. The novel concern in this chapter adds a new slant to this issue, namely that part of getting property rights right involves the commitment of governmental authority. Ambiguity and uncertainty surrounding this commitment, the product of discretion, may diminish the benefits of an appropriate property rights regime.[22]

NOTES

1. Elster (1979, p. 10) attributes to Schumpeter a similar maxim: "The maximal exploitation of present possibilities may often be an obstacle to the maximal creation of new possibilities." Also, in reference to a patent system, he quotes Joan Robinson

to the effect that "by slowing down the diffusion of technical progress, it ensures that there will be more progress to diffuse."

2. "Dynamic inconsistency occurs when a future policy decision that forms part of an optimal plan formulated at an initial date is no longer optimal from the viewpoint of a later date, even though no new information has appeared in the meantime. Dynamic consistency is equivalent to the game theory notion of subgame perfection" (Fischer 1986, p. 1).

3. In extensive form game theory, a strategy is a designated course of action at each node in the game tree at which a player has an opportunity to choose. A subgame is a subtree of the full tree (technical details omitted here). If an optimal strategy for the entire game tree consists of optimal strategies for each subtree, then the strategy for the full game is said to be *subgame perfect*. In this case, when the play of the game reaches a particular subtree—a node where the player has a choice opportunity—the choice made will agree with what the overall strategy dictates, even though the player could, at that point, exercise discretion and choose to deviate from the overall plan. It is in this sense that a motivationally credible plan is the same as a subgame perfect strategy.

4. In the PD game, the unique equilibrium is an inefficient, *dominant strategy* equilibrium, whereas the argument in the text applies to any inefficient *Nash* equilibrium.

5. Considering this as an extensive form game between the government and a real estate developer, there are *two* Nash equilibria: "no homes, no flood control" and "homes, flood control." But only the second is subgame perfect, inasmuch as the developer can force the second equilibrium point by exploiting the fact that an uncommitable government has the discretion to condition its optimization on moves already made. The developer, in short, can present the government with a *fait accompli*.

6. Giving a slightly different slant to this phenomenon is Elster (1979, p. 66): "Consistent planning is sophistication within the limits of the feasible; precommitment is sophistication amounting to a modification of the limits."

7. This provides an answer to the rhetorical question put by Brennan and Buchanan (1985, p. 67): "Any binding rule is, of course, a constraint on behavior. Hence the question, Why should a person, or persons, deliberately choose to impose constraints on his or their freedom of action?"

8. In his conference remarks, Professor Gary Becker emphasized this tension, suggesting that flexibility foregone may well be a substantial opportunity cost of a capacity to commit. I heartily concur, as the preceding paragraph suggests. In ignoring this tension, I believe I am making an even stronger case for the seriousness of the problem created by discretionary authority. I am claiming that the commitment problem is serious *even when there are no off-setting advantages to flexibility*. This may be seen most clearly in the accompanying diagram. In this game, Mr. 1 and Ms. 2 will only play once, and Ms. 2 has a commitment problem. She cannot assure Mr. 1 that she will not play r(ight), leading Mr. 1 prudently to play R(ight). The resulting suboptimal outcome derives directly from the discretionary authority Ms. 2 possesses, and there is no compensating advantage to her flexibility. In a world of imperfect and incomplete information, of which this diagram is *not* an example, flexibility will be positively valued, and rational individuals will be amenable to making tradeoffs between flexibility and commitment capacity. But in this perfect and complete information setting, there would not appear to be any advantage to flexibility.

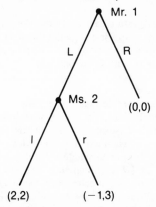

9. Before moving to collective credibility problems, let me note that individual-level credibility problems are not uninteresting. Parents often find themselves in "trigger strategy" situations, threatening their children with horrible consequences if certain forms of behavior arise. Children, alas, learn that many of these threats are incredible, that parents are paper tigers. Intellectually more interesting, perhaps, is Binmore's (1988a, b) critique of Rawls and Harsanyi on agreement behind the veil of ignorance. Can such individuals make credible promises, or, alternatively, once the veil is lifted and they know their respective intellectual, physical, and material endowments, can they renege on promises made behind the veil? The power of Binmore's critique resides in the fact that great ingenuity is required to devise the means to disable discretion or coerce compliance without giving "consent" to a rather authoritarian enforcement agent (assuming that the Rawlsian agreement is never motivationally credible for all agents).

10. A problem with bonds is that the bondholder might value the bond itself more than the commitment being bonded and therefore refuse to return it. The ideal bond is one that simultaneously is less valuable to the committee than the action promised. In giving hostages as a bond to make a commitment credible, therefore, a monarch is advised to offer his beloved, but ugly, daughter. On "ugly princesses" as bonds, see Williamson (1983) and Kronman (1985).

11. Capital markets in the Middle Ages are described in North and Thomas (1973, pp. 96 ff). The difficulties confronting the French and Spanish crowns over the selling of economic privileges in the fifteenth and sixteenth centuries are also found in this source at pages 120–131. A masterful analysis of the economic predations of the Stuarts in the period leading to the English civil war and subsequently after the Restoration is found in North and Weingast (1989). On the general phenomenon of the opportunistic appropriation of quasi-rents, see Klein et al. (1978).

12. Interestingly, if it were infinite, then the prize for finishing first in an R&D race would be enormous, but there would be no benefits to finishing second. If, on the other hand, patents had limited life, then it is conceivable that others who lost the initial race would have an eventual opportunity to capitalize on their investments. Thus, with risk-averse economic agents, it is not clear that lengthening patent life necessarily increases the incentives for investments in inventive activity.

13. Other forces may be at work, besides the disabling of discretion, that limit a legislature's capacity or desire to incur debt. For one, a current generation may incorporate welfare judgments about future generations in its current deliberations. For another, asset markets may impound future liabilities into the prices of current assets, thereby directly impinging on the welfare of a current generation and causing

the latter to factor these effects into current actions. Many municipalities, for example, underfund their pension funds, imposing huge liabilities on future municipal taxpayers. A controversy of great moment in municipal public finance involves the degree to which the depressing effects of unfunded liabilities on current property values are sufficient to moderate this tendency to incur future obligations. See Barro 1979; Epple and Schipper 1981; Inman 1982.

14. This example has considerable bearing on how we model coalition formation processes. In the nearly three decades of research, stretching from the classic treatment by Riker (1962) to the detailed summary and status report found in Laver and Schofield (1990), it is normally assumed that any "deal struck stays struck,"—that is, that coalition partners are bound to whatever agreement is reached. No attention is given to the credibility of such agreements, and no reference is made to the necessity of instituting enforcement mechanisms. As a consequence, this literature tends to assume that all coalition deals are possible, independent of their credibility or prospects for enforcement. The problem described here, and the implicit criticism directed at coalition theory, is the same as Binmore's criticism of Rawls and Harsanyi for failing to take into account the credibility of agreements arrived at behind the veil of ignorance (see note 9). For an effort to come to terms with this problem, see Laver and Shepsle (1990).

15. Coleman (1989, pp. 12–13) poses the problem as follows: "As the norms and sanctions that proliferated in primordial social organization come to be ineffective in a massive social system based on purposive organization . . . the task of overcoming anarchy without oppression remains elusive. . . . Is it possible to create a micro-structure of norms and sanctions?"

16. Axelrod (1981, 1984) offers the most accessible treatment of this subject for political scientists, although many of the ideas had been around in the technical game-theoretic literature for some years; see Aumann (1981) for a survey.

17. This, at any rate, is the opinion of Brennan and Buchanan (1985, p. 82): "Individual behavior in collective choice is likely to reflect shorter time horizons than comparable behavior in private . . . choice. . . . The person who may be willing to wait privately, to behave with prudence in order that he or his heirs may secure the fruits of long-term investment in human or non-human capital may, at the same time, be unwilling to wait collectively . . . because of the necessary attenuation of individually identifiable rights or shares in the fruits of collective or governmental 'investment'. . . . If this underlying hypothesis is valid, it would follow that as modern societies have become increasingly collectivized or politicized, there has been a shift toward a higher discount rate implicit in the allocation of the economy's resources." Also, see North and Weingast (1989) on the shortened time horizons of Stuart monarchs in the face of fiscal and military crises.

18. This is a simple statement of the famous chaos theorem for majority rule (McKelvey 1976, 1979), according to which any arbitrary commencement and ter-mination points may be linked by a sequence of majority votes. Thus, from any status quo, majority rule can drive the system to any other point. Hence, all alternatives are linked in one big cycle set, anything can happen, no point is stable, and the person who controls the agenda can determine the final result.

19. As Elster (1979, p. 88) describes it, "a direct democracy . . . will tend toward zig-zag policies and constant reevaluation of past plans; it will be incontinent, vacillating and inefficient."

20. For a fuller discussion of committee systems as division of labor arrangements, see Weingast and Marshall (1988).

21. This theme is developed in Shepsle (1988).

22. Several commentators on this chapter wish for further qualification. Professor Becker suggests, for example, that commitment problems, while tricky in theory, have in fact often been solved in practice. He gives as an illustration the example of the *family business*—a long-lived asset that "solves" the end-game commitment problems of a business that would otherwise die with its owner. I agree with the thrust of Becker's remarks—that various remedies for discretion have evolved. I would add, however, that our models are only just coming to appreciate these remedies as solutions because we are only just coming to appreciate the seriousness of the problems they solve.

Professor Hardin notes that a substitute for disabling discretion is proper motivation. He points, in the context of public institutions, to the proper motivation of public officials to maintain institutional commitments. I, too, have distinguished between motivational and imperative credibility. But Hardin, I believe, has taken the idea a step further by suggesting that, in some cases, an institution can solve its credibility problem, not by disabling its own discretion explicitly but rather by tying honorable performance on commitments directly to the career aspirations of its officials.

Finally, Professor Coleman has suggested that my overly simple characterization of commitment problems has glossed over complexities that might be of some interest to pursue. Specifically, he suggests that commitments may come in different sizes and shapes. One might wish to distinguish between individual and collective commitment. The first, he suggests, could be further subdivided into commitments to oneself and those to others. The second could similarly be subdivided according, for example, to the cardinality of decisive sets (simple majority, special majority, unanimity). I am pleased that he has drawn attention to these distinctions, and I believe he may be onto something important. I am struck, for example, at the combined impact of his comments and those reported above by Hardin—that institutions might resolve credibility problems by transforming collective commitments into individual commitments. In light of all these comments, I hope and expect that there will be further work on the subject.

REFERENCES

Abreu, Dilip. 1988. "On the Theory of Infinitely Repeated Games with Discounting." *Econometrica* 56:383–397.

Aumann, Robert J. 1981. "Survey on Repeated Games." Pp. 11–22 in Aumann et al., eds., *Essays in Game Theory and Mathematical Economics in Honor of Oskar Morgenstern.* Mannheim: Bibliograpfisches Institut.

Axelrod, Robert. 1981. "The Emergence of Cooperation Among Egoists." *American Political Science Review* 75:306–318.

_____ . 1984. *The Evolution of Cooperation.* New York: Basic Books.

Barro, Robert J. 1979. "On the Determination of the Public Debt." *Journal of Political Economy* 87:940–971.

Binmore, Ken. 1988a. "Social Contract I: Harsanyi and Rawls." Crest Working Paper No. 89-03, University of Michigan.

_____ . 1988b. "Game Theory and the Social Contract." ST/ICERD Discussion Paper No. 88/170, London School of Economics.

Brennan, Geoffrey, and James M. Buchanan. 1985. *The Reason of Rules: Constitutional Political Economy.* Cambridge: Cambridge University Press.

Coleman, James. 1989. "The New Social Structure and the New Social Science." Manuscript, Department of Sociology, University of Chicago.

Cukierman, Alex, and Allan H. Meltzer. 1986. "A Positive Theory of Discretionary Policy, the Cost of Democratic Government and the Benefits of a Constitution." *Economic Inquiry* 24:367–389.

Elster, Jon. 1979. *Ulysses and the Sirens: Studies in Rationality and Irrationality.* Cambridge: Cambridge University Press.

Epple, Dennis, and Katherine Schipper. 1981. "Municipal Pension Funding: A Theory and Some Evidence." *Public Choice* 37:141–178.

Epstein, Richard A. 1985. *Takings: Private Property and the Power of Eminent Domain.* Cambridge, MA: Harvard University Press.

Fischer, Stanley. 1986. "Time-Consistent Monetary and Fiscal Policies: A Survey." Manuscript, Department of Economics, MIT.

Fudenberg, Drew, and Eric Maskin. 1986. "The Folk Theorem in Repeated Games with Discounting or with Incomplete Information." *Econometrica* 54:533–554.

Gamm, Gerald, and Kenneth A. Shepsle. 1989. "The Emergence of Legislative Institutions: Standing Committees in the House and the Senate, 1810–1825." *Legislative Studies Quarterly* 14:39–66.

Inman, Robert. 1982. "Public Employee Pensions and the Local Labor Budget." *Journal of Public Economies* 19:49–71.

Klein, Benjamin, Robert G. Crawford, and Armen A. Alchian. 1978. "Vertical Integration, Appropriable Rents, and the Competitive Contracting Process." *Journal of Law and Economics* 21:297–326.

Kronman, Anthony T. 1985. "Contract Law and the State of Nature." *Journal of Law, Economics, and Organization* 1:5–33.

Kydland, Finn E., and Edward C. Prescott. 1977. "Rules Rather Than Discretion: The Inconsistency of Optimal Plans." *Journal of Political Economy* 85:473–491.

Laver, Michael, and Norman Schofield. 1990. *The Politics of Coalition in Europe.* Oxford: Oxford University Press.

Laver, Michael, and Kenneth A. Shepsle. 1990. "Coalitions and Cabinet Government." *American Political Science Review* 84:873–890.

McKelvey, Richard D. 1976. "Intransitivities in Multidimensional Voting Models and Some Implications for Agenda Control." *Journal of Economic Theory* 2:472–482.

———. 1979. "General Conditions for Global Intransitivities in Formal Voting Models." *Econometrica* 47:1085–1111.

Milgrom, Paul, Douglass C. North, and Barry R. Weingast. 1988. "Third Party Enforcement of Norms and Contracts: A Theoretical and Historical Analysis." Manuscript, Hoover Institution, Stanford University.

North, Douglass C., and Robert Thomas. 1973. *Rise of the Western World.* Cambridge: Cambridge University Press.

North, Douglass C., and Barry R. Weingast. 1989. "Constitutions and Commitment: The Evolution of Institutions Governing Public Choice in 17th Century England." Manuscript, Hoover Institution, Stanford University.

Riker, William R. 1962. *The Theory of Political Coalitions.* New Haven: Yale University Press.

———. 1980. "Constitutional Limitations as Self-Denying Ordinances." Pp. 85–91 in W. S. Moore and Rudolph G. Penner, eds., *The Constitution and the Budget.* Washington, DC: American Enterprise Institute.

Schelling, Thomas C. 1956. "An Essay in Bargaining." *American Economic Review* 46:281–307.

———. 1984. *Choice and Consequence: Perspectives of an Errant Economist.* Cambridge, MA: Harvard University Press.

Selten, Reinhart. 1975. "Reexamination of the Perfectness Concept for Equilibrium Points in Extensive Games." *International Journal of Game Theory* 4:25–55.

Shepsle, Kenneth A. 1978. *The Giant Jigsaw Puzzle: Democratic Committee Assignments in the Modern House*. Chicago: University of Chicago Press.

———. 1986. "Institutional Equilibrium and Equilibrium Institutions." Pp. 51–82 in Herbert Weisberg, ed., *Political Science: The Science of Politics*. New York: Agathon Press.

———. 1988. "Representation and Governance: The Great Legislative Trade-Off." *Political Science Quarterly* 103:461–484.

Weingast, Barry R., and William Marshall. 1988. "The Industrial Organization of Congress." *Journal of Political Economy* 96:132–163.

Williamson, Oliver. 1983. "Credible Commitments: Using Hostages to Support Exchange." *American Economic Review* 73:519–540.

Comments

Russell Hardin

Kenneth Shepsle argues that for individuals and for societies, the ability to commit ourselves is the ability to secure great benefits for ourselves. He is principally concerned with societal commitments, collective commitments. He argues persuasively that institutions often secure long-term commitments so that our efforts to do various things under the auspices of those institutions can be expected to bear fruit. He gives what one might suppose is his favorite example: the constraining influence of congressional committees that can largely guarantee the stability of their actions over a number of years. Since there are reasons to suppose that legislative bodies whose members have varied interests could produce volatile changes in policy from term to term, Shepsle's argument is an important corrective.

I wish to put the problem of institutional commitment and Shepsle's argument about committees into a more general strategic structure. When individuals keep their commitments, they may do so for one of two reasons that Shepsle discusses. They may find it costly to renege because they will suffer specific sanctions, or they may simply find it in their direct interest to do what they have committed themselves to do. When an institution keeps its commitments, the reasons are parallel but more complex in structure. An institution keeps commitments because relevant individuals in the institution can be motivated to do what is necessary for the institution to follow through. There are two ways the relevant individuals may be motivated: They may face sanctions, and they may find it of no interest to try to push the institution in other directions. The first of these may generally be necessary when the individual can be a free rider and when free riding can undercut institutional commitment. The second has more the character of a convention, a coordination on a mutually beneficial policy. The particular form the coordination takes, however, may be failure to coordinate on an alternative policy, a failure that stems from the high individual costs of organizing such coordination.

In his account of congressional committees, Shepsle implicitly assumes that the source of institutional commitment is based on this second form of motivation. He looks for structural reasons for why legislators in subsequent years will continue to support legislation from this year or, at the very least, why they will not succeed in overturning this year's legislation very easily even though there may be turnover in the legislative membership. Committees are an important structure for stability because, as Shepsle argues, they may be more stable over time than the larger legislative body, and they may have a clear interest in continuing support for their legislation. Of course, congressional committees can commonly block new legislation in their areas. Hence, if I wish to overturn last year's legislation, I may face an enormous burden of organizing enough support to override the relevant committee. If the relevant committee likes what I want to do, I can get my bill through with far less organizational effort.

Buy why does all this work when some majority might support a change in legislation? Because of the costs of changing the system from one in which committees play a central role to one in which committees can be turned over willy-nilly as majorities choose. These costs are far larger than merely the benefits a majority might receive this moment from getting a particular bit of past legislation changed. Hence, it will only be in the face of radically important changes that we can expect majorities to rise to strike against the committee structure. Typical legislative enactments will be allowed to continue as the relevant committees wish for want of a recoordination on an alternative.

This argument is roughly the same as the argument for why a particular constitutional regime works at all. Once it is in place and is working, no majority may object strongly enough to the way it works to go to the great effort that recoordination would require.

The other device, the invocation of sanctions to block free riding, may itself depend on coordination in the following way. It is through coordination that we elevate some people to the power to sanction others. I might strongly object to the use of sanctions against me, but I cannot motivate opposition to the sanctioning power to get us recoordinated on a system in which I would escape sanction. Indeed, because the costs of recoordination may be great, I may personally simply bow to the sanction without any effort to change the structure that supports it. The device of sanctioning is often used in Congress, although it may be far less important in the daily decisions on legislation than is the more direct failure of recoordination on alternative regimes to change legislative outcomes. It may be used more widely against subjects of an institution than against role holders within the institution. For example, a legal system that regularly uses sanctions against errant citizens may seldom use sanctions against role holders in the legal system itself.

This last point suggests an answer to the common question put to rational choice theorists: If people are rational, how then do we explain the success of public agencies in motivating officials to carry out public programs? Indeed, this is more nearly framed as a taunt than as a question because it is commonly assumed that there can be no rational choice answer to it. Rather, we must give a normative answer, a claim that people just are moral to a sufficient extent as to carry out their public duties properly. No doubt there is a great deal of morally motivated behavior by public officials, even as much on average as by ordinary people. But one wonders whether there is radically more than among ordinary people, as though we were somehow very good at selecting especially moral people for public roles. Conventional coordination, however, may be the chief answer to the anti-rationalist taunt.

People do not have to be fundamentally public spirited to be good public servants. They can be primarily interested in self, in income and career. As Madison advised, "Ambition must be made to counter ambition."[1] I block your wrong action because doing so benefits me personally. Once we have this system in place well enough, all will have strong motivation to do roughly what is right from an institutional perspective. We may occasionally judge, rightly or wrongly, that our interests can be furthered by acting against the institutional mandate. Then we may depend on direct sanction rather than on this conventional underpinning for our behavior.

In sum, there are at least two game theoretically distinct ways to stabilize commitments of collectives and institutions: (1) We may create structures, such as legislative committees, that can be changed only by coordinating a large group to vote or work against them in order to put alternative structures in place. The costs of such recoordination then weigh heavily against the change and in favor of the current structure and, hence, in favor of the general outputs of that structure. (2) We may create sanctions to punish or deter free riding. In both cases, the fundamental move is the prior coordination on a structure or a power, either for decision making or for sanctioning, that then stabilizes the policies or actions of the institution or collective. Contrary to the widespread view that our principal public difficulty may be the positive resolution of the prisoner's dilemma or collective action problems, the main grounding for social order and stability may be virtually the contrary. What we need are coordinating devices that make collective action too hard to be disruptive. And that is largely what we have in our public agencies. Otherwise, we are condemned to be victims of our momentary urges and passions rather than masters of our larger lives. The ironic twist here, of course, is that this dependency on commitment turns the supposedly conservative value of sticking with the status quo into a much more generally compelling value. Even one who wants constructive policies for change must want persistent and stable commitments to those policies. Such commitment requires stable institutional structures.

NOTES

1. "Federalist No. 51," in Philip B. Kurland and Ralph Lerner, *The Founders' Constitution*, Vol. 1 (Chicago: University of Chicago Press, 1987), p. 330.

9

Law Without Accidents

Kim Lane Scheppele

Accidents will happen, or so the saying goes. But as is the case with many maxims of common speech, the language structures as much as it appears to describe.

What are accidents? Many of those who study accidents proceed as though accidents were natural phenomena, existing in the world apart from our conceptions of them but ready and available to be classified, measured, *managed*. Seen this way, the crucial question to ask about accidents is how to prevent them, particularly how to design them away with institutions and rules that provide incentives for more careful conduct.

This conception presupposes that accidents have a particular nature in the world, a nature amenable to change. But accidents are social constructs, existing because we have chosen to see events in a particular way, to sort out the tangled but invisible web of connection among events into cause and effect relationships with a particular implicit ordering, to see particular occurrences as the unexplained and unexplainable residual of broader social patterns. Accidents are not supposed to happen. If they were planned and anticipated, they would not be accidents. The pain and suffering these events produce in the world would still exist, but the events would not be properly called accidents if everyone knew in advance what was going to occur.

The spirited discussion of the participants at the conference brought up many important issues, some of which I have tried to deal with in revision and some of which will have to wait for a later date for incorporation more fully into a larger project. I would like to thank Peter Bell, Carol Heimer, Rick Lempert, and Peter Manning for detailed comments and much helpful debate on these issues. I would also like to thank Bruce Frier, Larry Mohr, Eric Rabkin, Nancy Reichman, Peter Seidman, Jonathan Simon, Kent Syverud, and the audience at a roundtable discussion on accidents at the 1989 Law and Society meetings for providing more helpful suggestions than they were probably aware of making, particularly as many of their ideas and contributions came, often as lucky accidents, in the context of discussing something else.

Accidents are, crucially, surprises. The use of the passive voice ("accidents will happen"), however, leaves unstated the question: Surprises to whom? Does the accident have to be unexpected for the victim alone? Or does the actor (if there is one) who brings about the event also have to be unawares for the mishap to be an accident? And what if there are others who know in advance but are not saying? Or others who are surprised when the victim is not? As I will argue in this chapter, the point of view embedded in the idea of accident allows the conceptual construction of the social world to be carried out in some ways and not in others. Why things appear the way they do, who is thought responsible for these occurrences, and who should pay for them follow on these conceptual constructions. When we analyze point of view and work out the distribution of surprise, it helps us make sociological sense of some confusing policies that have been proposed to manage accidents.

Although I am ultimately interested in ways we can prevent pain and suffering in the world (and the limits on our capacities to do so), this chapter deals predominantly with the conceptualization of accidents in the law. Accidents are only one source of pain and suffering, but they are interesting precisely because they occur (by definition) at the limits of someone's knowledge, where mishaps come as a surprise. And the law is only one of the institutions for dealing with accidents, although it is the institution that tends to structure ground rules within which other institutions, such as insurance companies and engineering design firms, operate.[1] Studying the legal construction of accidents is a way of examining the production and distribution of knowledge in a particular social setting.

There are many knowledges in the social world, each produced and distributed differently. One of those knowledges, sociological knowledge, deals with aggregate social patterns and the ways in which individual intentions and actions are related to broader social forces. As we think about the role of social theory (and the sociological knowledge it provides) in the twenty-first century, the elimination of accidents appears as a recurring goal for social scientists who want to improve institutions with this new knowledge. The production of knowledge (or, we might say, the reduction of surprise) is itself a social process, and the types of knowledges that are produced as well as the ways in which institutions and individuals take these knowledges into account affect the capacity of social theory to produce changes in the world. Trying to understand surprises tells us about the limits of our practice. In order for sociological knowledge to have a deliberate effect on social life, it must find its way into those institutions and practices that shape what happens in the world.[2] And we can imagine that one effect of the spread of sociological knowledge would be the reduction of surprise and, along with that, a reduction in accidents.

Social scientists know much more than they used to about the sorts of things that produce what are seen as accidents at the level of the individuals affected. We know a great deal about how accidents come about and how often they do—so that, at the aggregate level, there are few surprises left.

If we imagine that social theory will give us more and more knowledge about the social world, particularly that part of the social world that is deliberately constructed, then we might be able to say that there are hardly any complete accidents anymore. From a sociological point of view, we understand quite a lot about how people get hurt in daily life.

But what happens when we look at accidents from a legal point of view? Tort law is the part of legal doctrine that is most centrally concerned with assessing liability for accidents. Traditional tort law, however, generally focuses narrowly on the individuals affected and the individual cause of the individual event; thus, many events predictable in the aggregate appear still to be surprises when seen from the affected individuals' perspectives. What if the legal system were to use the sociological knowledge that is available and find that there are no surprises left, leaving us law without accidents?

Here lies the problem in legal puzzles about accidents. Social science offers increased knowledge about accident rates and accident causes. But integrating this knowledge into tort models of accidents has proved to be quite difficult. In the next section, I show how traditional tort analysis differs from sociological strategies for thinking about accidents, and, in the sections to follow, I examine the ways in which some sociological knowledge has been taken into account in traditional tort doctrine and assess the ways in which two of the major recent institutional changes in that field—strict liability for products and the move to social insurance schemes—have improved the traditional tort track record in considering sociological knowledge.

In analyzing the concepts, categories, and assumptions of tort law, I take a sociology of knowledge approach to the study of legal doctrine. *Sociology of knowledge* is used here in two somewhat different senses. In one sense, my approach takes as central the ways in which the frameworks of thought in a particular professional field structure important understandings of the world and provide a well-marked trail to follow in analyzing new problems. Concern with the sociology of knowledge alerts us to the historical and contingent origins of concepts, categories, and assumptions of fields of practice and enables us to realize that situations may be seen in ways strikingly different from the accepted view. Legal doctrine generally, and tort doctrine in particular, is an intellectual structure for viewing problems in the world, and how problems are framed in law is an important element in determining when and how they are considered to be solved. In a second sense, though, a sociology of knowledge frame structures this inquiry so that the distribution and uses of particular knowledges themselves are taken to be crucial elements of the problem at hand.[3]

SOCIOLOGICAL AND LEGAL
PERSPECTIVES ON ACCIDENTS

Tort law in England and the United States is very much a product of the sociological age. Although its roots can be traced back to the old common-law actions in assumpsit, trespass, and action on the case,[4] tort law emerged as a separate body of legal rules in the second half of the nineteenth century, just as sociology was emerging as a discipline.[5] The timing is more than coincidental. Both tort law (White 1980, Chapter 1; Winfield 1926) and sociology were arguably responses to major changes occurring in Western societies as a result of industrialization and urbanization. But what is striking is how different the responses were. While sociologists were interested in general patterns of social interaction and in macro-historical changes, lawyers and judges in England and the United States were developing a very micro-motivational, anti-historical, generally unsociological framework for thinking about accidents.

That law should have developed a very different perspective from that of sociology should not be surprising when we think of the special institutional constraints within which lawyers and judges operate. In a common-law system, courts must wait for legal problems to come to them, always in the form of a specific harm arising in a specific situation, before they can work out the legal rules. Before the advent of an identifiable set of tort rules, most civil lawsuits arose either out of violations of agreements made by people who already knew each other or out of violations of property rules. These were cases in which the specifics of individualized agreements and arrangements had accustomed courts to look at each case as raising primarily local concerns. With the changes industrialization and urbanization brought, certain recurring patterns of harm started to become evident, but the case-by-case development of the common law did not provide a mechanism for registering and attending to such broad-scale social changes as *patterns.*[6] Common-law courts went on doing what they had always done, looking at each case as if it arose from primarily local causes with primarily local effects. The changes in the society around them forced common-law courts to deal with accidents among strangers, and the development of tort rules was the outcome of this process; but the already well-established common-law system got lawyers and judges to see each case as a unique event[7] with little connection to a set of broader causes in the social world.

How did English and U.S. courts decide whether one person was legally responsible for the injuries suffered by another in an accident? The ideas of causation and fault in individualized cases have been central to the development of tort doctrine, with most cases not seen (until quite recently) as instances of general social problems or as generalizable events. Tort cases are usually considered in all their idiosyncratic (and unsociological) glory, with cause and fault sought at a highly individualized level.

We can see this attention to idiosyncratic detail by examining the most famous U.S. accident case, read by every law student since it was decided in 1928, *Palsgraf v. the Long Island Railroad* (248 N.Y. 339, 162 N.E. 99 [1928]). The case is identified by, and the analysis proceeds from, its bizarre facts. Mrs. Palsgraf was waiting on a platform on the Long Island Railroad for a train to go to Rockaway Beach. As the train ahead of hers was pulling out of the station, two men raced across the platform to catch it. One man was able to get aboard without difficulty. The second man, who was carrying a wrapped package under his arm, jumped onto the steps but looked as though he were going to fall. A guard on the train grabbed the unsteady intending passenger by the arm, and a guard on the platform pushed him from behind; although all this activity succeeded in steadying the tardy passenger, it also succeeded in disloding the package from under the man's arm. The package contained fireworks, which fell between the train and the platform, causing a terrific explosion. The force of the explosion threw down some scales at the opposite end of the platform onto Mrs. Palsgraf, causing bruises and a lifelong stammer. She sued the railroad, claiming that the train company employees were at fault in this accident.

The majority opinion in the Court of Appeals, New York's highest court, was written by Benjamin Cardozo, one of the country's most respected judges. And although he is credited in this case with systematizing and putting on a more solid footing the area of negligence doctrine, he took his job to be announcing a general rule that made sense of the unusual particulars of this specific case and of similar cases. He began his analysis by announcing, "The conduct of the defendant's guard, if a wrong in relation to the holder of the package, was not a wrong in its relation to the plaintiff, standing far away" (248 N.Y. 341). And he continued in this vein, finding the principles to govern the specific conduct of the specific people at the specific time and place: "What the plaintiff must show is a 'wrong' to herself, i.e. a violation of her own right, and not merely a wrong to someone else, nor conduct 'wrongful' because unsocial, but not 'a wrong' to anyone" (248 N.Y. 343–344). Cardozo's opinion is best remembered for the general principle it developed: that defendants are liable for their negligent actions only to *foreseeable* plaintiffs.[8] Mrs. Palsgraf lost, on Cardozo's analysis, because the accident was a freak occurrence, a surprise to all, even though three of the seven high court judges and a majority of the intermediate appeals court judges thought that the cause-effect relationship was so clear in this case that Mrs. Palsgraf should win.

That cases should be considered in such an individualized way is deeply engrained in the common law. The common law had always analyzed cases one by one to look at the specific characteristics of a dispute, deciding each case on its own facts. The concepts of causation and fault, as they entered this frame of analysis, focused attention on the role of individual human agency in bringing about that particular injury in that particular place at that particular time, guaranteeing that accidents would come to be seen as freak occurrences where individuals in all their uniqueness were to blame for highly idiosyncratic events.[9] Anglo-American tort law developed on the principle that legal liability should follow personal fault in particularized circumstances, and so attention in legal inquiry focused on the activities of the alleged injurer and the victim and on the singular cause of the singular event.

The sociologist, of course, would see the matter quite differently, focusing not on what was idiosyncratic and unusual about the case but rather on what made the case typical of events of the day. *Palsgraf* was a railroad injury case, and railroads were probably the most common single source of accidents brought before the courts. As Lawrence Friedman noted, "From about 1840 on, one specific machine, the railroad locomotive, generated on its own steam (so to speak), more tort law than any other [machine] in the 19th century. The railroad engine swept like a great roaring bull through the countryside, carrying out an economic and social revolution; but it exacted a toll of thousands, injured and dead" (Friedman 1973, p. 262).

At the time Mrs. Palsgraf was hurt, railroads were still causing many injuries and deaths. In 1924, the year the fireworks exploded causing Mrs. Palsgraf's stammer, railroads in the United States killed 6,617 people and wounded 143,739 more (Noonan 1976, pp. 111–151). That would have been a little over 0.1 percent of the country's population at the time. Although not all of the accidents would have been quite so unusual as Mrs. Palsgraf's, clearly something more is going on here than a series of freak occurrences. Railroads brought with them a well-known toll of death and destruction. And examining liability, as Cardozo did, by looking at who was at fault in the particular accident seems to miss something crucial from a sociological perspective. The accident on the Long Island Railroad platform may have been a surprise to Mrs. Palsgraf, the trainmen, and perhaps even the mysterious man with the package of fireworks. But it was not a sociological surprise.

Ever since Emile Durkheim's study of suicide (1951), sociologists have known that *rates* of behavior—even highly idiosyncratic, personal behavior—follow regular patterns that are highly predictable. The regular patterns may be mysterious to the people whose individual actions and decisions find their way into the aggregate statistics, but the regular patterns have their own logic, their own ebbs and flows, their own apparent causes. The micro-knowledge of the individuals involved and the macro-knowledge of the social analysts are different knowledges, differently generated with different senses of relevant detail. Tort analysis traditionally incorporates the micro-knowledge but ignores the knowledge at the macro-sociological level. As a result, the legal system's capacity to understand the social patterns of accidents is greatly diminished.

We can now see the theoretical problem in the idea of accidents. Accidents are surprises, but surprises to whom? Events that may be surprises to injurers and victims may not be surprises when viewed in aggregate statistics. Events that are surprises in a statistical sense may not be surprises to the individuals involved, with their detailed local knowledge. The idea of an accident provides an important window on a central sociological problem: the generation and social distribution of different forms of knowledge.

TORT DOCTRINE
AND FIELDS OF KNOWLEDGE

To be able to see whether and how sociological knowledge might be brought to bear in legal thinking about accidents, we need to understand what legal doctrine in this area looks like. I will present tort rules framed in the way that they are taught to first-year law students, but I will discuss these rules in order to demonstrate that there is another, more parsimonious account of how torts might be organized conceptually. Let me indicate at the start what my point will be. Tort doctrine can be reconceived as an analysis of the fields of knowledge of the defendant and plaintiff, picking out the actual or constructive knowledge of the defendant and victim as central to assessing liability for accidents.

What is a field of knowledge? If we think of knowledge as being distributed unevenly across social space, then any individual or group will be located in the neighborhood of some information and far away from other information. For example, medical doctors are privy to some information that the rest of us do not know, and they can more easily understand and assimilate new medical information because they have had prior experience with such acquisition. Doctors, then, have a particular field of knowledge to which they are socially proximate and from which others are distant. Similarly, members of a particular family have a great deal of information about each other, information generally not available to those outside the family. Family news is more likely to be shared within the circle than outside it. And so on. We can map the distribution of knowledge across social positions and across social contexts and, in so doing, identify distinct fields of knowledge. A field of knowledge is the sum of all the knowledge to which a particular person has access, because of both the person's social positions and social contexts.[10]

I will argue that tort doctrine has already been centrally concerned with mapping the social distribution of knowledge and associating legal responsibility with access to operative knowledge that would make the accident less surprising. Those who have access to, and are in a position to make use of, knowledge that would be able to ward off the injuries accidents produce are generally found in tort law to be liable for the losses. Tort doctrine, then, requires an analysis of the social distribution of surprise. Those in the immediate vicinity of the accident who have access to the most knowledge about the relevant elements of the situation and who are in a position to do something about the impending disasters are generally the ones who have to pay for the consequences when the accident occurs.

I will also argue that discussion of fields of knowledge can greatly simplify the standard analysis of tort doctrine by reducing many of the tangled rules to a single conceptual scheme.[11] I will, further, assess the extent to which tort rules have been successful in describing accidents, arguing that they have worked well as long as the relevant knowledge has been in the social field occupied by the victims and defendants. But, as we will see later, this framework does not lend itself well to incorporating sociological knowledge that is not known to those involved in a particular accident but is only known in aggregate statistics to those who take a collective perspective.

Analyzing accidents by focusing on the social distribution of surprise represents a major departure from the traditional analysis of torts. Much has been written about the underlying structure of tort law, but suffice it to say that torts have usually been analyzed as a series of rules that establish when an agent's activity is said to be the legal cause of a mishap and when that activity is *blameworthy* in some way, leading to a judgment of legal liability (Hart and Honoré 1959). More recent economic analyses attempt to show that liability rules should and do assign the costs of losses to those who can most cheaply avoid the loss in the first place or who would be most affected by legal incentives to prevent the accident (Posner and Landes 1987; Calabresi 1970).[12]

Tort law itself does not operate idiosyncratically, even though the events it covers often seem very peculiar. Tort doctrine can be described as a set of general rules for deciding particular cases involving civil wrongs not elsewhere covered in the law. The last section established that the features of cases picked out by the general rules are the specific elements that connect the individual event with its unique cause under the particular circumstances. Although tort law operates according to general rules, and in this way it is patterned, many of the features identified by these general rules operate like indexicals[13] and so vary systematically with context.

Torts is a common-law subject,[14] which means that the rules that govern the field have been created slowly over time by judges trying to decide like cases alike. There is no official code that lays out in a straightforward fashion what the law is in the area, and so lawyers and judges (and nonspecialists, for that matter) generally have to consult many legal opinions to figure out the rules on a given point. Although not created by a body authorized to make law, the *Restatement (Second) of Torts* is the closest thing we have to a code laying out the rules of tort law. Drafted by law professors and practitioners who are members of the American Law Institute, the *Restatement* lists in orderly fashion rules that are the members' best guesses about what doctrine does and should look like in particular areas. It is often cited as authoritative by courts (and the eight-volume appendix to the four-volume work consists almost entirely of citations to cases that have cited the *Restatement*).

In the following sections, I will examine some of the basic rules of tort doctrine to see how the fields of knowledge of the defendant and the victim are evaluated and associated with liability for accidents. In doing this, I will show how an accident is constructed as a legal concept. Within the law, accidents are the special province of that part of tort doctrine called negligence. But, as I will argue, the same principles that animate negligence doctrine also work to explain why intentional torts, those injuries that are caused by the deliberate hurtful actions of an agent, are handled the way that they are. In considering these legal categories, I will discuss statements of the rules as they appear in the *Restatement (Second) of Torts*.

COMPARING FIELDS OF KNOWLEDGE

If my theory were correct, the more knowledge the plaintiff has of the circumstances giving rise to the accident, the more unsuccessful the plaintiff

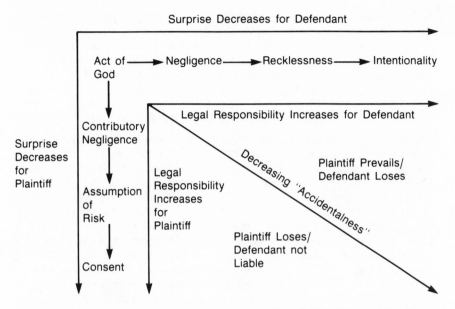

Figure 9.1   Tort liability and the fields of knowledge of plaintiff and defendant

should be in pushing off the costs of the losses to the defendant. The more knowledge the defendant has, the more likely the defendant should be to shoulder the burden. Any legal problem will require analysis of *both* of these fields of knowledge. These levels of knowledge, along with the legal rules that embody these levels, are displayed in Figure 9.1. Arraying the knowledge of the defendant along the top and the knowledge of the plaintiff along the side, we can map the dividing line (diagonally across the middle) where courts should flip in their judgments from one party to another, if the fields of knowledge theory is correct. Above the diagonal line, the plaintiff should prevail; below that line, the defendant should. The party that knows the most about the circumstances giving rise to the accident (or, conversely, the party who is least surprised by the accident)[15] should bear the costs of the accident if the law has a fields of knowledge logic.

If an accident is a complete surprise to both parties, then it may be held to be an "act of God," and the loss stays where it falls. And if it is a surprise to the victim while not to the defendant, then the defendant is liable. But if the event is a surprise to the defendant while the plaintiff knew what was happening, then the defendant is not legally responsible. The more knowledge each party to the accident has, however, the less "accidental" the accident becomes, and the more the law uses words not associated with the accident frame, such as "intentionality" or "consent." So, as we move from the upper left corner to the lower right corner in the figure, the event in question becomes less and less accidental and is analyzed in law under other headings, such as intentional torts or consensual encounters.

Each of the positions along the horizontal and vertical axes identifies a particular legal standard. We will examine each in turn to see how well the law implicitly follows the fields of knowledge model.

THE DEFENDANT'S KNOWLEDGE

An accident has happened. In deciding who should bear the cost of the loss involved, courts will first determine whether the elements of a "cause of action" (legitimate lawsuit) for negligence have been satisfied.[16] Those elements include: (1) whether the harm was something the victim was entitled to be protected against, (2) whether the defendant was negligent, (3) whether the defendant's actions *caused* the injury to the victim, and (4) whether the victim was partly responsible for the injury (*Restatement*, § 281). Whether the victim is entitled to be protected against harm is a complicated matter that I will not discuss here. Suffice it to say that for most of the cases with which we will be concerned, this will not arise as a problem, although it would need more careful consideration in any more general theory of tort law. We will not discuss the victim's role until the next section, and so we will focus here on negligence and causation as they affect evaluation of the defendant's conduct. We will then consider the separate standards for reckless and intentional torts.

Negligence

When is a person found to be negligent in causing injury to another? When his or her conduct "falls below the standard established by law for the protection of others against unreasonable risk of harm" (*Restatement*, § 282). And what is that standard? Tort doctrine invokes the "reasonable man" (*Restatement*, § 283). The *Restatement* says that the reasonable man is "a person exercising those qualities of judgment which society requires of its members for the protection of their own interests and the interests of others" (*Restatement*, § 283, Comment b). And when qualities of judgment are further explained, they are invariably described as qualities that tap the knowledge the defendant actually has or should have had, given the situation or the defendant's position.

For example, "The actor is required to recognize that his conduct involves a risk of causing an invasion of another's interest if a reasonable man would do so while exercising a) such attention, perception of the circumstances, memory, knowledge of other pertinent matters, intelligence, and judgment as a reasonable man would have; and b) such superior attention, perception, memory, knowledge, intelligence, and judgment as the actor himself has" (*Restatement*, § 289). And, the actor is required to know: "a) the qualities and habits of human beings and animals and the qualities, characteristics, and capacities of things and forces in so far as they are matters of common knowledge at the time and in the community; and b) the common law, legislative enactments, and general customs in so far as they are likely to affect the conduct of the other or third persons" (*Restatement,* § 290).

Clearly, this is a lot for anyone to have in mind, but the most striking feature of this legal analysis is the extent to which the liability of the defendant depends on the defendant's knowledge of the connection between his or her activities and the harm to the victim. Negligence doctrine focuses our attention on whether the defendant knew or could be expected to know whether the actions in which he or she was engaged would likely produce untoward consequences; often this is captured in the statement of the rule, originating in the *Palsgraf* case, that defendants are only liable to the foreseeable plaintiffs for their negligent acts. The negligence standard also extends liability to foreseeable *consequences* of negligent acts. But what is foreseeability if not an assessment of the defendant's position with respect to a field of knowledge? The knowledge clearly does not have to be known in fact by the defendant for the defendant to be liable. Instead, what the law engages in is an assessment of the social distribution of a particular sort of knowledge and the defendant's social position relative to that knowledge, mapping a field of knowledge in which the defendant is situated, regardless of what the defendant actually knows.

In the schematic cases that accompany the *Restatement's* announcements of rules, the procedure used by courts is clearer. For example, when a person is socially situated in such a position that someone *like* him or her probably does know of the existence of a risk, then that person will be found liable when his or her conduct results in injury. So, "A climbs a tree to look at bird's nest, and takes hold of an electric power line carrying a current of 110 volts, which runs through the tree. A is completely ignorant of the danger from the power line, although that danger is a matter of common knowledge in the community. A is negligent notwithstanding his ignorance" (*Restatement,* § 290 e, Illustration 1).

But the knowledge one is responsible for having is not just the stock of common knowledge in the community in which one resides; one may also have special obligations in light of the particular information to which one's social position gives one access. For example, when a defendant is a doctor, the relevant standard of knowledge is not just the stock of knowledge available to all (although the doctor as a community member is supposed to know that also) but is also that specialized stock of knowledge available primarily to doctors. So, "A is a physician. His child exhibits symptoms which A, because of his previous training and experience, should recognize as indicating that the child has scarlet fever. A fails to recognize them, and permits his child to go to school where the child communicates the disease to B, another pupil. A is negligent in not recognizing the risk, although if he were a layman he might not be negligent" (*Restatement,* § 289 m, Illustration 12). The special standards applicable to the practicing of particular professions are outlined later: "Unless he represents that he has greater or less skill or knowledge, one who undertakes to render services in the practice of a profession or trade is required to exercise the skill and knowledge normally possessed by members of that profession or trade in good standing in similar communities" (*Restatement*, § 299 a).

The "reasonable man"[17] of the *Restatement* is, thus, more sociologically sophisticated than he seems to be. The reasonable man is elaborated into the concepts of the reasonable doctor, the reasonable driver of a truck containing high explosives, the reasonable chemist, the reasonable stunt man. Each of these social statuses situates the occupant in a field of specialized knowledge, which becomes relevant for assessing the defendant's liability if the law, as I have argued, associates liability with knowledge of the connection between actions and harms. What tort law embodies is a sociological analysis of the links between knowledge and social position. But that sociological knowledge operates through the knowledge of individuals, as the law primarily analyzes the individual's access to particular knowledge, given the individual's social position.

Legal rules about torts also consider the specialized information associated with particular activities and not just specialized social roles. Defendants are found liable for injuring others when their conduct consists of especially dangerous activities, such as keeping tigers as pets or driving rapidly down winding mountain roads with little visibility. Here again, what the law seems to be picking out are activities in which there is reliable knowledge about the significant connection between the particular action and harm to others. In addition, defendants are found liable when they engage without reasonable care in activities that, while safe when performed normally, become dangerous when performed without competence, preparation, or warning (*Restatement*, § 297). And the same logic applies: Knowing an activity is likely to produce harm results in finding the defendant liable, even if the defendant herself did not actually know of the danger involved. If the knowledge were well-enough known in the social setting in which the defendant was located, then that knowledge is assumed to be possessed by the defendant also.

Defendants have special duties to potential victims in cases in which the defendant has special knowledge of the dangers lurking on land he or she controls (and thereby has superior knowledge of) (*Restatement*, §§ 328–387)[18] and in cases where he or she supplies another person with chattels (moveable property) he or she knows to pose risks of harm (*Restatement*, §§ 388–408). Although the precise specifications of these duties is complicated, it is clear that duties increase the more the defendant knows about the potentially dangerous character of the land or the merchandise and the more the defendant knows of the victim's possibility of being injured in the situation.[19]

Much of the idea of negligence, then, can be captured in assessing the level of knowledge present in the special part of the social world in which the defendant is acting. If the relevant knowledge is present in the defendant's social location, the defendant will be held to be liable for harm caused by acting in ways that ignore the available knowledge. The relevant information may be found in the common knowledge of the community, in the specialized knowledges of the defendant's social positions, in the knowledge that comes from ongoing practice of an activity, or in the specialized knowledge that attends possession of property. But standards of negligence clearly are rooted primarily in an assessment of the defendant's field of knowledge.

Causation

The other leading concept in assessing a defendant's liability for negligence is causation. For a defendant to be liable for harm, it must be established that the defendant's actions are a legal cause of the harm suffered by the plaintiff (*Restatement*, § 430). Legal cause is established if the defendant's conduct can be shown to be a "substantial factor in bringing about the harm" and "there is no rule of law relieving the actor from liability" (*Restatement*, § 431). In this assessment, courts are instructed to consider the number of other forces in play, whether the defendant's activities continued in active operation up until the time of the harm, and the amount of time that elapsed between the defendant's actions and the harm to the plaintiff (*Restatement*, § 433). In addition, liability is reduced in cases in which there are significant intervening or superseding causes, breaking the strong connection between the initial action and eventual harm (*Restatement*, §§ 440–452).

All of the signals courts are instructed to look for can be considered to be measures of the closeness of the connection between the defendant's actions and the victim's harm. Seen within the framework of the social distribution of surprise that we have been exploring, we can observe that all of these factors lessening causal attribution serve to make the defendant more likely to be surprised when a harmful event comes about. Multiple causes, effects at a distance, intervening causes, and a long time lapse all reduce the direct knowledge the defendant is likely to have of the potential effects of his or her actions, and liability decreases accordingly. Causation as constructed by courts tracks the field of knowledge of the defendant, even though the defendant's *actual* knowledge is often legally irrelevant. What matters to courts in determining causation is whether the knowledge of connection between cause and effect is clear enough and predictable enough to have been reasonably attributed to someone in the defendant's position.

Recklessness

Another factor affecting the defendant's liability is the degree of recklessness of his or her conduct. But consider the way in which the *Restatement* defines recklessness: "The actor's conduct is in reckless disregard of the safety of another if he does an act or intentionally fails to do an act which it is his duty to the other to do, knowing or having reason to know of the facts which would lead a reasonable man to realize, not only that his conduct creates an unreasonable risk of physical harm to another, but also that such risk is substantially greater than that which is necessary to make his conduct negligent" (*Restatement*, § 500).

This standard lays out a clear knowledge requirement: Recklessness of conduct implies an even more certain knowledge or reason to know of the relation between action and harm than is required for ordinary negligence. And, the more knowledge the defendant has, the more certain the defendant's liability. The defendant *must* know (actually or constructively) the facts that give rise to the risk in his or her conduct in order for a charge of recklessness to be made out, and, when the knowledge reaches this heightened level of certainty, courts hold defendants liable even when the victim contributed to the situation (*Restatement,* § 503). Recklessness, then, makes the defendant more likely to be found completely liable for the harm, and this reflects the connection I have been trying to demonstrate between knowledge and liability.

Intentional Torts

When a defendant *intends* to cause harm to someone, both the physical and legal consequences are more certain than they are when the defendant is either negligent or reckless. The *Restatement* explains the meaning of intent by indicating:

> All consequences which the actor desires to bring about are intended, as the word is used in this Restatement. Intent is not, however, limited to consequences which are desired. If the actor knows that the consequences are certain, or substantially certain, to result from his act, and still goes ahead, he is treated by law as if he had in fact desired to produce the result. As the probability that the consequences will follow decreases, and becomes less than substantial certainty, the actor's conduct loses the character of intent, and becomes mere recklessness. . . . As the probability decreases further and amounts only to a risk that the result will follow, it becomes ordinary negligence. . . . All three have their important place in the law of torts, but the liability attached to them will differ. (*Restatement,* § 8A, Comment b)

This explicit statement comes very close to reproducing the knowledge theory I have been trying to forward here. Intentional torts are different from cases of recklessness, which are different from cases of negligence not only in the quality of the actions but also in the quantity and certainty of knowledge possessed by the defendant. The various kinds of torts, usually thought to present very different legal principles, are actually, on the knowledge theory, different only in degree and not in kind.

THE VICTIM'S KNOWLEDGE

If a case of negligence can be made out against a defendant, the defendant may try to shift the blame to the plaintiff. In order for the plaintiff to prevail in the face of this defense, however, it is (under the classic common-law rules) not enough for the plaintiff to show that the defendant was negligent; the plaintiff must also be free from fault in the accident.[20] The legal standards used to assess the plaintiff's role in an accident parallel those used for the defendant and reveal that it is the plaintiff's knowledge that matters most in assessing whether negligent defendants can nonetheless avoid liability for the loss. I will consider contributory negligence, assumption of risk, and consent as standards for plaintiff's behavior.

Contributory Negligence

A plaintiff is barred from recovering for an injury inflicted negligently by a defendant if the plaintiff also contributed to the likelihood of the accident: "Contributory negligence is conduct on the part of the plaintiff which falls below the standard to which he should perform for his own protection, and which is a legally contributing cause co-operating with the negligence of the defendant in bringing about the plaintiff's harm" (*Restatement,* § 463).

What is this standard? Not surprisingly, the reasonable man appears again at this point (*Restatement,* § 464). While the reasonable plaintiff and the reasonable defendant are generally held to the same standards, there may be some important differences where the things one must do to protect oneself differ from the things one must do to prevent undue risk to others. Sometimes a person may be held to a higher standard in protecting him- or herself than he or she is held to in protecting others (*Restatement,* § 464, Comment f). But usually, a victim is held to the same knowledge, the same community standards, the same specialized knowledges associated with social positions, and the same knowledge of practices in which he or she may be engaged. Clearly, contributory negligence is meant to capture the same sort of knowledge as the initial judgment of negligence itself, and the *comparison* of the knowledges of the plaintiff and of the defendant is the main determinant of the final judgment about liability.[21] The person who either had the most knowledge of the conditions giving rise to the accident or was situated socially so as to have better access to such information is the person the court finds legally responsible.

Assumption of Risk

Sometimes it is said that a plaintiff has voluntarily assumed the risks involved in a particular setting and, as a result, cannot blame the defendant for the injury that followed. This assumption of risk doctrine is expressed in the *Restatement* as: "A plaintiff who voluntarily assumes a risk of harm arising from the negligent or reckless conduct of the defendant cannot recover for such harm" (*Restatement,* § 496A). Although assumption of risk and contributory negligence frequently overlap as defenses, it is generally held that contributory negligence involves some lack of care on the part of the plaintiff, while assumption of risk implies at least some consent to participate in the activities of the defendant. And while lack of care indicates that the plaintiff *might* or *should* be aware of the risk, consent implies that the plaintiff *is in fact* aware of the risk. As knowledge and certainty grow, so does legal responsibility. The plaintiff is unable to shift the burden of loss

to the defendant if the plaintiff knew of the risk involved in the activity
and participated anyway.

Consent

Assumption of risk implies consent to take a chance, but outright consent
implies even more "willingness in fact for the conduct to occur" (*Restatement*,
§ 892). While consent does not imply certainty that an event *will* occur, it
does imply knowledge of a high probability that the event will occur and
an unwillingness to take steps to avoid it.[22] Attention to the victim's consent,
then, can be seen as the court's concern for the knowledge possessed by
the victim as well as for the victim's disposition toward the event itself.
The only sort of knowledge that would render the victim more certain that
an event would happen occurs in the case of self-inflicted injuries for which
others are rarely responsible. Consent can make even intentional harmful
conduct by the defendant not tortious.

Just as we saw with the defendant's field of knowledge, then, analysis
of the victim's field of knowledge also produces the conclusion that the
more knowledge the actor has, the more he or she bears the burden of the
loss in tort. But what happens when we consider the fields of knowledge
of plaintiff and defendant together?

ASSESSING LIABILITY
AND THE SOCIAL
DISTRIBUTION OF KNOWLEDGE

We have seen how the standards for evaluating the individual conduct of
plaintiffs and defendants hinge on an assessment of the individual's position
with respect to a field of knowledge. But courts do not just assess what
each party knew separately. What courts do, in fact, is compare the *relative*
levels of knowledge of both parties. If one party knows more than the
other, that party bears all or more of the costs of the accident. In cases
where the knowledge is equal, courts do not intervene to change the way
the losses fall. So, for example,

> A is setting off dangerous fireworks in a public place with reckless indifference
> to a serious risk of harm to persons in the vicinity. B and C approach the
> place where A is acting. B, fully aware of the risk, approaches for the purposes
> of enjoying the spectacle. C is not aware of the risk, but in the exercise of
> reasonable care for his own protection should discover or appreciate it. B and
> C are injured by a rocket which goes off at the wrong angle. B is barred from
> recovery against A by his assumption of the risk, but C is not barred from
> recovery for A's reckless conduct by his contributory negligence. (*Restatement*,
> § 496A, d, Illustration 1)

This complicated case reveals how well Figure 9.1 describes what courts
do. A was being reckless, so it would take knowledge by a potential victim
equal to or in excess of A's knowledge to defeat A's liability for engaging

in such conduct. B knew the risk and so had knowledge equal to A's about the probability that B would be injured. (But note that if A *intended* to injure B, B's mere assumption of risk would not be enough to defeat A's liability because A would have had more knowledge about the probability of B's injury.) C did not know the risk, but placed himself in a position where he would be exposed to it, even though he should have known better. If A were merely being negligent, then C's claim against A would fail. But because A was being reckless and therefore knew just how risky the activity was, A was liable to C because A's knowledge was greater.

If I am right that this is a deep logic that runs throughout tort doctrine, then this theory should be useful to predict how courts will decide cases involving accidents. We would expect courts to be sensitive to the relative levels of knowledge of the two parties to the accident, and we would expect this analysis not to be confined to accidents but to extend to all occurrences of harm covered by tort law.

SOCIOLOGICAL KNOWLEDGE
AND THE CONCEPTION OF
ACCIDENTS AS "SURPRISES"

But notice the sort of knowledge we have been considering in analyzing tort doctrine. Although the reasonable man is a person assumed to have all the knowledge of his various social positions and all the knowledge embedded in his practices (whether he, in fact, knows these things or not), there is some obvious knowledge that is not well represented in the legal model of accidents: sociological knowledge of rates, causes, and aggregate patterns. The knowledge that traditional tort doctrine takes into account is the actual knowledge of individuals and the knowledge available in the social vicinity of the individual. Aggregate sociological knowledge has little place in these models. If social theory is going to find its way into the legal conceptualization of accidents, aggregate sociological knowledge must be taken into account in tort law.

Let me give one historical example of the way in which the traditional tort framework failed to incorporate sociological knowledge so that we can see how important it is to include it in our consideration of accidents. In the nineteenth century, as industrialized factories were providing new strategies of work organization, the emerging tort rules were not being designed to capture the importance and special knowledge of these collectivities. When one worker's actions caused injury to another, state courts announced the fellow servant rule, which held that a worker could only recover for an occupational injury from the fellow worker who caused it and could not sue the employer who employed them both. Using the traditional tort rules described above, Judge Lemuel Shaw, writing in the first U.S. case to use the fellow servant rule (*Farwell v. Boston & Worcester Railroad Co.*, 45 Mass. [4 Metc.] 49 [1842]), held that each worker assumed the risks of employment and could watch his or her coworkers so that not only were there knowledge and consent at the outset of employment but there was also constant vigilance in the workplace itself. The knowledge of plaintiff and defendant was taken into account, but the idea that relevant knowledge might exist elsewhere in the system was not easily incorporated in tort doctrine.[23] Although most state courts adopted the fellow servant rule, a number of legislatures tried to change it, only to find their statutes weakened by judicial interpretation (Auerbach et al. 1961). Courts generally did not acknowledge that the knowledge a company possessed and the way it chose to organize its workplace might also be considered to be relevant in determining why accidents happened and who should be liable (Friedman and Ladinsky 1969). Given that the knowledge of workplace accidents was so self-evidently patterned, probably more so than any other type of accident, it should not be surprising that workplace accidents were the first to be taken out of the traditional tort framework through the institution of workers' compensation plans. Since the tort framework did not adapt to recognize patterned accidents, the accidents had to be managed another way.

How might we conceive of sociological knowledge within the framework that has been advanced here? If we have considered accidents in light of the surprises they present to victims and injurers, then we should think of the surprises and nonsurprises accidents pose at the social level as well.

Knowledges relevant to the understanding and prevention of accidents exist in social organization above the level of the individual and his or her social positions and practices. And it is one important goal of social theory, as we confront an increasingly deliberately constructed social environment, to provide more insight into the generation and distribution of these various knowledges. When policies are being debated, for example, the policy makers often know the likely rate of accidents that accompany a policy shift. Whether changing the speed limit, requiring seat belts, controlling pollutants in the air and water, or setting standards in the fire code, social policies are often smarter than the individuals affected in knowing how accidents will happen, although it is usually difficult to pinpoint when the accidents will happen and to whom. Choices among policies are often made on the basis of comparative assessments of accident rates (which might be seen as error rates) associated with each policy. But tort law has been remarkably resistant to taking this other sort of knowledge, aggregate sociological knowledge, into account.[24] If knowledge about the cause and prevention of accidents is evident in policy decisions made by governmental officials or company executives in choosing how to construct social institutions, then following the logic we have been exploring in traditional tort law, these supra-individual agents should be part of the pool of candidates who should be considered in assessing who has the most knowledge relevant in managing accidents, even if they are not the direct injurers or the victims.[25]

Three sorts of surprises, then, need to be considered in working out how to think about accidents. Accidents may be surprises to the victims, to the injurers, or both. But they may also be social surprises.[26] And just as accidents may be surprises at all of these levels, so we may find knowledge at all of the levels that helps us to understand when and how accidents happen, as well as when and how accidents might be prevented.

The plea for incorporation of sociological knowledge does not imply that we should ignore the other knowledges the law has always considered. Sociological knowledge may tell us about aggregate patterns, but it often gives us little information about who the victims will be and when they will suffer. Local knowledge, closer to the scene, may tell us that, although that close-up knowledge will not reveal the larger social forces that come into play in determining the aggregate rates. A full understanding of accidents requires that all these knowledges be taken into account, but tort law has generally only considered the micro-knowledge while social explanations typically have only considered the macro-knowledge.

Although not expressed in quite this way before, dissatisfaction with the tort system for inadequately taking social knowledge into account has led to a variety of reforms of the tort system. To remedy the situation, many changes have been proposed and experiments tried to better manage accidents. I will consider two of these here and will show that these bold efforts have had uneven success because they failed, at least initially, to consider crucial sources of knowledge: (1) U.S. courts have been progressing steadily toward a system of strict liability in areas where many injuries are caused by a single defendant's actions, particularly in products liability; and (2) New Zealand acted in the mid-1970s to abolish its tort law altogether, replacing accident law with a social insurance scheme. Both policy changes were attempts, I will argue, to better take into account sociological knowledge; unfortunately, the new policies also ceased to take into account knowledge that tort doctrine once incorporated, and their failings can be traced to this ignorance of crucial sources of knowledge.

Strict Liability for Products

Strict liability, holding someone liable for actions that harm others even if the injurers have exercised due care and have not been negligent, is not new. Selling impure food has long subjected the vendor to strict liability, but the expansion of the doctrine to cover many other products took place in the second half of the twentieth century. As I have argued elsewhere (Scheppele 1988, Chapter 14), there are good reasons to hold manufacturers liable for the damage their products cause; manufacturers generally have more knowledge about the products they make than consumers do. Following the framework we have been outlining here, this rule seems broadly consistent with traditional tort doctrine, which allows liability to flow from knowledge. And it also seems to make good use of sociological knowledge; after all, manufacturers have access to information about the rates of accidents their products cause, rates that indicate patterns in their manufacturing processes that might be altered to make the products safer.

But strict products liability has received a good deal of criticism, particularly in a stinging attack by Peter Huber (1988). Huber argues that tightened liability rules for manufacturers have dampened the innovative spirit of U.S.

business by placing what amounts to a huge liability tax on all products. Because of what Huber sees as the tendency of juries to make huge damage awards and the expansion of grounds on which businesses can be found liable for even the most bizarre accidents, the "tort tax," according to Huber, is driving innovation out of the marketplace.

Huber's analysis of the law run amok may or may not be accurate on the question of incentives to innovate or the causes of the insurance crisis, but what his many examples reveal is a legal system that has changed to take into account patterned knowledge at the level of the firm, while not taking into account knowledge in other relevant locations.

For example, what becomes of strict liability when there are important intervening causes between the sale of a product and its eventual use in injuring someone? Strict liability often shifts the loss to the manufacturer, even if the local knowledge would have or should have informed consumers of the danger. For example:

> A Maryland court held the manufacturer of a "Saturday night special" liable to Olen Kelley, a store employee who was shot in the chest during an armed robbery. A Michigan court ruled that a manufacturer could be held liable for selling a slingshot to children. . . . A manufacturer was sued successfully for installing a telephone booth in a place where a drunk driver could and subsequently did collide with it, injuring the person inside. A pawnshop that sold a pistol later used in the murder of an automobile-dealership employee paid $1.9 million to the widow. (Huber 1988, p. 75)

With examples such as these, it is easy to criticize a strict products liability system. But the framework I have been developing here allows us to see precisely what is wrong with this system. In the examples Huber cites, the knowledge most relevant to the occurrence or prevention of the accident is not taken into account in the determination of liability. Agents other than the manufacturers provided a crucial intervening cause of the events in question, but with the growth of strict liability, the old search for the relative knowledge of all the parties on the scene was abandoned. Strict liability allows us to take into account the special knowledge of a company, but, in doing so, it takes away the knowledge base that once provided more finely tuned assessments of liability and knowledge at the individual level. So, while courts used to look at the actions of individual consumers as well as the actions of agents, if there were any, setting in motion the events that led to a disaster, they now look only at the nature and defects of the product itself. In the old tort regime, the scrutiny of the actions of the specific individuals on the scene left out consideration of the decisions and policies that made accidents more likely. Under the new regime, the consideration of only aggregate risks leaves out the crucial information about the way the product is being used, which affects the likelihood of injury. Strict liability schemes do produce a certain rate of strange decisions because the local knowledge of micro-motives and micro-actions is omitted.

Strict liability, then, allows some important information that prior rules excluded, particularly information about firm-level knowledge, but it still does not guarantee that liability will track the best available knowledge for understanding the particular accident.

New Zealand's Tort Reform

New Zealand, another country that has adopted and adapted the common law of England, reconsidered its workers' compensation scheme in the 1960s (Palmer 1979). When the reconsideration was done, New Zealand had enacted a sweeping change in tort law, abolishing all personal actions in law for negligence and replacing the old tort actions with a general scheme of social insurance. As the New Zealand scheme works, a person who has been injured in an accident has only to go to his or her general practitioner, who fills out the forms certifying that the medical condition has been caused by an accident, and the Accident Compensation Commission handles the case much as an insurance company would, reimbursing the accident victim for medical expenses, lost wages, and lump sum payments for physical injury and emotional suffering.

Aside from the fact that this plan reduced the costs of administering accident compensation from over half the total collected funds to a little less than 10 percent (Gellhorn 1982, p. 193), there is a great deal we can learn from this scheme about managing accidents well. First, "accident" was never defined in the statute, and so judicial elaboration came to view accidents as all those injuries that came as a surprise to the victim. As we have seen, having an injury be a surprise to the victim is one element of an accident, but it is not the only one in usual legal parlance. And so, faced with its own rather unusual definition, the New Zealand courts came to see intentional torts as species of accidents. In *Donselaar v. Donselaar* (New Zealand Court of Appeals, 19 March 1982, cited in Love 1983, p. 231), for example, a man attacked his brother with a hammer. The court ruled that this was an accident because it came as a surprise to the victim, even though it was an intentional act on the part of the hammer-wielding sibling.

In another area formerly covered by negligence law, medical malpractice, other peculiar consequences flowed from taking only the knowledge of the victim into account. If a patient were told before an operation that certain side effects—say, severe and life-threatening blood clotting—might occur after surgery and the patient agreed to the surgery anyway, the patient was held to have not been the victim of an accident when blood clotting occurred because he or she had been told about the possibility beforehand. The event was not a surprise. But if the patient underwent surgery and suffered nerve damage that had not been mentioned in advance, then the patient could be said to have suffered an accident (Vennell 1981). It did not matter whether the doctor might have known more about how to prevent blood clotting than about how to avoid the nerve damage. Without some way to take into account the special knowledge of the potential injurers, the system is likely to generate some peculiar results.

The New Zealand system is generally good about taking into account sociological knowledge, however, because it works as insurance does from an actuarial account of rates of different sorts of accidents, and it takes into account victims' knowledge in its ideas about accidents as surprises. But by failing to take into account the knowledge of the injurer, strange things occur. For example, after the passage of the Accident Compensation Act, accidents in some industries—most notably the refrigeration industry— skyrocketed (Klar 1983). Because a flat tax was placed on all employers to cover their employees' injuries, there was no way to take into account the knowledge relevant to accidents in the manner in which employers organized their workplaces, and so some employers apparently felt free to let safety slide as a consequence. Failing to take this knowledge into account produced another gap in pegging liability to knowledge, and it made the New Zealand scheme less exemplary than it might have been at the start, although it clearly goes a long way toward taking multiple knowledges into account. This particular problem has been corrected by the imposition on companies of an accident tax that is responsive to the accident rate in their particular industry, dealing with the problem of moral hazard.

Of all the attempts to reform tort law, the New Zealand system seems to work the best. It takes into account the knowledge of the victims, and it uses sociological knowledge effectively. Although there were a few problems in taking into account the knowledge of potential injurers, the recent reforms (adjusting the tax code to provide incentives for careful conduct) have gone a long way toward addressing that gap in knowledge.

CONCLUSIONS: KNOWLEDGE AND ACCIDENTS

One premise of this conference, forcefully stated in James Coleman's introductory chapter to this book, is that society is changing in such a way that the deliberately constructed environment will increasingly be a much bigger part of individuals' lives than will the primordial organization of families and neighborhoods. If this is true, the sociological knowledge embedded in these newly constructed forms will have to work its way into our models for handling the rates of injury social planning produces. If social theory is going to make a difference as society changes, we need to think about how to ensure that this new level of knowledge filters into the governance, maintenance, growth, and change of the new forms. As I have argued here, tort law—an important legal framework for handling accidents—is currently not close to incorporating such sociological knowledge, and attempts to use sociological knowledge in revising traditional tort doctrine have not been as successful as they might have been at blending sociological knowledge with important local knowledge the current tort system provides.

But I have tried here to reframe traditional tort law, those rules that have long exercised a powerful force over legal thought about accidents, as an attempt by courts to assign liability for accidents where the knowledge is. I hope this reframing will enable legal analysts to see how sociological insight might fit into the traditional tort concepts and categories without requiring radical reforms. If liability tracks knowledge, and there is more knowledge in the social system that generates accidents than has previously been considered, there is no reason why courts should limit themselves to the knowledge of the victim and the injurer in making this assessment in tort law.

This may lead to what some would see as an uncomfortable shift in liability away from individuals and direct injurers to those collectivities that create the policies for which the accident rates represent known risks. But if those who might have some control over lowering the accident rates are to be encouraged to do so, then liability should track knowledge in this way, even when it is aggregate and collective knowledge. Policies and institutions designed with a particular accident rate in mind cause untoward events no less injurious than the harms caused by direct physical assault. With the knowledge and certainty usually associated with intentional torts, policy makers may make use of social theory to design more intensive, deliberately constructed environments. And with this increased control that sociological knowledge makes possible comes responsibility. In a world increasingly occupied by deliberately constructed social forms, the accidents we see are more often than not planned—if not individually, then collectively. Predictable in advance, these "accidents" are no longer accidental. Although they may be surprises to the victims and injurers, they are usually no longer social surprises. And the legal system needs to adapt to take this new knowledge into account, creating a system of law without accidents.

NOTES

1. Liability rules in tort will clearly have an impact on the incentives of those who might prevent accidents. So, even though other institutions may care about accident prevention independently of law, some of their incentives to do so and the strategies they use may be quite responsive to the extent of their liability in law. Still, tort law provides only one way among many to think about accidents. See, for example, Heimer 1985.

2. Insofar as sociological knowledge is merely descriptive of what is already happening, it may be implicit in institutions that already operate on other stated principles. But if sociological knowledge is to be used to direct planned change, there must be some mechanism through which the knowledge can have an influence on actions or attitudes. Tort law provides one important mechanism that might be quite open to changes in the level of knowledge in specialized professional communities.

3. I will be discussing in this chapter *unwanted* accidents: those unexpected events the injured victims would rather not experience. Lucky accidents, so-called when they appear, may have a different logic, but that does not mean they are any less patterned (see Short 1984). The accidents I will discuss here are the ones that hurt. I limit myself in this way because I will be examining the law, one social institution that is in charge of managing hurtful accidents. No one, to my knowledge, tries to

sue when something unexpected and wonderful happens. Nor could they, given requirements of legal standing.

4. Assumpsit eventually developed into the modern law of contract, out of which tort law grew. Trespass originally covered direct forms of injury to person and property, while action on the case covered more indirectly caused injuries. While the elements of tort claims were long present in the common law, the specific combination of claims tort law represents was not made available in organized form until the second half of the nineteenth century (see Baker 1979, pp. 336–350; and Maitland 1909, pp. 53–58).

5. I do not, in this chapter, deal with the development of similar rules in civil law systems. Instead, I confine myself to the evolution of tort doctrine in common-law systems, particularly in the United States. The civil law category of delicts (parallel to Anglo-American torts) was present in Roman law, and it was taught along with contracts in the European civil law under the general heading of *obligations*. Nineteenth-century social theorists trained in the civil law—such as Marx, Durkheim, Weber, and Simmel—would have been familiar with concepts such as negligence and fault, which had long been rooted in civil law tradition, even though they were still new and controversial in Anglo-American law. Tort doctrine may have emerged much later in England and the United States than it did on the Continent because of the retroactive quality of the common law, which creates legal principles only after cases have been brought. The more forward-looking civil law system may have developed an intellectual structure for accidents before many of them were brought before the courts as mishaps of a modern age. I am indebted to Bruce Frier for explaining the continental history to me.

6. The common law does see certain sorts of factual regularities as patterns when these regularities involve various disparate circumstances being placed in the same legal category. In addition, common-law courts are subject to control through legislation, which is prospective in character and can anticipate particular patterns arising. It is not surprising that in areas where the patterns of accidents have been the most visible, legislation has been central. Statutes were drafted to cover areas such as general workers' compensation precisely because they were areas in which data collection was centralized in a specific location and interest groups of those likely to be injured could more easily be organized to bring the patterns to the attention of the legislature. But in most types of accidents covered by tort law, legislation has played a very minor role in developing policy.

7. Just *why* courts did not change in this regard needs further investigation, but what is clear is *that* they did not. Some judges, however, like Lord Mansfield in England, did see the influence of broader social forces and made more policy-oriented decisions. But they were the exception that proved the rule.

8. The way the general rule is framed indicates that Cardozo was not just concerned with deciding *only* the particular case in front of him. But the general rule instructs future judges to look at whether each particular defendant could have foreseen injury to each particular plaintiff. And so, the general rule picks out locally relevant features for further examination. See W. Page Keeton (1984, pp. 284–290) for a discussion of the development of the rule.

9. This tendency is magnified by tort law casebooks, from which all law students learn. In compiling casebooks, authors generally select cases *because* they have very unusual facts on the grounds that the principles illustrated by the case will be more memorable when set in a strange landscape.

10. The idea of a field of knowledge here borrows heavily from Pierre Bourdieu's concept of a field as an area of structured, socially patterned activity. See, for example, Bourdieu (1987).

11. I do not think this scheme captures all that is going on in tort doctrine, but I think it can provide the core of a more complicated general theory of torts.

12. Although these approaches do not necessarily recommend results inconsistent with the ones discussed here for many cases (and it would be surprising if they did, given that we all intend to describe the same landscape), the economic theories are organized around different operating principles and are justified in very different terms than the approach advocated here. Most significantly, the fields of knowledge approach would justify assigning the costs of losses more frequently to actors with sociological knowledge than the economic approaches would recommend.

13. An indexical is a term whose specific referent depends on context. When I say *I*, it identifies a different person than when you say *I*, even though *I* has a general and clear meaning. Terms such as *this*, *that*, and pronouns are indexicals. In tort law, legal language such as "the standard to which one should perform for one's own protection" operates like indexicals, picking out different standards of conduct in different circumstances.

14. A word about audience: I assume here that my audience has no prior knowledge of the law. Lawyers, clearly, will know more detail about how these rules operate and may find the following description overly simplistic. For each of the rules I explore here, there are countless qualifications, specifications, and exceptions, and no one should assume that this is all there is to torts. But I hope, nevertheless, to have captured the general picture accurately, as far as it goes.

15. Knowledge here means operative knowledge, knowledge that the person who possesses it can *use* to affect the probability of injury to him- or herself or others.

16. The case might be covered by special rules, such as no-fault laws in the case of auto accidents in many states. And although these special provisions may cover the empirically most frequent cases, my discussion here pertains to those accidents that will enter the traditional tort system. The cases that are decided in tort may not be representative of all accidents because those that are particularly patterned may be taken out of the tort system earlier than those in which the patterns are less clear. But the tort system has a powerful role in structuring legal and extra-legal thinking about accidents, and so its internal logic matters a great deal.

17. As Carol Heimer has pointed out to me, standards such as this have multiple functions. They are flexible and evolving, thus allowing the standards to have different meanings in different times and places. They also provide some policing of moral hazard problems by requiring individuals to engage in an effort to find out what they need to know and assessing liability even when individuals do not, in fact, know. Finally, such standards require that individuals adapt their actions to specific contexts, as the judgment of a court will involve consideration of a wide variety of specific attributes of the situation in which the offending behavior occurred.

18. See also the argument I make about the superior knowledge that comes with the possession of goods (Scheppele 1988, Parts III and V).

19. This may entail assessing whether the defendant knows that the potential victim does not know of the danger.

20. In the discussion that follows, I assume that jurisdictions still use the rule that *any* contributing actions to the accident on the part of the plaintiff act as a complete bar to recovery. Most jurisdictions have switched from this rule to one in which damages are assessed according to the proportion in which each of the parties contributed to the accident, the so-called comparative negligence rule. I use the old rule (contributory negligence) rather than the new rule (comparative negligence) because it greatly eases presentation of the judgments courts make. In Figure 9.1, the diagonal line can be seen as a switching point where liability of the defendant

switches to plaintiff's complete loss. A comparative negligence perspective would require assessment of damages to be made proportional to the distance from the upper left corner that both plaintiff and defendant are located. In most jurisdictions, the standards used in judging plaintiff's actions for the purposes of assessing comparative negligence are the same as those used for the purposes of assessing contributory negligence; thus, all that is affected by using the contributory negligence rule here is the ultimate assessment of damages, not the basic structure of the problem.

21. This formulation may show why the move to comparative negligence from contributory negligence was not as disruptive of basic legal logic as one might imagine. If I am right, courts were always engaged in a sort of comparison of the two parties, even under the old rule.

22. If a person is not *able* to avoid a harmful occurrence, we cannot say that the person meaningfully consented.

23. Some courts did try to work around some of the obvious absurdities of the fellow servant rule by announcing different rules when the injurer was a supervisor or the two employees were otherwise not equals in the workplace. But this still did not get to the special knowledge and responsibility of those in charge of organizational design.

24. Legislation has been far better in this regard than has tort law. But often legislation is gutted by the practice of common-law courts reading old tort standards into similar statutory language.

25. Sovereign immunity generally limits the extent to which governmental officials should be sued for the harm their decisions cause (Schuck 1984), but this logic of the surrounding doctrine argues against such exceptions.

26. We might expect to see social surprises in areas where there is not enough experience to confidently calculate base rate information, as in the Challenger disaster or Three Mile Island's partial meltdown. For a dissenting view, see Perrow (1984).

REFERENCES

Auerbach, Carl A., Lloyd K. Garrison, Willard Hurst, and Samuel Mermin. 1961. *The Legal Process.* Boston: Little, Brown and Company.

Baker, J. H. 1979. *Introduction to English Legal History.* London: Butterworths.

Bourdieu, Pierre. 1987. "The Force of Law: Toward a Sociology of the Juridical Field." *Hastings Law Journal* 38:805–853.

Calabresi, Guido. 1970. *The Cost of Accidents,* 2d. ed. New Haven: Yale University Press.

Durkheim, Emile. 1951. *Suicide.* New York: The Free Press.

Friedman, Lawrence. 1973. *A History of American Law.* New York: Simon and Schuster.

Friedman, Lawrence, and Jack Ladinsky. 1969. "Social Change and the Law of Accidents." *Columbia Law Review* 67:50–82.

Gellhorn, Walter. 1982. "Medical Malpractice Litigation (U.S.)—Medical Mishap Compensation (N.Z.)." *Cornell Law Review* 73:170–223.

Hart, H.L.A., and Tony Honoré. 1959. *Causation in the Law.* Oxford: Oxford University Press.

Heimer, Carol. 1985. *Reactive Risk and Rational Action.* Berkeley: University of California Press.

Huber, Peter. 1988. *Liability: The Legal Revolution and Its Consequences.* New York: Basic Books.

Keeton, W. Page. 1984. *Prosser and Keeton on Torts*, 5th ed. St. Paul: West Publishing Co.

Klar, Lewis. 1983. "New Zealand's Accident Compensation Scheme: A Tort Lawyer's Perspective." *University of Toronto Law Review* 33:80–107.

Love, Jean. 1983. "Punishment and Deterrence." *University of California at Davis Law Review* 19:229–245.

Maitland, F. W. 1909. *Forms of Action at Common Law*, edited by A. H. Chaytor and W. J. Whitaker, Cambridge: Cambridge University Press.

Noonan, John. 1976. "The Passengers of Palsgraf." Pp. 111–151 in *Persons and Masks of the Law*. New York: Farrar, Straus and Giroux.

Palmer, Geoffrey. 1979. *Compensation for Incapacity*. Wellington, New Zealand: Oxford University Press.

Perrow, Charles. 1984. *Normal Accidents*. New York: Basic Books.

Posner, Richard A., and William Landes. 1987. *The Economic Structure of Tort Law*. Cambridge, MA: Harvard University Press.

Restatement (Second) of Torts. 1965–1979. St. Paul: American Law Institute.

Scheppele, Kim Lane. 1988. *Legal Secrets: Equality and Efficiency in the Common Law*. Chicago: University of Chicago Press.

Schuck, Peter. 1984. *Suing Government*. New Haven: Yale University Press.

Short, James. 1984. "The Social Fabric at Risk: Toward the Social Transformation of Risk Analysis." *American Sociological Review* 49:711–725.

Vennell, Margaret. 1981. "Medical Negligence and the Effect of the New Zealand Accident Compensation Scheme." *Zeitschrift fur Vergleichende Rechtswissenschaft, Einschliesslich der Ethnologischen Rechtsforschung* 80:228–240.

White, G. Edward. 1980. *Tort Law in America*. Oxford: Oxford University Press.

Winfield, R. 1926. "The History of Negligence in the Law of Torts." *Law Quarterly Review* 42:184–226.

Comments

Jack Goldstone

I appreciate the opportunity to discuss Kim Scheppele's chapter, even though I am not an expert on law. The chapter is so clear and addresses so many crucial social issues that it is easy to have an immediate response. That is fortunate because it was faxed to my office just hours before I was to comment on it. But I thought perhaps this is an importation of Japanese just-in-time inventory techniques, and there may be something to learn from that. What just-in-time inventory does is to force suppliers to provide parts of such reliability that they can be used right away. There is no time to sort through parts and throw out the defectives. I think it might upgrade the quality of social research if every article had to be so clear and to the point that a discussant could read it and respond within twenty-four hours of receiving it. Scheppele's chapter is commendable on that score.

She addresses two issues that I think cut across social theory. One is that many events that are surprises to individuals become predictable when large numbers of individuals are considered as the unit of observation. And

these incidents—whether they are thefts or suicides or other casualty incidents—are often quite predictable as to their frequency and magnitude,
not just in the sense that we know that something will go wrong. A large
actuarial base can give one quite precise knowledge of things that appear
as accidents from the point of view of the individual. That is a classic
Durkheimian argument, but one that is necessary to remind us that we can
use social science to get a handle on things that are difficult to analyze at
the individual level.

There is a second issue that Durkheim did not address, which is that a
lot of these incidents have costs—social costs. And one of the issues in this
conference, I think, is how to better deal with socially incurred costs. There
was a great example of this with the oil tanker the Exxon *Valdez* running
aground in Prince William Sound. It is a marvelous example of an accident
that has created a great deal of difficulty for liability law, and I will return
to that case as I deal with this problem of social cost. The issue with these
costs, of course, is how to make them payable. Who pays, and who has
responsibility?

Scheppele has taken that a step further and said that perhaps we should
say who has the relevant knowledge. There is a problem with that formulation,
although it is extremely useful. The problem is that knowledge is often
broken up into bits and pieces that are widely diffuse. There is knowledge
at the level of individuals, knowledge at the level of organizations, and
knowledge that adheres variously in members of society. And while it is
desirable to bring all of this knowledge to bear, averting accidents and
properly assessing costs, there is a great problem if knowledge, and therefore
responsibility, is diffused.

For example, in the Exxon *Valdez* accident, many people claim to have
knowledge that was relevant to averting that accident. The Coast Guard
has a navigation tracking station and should have been able to observe that
the ship was off course and headed for a reef. Does the Coast Guard have
responsibility for sending a helicopter out to the ship or breaking through
in some sense and notifying an unresponsive helmsman that he is off course?
Does the oil industry have collective responsibilities? Certainly, the oil
industry is aware that accidents happen. But is the industry as a whole
able to patrol individual ships' captains, or is that the responsibility of a
particular company or a particular port master? One might even conclude
that the Sierra Club and other environmental organizations might have
better knowledge of accident conditions than the oil industry. The oil
companies claim that such an accident was a one-in-a-million possibility.
Environmental groups complain that it was more like a one-in-ten-thousand
chance and therefore was quite likely to occur, given the volume of tanker
traffic. Now, *ex post facto*, if we are judging the probability distribution, the
accident having occurred would shift us in favor of saying that perhaps the
environmental organizations had superior knowledge of the chances of such
an event occurring. But I do not think we would therefore want to indict
them with superior responsibility and, perhaps, liability.

So, there is a combination, I think, of factors that have to be used in discussing liability. Certainly, knowledge is one crucial component, but a second is the capacity to avert the harm. I am sure Scheppele agrees, although this was underemphasized in the chapter. The *combination* of knowledge and being in a position where one has the capacity to avert the harm, together, I think, constitute liability.

If that is the problem, and it is a marvelously provocative problem to raise, if we view it as social scientists, two broad issues in social theory arise. One is the importance of scale, and the second is the nature of social structure.

First, we have to ask: Was the tort law designed to deal with accidents on a scale of the Exxon *Valdez* disaster? It used to be the case that it was very hard to kill people or to destroy property in large volumes. Technology has now made it possible for one individual to create damage on the scale of the gross national product of a small country. Or in the case of something like the safety operator at the Three Mile Island nuclear plant, one individual's negligence endangered millions of people. Tort law was developed at a time when individuals usually created damage or hurt on a scale relevant to other individuals or small groups. Technology has changed that to a degree where tort law no longer makes sense. What does it mean to hold the captain liable for the effects of the oil spill? This difficulty was felt by the judge at the bond hearing, where a $1 million bail was initially posted for the captain of the tanker. But that was overturned because it was considered by law that the accident was a misdemeanor—taking your ship off course and running aground—and there cannot be a $1 million bail for a misdemeanor. The legal system is obviously in confusion over how to deal with very large-scale accidents. So the scale of negligence and casualty has changed, and I think this means liability has to be parcelled out. And here we get to the issue of social structure.

The convention of law is usually directed at micro-level social structure, and even corporate actors are reduced to individual actors in law, although they are fictitious actors with special conditions. The alternative is to look perhaps to the macro-level, at statistical knowledge of accidents, and fix responsibility with organizations. But I have argued in a number of comparative papers that the way to view social structure is neither strictly from a micro- nor macro-point of view, but as having *multiple* levels. That is, society has national, regional, local, business, and individual levels at which action is initiated and decisions are taken. Therefore, I think we need to think of liability as also extending through multiple levels. So, for instance, fiscal liability might be lodged at a different level than individual liability. One might say that the tanker captain is responsible for losing his position or his license, but that financial responsibility cannot be lodged at that level. So perhaps fiscal liability should be lodged at the level of the company or the oil industry.

Now, this notion that accidents have to be regarded as yielding multiple levels of liability means that agency needs to be reexamined. We have notions of what a reasonable actor should be held liable for. But do we have clear notions of what a reasonable organization should be held liable for? Under what conditions is it reasonable to hold Exxon liable for the actions of its tanker captain? Should the personnel manager who did not act on the record be responsible? Should it be top management? Should it be shareholders? I would say that the way Scheppele has posed this theory of liability as knowledge requires, therefore, not only a reapportioning of liability in terms of the social distribution of knowledge but also a reconceptualizing of the reasonable actor in terms of a reasonable organization. We need to ask how knowledge is reasonably dispersed and how the capacity to act *and control subordinates* is reasonably dispersed. Otherwise we will be unable to address the type of complex organizations in which accidents will, in the future, increasingly occur.

Comments

Michael Hechter

I should preface my remarks by confessing that prior to reading this chapter, torts made me think more about the dessert menu at Vienna's Hotel Sacher than about anything related to the law. Despite this initial predisposition, I did find this chapter stimulating. It proposes nothing less than a fundamental modification in the structure of a major social institution, the law of torts, based on implications drawn from social theory.

At the most general level, law is an institution designed to bring about cooperative social outcomes among individuals who otherwise might behave in a nonsocial or anti-social fashion. The law of torts contributes to this end by ensuring that the people who are responsible for causing accidents, injury, or loss are liable to make redress. This redress can be regarded as a form of punishment.

Just as Adam Smith viewed the market as a force that disciplines producers, at least two similar kinds of purposes are served by the law of torts. On the one hand, it provides incentives for people to act responsibly. On the other hand, it provides a mechanism by which the injured get compensated, and this compensation only comes from those who actually cause the loss—not from the members of society at large. In short, the law of torts, as traditionally understood, turns out to be a remarkably cost-effective means of providing social discipline and resolving disputes.

Scheppele thinks this law can be improved by employing social theory to determine the foreseeability of loss. She believes that with the aid of theory, we can predict that the coming of the railroad (to take her example) will cause n deaths and x injuries. The availability of this knowledge presumably could alter the determination of liability in certain kinds of legal cases. Regrettably, just how this knowledge would change the application of the law of torts is left unclear in the chapter, and this is a vital omission.

Who assumes liability under Scheppele's interpretation? Under her scheme, does the railroad company compensate Mrs. Palsgraf for the bizarre accident that befell her? Or does somebody else compensate Mrs. Palsgraf? There is simply no answer to these questions in the text. Scheppele discusses cases in New Zealand and elsewhere, but her argument would be immeasurably strengthened were she to recommend a new institutional design that is better able to handle these issues. (It might also help to know how we are supposed to select normative criteria to evaluate legal institutions.)

The chapter raises several ancillary questions as well. Is social theory sufficiently developed to predict how many injuries and deaths are likely to be caused by the advent of a new technology? Do we even have the requisite knowledge to predict the damages that can be expected to occur using an *existing* technology? So many of the papers at this conference focused on the phenomenon of unintended consequences that this argues for a healthy dose of skepticism regarding such claims.

Further, how could we ever determine when a particular accident falls within the domain of the theoretically foreseeable and when it does not? Obviously, the plaintiff and the defendant will have directly opposing interests in each case. Resolving their differences would constitute a very difficult bargaining problem, one for which no solutions may exist in current theory.

Given the ambiguity of the outcome of this kind of bargaining game, one potential danger in modifying the law of torts obviously entails moral hazard, and the chapter does mention this possibility, albeit indirectly. That is, if the railroad company is going to be held responsible for some set of accidents that occurred in the wake of the establishment of railroads and the dissemination of railroad technology, then this might give the company an incentive to act less responsibly than it would under the current interpretation of the law.

However, there is also the danger of precisely the opposite problem. In other circumstances, the railroad company might be punished for losses for which (by the application of some consensually determined criterion) they should bear no responsibility.

Anyone arguing for major changes in the interpretation of the law of torts must be concerned with balancing these different sources of judgmental error. Evidently, analytical problems such as these have to be addressed before Scheppele's interesting idea of using theory to modify legal institutions can be more persuasive.

PART FOUR

New Political Boundaries and New Political Forms

10

Bounded States in a Global Market: The Uses of International Labor Migrations

Aristide R. Zolberg

Within a world of bounded states containing human aggregates that consider themselves family-like bodies with a common ancestry and a common destiny, international migration constitutes a deviance from the normal order of things. Both aspects of the process, emigration and immigration, therefore tend to elicit considerable public concern and provoke political contention within and between countries. The prevention of emigration was a sine qua non for the erection of twentieth-century absolutist states with command economies; and concomitantly, the difficulty of maintaining this policy in the face of changing circumstances fostered among them a generalized regime crisis. Today, in both Western Europe and North America, issues arising from immigration and its consequences have moved to the fore of the political agenda. They encompass law enforcement, the organization of economic life, and the conduct of foreign affairs, and they ultimately reach into the very basic question of what obligations the members of affluent national communities have toward strangers in dire need abroad or who come knocking at their doors. In a number of countries, these issues have fostered new alignments across classes and established political parties, pitting humanitarians against realists and those who believe immigration threatens the identity and integrity of the receiving communities against others who believe these communities must adapt and change. Widespread anti-immigration sentiment also sometimes provides a basis for mobilization against democratic institutions more generally.

Yet the subject has been of only marginal interest to social scientists, who have left it largely to population specialists. Although the general import of migration is well recognized by demographers, who rank it alongside birth and death as one of the basic determinants of any human population, they tend to view it narrowly, as a process of relocation in physical space. Within that perspective, there are no grounds for making a conceptual distinction between internal and international movement. Pre-dicating their theoretical undertakings on the assumption that individuals are free to stay or to move, migration theorists have treated obstacles to movement or forced migrations as an "error term" for which the theoretical equation does not account.[1] But this is self-defeating because with regard to international migrations, the explanatory weight of the error term is at least as great as that of the variables included in the equation.

An ineluctable reality throughout modern history, the pervasiveness of control by states over the movement of people across their borders fosters a fundamental distinction between the internal and external segments of the global migratory stream. Whereas all migration entails relocation in physical space, international migration is distinctive in that it entails, in addition, a change of jurisdiction from one sovereign state to another and, should the move be permanent, also a change of membership from one political community to another (Zolberg 1981). Transfers of population between territorial states thus difffer in kind from other forms of human migration, particularly the secular movement of communities across space before the earth was carved out into exclusive territories and the voluntary movement of individuals within the confines of the state to which they belong.[2]

My theoretical starting point is the aphorism with which Kingsley Davis concluded a masterful overview of human migrations from prehistoric times to the present: "Whether migration is controlled by those who send, by those who go, or by those who receive, it mirrors the world as it is at the time" (Davis 1974, p. 96). The bewildering array of disparate movements observable at any given time can be thought of as forming identifiable patterns shaped by a changing configuration of world conditions. But these conditions come into play in two distinct ways: They shape the dispositions of individuals toward movement and, simultaneously, the migration policies of their states of origin and of potential destination. Conceptualized in this manner, transnational migration emerges as a worldwide arena of contention between individuals, seeking to maximize their welfare by staying or leaving, and the states in which they live or that they seek to enter, promoting objectives of their own.

Each epoch produces characteristic emigration and immigration policies, with local variations (Zolberg 1978a). Generally, whereas exit policies vary widely (Dowty 1987), states normally maintain severely restrictive immi-gration policies, with little variation between regimes. The major exceptions were the United States and other "colonies" (in the sense used by Adam Smith and John Stuart Mill) until the early twentieth century; but even then the United States qualified its generally pro-immigration, laissez-faire stance by means of regulations designed to keep out those deemed unpro-ductive (paupers) or considered unsuited for membership in the body politic— notoriously nonwhites and felons. As a consequence of the political liber-alization of the Warsaw Pact countries in the late 1980s, the present world configuration is characterized by a fundamental asymmetry between liberal exit policies and highly restrictive immigration policies amounting to a general prohibition of entry for purposes of permanent settlement. In relation to this tacit baseline, some specific exceptions are made, commonly including the selective recruitment of foreign labor, often for a limited period; the possibility for members of the community to bring in close relatives; and the granting of asylum to a small number of people who qualify as refugees and have no other place to go.

Within a capitalist world economy founded on free market principles, the persistence of barriers to population movement between countries constitutes an anomaly. As the international trade theorist J. N. Bhagwati has observed, "A somewhat remarkable hierarchy obtains in terms of the extent to which the operation of liberalism in the economic sphere is considered to be acceptable in modern national states" (1984, p. 678). International trade in goods, governed by the rules of the General Agreement on Tariff and Trade (GATT), comes closest to operating according to the unfettered dynamics of the market, with only limited intrusion of what Bhagwati terms "political considerations." In the sphere of services (notably finance), political considerations are somewhat more pervasive. But with respect to labor, practices shift decisively away from liberalism: "There is practically universal agreement, among modern states, that free *flows of human beings*, no matter how efficacious for world efficiency, should not be permitted. Today, immigration restrictions are virtually everywhere, making immigration the most compelling exception to liberalism in the operation of the world economy" (Bhagwati 1984, p. 680; emphasis in original). Bhagwati points out further that in contrast with trade and finance, within the sphere of population movement state sovereignty remains unfettered by any supra-national norms or institutions: "There is virtually no international Code of Conduct in regard to the question of how immigration ought to be operated" (Bhagwati 1984, p. 697). Believing this situation to be undesirable, he concludes with a plea to establish a code of conduct in this sphere as part of the currently envisaged reform of international economic management.[3]

Any explanation of this situation must center on the state as the principal instrument through which a variety of groups seek to achieve certain goals. Previous analyses of the determinants of immigration policy have focused mostly on domestic factors, particularly the impact of classes and interest groups. But given that the state is an organization with two faces—one turned inward toward civil society and the other outward to other states— a framework that takes into consideration the external side as well is likely to provide a better understanding of the determinants, significance, and consequences of immigration policies than can be achieved by way of an internalist approach alone (Zolberg 1987c).

The classic work of Karl Polanyi (1957) provides a heuristic solution to some of the perennial theoretical difficulties we face in conceptualizing the interpenetration between the national and international levels and the interaction between the economic and political spheres at both levels. In short, conceiving the two world wars, the Great Depression, and the emergence of totalitarian regimes in inter-war Europe as episodes in a single cataclysm, Polanyi attributes the origins of this catastrophe to the "utopian endeavor of economic liberalism to set up a self-regulating market system," which entailed a thoroughgoing commodification of land and labor (Polanyi 1957, p. 29). Because the market violates human needs, Polanyi asserts that "such an institution could not exist for any length of time without annihilating the human and natural substance of society." A dialectical effect ensued: "Inevitably, society took measures to protect itself," notably to prevent the transformation of labor into a commodity pure and simple; but in turn, "whatever measures it took impaired the self-regulation of the market, disorganized industrial life, and thus endangered society in yet another way" (Polanyi 1957, p. 3). No escape was found out of this double bind; after self-regulation was impaired in the 1880s, the disruptions subsequently grew ever more intense throughout the domain of a vastly expanded international economy: from protectionism to imperial rivalries, from imperial rivalries to world war, from world war to closed political regimes, economic autarchy, and world depression, and then again world war.

Polanyi analyzes the complex consequences of the market dynamic by constructing a comprehensive framework sketched out in his opening lines:

> Nineteenth century civilization rested on four institutions. The first was the balance-of-power system which for a century prevented the occurrence of any long and devastating war between the Great Powers. The second was the international gold standard which symbolized a unique organization of world economy. The third was the self-regulating market which produced an unheard-of material welfare. The fourth was the liberal state. Classified in one way, two of these institutions were economic, two political. Classified in another way, two of them were national, two international. Between them they determined the characteristic outlines of the history of our civilization. (Polanyi 1957, p. 3)

While it is impossible to trace here in detail the complex interrelationships among the four institutions, it should be noted that Polanyi conceives each of them as being relatively autonomous and tending toward an equilibrium of its own, but not as a closed system: "Whenever this balance was not achieved, the imbalance spread over into the other spheres. It was the relative autonomy of the sphere that caused the strains to accumulate and to generate tensions which eventually exploded in more or less stereotyped forms" (Polanyi 1957, p. 211). At the level of the national economy, the Concert of Europe took the form of massive unemployment; in the sphere of national politics, more acute class struggles; at the level of the international economy, pressure on currencies; and finally, in the international political arena, it gave way to imperialist rivalries. The tensions engendered within each sphere contributed to a negation of established structures and to the emergence of an alternative set; together, these constituted a new global configuration whose components interacted in a similar manner.

TOWARD A POLANYIAN PERSPECTIVE
ON THE CONTEMPORARY SITUATION

From 1970 onward, in one advanced industrial society after another, the relationships between state, market, and citizens institutionalized in the wake of the Great Depression and World War II have been called into question. Explanations for this phenomenon initially focused almost entirely on what, for one sociological tradition, were "dysfunctions" or "perverse effects" within each of the societies involved or, for another, "contradictions" at the level of capitalist society as a whole. However, Karl Polanyi's admonition concerning the rise of fascism in the 1930s is applicable: "The appearance of such a movement in the industrial countries of the globe, and even in a number of only slightly industrialized ones, should never have been ascribed to local causes, national mentalities, or historical backgrounds as was so consistently done by contemporaries" (Polanyi 1957, p. 237). Instead, the explanation must be sought at the global level.

A decade and a half after the first oil crisis, hardly anyone needs persuading that events emanating from the international economy can penetrate even the most self-sufficient advanced industrial societies and wreak havoc with their economies. Analysts in 1990 agree that this crisis was more than a conjunctural event but was rather the manifestation of structural changes that signaled the breakdown of the post-war international economic system, or at least profound modifications within it. The critical turning point was the collapse of the financial regime established at Bretton Woods—the exchange system founded on a U.S. dollar convertible into gold—as the result of a unilateral declaration by the United States in 1971; subsequent actions by OPEC can be seen as a rational response to what was in effect a major devaluation of the U.S. dollar, of which its members held considerable reserves.

But the U.S. action itself was as much an effect as a cause. Beginning in the late 1960s, a number of capitalist democracies began experiencing severe difficulties in reconciling obligations of the welfare state with the maintenance of international competitiveness in a vastly enlarged international market. In Great Britain, which was the weakest link in the Bretton Woods system, Harold Wilson's Labour government was forced into an undesired devaluation in 1967 and subsequently found it necessary to adopt a deflationary policy (Thomas 1988). Concurrently, attempts by the United States to manage the Great Society and the Vietnam War without extracting additional revenue steadily undermined the dollar; this situation caused the Nixon administration to administer the coup de grace to the Bretton Woods system.

The significance of this turning point went well beyond the economic sphere. The protracted crisis that followed revealed, in retrospect, that the consensual equilibrium that prevailed in Western societies on both sides of the Atlantic in the late 1950s and that was extrapolated into a systemic characteristic of that type of society was a contingent state of affairs, rendered possible by the initial configuration of the post-war international economy;

its stability depended on the maintenance of that situation. There is a concurrence in 1990 that the "consensus" that provided the major theme of political sociology a generation ago has become history.

Somewhat unexpectedly, it is within the field of international relations, hitherto developed in splendid isolation from the other social sciences, that the Polanyian tradition experienced its most vigorous revival. In the early 1970s, a new generation began pointing out the inadequacy of a conceptualization of the international field as a sort of billiard table with sovereign states as the balls. Observing the growing importance of economic concerns in foreign policy alongside more traditional strategic ones, this new generation was led to pay attention to the role of other significant actors in the international field, particularly transnational corporations, and to the interactions of the various actors in attempts to manage international markets. Attention was focused on interdependence and transnational relations and on conditions for cooperation among essentially selfish actors (Keohane and Nye 1972). The emerging discipline of international political economy was thus founded on a conceptualization of the international field as subject to co-determination by two structures of global domain—the market and the state system. From the vantage point of the market, there is an evident continuity of processes between the domestic and international levels. Hence, the emergence of international political economy contributed to an attenuation of the traditional separation between the study of international relations and internal politics (for example, Gourevitch 1986). This movement, which was vastly reinforced by observation of trends in the world at large and their domestic consequences, entailed a remarkable convergence with contemporaneous developments in the reviving field of historical sociology noted earlier.

The dominant motif in the international political economy literature is the conflict between the evolving economic and technical interdependence of the globe and the continuing compartmentalization of the world political system composed of sovereign states (Gilpin 1987, p. 11). The logic of the market is to locate economic activities where they are most productive and profitable; accordingly, market economies tend to expand geographically and functionally, encompassing both peripheral zones and previously domestic sectors of society—that is, the "commodification" of land and labor that constituted "the great transformation." Market forces tend toward dualism; both individual national economies and the international economy as a whole came to be structured into core and periphery.

As against this, Robert Gilpin suggests, the logic of the state is to capture and control the processes of economic growth and capital accumulation in relation to particular territories. This view is congruent with A. Przeworksi's conceptualization of the state in capitalist democracies as the expression and agent of a specific class compromise achieved by capitalists and organized workers at some previous time (Przeworksi 1985, p. 202). But its commitment brings the state into conflict with other states with similar goals because one of the means normally used to achieve its objective is to pass on economic difficulties to other societies. This is particularly likely to be resorted to in times of economic crisis and is obviously more available to powerful states than to weaker ones.

Ultimately, actions of this sort jeopardize the survival of the capitalist system at the international level, with negative feedback effects on the domestic economies of all the units in the system, as occurred in the wake of World War I. But even in the absence of crisis, the logic of the market economy as an inherently expanding global system collides with the logic of the modern welfare state: "While solving the problem of a closed economy, the welfare state has only transferred the fundamental problem of the market economy and its survivability to the international level. The problem of reconciling welfare capitalism at the domestic level with the nature of the international capitalist system has become of increasing importance" (Gilpin 1987, p. 63).

A related theme concerns conflict and cooperation among component states. Here, the theoretical starting point is the reinterpretation of the causes of the Great Depression set forth by Kindleberger (1973), who attributes the collapse of the international economy founded on free trade and the gold standard less to inherent flaws in the system—as argued by both Marxist and non-Marxist predecessors, including Polanyi—than to the absence of leadership at a critical moment. By the end of World War I Britain no longer had the strength to lead the system; when crisis came, the United States sought to solve its problems without any regard for external consequences and thereby precipitated world-wide depression with catastrophic political as well as economic consequences. It was only in the post-war period that the United States acceded to the role of hegemon with the institutional consequences noted earlier.

The structures established in the wake of World War II entailed something beyond ordinary agreements among states, such as treaties—which reflect a particular configuration of power and interests, and change in accordance with shifts in these components. Termed *international regimes,* these structures constitute a set of more enduring rules that, once adopted, impose certain constraints on the actions of sovereign states within the specified sphere (Krasner 1983, pp. 1–22; Haggard and Simmons 1987). In the absence of constituted society beyond the nation-states, regimes mitigate the prevailing anarchy of international relations. Distinctive regimes were established after World War II in the spheres of international trade and finance when the United States rose to global hegemony and assumed the mantle of economic leadership from a weakened Great Britain. Implemented by way of the GATT and the establishment of the International Monetary Fund (IMF) as well as cognate institutions, together these regimes constituted what is generally known as the Bretton Woods system.

The system marked the end of unfettered capitalist internationalism as governments learned that international automaticity stands in fundamental and potentially explosive contrast to the domestic objectives of the active state. Ruggie (1983, p. 198) has dubbed the post-war system "embedded liberalism," using the Polanyian term to indicate its anchoring in the social order of the component societies. In effect, it entailed a recognition of some form of the welfare state as the national norm of capitalist states. Although this was not to the liking of orthodox financial circles in the United States, in order to secure adherence to the principle of multilateralism in trade, the United States had to provide an acceptable resolution of the dilemma between internal and external stability by mitigating obligations under the GATT system to provide for full employment policies and by allowing price supports in agriculture (which arose as a domestic political requirement in the United States itself). The IMF was constrained in the same manner as well, at least with respect to the more developed countries. Hence, participants were able to pursue domestic demand-management policies and international trade policies in partial isolation from one another: As Gilpin has put it, it was to be Keynes at home, Adam Smith abroad (1987, p. 355).

The new system rested on a U.S. foundation. Its basic formula arose out of the terms in which Americans resolved their own organization of economic power in the course of New Deal and wartime controversies—by way of an apolitical emphasis on output and growth, which allowed for high wages that transformed workers into affluent consumers (Maier 1987a). This orientation also guided the U.S. foreign economic policy in the aftermath of World War II: The free movement of capital and of goods worked to the advantage of the most productive economy, as had been the case for Great Britain in the preceding century. But the outward reach of U.S. capital also provided the wherewithal for the reconstruction of Europe on a more stable foundation. In effect, the United States extended to European economic and political elites an offer they could not refuse. *Mutatis mutandis*, the U.S. formula—sometimes referred to as Fordism—was successfully domesticated and institutionalized, with minor variations, in national sociopolitical settlements throughout the region (Maier 1987b; Lipietz 1988). Its success was confirmed by the observations of social scientists on both sides of the Atlantic, as indicated, for example, by a 1963 symposium *A New Europe?* which emphasized the mitigation of class conflict (*Dædalus* 1964). There is no gainsaying that Europe's societies, economies, and political systems were truly modernizing; but social scientists failed to understand that the process was guided by a visible hand.

However, the combination of a continually rising real wage rate with low unemployment, which facilitated class compromise, also made for a structural inflationary problem. As Gilpin points out, global Keynesianism worked largely because the United States was unconcerned about its own payments and trade position—or, rather, was able to remain unconcerned by virtue of its hegemonic position and the role of the dollar in the international financial system. More generally, Ruggie suggests that a central element in the success of embedded liberalism was its ability to accommodate and even facilitate the externalizing of adjustment costs through inflation and private markets (leading to higher domestic interest rates) and by shifting the costs from "regime makers" to "regime takers"—that is, developing countries, to which embedded liberalism was never fully applied (Ruggie 1983, pp. 229–231).[4] Another adaptive mechanism was the use of foreign labor.

INTERNATIONAL MIGRATION
IN THE CONTEXT
OF EMBEDDED LIBERALISM

Regarding the absence of a code of conduct—synonymous with regime—in the sphere with which we are concerned, Bhagwati comments: "It is . . . remarkable that none of the architects of Bretton Woods thought that the superstructure we would provide for international economic governance in an interdependent world should extend to an agency that would oversee international migration questions" (1984, p. 698). However, there is some evidence that suggests that the architects of the post-war international economic order *did* give thought to the subject of international migration and, in particular, that they were committed to promoting greater international movement of labor, much as they were to the revival of international trade and the promotion of capital movement. While it is true that no international regime arose in this sphere, this was the case because the states that participated in the formation of the post-war capitalist political economy shared a common outlook with respect to the procurement of foreign labor and were in a position to achieve their objectives by acting individually to maximize their interests without having to cooperate with one another.

As will be elaborated below, notwithstanding variations in policy ways and means, in the expansive post–World War II decades the more developed countries (MDCs) of the capitalist world shared a major overall objective: to procure a limited supply of *cheap and disposable alien labor* so as to facilitate the structural adjustments participation in the international economy entailed. Given this objective, cooperation was unnecessary because—individually and collectively—these states had, in effect, an unlimited supply of such labor at their disposal. In short, they faced a buyers' market for what they sought.

It is the *suppliers* who faced an agonizing prisoners' dilemma, paralleling the one with which workers are confronted in capitalist economies. They shared an interest in improving terms of trade for the sale of labor to the MDCs; in order to bring this about, cooperation was required to control the supply (which workers were able to achieve historically through trade unions). But, in the absence of guarantees of compliance, each individual supplier was best off selling its labor for what it could get. The supply of labor was so vast and so widely distributed that cooperation among suppliers was unlikely, and there was no authoritative political apparatus at the international level by way of which a code of conduct could be imposed on unwilling users of labor. This accounts for the extremely limited success of the International Labor Organization's efforts to devise a regime on behalf of the migrants and the sending countries.

Since it is so easily explained, the absence of a code of conduct with respect to the international movement of labor does not constitute a very heuristic theoretical question, and the focus must shift to an explanation of the pattern of immigration policy observed among the MDCs. But what, precisely, is to be explained? Bhagwati characterizes the pattern simply as "restrictive" and suggests that it arose because, in the sphere of population movements, non-economic considerations are paramount. He identifies the key concern involved as "territoriality," a sort of "natural right," paralleled by the notion that groups have the right to maintain their distinctive identity. I shall discuss this explanation below. For now, however, it should be noted that it accounts at best for only one aspect of the pattern in question. While it is true that the receivers have erected protective walls against foreign populations, it is equally evident that substantial labor migrations *have* taken place since the end of World War II and, in particular, that during the period of sustained economic growth from about 1950 onward, the leading actors within the capitalist world economy—with the singular exception of Japan—steadily increased their use of foreign labor.

Any explanation of the prevailing patterns of immigration policy must therefore account simultaneously for the restrictive wall and the openings in it. Since the formation of a limited regime pertaining to refugees has been dealt with elsewhere, this chapter will focus principally on the pattern of policy pertaining to labor migrations.[5] I will demonstrate that these policies were founded on a common doctrine and implemented individually, but with some international concertation as a mechanism for resolving tensions between the requirements of domestic management and of external economic performance. However, the policies were cast against a restrictive baseline established in the late nineteenth century. In conclusion, I shall examine the crisis of the 1970s and discuss the trends that have arisen in its wake.

THE ROOTS OF
IMMIGRATION RESTRICTION[6]

In seeking to account for immigration restriction, Bhagwati points to territoriality but he does not ground this in anything except some sort of psychological need.[7] Matters might be clarified by shifting the emphasis away from physical space to the human aggregates territories contain, which have constituted themselves into mutually exclusive membership groups. In this perspective, the defining feature of international migration emerges as not mere movement across space but as movement from one political jurisdiction to another, with a concomitant change in political membership.

The contemporary emphasis on restriction is often contrasted with an earlier "liberal" situation. However, the liberal moment in the history of international population movements was extremely short-lived and geographically limited. First, during the mercantilist era—under conditions of slow population growth, which made for scarcity—states interacted in a competitive constant-sum game: On the one hand, they imposed strict prohibitions on exit to prevent loss, and, on the other, they engaged in the rapacious procurement of valuable populations from other states. Emigration to the colonies was encouraged so long as the colonies did not compete with the metropole. We should add to this discussion procurement from the periphery, especially the "external" world, by way of purchase or conquest (the slave trade) and the forcible relocation of populations to where they were thought to be more productive (colonial transportation).

The emergence of the United States as an independent state with an unlimited (in a theoretical sense) supply of land that could be rendered valuable only with a large input of labor altered the basic parameters of the ongoing system. The first century of U.S. immigration policy may be characterized as assisted laissez-faire, with incentives to attract self-capitalized agricultural middle classes and skilled workers, together with some protection against landing people deemed likely to become a public burden and ad hoc actions to reduce immigration in times of economic downturn. This orientation generally expressed the interest of the leading sectors of the U.S. economy, including a variety of entrepreneurs as well as the federal and state governments, which were in the business of selling land. Objections to massive immigration were voiced perennially by organized labor, port-of-entry welfare agencies, and conservative cultural elites, but with limited success.

As was to be expected, European states reacted initially by reinforcing prohibitions on exit. However, the formation of the United States coincided with the transformations that resulted in the emergence of the liberal international economy as well as with the onset of rapid population growth throughout Europe (arguably, these several processes were related). In the late 1820s, Great Britain relinquished mercantilist controls over emigration to the United States; combined with a vast flow of capital, this fostered the formation of a transnational "Atlantic economy" (Thomas 1973). With only minor exceptions, over the next several decades other European states followed suit as they in turn began to experience population growth and industrialization.

It is noteworthy that during this period, European industrializers also expanded the domain of their labor reserves beyond the confines of the state. Great Britain's main source of labor was Ireland, which was formally incorporated into the United Kingdom in 1801 but remained a distinctly colonial country. The Irish in Great Britain were tantamount to "guest workers"; although there were no formal regulations governing their movement, in times of unemployment many who sought to remain in Great Britain were forcibly ejected by local authorities. Similarly, from the boom years of the Second Empire onward, France drew considerable amounts of labor from Italy on the one hand and Belgium on the other, and Germany subsequently obtained labor from Poland.

These developments determined, for the first time since the international state system came into being, the nearly free movement of population in that sector of the world, which was also coming to be linked by way of the gold standard into a free trade system. The achievement by the industrial states of their objectives with respect to foreign labor did not require the creation of an international regime because they could achieve their goals by acting individually in accordance with their self-interest; expansion of the market system fostered the transformation of the outlying regions of Europe into a periphery whose growing population was propelled by the processes of the great transformation into the national and international industrial reserves. However, in the colonial world, where these processes had not yet come into effect, the mobilization of manpower required coercion, especially when it entailed long-distance relocation. Hence, expansion of the market economy also stimulated considerable migration within the periphery, but under unfree conditions (Zolberg 1987b, pp. 45–60; Cohen 1987).

In the United States, the thrust to regulate immigration in a restrictive direction achieved some successes in the 1880s and steadily gained ground in ensuing decades. Action was taken early on to prohibit the entry of Chinese immigrants; by the 1890s, a congressional majority emerged on behalf of proposals designed to reduce incoming numbers from Europe, but the most concerned segments of the business community managed to delay enactment of such proposals for another two decades. The dominant interpretation provided by U.S. historians for the rise of restrictionism is rooted in psychology.[8] However, much as with Polanyi's observations concerning fascism, synchronic developments of a similar sort in otherwise very different states suggest that a more general explanation might be found at the level of the international system of which these states were a part.[9] In short, this was a period of severe economic crisis throughout the system, to which states responded largely by way of protectionist measures that were related as both cause and effect to greater political tensions among the component states as well (Gourevitch 1986, pp. 71–123).[10]

Under these conditions, restrictive measures were designed to achieve two distinct but complementary objectives: (1) to protect domestic society against deleterious processes generated by international market forces; and (2) to enhance national security in the face of rising international tensions. Protection was of concern to both workers threatened by unemployment and elites faced with the mounting burden of maintaining and managing populations that were no longer self-subsistent in a period of economic crisis. National security entailed reinforcement of the domestic and international capacities of the states. In particular, limiting immigration facilitated the construction of national identity, which served as an instrument of hegemony at a time of growing class tension and was also of vital importance with respect to mobilizing populations for military service in prospective international conflicts.

Yet, foreign workers were obviously useful to offset pressure on wages in times of rising demand, both cyclical and seasonal. Similar solutions appeared throughout the system. As noted, Great Britain had already informally constituted the Irish into a disposable migratory reserve; in the 1890s, Germany devised the first regulated guest-worker system, designed to secure the economic benefits of imported labor while minimizing social and political costs; and other European countries followed suit, among them Switzerland and France. Attempts were made in the United States to devise a similar system with respect to Chinese workers in the Southwest; after this failed in the face of strong opposition, an *informal* system arose involving Mexicans. Morover, an increasing proportion of European immigrants consisted of "birds of passage," while French Canadians constituted a disposable reserve for New England (Piore 1979). It is noteworthy that in the 1920s, when the United States drastically reduced immigration from Europe to approximately one-seventh the ongoing levels, no quantitative limit was established for the Western Hemisphere, despite restrictionist clamors that Mexicans were racially undesirable. This action, in effect, institutionalized a policy of temporary labor procurement from neighboring countries.

EMBEDDED LIBERALISM
AND THE "CONJUNCTURE BUFFER"

The use of imported labor should be added to the externalization mechanisms mentioned earlier for inducing growth while minimizing inflationary pressure. During World War II, albeit refusing to depart from a strict restrictionist stance on behalf of refugees, the United States organized the massive importation of temporary labor from Mexico. A similar approach was applied to the reconstruction of Europe: "There was a certain measure of agreement between ethical and legal principles and the practical interests of the international community, that manpower shortages which were holding up the repairs to the productive apparatus should be alleviated by improving the use of human resources and transferring these from 'surplus' countries to 'deficit' countries" (Organization for Economic Cooperation and Development 1979, p. 7).

This approach was founded on a theory, originating with J. M. Keynes and A. Sauvy but formalized by W. Arthur Lewis, which stated that growth and full employment in the more industrialized countries depend on the availability of an abundant supply of labor—as in the United States in the second half of the nineteenth century—and that the problems of the poorer countries could be more easily overcome if they were able to reduce the pressure of their manpower surpluses on their society and economy—as was said to be the case with Mexico thanks to the *bracero* program (Kindleberger 1967, p. 9, Note 1; pp. 20–21; Craig 1971).[11]

Incorporated into the terms of reference of the Organization for European Economic Cooperation (OEEC), established under U.S. leadership to coordinate the distribution of Marshall Plan aid, the promotion of the international labor movement was explicitly designed to complement the other nascent international regimes: "Since the Organisation [OEEC] was elaborating 'Codes' of liberalisation of trade and payments, it was natural to try and do the same for manpower movements" (OECD 1979, p. 8); accordingly, the contracting parties undertook explicitly to "cooperate in the progressive reduction of obstacles to the free movement of persons" (OECD 1979, p. 7).[12] Mechanisms to implement the doctrine were subsequently consolidated into a set of recommendations passed on to the OEEC's successor, the Organization for Economic Cooperation and Development (OECD), launched in 1961 to provide the Bretton Woods system with "a much-needed talking-shop on policy, and a clearing-house for economic information" (*The Economist* 1988, p. 57).[13]

The validity of the Lewis model of growth as applied to Europe was verified in a study launched in 1964 by Kindleberger, who had served as an adviser to the European Recovery Program. He found that the major factor shaping the remarkable economic growth most of Europe had experienced since 1950 was not a change in demand but rather the availability of a large supply of labor from (1) a high rate of natural increase as in the Netherlands, (2) transfers from agriculture (Germany, France, and Italy), or (3) immigration—refugees in the case of Germany and unemployed or underemployed workers from the Mediterranean countries elsewhere (France, Germany, and Switzerland). In contrast, those countries with no substantial increase in the labor supply—Great Britain, Belgium, and the Scandinavian countries—had, on the whole, grown more slowly. Concomitantly, the Mediterranean rim of less developed countries "has benefited in growth from the loss of labor (a different though in some ways complementary model)" (Kindleberger 1967, p. 4).

However, with the exhaustion of Europe's excess supplies of labor in the early 1960s, the high rates of growth of the 1950s were grinding to a halt; although a number of countries "have tried to substitute control of wage rates, or incomes policy, for the assistance to growth furnished by unlimited supplies of labor," Kindleberger thinks "it seems unlikely that they will succeed" (1967, p. 5). Hence, migration remained the most effective solution for the forthcoming period. With the waning of population surpluses within Europe itself, the receivers recruited further afield, mostly in the Mediterranean periphery.

Assessing the overall costs and benefits of the process, Kindleberger noted in 1967 that "on a short-term basis . . . the benefits greatly outweigh the costs. Migration, like mercy, blesses him that gives and him that takes" (p. 202). Although some costs do emerge, the risks are limited "until some considerable percentage of the labor force is foreign. Thirty percent is too high. Ten percent seems acceptable, particularly where there is cultural similarity. To locate the discontinuities more precisely is probably impossible" (Kindleberger 1967, p. 213).[14] In conclusion, therefore, "Where immigration is politically acceptable . . . It provides a margin of effective mobility to the labor force, which, in the absence of a bulge of new native recruits to the labor force or a heavy movement of educated farm children or adults to the city, can hardly be achieved by active manpower policy" (Kindleberger 1967, p. 223). Given fundamental agreement among the actors and an absence of competition, no regime arose beyond the minimal policy concertation provided under OEEC and, subsequently, OECD because none was required.[15]

Within this general framework, it is possible to analyze how, at the national level, each of the receivers resolved somewhat differently the problem of reconciling the use of foreign workers with the provision of protection to the indigenous labor force. Countries varied considerably with respect to the externally generated constraints under which they operated, with the United States benefiting from the greatest autonomy by virtue of its hegemonic position.

On the domestic side, one important variable was the status of organized labor in the overall policy apparatus. In the United States, for example, a compromise was achieved around 1950 within what was termed at the time the "liblab" camp, whereby the reformists who sought to eliminate the egregiously discriminatory national origins quota agreed to extend the *numerical* quota to encompass the hitherto-unrestricted Western Hemisphere as well as to restrict agricultural labor procurement in the Southwest (for example, the 1948 campaign against "wetbacks" and termination of the war-time *bracero* program) and impose sanctions on employers of illegal foreign workers. However, implementation was impeded by dependence of the Democrats on southern support for achieving a congressional and presidential majority. Beyond this, protection was provided by the unions, which by and large kept undocumented aliens out of the primary segment of the dual labor market (Piore 1979). Consequently, the deleterious effects of the additional labor supply fell mainly on the secondary segment and thus contributed to a further weakening of those already the worst off— minorities, youths, and women.

In Great Britain, the post-war Labour governments inherited the protective restrictions on immigration established in the 1920s. Limited attempts to use temporary foreign workers for reconstruction, particularly in mining, were defeated by the miners; consequently, immigrant labor was limited to the traditional free flow of Irish, whose economic significance probably outweighed that of the more controversial blacks from the Commonwealth. France resumed its traditional pro-immigration stance in the name of population growth and to facilitate reconstruction, with workers initially coming mostly from Italy and Spain and later from Algeria and Portugal. Paradoxically, despite the state's prominence in the economy generally, labor immigration remained largely unregulated and was controlled essentially by employer demand, as in the United States. This state of affairs is probably attributable to the marginal role of French organized labor in economic policy-making.[16]

Within Europe, immigration had the greatest impact in West Germany, contributing to the "economic miracle" of the late 1940s. Initially, this was not the result of an immigration policy harnessed to economic objectives but a by-product of the open door to Germans from the Russian occupation zone and Eastern Europe. From the mid-1950s, some southern Europeans appeared on the scene as well, and after the Berlin Wall was erected, foreign recruitment became a major policy. This was cast within the framework of neocorporatist concertation among labor and management under the aegis of the state, which provided protection to indigenous workers by imposing tight controls on the mobility of foreign workers.

The arrangements that arose throughout the OECD were predicated on an expansion of the world economy to encompass a vast periphery and the subjection of this periphery to the great transformation. The underlying processes have been well analyzed and need not be restated here (see especially Burawoy 1976; Portes 1978, 1983; Sassen 1988). In effect, each segment of the core developed a special relationship with a segment of the periphery. The expanse of the peripheries—rendered steadily more accessible by the secular reduction in the costs of long-distance transportation—and the acceleration of the disruptive processes within them—compounded by considerable population growth—provided the privileged few with a situation approximating the unlimited supply of labor ideally called for under the doctrine. In the Western Hemisphere, these processes were induced by the regional hegemony of the United States; in the case of Europe, relationships were often established during the colonial period—notoriously in Algeria—presenting newly independent governments with a *fait accompli*. Among the senders, the labor-exporting solution was generalized in part because it provided an important source of foreign exchange by way of remittances; this was rendered more necessary by the IMF and World Bank requirements of a sound balance as a condition for loans. Pressures to engage in export agriculture also contributed to population displacement and emigration.

The exchange undoubtedly brought benefits to senders as well as receivers; but there is little doubt that the receivers benefited more and that, except in a few cases within Europe itself involving senders that were already within reach of the privileged group, labor export contributed little more than stopgap revenue, insufficient to overcome the underdeveloped status quo. The balance might have been redressed by way of some code of conduct, such as a compensatory payment by the receiving to the sending states; but although a number of proposals to this effect were put forward by international organizations (the ILO under the leadership of R. Böhning) or individuals (J. N. Bhagwati), the privileged group had no reason to acquiesce in such a regime, and the poor lacked the clout to impose it on the willing.

CRISIS AND ADAPTATION

Much as generals are best at theorizing about the last war, social scientists developed a *problematique* viewing international migrations from less to more developed countries as epiphenomenal to their relationship in the international economy at the very moment when, under the impact of changing conditions, the receivers questioned the further suitability of ongoing arrangements. In retrospect, however, it is evident that both orthodox economists and a number of Marxists "became trapped into a timeless functionality and exaggerated the extent to which migrant labour was a permanent solution for European capital" (Cohen 1987, p. 144). Considering the changing uses of foreign workers by capitalist economies from their inception, Cohen concludes: "The mix between free and unfree labour is spatially redistributed in a complex and continuously *changing* way in response to the mix of market opportunities, comparative labour-power costs, the course of struggles between capital and labour and the historically specific flows and supplies of migrant and other forms of unfree labor" (1987, p. 144; emphasis in original).

The system ground to a halt much as it had begun, as the result of the concurrent but uncoordinated actions of the receivers; once again, the modalities varied in accordance with local situations and the freedom of action of the policymakers. Under the impact of the energy crisis and the subsequent economic downturn, most European countries—where labor immigration fell within the domain of executive regulation—quickly imposed a freeze, followed by repeated attempts to repatriate at least a portion of the workers; when this did not succeed, there was reluctant movement toward incorporation, accompanied by a reinforcement of barriers to entry. In the United States, there was considerable early agreement with respect to the general objective—to drastically reduce the labor-procurement segment governed by laissez-faire (undocumented migration)—but because of the complexities of the decision-making process, requiring legislation and hence involving congressional action, it took over a decade to pass employer sanctions, the regulatory instrument of the new policy (Zolberg 1990a).[17]

Although these changes were triggered by conjunctural factors, the new situation also fostered a reconsideration of the overall balance of costs and benefits of the system, with special attention to two unanticipated consequences. The first, expressed in economic terms, pertained to the inelasticity of the supply of foreign labor on the downside—that is, the difficulty of regulating the supply so as to avoid a surplus in hard times. This can be disaggregated into two components: (1) the inability of the receivers to send workers back to their country of origin; and (2) the inability to prevent additional entries.

Most obviously, by virtue of the prevailing level of social rights in contemporary capitalist democracies, in many cases foreign workers were able to overcome their commodification and stay in the receiving country despite growing unemployment among natives and within their own ranks. Excess entries occur in good times as well as bad but are, of course, particularly objectionable in the latter situation. Portes and Walton (1981) have accounted for the process by way of social networking—a sociological restatement of Marcus Hansen's historical observation that "emigration begets emigration" (Hansen 1961). In addition, the gap in the income of workers in the two sets of countries is often so extreme (for example, the United States versus Mexico, France versus Mali) that foreign workers are better off in the receiving country under almost any circumstances. This income gap stems not only from wage differentials but also from substantial differences in the income derived from the different bundles of collective goods provided by the respective countries (Carruthers and Vining 1982; Freeman 1986).[18] Given the structure of the international economy, the impact of downturns is amplified in the peripheral countries, so that in bad times the incentives to move become even greater than before. Together, these factors concur to generate permanent pressure for entry. The transformation of foreign workers into permanent residents induced the immigration of family members. This was sometimes facilitated by the receivers' desire to defuse the tensions triggered by the presence of ghetto-like concentrations of young, somatically distinct males.

The sedentarization of migrants in turn occasioned the second unanticipated consequences of the system, namely, a marked heterogeneization of European societies. The issue of incorporating culturally distinct populations subsequently rose to the fore of the political agenda.

The problem was already in evidence before the energy crisis. Commenting on the European freeze, a group of independent experts reviewing policy trends for the OECD dealt first with the economic explanation, and then went on: "The second primary objective of implementing restrictions . . . was a desire to minimize the growing social tensions created by the presence of a large number of foreigners. It is hard to be precise about such a nebulous topic, but history is replete with examples of the seriousness of problems resulting from cultural conflicts, competing claims for jobs, or miscommunication due to language problems" (OECD 1979, p. 22). The "growing social tensions" alluded to reflect in large part the responses of xenophobic and racist segments of the native populations. However, that is not the whole story.

International migration *does* bring about the encounter of culturally different groups hitherto separated from each other in space. Even under the best of circumstances, the arrival of a relatively large wave of immigrants who speak a different language, practice a different religion, or merely have very different habits *does* challenge the cultural status quo of the receiving country and induces some collective stress. As it happens, however, these are not just *any* groups. In the course of establishing their hegemony over the world at large, Europeans and their descendants stressed their common distinctiveness from the subjected populations, founded in part on phenotypical distinctions, and assigned to these differences values that legitimized domination. *Mutatis mutandis*, a similar process of cultural coding tends to develop with respect to labor imported from the periphery. Once established, this configuration of beliefs serves as a foundation for calculations concerning the putative political and cultural impacts of various groups on the receiving countries. In effect, the very characteristics that make these human beings suitable for labor render them undesirable from the perspective of membership in the receiving society. This also has the effect of a self-fulfilling prophecy: The conditions to which the workers are subjected in fact render their incorporation more difficult.[19]

The problems of membership evoked by Michael Walzer (1981) in his exploration of the moral justification for maintaining national boundaries and restricting access thus have a basis in reality; but because this reality is itself the result of inequity, it does not provide legitimate grounds for exclusion but is rather the source of an obligation to provide the newcomers with the means to qualify for membership.[20]

CONCLUSIONS

It is evident that the changes in the international political economy have altered in important ways the elements of the formula that governed post-war settlements and, hence, triggered disturbances among all the states in question. Paradoxically, this has precipitated simultaneously a broadening of the debate over possible alternatives but also a narrowing of actual policy choices (Gourevitch 1986). As the consequences of the collapse of Bretton Woods continue unraveling, none of the scenarios regarding the future of the international political economy suggests a return to the pre-1970s massive procurement of low- to medium-skilled foreign labor by the countries of the core. The burdensome legacy of the Bretton Woods pattern has contributed to a drastic reevaluation of costs and benefits, leading to a negative assessment of the overall balance and, hence, the establishment of a higher threshold before resorting to foreign labor.

Beyond this, indeterminacy prevails. The negative prospect is strengthened by changes in the structure of national manpower demand. According to the recently elaborated theory of a new international division of labor, capital from the core is establishing factories in the cheaper-labor periphery to produce manufactured goods for export to the worldwide market (for example, Froebel et al. 1980). Concomitantly, structural changes in the labor markets of both Europe and the United States would tend to reduce the demand for industrial labor of the sort hitherto filled by immigrants (Piore 1986). By the same token, some of the new industrial countries (NICs) might adopt some version of the Bretton Woods pattern, as is already manifest, for example, in Singapore.

However, the much-touted new international division of labor still leaves the bulk of industrial production within the core, and some analysts have pointed out that the rates of growth of industrial production that have fostered the emergence of NICs fall well within the norm of earlier long-cycle adjustments, so that past performance should not be projected into the future (Cohen 1987, pp. 233–251; Gordon 1988). In light of this, one might hypothesize that core economies will have a renewed incentive to use foreign labor in order to maintain their competitiveness in the older sectors of manufacturing. Saskia Sassen (1988) projects a continuing polarization of the employment structure of global cities, with the lower segment to be filled largely by immigrants; but it should be noted in turn that this can be met by internal sources as well, partly as a consequence of the new labor reserve constituted by the legacy of recent waves of immigration. To the extent that changes in the international political economy impose greater constraints on the externalization of the costs of the welfare state, there are likely to be additional pressures to reduce costs by forcing "idle" natives and recent immigrants to work.

If Gilpin's vision of the regionalization of the international political economy is correct, this is likely to be accompanied by lowering barriers to the international movement of labor within each region, together with maintaining or even reinforcing barriers to movement between them. The most noteworthy development in this respect is the expanded European Community, which does provide for the free movement of labor and incorporates poorer countries from which a limited "conjunctural buffer" can be constituted if need be. In the United States, there has already been talk of providing higher national quotas for neighboring countries, and the provision for agricultural workers under the Immigration Reform and Control Act of 1986 in effect accords privileged treatment to a segment of the periphery that comes close to being incorporated into a comprehensive North American economy. A generalization of these developments would constitute a step toward an epochal change in the basic unit of political membership, comparable to the transition from the feudal unit to the modern state fostered by the growth of the money economy and the bursting out of productive processes beyond the confines of the manorial system (Anderson 1974).

That is as far as the world is likely to evolve toward greater freedom of movement. Under prevailing world conditions, the unimpeded flow of population across international borders would probably produce worldwide gains in efficiency and, hence, higher annual gains in the worldwide gross national product than under restricted conditions. A relatively greater share of these gains would accrue to the population of the less developed countries (including the portion that would relocate), while the resident labor force of the affluent countries would incur some losses (Hamilton and Walley 1984). Thus, there is every reason to expect that the affluent group will consolidate its protective wall. In short, the outlook for a more equitable code of conduct in the sphere of international migrations is as negative as that for the institutionalization of a new international economic order more generally.

NOTES

1. Transnational human flows have received much less attention from economists and political scientists than have trade or strategic interactions. Within sociology generally, migration was traditionally conceptualized as an aggregate of individual movements patterned by choices based on available information regarding economic and social conditions in the places of origin and of putative destination, usually termed "push" and "pull" (see, for example, Stouffer 1940; Ziff 1946; Anderson 1955; and Hoffman-Novotny 1970). The tradition can be traced back to the classic papers entitled "The Laws of Migration," read before the Royal Statistical Society of England over a century ago (Ravenstein 1885, 1889). As recently as 1966, Everett S. Lee, who quoted Ravenstein's propositions in systematic detail at the outset of his own oft-cited attempt to construct a theory of migration, stated that not only

have "Ravenstein's papers . . . stood the test of time," but, in the intervening period, "few additional generalizations have been advanced" (Lee 1966, p. 47). In the mid-1970s, the sociological tradition was modified by more structural approaches, which reconceptualized the "pull" in terms of the initiatives of capitalists in developed countries, motivated by the singular profitability of foreign labor, and the "push" in terms of displacement effects occasioned by dependent development (for example, Castles and Kosack 1985; Burawoy 1976; Portes 1978; Sassen 1988). However, the problem of accounting for obstacles and forced migrations remained intact.

2. This is not to say that either domestic or international migration can be analyzed without reference to the other. On the contrary, their conceptualization as distinct processes should foster a better understanding of the relationship between them. The distinction is also applicable to involuntary movement. People displaced by violence are generally termed "refugees" whether they are inside or outside their country, but only if they are outside of their country and deprived of its protection do they come under the jurisdiction of the international community and become eligible for protection and assistance.

3. Susan Strange (1983) has noted the anomaly as well. She refers to the contemporary system as a "world economy in which relationships between states are largely determined by relations of production and other prevalent structural arrangements for the free movement between states of capital, knowledge, and goods (*but not labor*) that make up a world market economy" (p. 338; emphasis added).

4. Instead, these countries were subject to the orthodox stabilization measures of the IMF, often with no beneficial results in export earnings but substantial increases in import bills and consequent increases in domestic prices. Concomitantly, the liberalization of trade fostered by GATT benefited only the few among them that have evolved into NICs.

5. On the refugee regime, see in particular Gordenker 1987; Zolberg et al. 1989.

6. Material for this section has been drawn from a forthcoming work, of which previews are presented in Zolberg 1978a, 1987a.

7. "Although socio-biological and similar deterministic models of human behavior are, in my judgment inappropriate, it is nonetheless suggestive that 'territoriality' is a widespread (though not universal) behavioral pattern among animals, suggesting that similar territoriality, and unwillingness to permit entry into one's space at will to strangers outside the pack, appears to many as a 'natural' right, compatible with basic human decency in a civilised society" (Bhagwati 1984, p. 681). Bhagwati's only reference in this respect is to Robert Ardrey, an early popular advocate of the application of the observations of Konrad Lorenz to human behavior; however, he comments that this is "an overdrawn parallel" (1984, p. 181, Note 1).

8. The leading historian of the subject (Higham 1970) attributes the rise of restrictionism mainly to xenophobia and views the growth of this disposition largely in psychopathological terms as the conversion of frustrations induced by social change into aggression toward external objects.

9. In Great Britain, despite a stalwart defense of free entry by the Liberal party on Manchesterian grounds, a restrictive Aliens Act was adopted by the Conservatives in 1905 (Gainer 1972, pp. 144–165); despite pleas from eastern landowners, the German government barred entry to most immigrants in the 1880s as well. The major exception was France, whose elites valued immigration as a way of overcoming economic and military manpower shortages induced by the precocious achievement of population stability; France maintained an open door but, in the face of restrictionist agitation, piled up regulations on incoming foreigners (de Wenden 1988, pp. 17–29).

10. The trend was further amplified by the security issues during World War I and social upheavals in its aftermath. In the 1920s, in the face of persisting

unemployment, Great Britain required evidence of prospective employment as a requirement for admission; this appears to be the first instance of what subsequently became common practice throughout the international system. The British overseas dominions (Canada and Australia) also restricted entry, except for a limited flow of British settlers with appropriate capital.

11. At the time, the relevant surplus countries included Italy and the Netherlands, with high rates of natural increases in population, as well as what was known as West Germany, with a large influx of refugees from the east.

12. Over the next several years, the doctrine—shared by all members—was translated into organizational policy, which further stimulated the expansion of labor migration in Europe. For example, an OEEC Council Decision of 1953 stated that the national labor force enjoyed priority over new immigrants but consecrated the "obligation" of governments to issue or renew work permits to nationals of member countries and to integrate into the national labor market foreign workers who had been employed for a certain time on that market (OECD 1979).

13. It "can encourage a consistent way of thinking about international economic problems" and "can help to make countries aware of the impact of their national policies on each other."

14. On the matter of non-economic costs, Kindleberger relies heavily on John Commons, *Races and Immigrants in America* (3d ed. 1924. New York: Macmillan), a classic work of labor economics, which argued on behalf of limited immigration guided by manpower criteria.

15. The OECD sought to persuade reluctant Europeans to go along with the trend. For example, Kindleberger reports that "the point was put strongly by the OECD examiners of Swedish manpower policy" who "raised the question of whether Sweden should not consider a more active immigration policy" and pointed out that "increased migration to Sweden with its high level of productivity would be a contribution to the common growth target of O.E.C.D." (1967, p. 223). He comments further that "Long after this manuscript was finished, it has been learned that Sweden in fact did experiment with a much more liberal policy of immigration, presumably in 1965, but abandoned it in 1966 because of social problems" (1967, p. 224, Note 16a). Yet we know that a few years later, Sweden was prevailed upon to revise its views and did indeed adopt a modified version of the prevailing pattern, as did the other Scandinavian countries (Hammar 1985).

16. The leading labor federation in the post-war period was the CGT; although it played an important role in *political* affairs by way of its links with the Communist party, the Confédération Générale du Travail refusal to participate in planning and policy-making on the grounds that this would constitute "class collaboration" left things to the employers by default.

17. It is worth stressing the historical irony of this enactment, advocated in vain by organized labor as early as 1950 but ultimately achieved when it reached the nadir of its political clout in the Reagan era with the support of conservative Republicans for whom business regulation is ordinarily anathema.

18. Affluent welfare states provide their residents with many more of the universally prized conditions than do LDCs, ranging from abundant and safe water to relatively disease-free environments, educational facilities, and protection from arbitrary exactions by government officials.

19. I have elaborated this analysis in Zolberg 1990b.

20. For further discussion of the ethical issues, see Gibney 1986; Zolberg 1987b; Carens 1988.

REFERENCES

Anderson, P. 1974. *Lineages of the Absolutist State*. London: New Left Books.

Anderson, T. R. 1955. "Intermetropolitan Migration: A Comparison of the Hypotheses of Ziff and Stouffer." *American Sociological Review* 20 (June):287–291.

Bhagwati, J. N. 1984. "Incentives and Disincentives: International Migration." *Weltwirtschaftliches Archiv* 120 (4):678–701.

Burawoy, M. 1976. "The Functions and Reproductions of Migrant Labor." *American Journal of Sociology* 81 (March):1050–1087.

Carens, J. H. 1988. "Immigration and the Welfare States." Pp. 207–230 in A. Gutmann, ed., *Democracy and the Welfare State*. Princeton: Princeton University Press.

Carruthers, N. R., and N. Vining. 1982. "International Migration: An Application of the Urban Location Choice Model." *World Politics* 35 (1):106–120.

Castles, S., and G. Kossack. 1985. *Immigrant Workers and Class Structure in Western Europe*, 2d ed. London: Oxford University Press.

Cohen, R. 1987. *The New Helots: Migrants in the International Division of Labor*. Aldershot: Avebury/Gower.

Craig, R. 1971. *The Bracero Program*. Austin: University of Texas Press.

Davis, K. 1974. "The Migrations of Human Populations." *Scientific American* 231 (3):93–102.

de Wenden, C. W. 1988. *Les Immigrés et al Politique*. Paris: Presses de la Fondation Nationale des Sciences Politiques.

Dædalus. 1964. (Special issue: *A New Europe?* ed. S. Graubard) 93 (1):6–566.

Dowty, A. 1987, *Closed Borders: The Contemporary Assault on Freedom of Movement*. New Haven: Yale University Press.

The Economist. 1988. London. 315:38.

Freeman, G. P. 1986. "Migration and the Political Economy of the Welfare State." *Annals of the American Academy of Political and Social Science* 485 (May):51–63.

Froebel, F., J. Heinrichs, and O. Kreye. 1980. *The New International Division of Labour*. Cambridge: Cambridge University Press.

Gainer, B. 1972. *The Alien Invasion: The Origins of the Aliens Act of 1905*. London: Heinemann Educational Books.

Gibney, M. 1986. *Strangers or Friends: Principles for a New Alien Admission Policy*. Westport, CT: Greenwood Press.

Gilpin, R. 1987. *The Political Economy of International Relations*. Princeton: Princeton University Press.

Gordenker, L. 1987. *Refugees in International Politics*. New York: Columbia University Press.

Gordon, D. M. 1988. "The Global Economy: New Edifice or Crumbling Foundations?" *New Left Review* 168 (March/April):24–64.

Gourevitch, P. A. 1986. *Politics in Hard Times: Comparative Responses to International Economic Crises*. Ithaca: Cornell University Press.

Haggard, P., and B. A. Simmons. 1987. "Theories of International Regimes." *International Organization* 40 (3):707–744.

Hamilton, B., and J. Walley. 1984. "Efficiency and Distributional Implications of Global Restrictions on Labour Mobility: Calculations and Policy Implications." *Journal of Development Economics* 14:61–75.

Hammar, T., ed. 1985. *European Immigration Policy: A Comparative Study*. London: Cambridge University Press.

Hansen, M. L. 1961. *The Atlantic Migration 1607–1860*. New York: Harper Torchbooks.

Higham, J. 1970. *Strangers in the Land*. New York: Atheneum.

Hoffman-Novotny, H. J. 1970. *Migration: Ein Beitrag Zu Einer Soziologischen Aufklärung.* Stuttgart: Enke.

Keohane, R. O., and J. Nye, eds. 1972. *Transnational Relations in World Politics.* Cambridge, MA: Harvard University Press.

Kindleberger, C. P. 1967. *Europe's Postwar Growth: The Role of Labor Supply.* Cambridge, MA: Harvard University Press.

———. 1973. *The World in Depression, 1929–1939.* Berkeley: University of California Press.

Krasner, S. D., ed. 1983. *International Regimes.* Ithaca: Cornell University Press.

Lee, E. S. 1966. "A Theory of Migration." *Demography* 3:47–57.

Lipietz, A. 1988. "Gouverner l'Economie Face aux Defis Internationaux: Du Developpementisme Nationaliste a la Crise Nationale." Paper presented at conference *In Search of the New France: State and Society in France, 1962–1987*, Brandeis University.

Maier, C. S. 1987a. "The Politics of Productivity: Foundations of American International Economic Policy after World War II." Pp. 121–152 in Charles S. Maier, ed., *In Search of Stability: Explorations in Historical Political Economy.* Cambridge: Cambridge University Press.

———. 1987b. "The Two Postwar Eras and the Conditions for Stability in Twentieth-Century Western Europe." Pp. 153–184 in C. S. Maier, ed., *In Search of Stability: Explorations in Historical Political Economy.* Cambridge: Cambridge University Press.

Organization for Economic Cooperation and Development. 1979. *Migrations, Growth, and Development.* Paris: OECD.

Piore, M. J. 1979. *Birds of Passage: Migrant Labor and Industrial Societies.* Cambridge: Cambridge University Press.

———. 1986. "The Shifting Grounds for Immigration." *Annals of the American Academy of Political and Social Science* 485 (May):23–33.

Polanyi, K. 1957. *The Great Transformation.* Boston: Beacon Press.

Portes, A. 1978. "Migration and Underdevelopment." *Politics and Society* 8 (1):1–48.

———. 1983. "International Labor Migration and National Development." Pp. 71–92 in M. Kritz, ed., *U.S. Immigration and Refugee Policy: Global and Domestic Issues.* Lexington, MA: D. C. Heath.

Portes, A., and J. Walton. 1981. *Labor, Class, and the International System.* New York: Academy.

Ravenstein, E. G. 1885. "The Laws of Migration." *Journal of the Royal Statistical Society* 48:167–235.

———. 1889. "The Laws of Migration." *Journal of the Royal Statistical Society* 52:241–305.

Ruggie, J. G. 1983. "International Regimes, Transactions, and Change: Embedded Liberalism in the Postwar Economic Order." Pp. 195–231 in S. Krasner, ed., *International Regimes.* Ithaca: Cornell University Press.

Sassen, S. 1988. *The Mobility of Labor and Capital: A Study in International Investment and Labor Flow.* Cambridge: Cambridge University Press.

Stouffer, Samuel A. 1940. "Intervening Opportunities: A Theory Relating Mobility and Distance." *American Sociological Review* (December):845–857.

Strange, S. 1983. "Cave! His Dragones: A Critique of Regime Analysis." Pp. 337–354 in S. D. Krasner, ed., *International Regimes.* Ithaca: Cornell University Press.

Thomas, B. 1973. *Migration and Economic Growth: A Study of Great Britain and the Atlantic Economy.* Cambridge: Cambridge University Press.

Thomas K. P. 1988. "The Weakest Link: Britain and the First Crisis of Embedded Liberalism." Paper presented to the Conference Group on Political Economy, American Political Science Association, Washington, DC.

Walzer, M. 1981. "The Distribution of Membership." Pp. 102–128 in P. G. Brown and H. Shue, eds., *Boundaries: National Autonomy and Its Limits*. Totowa, NJ: Rowman and Littlefield.

Ziff, George K. 1946. "The P1 P2/D Hypothesis: On the Intercity Movement of Persons." *American Sociological Review* 11 (December):677–686.

Zolberg, A. R. 1978a. "International Migration Policies in a Changing World System." Pp. 241–286 in W. McNeill and R. Adams, eds., *Human Migration*. Bloomington: Indiana University Press.

_____. 1978b. "The Main Gate and the Back Door: The Politics of American Immigration Policy, 1950–1976." Unpublished manuscript, Council on Foreign Relations.

_____. 1981. "International Migrations in Political Perspective." Pp. 15–51 in M. C. Kritz, C. Keely, and S. Tomasi, eds., *Global Trends in Migration*. New York: Center for Migration Studies.

_____. 1987a. "Wanted but Not Welcome: Alien Labor in Western Development." Pp. 36–74 in W. Alonso, ed., *Population in an Interacting World*. Cambridge, MA: Harvard University Press.

_____. 1987b. "Keeping Them Out: Ethical Dilemmas of Immigration Policy." Pp. 261–297 in R. Myers, ed., *International Ethics in the Nuclear Age*. Washington, DC: University Press of America (Ethics and Foreign Policy Series).

_____. 1987c. "Beyond the Nation-State: Comparative Politics in Global Perspective." Pp. 42–69 in J. Berting, W. Blockmans, and U. Rosenthal, eds., *Beyond Progress and Development*. London: Bowker.

_____. 1990a. "Reforming the Back Door: The Immigration Reform and Control Act of 1986 in Historical Perspective." Pp. 293–339 in V. Yans-Johnson, ed., *Immigration Reconsidered: History, Sociology, and Politics*. New York: Oxford University Press.

_____. 1990b. "Stranger Encounters." Pp. 178–193 in I. Simon-Barouh and P.-J. Simon, *Les Etrangers dans la Ville: Les Regard des Sciences Sociales*. Paris: L'Harmattan.

Zolberg, A. R., A. Suhrke, and S. Aguayo. 1989. *Escape from Violence: The Refugee Crisis in the Developing World*. New York: Oxford University Press.

Comments

Charles C. Ragin

Professor Zolberg presents a creative analysis of how international inequality is sowing the seeds of its own undoing. The mechanism of choice is international migration, with special attention to state attempts to manage human capital flows across national boundaries within a context of established social policy practices and uncontrolled macro-economic changes, both national and global. The framework for the analysis, according to Zolberg, is thoroughly Polanyian. This framework represents an attempt to avoid the narrowness of both internalist perspectives (which now seem hopelessly outdated) and externalist perspectives such as world-system theory, criticized for their infatuation with global-level processes and changes and their willful ignorance of national-level structures and forces.

A Polanyian framework combines complementary substantive and methodological foci. With respect to substantive foci, primary attention is directed to the political and economic spheres at both the national and international levels. Crossing these two dichotomies yields four different arenas for analysis and six basic relationships (for example, one is the relationship between international economic changes and national political outcomes). The methodological focus takes the form of a directive: Examine the origins of parallel developments (for Polanyi the emergence of fascism) in countries that are similarly situated in the international system. This methodological strategy provides a context for giving proper weight to international factors and conditions but takes national-level phenomena as the starting point. What separates this perspective from externalist perspectives is the *equal weight* given to political and economic phenomena and the interest in the *interpenetration* of national and international phenomena.

Zolberg implements this framework in an analysis of how most advanced countries have changed over time, especially in the post–World War II period, in their willingness to accept surplus labor from other countries. On the one hand, national governments want to avoid having labor shortages because such shortages seriously undermine economic growth and international competitiveness. Economic expansion typically requires a labor force that can be quickly enlarged. On the other hand, however, migrants that might be welcome in times of labor shortage pose serious political, economic, and social problems in times of labor surplus, resulting in ethnic and racial conflicts, pressures for highly restrictive legislation from organized labor and other groups, heavy burdens on social welfare programs, and lower living standards for the national population as a whole. And the economic forces that push migrants out of less developed countries are strong, even when economic growth in less developed countries outpaces economic growth in developed countries.

All the ingredients for Polanyian social science are in place. What is needed in Zolberg's analysis, however, is more attention to national-level variation. North Atlantic countries have moved together in enacting more restrictive legislation—the changes are parallel, and the origins can be traced to international forces. But what about differences among these countries? The goal, as stated, was to implement a Polanyian approach and avoid the sins of internalist and externalist approaches. The end product, however, seems all too consistent with externalist approaches. International economic changes are the primary cause; relatively uniform directional changes in the immigration policies of developed countries are the result. It is as though Zolberg's main focus is on how the average level of restrictiveness has changed over time, and it all but excludes the possibility of differences among these countries, both in terms of their enduring degrees of restrictiveness and in the responses to international forces. The little cross-sectional variation in restrictiveness among advanced countries that is charted is credited almost entirely to variation in the national political strength of organized labor.

Why should this inattention to national-level variation matter? First, it seems clear that enduring differences among advanced countries in restrictiveness are far more profound than the temporal variations generated by swings of the international economy. The strong contrast between North American countries on the one hand and Scandinavian countries on the other provides a snapshot of the wide range of cross-sectional variation. Enduring differences in restrictiveness have their origins in a variety of historical arrangements and compromises, including immigration history, social policy system and welfare state development, employment practices, strength of labor organizations, and so on (which, in turn, may be linked to differing histories and pressures of international competition and involvement, bringing the Polanyian framework full circle). Among developed countries, several extreme cases stand out and beg attention. Japan, for example, compared to virtually all other developed countries, has always been highly restrictive. This stance has not inhibited economic growth. (Indeed, Japan's practice of lifetime employment in some sectors would seem to pose a more serious obstacle to economic vigor than that posed by excess immigrants in North Atlantic economies.)

Second, there are also strong differences in the degree of restrictiveness and changing levels of restrictiveness induced by imperialist legacies. Some advanced countries have sizeable immigrant populations and remain relatively open to new immigration because of their history of involvement in Third World economic and political affairs. For example, both France and the United States have been more open to Vietnamese immigrants precisely because of the military involvement of these two countries in Southeast Asia. In this chapter, Zolberg ignores this aspect of restrictiveness, emphasizing economic causes and skirting the international political causes of international migration. Massive human flows have occurred for predominantly political reasons, especially in the aftermath of anti-neocolonial struggles. These flows are well within the Polanyian framework (the crossing of the two dichotomies) and should be examined as well. After all, Zolberg's chapter concerns international migration within the context of international inequality, and international inequality is one of the main causes of international political conflict. Such flows are not mechanical reactions to fluctuations in national and international economies, and barriers to flows with predominantly political origins cannot be erected as easily as barriers to other types of immigration. North Atlantic countries vary widely in their exposure to immigration induced by international conflict and imperialist legacies, and this exposure is outside Zolberg's economistic analysis.

Third, North Atlantic countries also differ in the degree to which they contain untapped internal labor pools. Some, for example, have "peripheral" areas within their national borders, with surplus labor awaiting economic absorption. There are also other internal labor pools (housewives, youths, the retired, and similar groups), and countries vary considerably in how these pools of employables are treated, both in employment and as clients of the welfare state. The status and treatment of these internal labor sources have an impact on restrictiveness and the treatment of immigrants.

Finally, North Atlantic countries differ a great deal in racial and ethnic diversity and in how they treat ethnic and racial minorities. This variation has an impact on immigration policy and is confounded with other differences that are also relevant to immigration policy (for example, labor organizations, employment practices, and welfare state structures). Existing racial and ethnic diversity also affects how new immigrants are treated. Some North Atlantic countries are profoundly multi-ethnic and multi-racial and have a history of absorbing diverse immigrant groups. Some are more insular and lowered their considerable barriers to immigration—thus allowing the possibility of culturally distinct minorities—only in response to international pressure. Not surprisingly, the more multi-ethnic and multi-racial countries also tend to be among those with weaker labor movements and less extensive welfare states. Furthermore, having a weak social welfare net lowers the potential costs of a liberal immigration policy.

Viewed in this light, each country appears as a complex configuration of characteristics, embracing ethnic and racial composition, welfare state development, labor organization, employment practices, immigration history, and immigration policy. These different traits cohere in diverse and unique, but penetrable, ways, and the different configurations they form should be seen as a backdrop for examining the impact of international economic changes. At least this way of approaching the problem would be more faithful to Polanyi.

The best way to move Zolberg's analysis away from the clutches of externalist perspectives is to treat these configurations seriously and examine how different patterns of response to international economic forces are embedded in these national-level configurations of characteristics. For example, in some countries the impact of changed international economic conditions may be felt more profoundly in welfare policy than in immigration policy. This outcome might have its origins in the weakness of welfare state development, a history of contention over immigration policy, or some combination of conditions. Another possible response would be to leave both welfare policy and immigration policy relatively untouched but block the further integration of internal labor sources (such as women) and speed the exit of others (such as the elderly). The conceptual framework for examining these different patterns of response is ready-made—in Polanyi— and invoked by Zolberg himself.

Because of their shared characteristics, North Atlantic countries can provide a rough, quasi-experimental framework for the analysis of the impact of international economic pressures. The same general "treatment" is applied in different settings with sometimes similar, sometimes different, consequences, depending on the configuration of elements present in each country. In effect, changes in the international economy give this type of investigation structure and provide a methodological tool for prying open the circumscribed configurations represented in bounded national units. Examining the different responses of different configurations helps us understand each configuration—its specificity; examining the pattern of responses helps us understand the nature of national political economies, North Atlantic especially, in the international system.

These suggestions concern unrealized potential in Zolberg's chapter and are not meant to detract from the strength of the arguments and the insights that are presented. Indeed, it would take a book-length manuscript to implement the approach suggested here. Zolberg's principal argument—that international migration can be a key mechanism undermining international inequality, and that nations act to prevent this eventuality—is important and stands on its own. The boundedness of states with respect to labor flows seems both primordial—a curious anomaly in an increasingly international system—and modern—as an essential and defining feature of that system.

Comments

George Steinmetz

Aristide Zolberg has introduced advanced theories of the international political economy into the study of migration. The recent work of Zolberg and other historical sociologists has also begun to restore the state to the central place it occupied in the classical writings of Marx, Weber, Hintze, and even Durkheim.[1] Zolberg defends an integrated Polanyian perspective, one that pays attention to the systemic effects of both international and domestic politics and economics and examines their relationships to one another. In sharp contrast to methodological individualism, Zolberg's analysis begins at the level of the world political economy, the furthest extreme from the realm of individual decision-making. From here, Zolberg proceeds to examine national-level developments and contrasts, exploring the ways in which global pressures are differentially experienced, inflected, and responded to in various countries. This strategy of interweaving general theory and case-specific interpretation and emphasizing the intersection of broad trends with local and historical contingencies is respresevive of much of the best work in the burgeoning field of historical sociology. Many historical sociologists, of course, would attend more closely to the systematic explanation of national differences; I will return to this point below.

Zolberg argues that sweeping historical changes in migration patterns cannot be understood, as in traditional population studies, as aggregations of individual "choices based on available information regarding economic and social conditions in the places of origins and of putative destination" (Note 1). Migration is profoundly shaped by structural economic and political factors that are beyond the control of individuals. These "irreducibly structural" variables influence not only the cost-benefit calculations and information available to potential migrants but determine the very possibility of migration.

Zolberg also goes beyond the structural Marxist approaches to labor migration developed since the 1970s, which mainly emphasized the imperatives of capitalist development. The reasons for obstacles to immigration must remain obscure within an overly economistic account: While employers have a basic economic interest in procuring an unlimited supply of cheap labor, the history of immigration reveals that restrictions have been as common as liberalization. Even in the United States restrictions were eventually enacted after the turn of the century, although "the business community managed to delay enactment of legislation" for two decades. While the "unimpeded flow of population across international borders" would benefit both First World employers and migrants and would "probably produce world-wide gains in efficiency," Zolberg acknowledges that "the resident labor of the affluent countries would incure some losses." The implication is that these perceived losses are the main reason for restrictive legislation. The state in the more industrialized world would thus appear to be less the instrument of the dominant class than of wage earners, at least with respect to immigration policy.

Yet Zolberg suggests that even this image of the state is too simple. A specific theory of the state is necessary precisely because the state is more than a simple reflection of societal pressures and interests, pluralist and instrumental Marxist theory notwithstanding (Elkin 1985). Until recently, when sociologists discussed the state (usually employing some related term such as *government*) they typically treated it as an entity without efficacy or interests of its own. The term *state* has historically implied, however, that governing is not merely an aggregation of the wills of individuals and social groups (even if the state's autonomy from society is only relative).

Even more important for Zolberg, the state has an "external face" and is influenced by *international* economics and politics. Zolberg actually downplays the significance of national factors in accounting for long-term shifts in immigration policy, arguing that groups of states shift in tandem from liberalization to restrictiveness and back again. States' individuality is limited by the internationalization of the economy. At the same time, Zolberg affirms that states are not merely epiphenomenal by showing that they exercise effective control over the exit and entry of migrant labor. Even if the political compartmentalization of the world is now incapable of impeding the international flow of capital and commodities, it still matters enormously for movements of population. States are relatively autonomous from both the international and domestic environments.

My two criticisms of Zolberg's chapter concern the weakness of his account of the state and his inattention to cultural factors.

Zolberg's analysis of the national or internal dimension is relatively underdeveloped, especially with respect to the state. In his fully justified attack on sociology's "axiomatic internalism," Zolberg seems to have bent the stick too far in the other direction. To return to one of Zolberg's examples,

while it is true that the appearance of fascist movements across the industrialized world in the 1930s "should never have been ascribed to local
causes, national mentalities, or historical backgrounds" (quoting Polanyi
1957, p. 237), the German variant, for example, was undeniably unique and
cannot be ascribed to that country's location in the international system
alone. The same problem exists with Zolberg's analysis of international
trends in immigration policy. Even if the surplus of people trying to emigrate
and the pressures on the labor forces in the advanced countries are the
products of global economic forces, the determinants of entry regulations
are partially specific to each country. Zolberg briefly discusses such cross-
national differences but offers only ad hoc explanations. A theoretical account
of the state should be able to address both similarities and differences in
policy-making.

The need for such a theory is illustrated by Zolberg's discussion of the
movement in the United States and Europe to restrain immigration that
began during the last two decades of the nineteenth century. Zolberg attributes
this shift to the common experience of a severe economic crisis. While he
recognizes that the resultant policies are partially specific to each country
and discusses some of the variables affecting cross-national variations, Zolberg
does not specify the relative importance of such variables or the precise
form of their influence. The sole general theoretical statement concerns the
impact of the world economic crisis. That this explanation is inadequate is
shown clearly by the divergent timing of each country's move toward
restrictiveness. Moreover, the *lag* between the crisis and eventual policy
restrictions on immigration underscores the typically indirect translation of
economic events into politics. Bismarck's extradition of Poles from Prussia
in 1885–1886 began twelve years after the economic crisis, and by the time
restrictive legislation was passed in the United States, the long-wave crisis
(1870s–1890s) was already over. The specific *form* taken by restriction in
each country—its severity and ideological framing—also varied. The Bis-
marckian restrictions, for example, had a specifically antisemitic slant, which
the general economic model fails to capture (Neubach 1967). To take a
current example, the debates over restricting the immigration of Poles,
Eastern European gypsies, and Soviet Jews to Germany take on a very
particular cast due to the Nazi state's assault on these groups. Even if all
governments attempt to curtail immigration at the same time and for the
same economic reasons, the actual policies that finally emerge reflect a
variety of nationally specific factors, including the nature of the state and
of the political system more generally.

Other cross-national variables discussed by Zolberg include the stance
of labor and employers toward immigration and their degree of involvement
in the policy-making process. Zolberg notes that French labor's ability to
influence immigration was undermined by the CGT's unwillingness to enter
into neo-corporatist forms of policy-making, in contrast to the national labor
federation in West Germany. He has calculated that fifty bills were presented
to the French National Assembly between 1883 and 1914 calling for re-

strictions on immigration (Zolberg 1978, p. 278), but all of them were defeated due to the opposition of employers and state elites. Despite the continuous history in France of xenophobic movements against foreign workers, stretching from the French Revolution through Boulangism in the 1880s to the present, the weak political influence of labor and populist parties has contributed to relatively open immigration policies.[2] But how can one account for the enactment by Reagan and conservative Republicans of sanctions on employers for hiring illegal immigrants, for example? Zolberg mentions this paradox without elaborating on it. Which political conditions lead employers to defer their interest in cheap labor and play the role of social peacemakers by supporting immigration cutbacks?

Other variables referred to in passing as influences on immigration policy include demography, party systems, and contingent features of national history, such as relationships to former colonies. The German Christian Democratic party (CDU) provides an example of the impact of the party system. The presence of an extreme right wing in the CDU's electorate, at least until the recent formation of the Republican party, made its leaders hypersensitive to demands for restrictions on immigration. Again, this diverges from the French party system, with its long history of separate anti-immigrant parties. The effects of France's early demographic transition and low birth rate on immigration policies illustrate the importance of another national-level variable. The significance of access to "nondisruptive" sources of immigrant labor is illustrated by the contrast between the German Federal Republic and France. The influx of East German immigrants between 1945 and the construction of the Berlin Wall in 1961 provided a plentiful source of cheap labor that was less problematic than immigrants from (former) colonies or the European periphery, given the social-cultural similarities between East and West Germans.[3]

An elaboration of the concept of Fordism might prove capable of integrating these various factors into a coherent model that could account for national policy differences. Fordism ordinarily refers to a specific form of accumulation, economic growth, class relations, politics, and culture that was constructed in Western Europe and North America between the post–World War II period and the early 1970s. Fordism is characterized by a systematic relationship between mass production and mass consumption. Fordism is also said to be accompanied by a series of changes in *culture*—such as productivism, consumerism, and the spread of the mass media—and in *politics*—such as the prevalence of neocorporatism and the Keynesian welfare state.[4] Zolberg writes that Fordism was institutionalized "with minor variations in national sociopolitical settlements" throughout Europe. The more recent empirical work using the concept of Fordism, however, emphasizes rather large national variations within the contours of the general model (cf. Jessop 1989). Nationally specific factors determined which aspects of the model were adopted, the manner in which "national" Fordism has broken down, and what mode of regulation, if any, has been replacing it.

Such a fine-tuned analysis might provide systematic tools for understanding cross-national differences in immigration policies.

My second criticism of the Polanyian perspective as developed by Zolberg is that it pays too little attention to the role of culture and ideology at both the national and international levels. Nationalism will serve as an example of a cultural variable at the national level, one Zolberg touches upon only briefly. State managers' concern with constructing and solidifying a *national identity* is a reason for restrictions on immigration cited in some of the literature. The official obsession with national identity in the second half of the nineteenth century (Anderson 1983) undoubtedly played a role in the simultaneous move to restrictive legislation. But where does this concern with national identity come from? The call to preserve a distinctive identity through control of a territory may merely mask more material underlying protectionist motives. Yet evidence suggests that waves of nationalism are more than simple responses to economic pressures. The recent resurgence of nationalism in Eastern Europe seems to have been triggered by a specifically political factor—the collapse of the state-socialist regimes (even if economic deprivation has subsequently played a role).

Despite its internationalist orientation, the resolutely Polanyian perspective also ignores international forms of culture. Even as states throw up protective walls against migrants, they are less able to keep out international cultural forms, which may in turn influence local understandings and, thus, immigration policies. The "common doctrines" on labor migration discussed in Zolberg's chapter illustrate one "expert" version of such cultural diffusion. Manchesterist free trade doctrines circulated throughout Europe in the nineteenth century, urging the elimination of restrictions on the movements of people as well as goods. Modern European nationalism itself, which ultimately worked to hinder international migration, was arguably a partially international doctrine at the outset. Even if social ideas or concepts (Fordism), theorists (Bourdieu), artists (Anselm Kiefer), and mass-cultural artifacts (the U.S. techniques and products whose inundation of Europe in the interwar years first gave rise to the notion of Fordism) are understood differently when torn out of their national contexts, the very fact of their widespread diffusion points to a heightening of cultural internationalization whose political influence should not be ignored. Although it is impossible to predict how the current debates over multiculturalism in the United States and Western Europe will be resolved, a possible indirect effect would be the erosion of certain ideologies underpinning restrictions on immigration.

Zolberg is a leading voice in a rising chorus calling for an international agreement on migration that would oblige all countries to provide "newcomers with the means to qualify for membership." Such an international code would help combat the xenophobic movements and political parties that have sprung up across Europe in recent years. Zolberg's conclusion offers little hope for such a development, however, predicting instead that the affluent countries will "consolidate their protective walls" against further immigration.

NOTES

1. This is not to imply that Durkheim's analysis of the state is adequate; see the assessment of Birnbaum (1976). On Weber and Hintze, see Kocka (1983); on Marx, see Jessop (1982). In addition to Zolberg's papers cited in his article, see especially Zolberg (1980). The recent "turn toward the state" in U.S. sociology is exemplified by Skocpol (1979) and Tilly (1990).

2. On these movements, see Gossez (1967, p. 64) on petitions in 1848 demanding exclusion of foreigners; Newman (1975) on efforts to expel foreign and provincial workers in 1830; Perrot (1974, p. 171) on limitation of foreign labor as a common strike demand in the early Third Republic; and Néré (1959, Vol. 2, p. 90) on the 1880s.

3. The vast westward immigration of Germans from the former German Democratic Republic, which began in October 1989 and has continued to the present, is a different matter. The rising costs of German unification to West German taxpayers and the already high levels of unemployment in the Federal Republic before the immigration have contributed to widespread popular resentment of the Ossis. (In an interview broadcast on U.S. television on October 4, 1990, a West Berlin worker said he wished the East German government had raised the Berlin Wall rather than opening it.) The greatest anger, nonetheless, has been reserved for gypsies and other "non-Germans."

4. These and other aspects of Fordism are discussed in Aglietta (1987); Lipietz (1987); Boyer (1990); Harvey (1989); and Hirsch and Roth (1986).

REFERENCES

Aglietta, Michel. 1987. *A Theory of Capitalist Regulation. The US Experience.* London: Verso.

Anderson, Benedict, 1983. *Imagined Communities: Reflections on the Origins and Spread of Nationalism.* London: Verso.

Birnbaum, Pierre. 1976. "La Conception Durkheimienne de l'État: l'Apolitisme des Fonctionnaires." *Revue Française de Sociologie* XVII(2):247–258.

Boyer, Robert. 1990. *The Regulation School: A Critical Introduction.* Trans. Craig Charney. New York: Columbia University Press.

Elkin, Stephen L. 1985. "Between Liberalism and Capitalism: An Introduction to the Democratic State." Pp. 1–18 in Roger Benjamin and Stephen L. Elkin, eds., *The Democratic State.* Lawrence: University Press of Kansas.

Gossez, Rémi. 1967. *Les Ouvriers de Paris, Livre 1: L'Organisation.* La Roche-sur-Yon: Imprimerie Centrale de l'Ouest.

Harvey, David. 1989. *The Condition of Postmodernity. An Enquiry into the Origins of Cultural Change.* New York: Basil Blackwell.

Hirsch, Joachim, and Roland Roth. 1986. *Das Neue Gesicht des Kapitalismus. Vom Fordismus zum Post-Fordismus.* Hamburg: VSA-Verlag.

Jessop, Bob. 1982. *The Capitalist State.* New York: New York University Press.

———. 1989. "Conservative Regimes and the Transition to Post-Fordism: The Cases of Great Britain and West Germany." Pp. 261–299 in M. Gottdiener and Nicos Komninos, eds., *Capitalist Development and Crisis Theory: Accumulation, Regulation and Spatial Restructuring.* New York: Macmillan.

Kocka, Jürgen. 1983. "Otto Hintze, Max Weber und das Problem der Bürokratie." *Historische Zeitschrift* 233(1):73–77.

Lipietz, Alain. 1987. *Mirages and Miracles. The Crises of Global Fordism.* London: Verso.

Néré, Jacques. 1959. "La Crise Industrielle de 1882 et le Mouvement Boulangiste." Paris, unpublished Thèse de lettres.

Neubach, H. 1967. *Die Ausweisungen von Polen und Juden aus Preussen 1885–1886.* Wiesbaden: Otto Harrassowitz.

Newman, Edgar Leon. 1975. "What the Crowd Wanted in the French Revolution of 1830." Pp. 17–40 in John M. Merriman, ed., *1830 in France.* New York: New Viewpoints.

Perrot, Michelle. 1974. *Les Ouvriers en Grève,* 2 Vols. Paris.

Polanyi Karl. 1957. *The Great Transformation.* Boston: Beacon Press.

Skocpol, Theda. 1979. *States and Social Revolutions.* Cambridge, MA: Harvard University Press.

Tilly, Charles. 1990. *Coercion, Capital, and European States, A.D. 990–1990.* New York: Basil Blackwell.

Zolberg, Aristide R. 1978. "International Migration Policies in a Changing World System." Pp. 241–286 in W. McNeill and R. Adams, *Human Migration.* Bloomington: Indiana University Press.

———. 1980. "Strategic Interactions and the Formation of Modern States: France and England." *International Social Science Journal* 32(4):687–716.

11

Intellectuals and Domination in Post-Communist Societies

George Konrad and Ivan Szelenyi

We completed our book, *The Intellectuals on the Road to Class Power*, in September 1974. In the last paragraph of the manuscript, we concluded: The publication of this book by an official publishing house in a Central European country will be the empirical proof that socialism has entered its third period[1] in which the intellectuals, rather than the bureaucratic elite, exercise class power.

Fifteen years later, in November 1989, our book was published in Hungary by a respectable, government-owned publishing house, Gondolat Kiadó. We wish to answer at least three important questions our readers may pose. (1) Are current events proof of the decline of bureaucratic domination and the growth of power of the intelligentsia? Is the intelligentsia the new ruling elite, the new dominant class of post-Communist Hungarian society? (2) Is the clearly increased political activism and influence of the intellectuals a lasting phenomenon or just a brief interval between Communist bureaucratism and a new, possibly bourgeois class domination? In other words, are we observing an epoch in the making or just a brief period of transition? (3) If the current stage is not just a brief transition period but is likely to be

---

The paper presented at the conference was titled "Intellectuals and the Politics of Knowledge" and was by Ivan Szelenyi alone. Events in Eastern Europe shortly after the conference made a portion of that paper obsolete, and Ivan Szelenyi has, jointly with George Konrad, extensively revised, retitled, and refocused the paper, resulting in this chapter.

However, this means that certain valuable parts of the original paper, on which both commentators, Seymour Martin Lipset and Klemens Szaniawski, made comments, have been excluded. In order that these points, and the comments upon them, not be lost, Szelenyi's abstract of the original paper is printed on p. 362, followed by the comments upon the original paper by Lipset and Szaniawski. [Editors' note]

a new epoch, is this third "epoch" socialist at all in any meaningful sense of the term?

We need a book-long manuscript to answer all these questions in any serious manner. We would like to write this book eventually, but since we can only spend a few weeks together now, this chapter will present our argument in only a few theses. Briefly, we offer the following answers to the questions above.

Currently, indeed, the intellectuals play the most fundamental role in the transformation of state socialist societies (this was particularly true for Hungary in 1989–1990, but it is also true for the USSR, Poland, and Czechoslovakia). The foundations of bureaucratic domination were eroded, and, with the decline of the old elite, the only viable candidates for membership in the new elites are intellectuals. Never before in central European history have intellectuals exercised more collective power than they do today in Hungary.

The power of intellectuals may only be a transitory phenomenon—like their predecessors during the French Revolution, they may only lay the foundations of a new type of domination for a class other than their own. This domination, at the least, should not exclude the possibility that the new intellectual class, which is just appearing on the historical scene, may be able to reproduce itself in a uniquely central European configuration of economic and political institutions and social agents.

We are the least certain about our answer to the third question. We prefer to call the social and economic orders we see emerging in Hungary today *post-Communist*.[2] With the term *post*, we want to express our belief that we better know what we are leaving behind than what lies ahead. The emergent new social formation may be socialistic, but it may also represent a convergence with Western capitalism. It may also be of a different quality: It may be located on some kind of "third"—or central European[3]—way that is as different from Western capitalism as from any form of socialism presently known to us.

In this chapter, we summarize our theses on three subjects. First, we offer a general diagnosis of the current social and economic changes and a sketch of the anatomy of post-Communist society as we currently understand it. Second, we explore the position of intellectuals in such a post-Communist society, and we try to measure along three dimensions how far the formation of an intellectuals class has progressed.[4] Finally, we will briefly consider how lasting the newly gained power of the intellectuals is likely to be.

TRANSITION TO POST-COMMUNISM
AND THE EROSION OF COMMUNIST
BUREAUCRATIC DOMINATION

The changes we are experiencing in virtually all central European countries and, at least in certain ways, in the USSR and China are of epochal significance. Communism as we knew it for seventy years is disappearing.

Although Western scholars disagree about what to call these societies (Communist, socialist, totalitarian, state capitalist, Marxist-Leninist, bureaucratic collectivist, "Soviet type of societies," or whatever), commentators usually agree in descriptive terms on the major characteristics of these formations. It is probably quite uncontroversial to suggest that these socio-economic systems can be described by the following:

1. The state has a monopoly in the economy, particularly in the spheres of production of key goods and ownership of the most important means of production.
2. Correspondingly, the social structure of these societies can be characterized by a single hierarchy, by a single pyramid, which operates as a single bureaucratic rank-order. Ascent and descent in this order are regulated by two criteria: political loyalty (loyalty to the boss or the party, dedication to Marxism-Leninism; we will call it, in a Bourdieusque manner, *political capital*) and educational credentials (*cultural capital*). Few made it to the top without having an abundance of both of these capitals. Those who had neither political nor cultural capital were likely to find themselves at the bottom of the hierarchy.
3. Finally, and most obvious in all these societies, one party, trying to legitimate itself with reference to the teachings of Marxism-Leninism, had the political monopoly.[5]

In light of the above description, it is reasonable to suggest that central European countries are in a transition to post-communism in all these respects. The monopoly of the state in the economy has been undermined gradually since 1970, first by the emergent second economy and since 1988 by an accelerating transformation of the statist economy. A new legal framework was created that introduced a "sector neutral property law." Thus, for the first time since the Communist takeover, private property is accepted as equivalent to public property. A statist economy with a secondary sector where private activities are tolerated is being transformed into a mixed economy with a fully fledged private sector that not only exists but is the major source of economic dynamism.

In conjunction with these economic changes, the Hungarian social structure was also transformed. From the mid-1960s onward, through participation in the second economy, a gradual embourgeoisement,[6] or petty bourgeoisification, occurred. Between one-third and one-half of the Hungarian working class, instead of being fully proletarianized, increasingly looked for its fortune outside the state sector in part-time private ventures.[7] With the recent liberalization of the private sector, one can reasonably expect the development of a bourgeoisie proper. Some people will remain small entrepreneurs. Others may become members of a new, big bourgeoisie. The single social hierarchy of communism, based on bureaucratic rank, is now being complemented by a second social hierarchy in which ascent and descent are determined by private wealth and market capacities.

Finally, the Marxist-Leninist party lost its political monopoly. Hungary today has a multiparty system. In February 1989, even the Communist party had to accept the principle of a multiparty parliamentary democracy. The new constitution deleted the idea of the "leading role" of the Communist party. Instead, it offers legal guarantees to the formation and functioning of different political parties. The first competitive elections were held in March and April 1990, and the Communist party is now in opposition, with bourgeois parties forming the government.

The most spectacular changes were those in the political system. While the transformation of the economic system and social structure through the process of petty bourgeoisification stretched over two decades, the bourgeoisification of the political system—particularly the disintegration of the old cadre elite—has occurred since early 1989. This chapter focuses on these changes, trying to explain how and why the cadre elite lost its grip on power. It also tries to comprehend the recent politicization and mobilization of the whole of the intelligentsia. We are, of course, fully aware that these recent changes were prepared by the slower, more silent revolution from below, which has gradually undermined the Communist system since the mid-1960s. The suddenly politicized and radicalized Hungarian intelligentsia today is often impatient with unresponsiveness by society, or the masses. Indeed, the newly formed political movements or parties meet with a great deal of skepticism, if not with outright and total apathy. We do not share this impatience of our colleagues and friends. A key theoretic assumption of this chapter is the unevenness of the embourgeoisement process in Hungary and generally in central Europe, both today and historically.

German nineteenth-century social history got a lot of mileage out of a distinction between *Bildungsbürgertum* (referring to the educated middle class) and *Besitzbürgertum* (basically meaning the propertied bourgeoisie). In both North America and Western Europe (especially in countries such as England or Holland but also to a significant extent in France), the embourgeoisement process was led by the *Besitzbürgertum*. In Germany, by contrast, the educated middle class emerged as the new capitalist class, and the market economy absorbed highly skilled professional labor. In central Europe, in the Habsburg Empire—in countries such as Hungary, Poland, or Bohemia—this was even more pronounced. In the dialectics of *Bildungsbürgertum* and *Besitzbürgertum*, the emphasis was on the *Bildungsbürgertum*. Thus, in some places, the bourgeois transformation was attempted without a proper bourgeoisie—by a bourgeoisified *Bildungsbürgertum*, which in several ways had a rather mixed attitude toward the propertied bourgeoisie it was supposed to create.

Interpreting recent Hungarian history in these terms, one may suggest that, in the two decades since the mid-1960s—in a historically unusual way for central Europe—a *Besitzbürgertum* developed (although this was emphatically "petty," part-time, small-scale, consumption, not accumulation, oriented). On the one hand, with the exception of a gradually growing but numerically insignificant group of dissidents, a majority of the intelligentsia remained statist, or cadre, in its social and political character. On the other, a very large section of the population gained significant petty bourgeois autonomies from the bureaucratic center. For some two decades, Hungarian embourgeoisement was uneven. Petty bourgeoisification was reasonably extensive (involving the development of a new, although small, *Besitzbürgertum*), while the educated middle class was less bourgeoisified, remaining more cadre than the *Bildungsbürgertum*. This petty bourgeoisification gradually undermined the dominant bureaucratic system of domination, and, beginning in early 1989, the political reform exploded through the holes thus created in the system of bureaucratic power. This resulted in a rapid bourgeoisification of the educated middle class, and today a new unevenness of the Hungarian embourgeoisement process can be observed: The *Bildungsbürgertum* regained its dominant role and jumped ahead of the *Besitzbürgertum*. As in the nineteenth century, Hungary again is faced with the paradox: attempting a bourgeois transformation without a propertied bourgeoisie.

Although we are aware that the collapse of communism was the result of popular resistances to bureaucratic power and to pressures of socialist proletarianization, in this chapter we focus our attention on this *Bildungsbürgertum*. In the current conjuncture, the unique feature of social change in this part of the world is again the exceptional role played by the intelligentsia. Our aim here is to understand these agents and to explore whether their power is only transitory or whether they have a chance to consolidate it into a class power of their own.

INTELLECTUALS IN THE
SOCIAL STRUCTURE
OF POST-COMMUNIST SOCIETY

The Intellectuals on the Road to Class Power was not a particularly popular book among our central European friends and colleagues. Our contention that the entire intelligentsia may eventually share power with the bureaucracy sounded unpersuasive, if not insulting, to most of our fellow central European intellectuals. Indeed, they felt neglected, unrewarded, and sometimes even persecuted by Brezhnevism (frequently called neo-Stalinism or just Stalinism). The central European intelligentsia, which expressed considerable enthusiasm during the 1960s for the projects of the humanization and rationalization of socialism, felt cheated during the 1970s and early 1980s as the promised reforms were sabotaged. Thus, the Zagorskis claimed that under these conditions, the East European intelligentsia was more on the road to dissent than to class power.

However, by the late 1980s, our initial analysis seemed to offer more insights than central European commentators usually acknowledge. The East European intelligentsia found an effective strategy against the counteroffensive of the old bureaucratic elite. It transformed the nature of the ruling bureaucracies and appeared to emerge victorious from its long war against the ruling bureaucratic estate. It forced the bureaucracy to accept the rules of the culture of critical discourse in the Gouldnerian sense of the term[8] while learning how to seek allies among the petty and not so petty bourgeoisie. No doubt in the near future, it will have to do much more learning along these lines. Still, with a decaying bureaucracy and an ascending—but so far quite weak—propertied bourgeoisie, the educated middle class is undoubtedly the current ruling elite, if not the ruling class.

The rest of this chapter analyzes the process of the formation of this intellectual class in three dimensions. First, it focuses on the critical relationship between the cadre elite and intellectuals and tries to explain the sudden melting away of the cadre elite. Next, it looks at the linguistic victory of the intelligentsia—how, through the establishment of the culture of critical discourse, the intellectuals fatally wounded the cadre elite by assuring that the future political agenda can only be set by those who share this culture. Finally, we look at the social positions intellectuals occupy in the post-Communist transition. In particular, we focus on the role of intellectuals in the pluralistic political process and in the mass media, and we explore the conditions and the degree to which the intelligentsia can exercise power from such positions.

We do not claim that the intellectual class has been fully formed in all these dimensions. We do not make such a claim because we do not think any class was ever "fully" formed. Even the most successful class formations in history—for instance, that of the bourgeoisie—have been incomplete. By the time the bourgeoisie established itself, its disintegration had begun. Even more important, the social reality from which we try to generalize—namely, the Hungarian social reality during the summer of 1989—is a highly fluid one. Hungary is not quite a post-Communist society. It is well on the way toward the third, or post-Communist, stage of socialism, but it certainly has not been stabilized in a new social formation. Thus, we intend to present pros and cons, indicators of the weaknesses and strengths of the class formation process. For the class analyst, the right question is always: To what extent can these agents be understood as members of a class?[9] The answer to such a cautious question is necessarily tentative.

Problem of the Agency:
Cadre Elite Versus Intellectuals

The Intellectuals on the Road to Class Power was particularly controversial for many of our readers because we predicted a rapprochement between the cadre elite (the ruling estate) and the rest of the intelligentsia, which primarily included the technocracy but also the ideological intellectuals. In sharp contrast to conventional wisdom about Communist social structure, we believe that the major cleavage is not between intellectuals and cadres but rather between workers on the one hand and intellectuals and cadres on the other.

We believe this diagnosis and prediction proved to be powerful. At least in Hungary since the mid-1970s with the last ten to fifteen years of the decaying Kadar regime, despite the stubbornness and counteroffensive of the cadre elite, the cadre bureaucracy proved to be the loser in more ways than one. Interestingly, from the point of view of our analysis, while stubbornly resisting the strategic compromises with the intellectuals, the cadre bureaucracy became assimilated into the intelligentsia. It was increasingly recruited from highly skilled professionals, and it became in its habitus (in Bourdieu's sense of the term) almost indistinguishable from the classical central European *Bildungsbürgertum*.

Changes in the Composition of the Cadre Elite. Much in accordance with the predictions we made in *The Intellectuals on the Road to Class Power*, the patterns of recruitment into the cadre elite changed quite drastically in Hungary in the early or mid-1970s. During the Stalinist epoch of socialism, exceptional emphasis was put on the anticipated loyalty of future cadres. Thus, people with less self-confidence or fewer marketable skills were preferred to the professionalized intellectuals, who were distrusted due to their potentially greater autonomy. During the 1960s, this phenomenon was frequently referred to as *counterselection*, the process in which the less qualified have a systematically better chance of occupying decision-making positions.

After 1968, during the last two decades of Kadarism in Hungary, this changed significantly. (We are hesitant to generalize our statement for the whole of the region, as we do not have comparable data from other central European countries.)

In the mid-1970s, Pal Juhasz,[10] for instance, had already noticed a dramatic shift in the composition of management of agricultural cooperatives. Following the forced collectivization of Hungarian agriculture in 1960–1961, peasant cadre people were characteristically appointed into managerial positions. According to Juhasz, during the 1960s, a new generation of technically highly skilled agricultural engineers was trained in the agricultural colleges and, during the early and mid-1970s, systematically removed the old peasant or cadre elite. A new intellectual class seized the management of agriculture. Its members became the presidents and chief agricultural engineers of cooperatives. They headed the departments of agricultural affairs in the county governments and moved into executive positions in the Ministry of Agriculture. Through their ties with agricultural colleges and the research establishment, they controlled the Hungarian agriculture from training and research to production, domestic and foreign trade, labor organization, and technological development.

But agriculture was not exceptional. Both the Communist party and the government made a concerted effort to recruit the best young university graduates to the party apparatus and to government positions. Emphasis on technical competence began to override considerations of political loyalty. Paradoxically, some of these new apparatchiks were not even required to join the Communist party. Some of the best researchers at the Social Science Research Institute of the Hungarian Communist party were not party members. Recently, this process has greatly accelerated. For example, during the summer of 1989, of the thirteen journalists who worked in the economic policy section of *Nepszabadsag*, the daily newspaper of the Hungarian Communist party, only three were party members. Beginning in 1970, a new kind of recruitment began in which the apparatus was filled with university-trained professionals. These people, often quite competent, would have little difficulty finding jobs in the marketplace as architects, economists, or engineers if the party or state apparatus were significantly reduced.[11] One would like to see more systematic evidence and comparisons over time, of course, but the evidence available to us at this point seems strongly to suggest that intellectuals have entered positions of bureaucratic decision-making in great numbers since the early 1970s.

As one watches the sudden collapse of Hungarian bureaucratic domination, one inevitably begins to wonder how all this is possible. This, of course, has to be explained by a variety of factors, but the changes in the social and educational composition of office holders sketched above may play a role. The qualitative change in the Hungarian social system and political regime coincides with the aging of the old guards, who came to power with Janos Kadar right after 1956. Many of them are now retired, or are ready to retire, while the new recruits are not as stuck in bureaucratic positions of power and privilege as their predecessors. During the summer of 1989, we interviewed a thirty-five-year-old official of the Budapest Communist party apparatus. When asked what will happen to him if the Communist party loses the next elections and the apparatus is reduced, he expressed no concerns. "I am a good architect," he told us. "I was designing buildings before I came to this office. I will actually enjoy going back to my profession." People such as our respondent—who is in charge of housing and urban policy in the Budapest Communist party apparatus—have relatively little personal stake in preserving the power of their offices. They can find alternative jobs. These may offer somewhat less office power but will provide better incomes with more professional, ethical, and political autonomy. Thus, the positions of bureaucratic power are occupied by these new agents, professionalized intellectuals, who are less dependent on preserving the old rank order, paternalism, and estate-type domination. Instead, they are more tempted to test their abilities on markets and in meritocratic competition among classes.

The Embourgeoisement of the Cadre Elite. But the transformation of the cadre elite starting in 1970 was far-reaching. Not only have new agents occupied the positions of bureaucratic power, but incumbent office holders have changed as well. These incumbents became deeply bourgeoisified, with their habitus changing irreversibly, resembling that of the old educated middle class in striking ways. This may be the most important reason a neo-Stalinist restoration seems so unlikely in Hungary.

This inner, one may say spiritual, transformation or embourgeoisement happened gradually and in several dimensions. The petty bourgeoisification of Hungarian life and patterns of consumption since the mid-1960s is the most pedestrian, but not the least important, reason or indicator of such a change. Like the rest of the society, the Hungarian cadre began to appreciate the pleasures of the greater supply of high-quality food, other consumer goods, and polite service in private shops and restaurants. The Hungarian cadre elite also learned how to use markets for its own benefit.[12] The most important change from this point of view was in housing. Since 1980, the members of the elite began building solid bourgeois housing for themselves and often for their children. The villas that were built on the Buda hills or in prestigious suburban areas of provincial cities would be envied by Western professionals. With their two-car garages, two bathrooms, marble floors, wood and copper works, fancy gardens with spotless lawns and neatly planned trees, they have a touch (with possibly a little understatement) of the taste of the *nouveau riche*. However, a nostalgia for the lifestyles of the educated middle class during the inter-war years or at the turn of the century is also clearly recognizable. The interiors of these houses are no less telling. Antique furniture, china, silver, and paintings purchased from the impoverished, aging widows of the old middle class are mixed harmoniously with old family photographs (suddenly, even the photographs of a rabbi grandfather or a Calvinist minister uncle are shown to visitors with some pride) and computers, VCRs, or even telefax machines purchased on trips to the West.

Indeed, the massive and systematic exposure of this elite to the West in the transformation of their habitus should not be underestimated. One important force that operated toward the assimilation of the cadre elite into the intelligentsia was their common exposure to the West—to Western lifestyles, manners, and technologies. Official and private trips to the West became routine, often extending beyond a two- or three-day visit with a delegation to conferences or meetings or a one- or two-week vacation on camping grounds to longer stays as IREX fellows, Fulbright scholars, trade representatives, and visiting professors. The members of the cadre elite, and particularly their children, learned languages and began to feel at ease with living in the West and communicating with Western colleagues. Many of them even realized that they have marketable skills in Western markets. If they wish, they can find employment in either large corporations or universities. Many of these state intellectuals, rectors, leading economic bureaucrats, and academicians have impressed their Western colleagues. They are so unlike the old cadre academics from the Soviet Union, East Germany, or, previously, from Hungary and Poland. They have and dare to express interesting ideas. To cultivate contacts with them is not only useful in terms of academic politics but has also proved to be intellectually stimulating and socially rewarding.

The cultural cleavage between the "dumb cadre" and the "smart intellectual" is also disappearing. Such a convergence, through bourgeoisification of the habits of the elite, is another reason why reformism became the hegemonic ideology and why the old cadre existence offers so little attraction to most of those who hold power in Hungarian society today.

Limits of the Class Formation: Alternative Strategies of Cadres and Intellectuals. The rapprochement, in terms of personnel and habitus, between office holders and professionally competent, highly educated citizens is an important indication that the formation of a new elite, or even a new class, is well underway. But there are limits to this process as well, and we present a few counterarguments now. Cadres and intellectuals have their differences as well as their similarities. The cleavages between them have narrowed but have not disappeared, and the highly educated are also internally quite diversified, if not divided.

The Fearful Cadre. Despite all the embourgeoisement of the cadre and its rapprochement with the professionally competent, highly educated citizens, we sense that the cadre intelligentsia is greatly concerned about the post-Communist transformation of Hungary. It is undoubtedly less threatened by these changes than its predecessors would have been twenty or even ten years ago, but it still sees itself entering a new, somewhat alien world. One major attraction of Kadarism (not unlike the post-1968 Czechoslovakian regime) was its predictability, its paternalistic security.[13] For decades, close-knit networks of cadre bureaucrats in counties, firms, and whole branches of the economy were loyal, friendly, and even protective of each other. Even academic and cultural cadres exhibited these networks. In an academic discipline, one could identify the five or six individuals who presided over all committees, edited all the journals, distributed among each other attractive trips abroad, queued each other up for membership in the Academy of Sciences, and waited patiently for their turns, rather than back-stabbing each other in the old Stalinist way of bureaucratic careerism. Although they did not necessarily like each other (despite being "friends," spending their vacations together and dining together), they learned from Stalinism that they would collectively benefit it they ran their shops in a coordinated manner, did not betray each other, and thus achieved some collective security.

Now this old paternalistic careerism is being seriously threatened. Even the reasonably professionally competent office holders take advantage of party membership in their careers. They, therefore, may be quite competent, but they are not necessarily the most competent persons to fill the jobs they currently hold. They look with some anxiety toward the future, where they are compelled to compete with everyone in a merciless rat race. They are also not thrilled by the prospect of future competitions in which former Communist party membership becomes a slight handicap, casting doubt on their moral, professional, and scholarly integrity. The "old boy networks" are already breaking up. For example, in scholarly or cultural establishments, some persons have begun to look for new starts and search for new alliances, doubting the chances of their former mates to really make it in the competitive academic or cultural marketplace.

We see a lot of concerned cadre intellectuals who are not necessarily dangerous anti-reformers. Rather, they are confused, not knowing themselves what they want. Few of them would like to go back to the "good old days"; they value their new lifestyles too much. They enjoy being able to say or write what they want. Fundamentally, they are much more comfortable in their new role as liberal, *Bürgeliche* intellectuals than they were in the roles of officials or state intellectuals. Still, they look forward to the future with justified anxiety. These are the people who—half concerned, half hopefully— talk to us about the dangers of restoration; who are likely to think that the collapse of communism is more the result of the rise of Gorbachev to power than of internal developments in Hungary; who doubt that Gorbachev can succeed; who talk at length about the dangers of a military coup d'état and the dedication of the party militia to restore Stalinism by force. Few of them really want these things to happen, but many could probably learn how to live under such circumstances if they occurred.

There are also moralizers among the fearful cadre intellectuals. As we will elaborate soon, the change in the political discourse was indeed dramatic. Virtually overnight, multi-party system, parliamentary democracy, market economy, reprivatization, and deregulation became the hegemonic way to speak about the future. Still, many find this rapid change difficult to follow, and while they are skeptical about the possibility or desirability of communism, they find it difficult to out-Thatcher Thatcher in liberalism and anti-socialism.

The main point we are making here is this: While the old bureaucratic or cadre elite indeed lost its ability and will to rule in the old way and was softened up too much by *Bürgerliche* values and manners, many of its members are sufficiently anxious about the unpredictable rat race of the future that they, while not initiating it, may not find it too difficult to live with a Communist restoration.

Entrepreneurship or Professionalism as an Alternative to the Class Power of Intellectuals. From the above description, it follows that we could not find in Hungarian society a large and coherent enough group to initiate, lead, or actively participate in a restoration. Such a restoration could only come from the outside. The current Hungarian elite—without some major change in the international situation—is losing its war against the only serious challengers for the power of the intellectuals.

But it is not clear what kind of power these intellectuals have and how the cadre elite may succeed in rescuing its own privileges. We can propose several scenarios. The class formation of intellectuals is one possibility. It is not impossible for the cadre elite to attempt or even succeed in transforming itself into a new propertied class. And it is far from impossible that the professionalized strata within the intelligentsia, rather than undertaking a domestic class project, will choose well-paid professional, managerial, and engineering jobs in multinational concerns that they may try to attract to Hungary. Let us briefly speculate on the probability of both these alternatives.

Two Hungarian scholars, Elemer Hankiss and, more recently, Erzsebet Szalai have suggested that the cadre elite, particularly the top management of large state firms, may try to transform itself into a propertied class to become, in Hankiss's terminology, a new "big bourgeoisie." Indeed, in a late spring 1989 session of the Hungarian Parliament, a new law was passed allowing the "transformation of state ownership." State companies would be reprivatized by creating joint stock-holding companies out of them and offering enticements for the employees of the firms to purchase these stocks. Although the text of the law does not distinguish between management and other employees of the firms, some commentators believe that this is really a way to pass state property on to managers. The etatization of Hungarian industry happened virtually overnight in 1949. One day, around one thousand people were invited to a meeting and told that the firms for which they had previously worked had just been nationalized and that they had been appointed as state managers. A friend of ours has suggested that a similar strategy of reprivatization cannot be excluded. What if, one day, the managers of the one thousand largest firms were called to a meeting and told that, as of today, they were the private proprietors of these firms?

This scenario is far from absurd. Indeed, in the current post-Communist transformation of the Hungarian society and economy, reformers are desperately seeking identifiable owners. (Recently at a conference, we heard a Polish economist half-jokingly recommend that stocks of state firms should be distributed in a state lottery to private individuals.) It is also reasonable to assume that the old elite will make an attempt to convert its old privileges into new privileges. It has certainly proved that it has the skills to do this, and, acting from a position of power and authority, it is likely that such an attempt may be successful.

Still, we find the Hankiss-Szalai scenario a bit too adventurous. The empirical evidence suggests that the commodification of bureaucratic privileges is much more modest, more petty bourgeois than big bourgeois, in character. What is this evidence? To be sure, the cadre elite reprivatized some of the formerly nationalized housing for itself at highly subsidized prices. It may have accumulated a few million forints or, at best, a few hundred thousand dollars of family wealth in terms of villas, luxurious condos, or antique furniture. More important, there is some evidence that the cadre elite directs its children toward entrepreneurship and the private sector and advises them against a cadre career. But many of the cadre children do not even complete college, choosing instead to enter the business world. We analyzed the 1983 Hungarian Central Statistical Office social mobility data to identify patterns of three-generational mobility. Our data seem to indicate that among those who became first-generation professionals between 1945 and 1965, there is relatively great outward mobility from the professional class: Only about half of their children finish college. Interestingly, the proportion of college graduates is not only higher among those families that are highly educated and, thus, already in their third generation as professionals, but it is also higher among those who became déclassé during 1945–1965. The children of the déclassé, children of those born in the educated middle-class families but who failed to get to college themselves during the Stalinist years, finish college in greater proportion than do children of the first-generation cadre intelligentsia. While statistically we could not identify what is happening to the children of the first-generation cadre, it does not seem unreasonable to assume that many of them may try business. Even the son of the most conservative previous party boss,

Karoly Grosz, is working for a private Western firm, and many cadre children own small businesses of different sorts.

But we would like to underline the primarily petty bourgeois character of this process. These cadre children take advantage of their parents' bureaucratic connections, get licenses from authorities more easily, and may have advantages when they apply for bank loans and the like. Still, they are typically owners of boutiques and small restaurants or are middle-level rather than top executives of foreign firms. They remind us more of an English or French petty bourgeoisie than of Rockefellers and Gettys. In other words, while some cadre members—in the diversifying social structure of post-Communist society—will undoubtedly leave the intelligentsia, they are more likely to become small or middle-sized entrepreneurs with relatively little personal wealth and political influence.

So, professionalization or expert jobs in large multinational or other Western firms may be a more attractive proposition for many cadre or state intellectuals. Indeed, high technology, the information industry, computing, biotechnology, software production, consulting, or a variety of "yuppie" jobs seem much more likely to divert the cadre from an intellectual class project than does the new position of big bourgeoisie. Large firms may be attracted to central Europe, and Hungary or Poland might become alternatives to South Korea or Taiwan for West German, French, Swiss, or Italian capital. This may create jobs for locals who have local knowledge and networks and enough technical knowledge to make themselves useful to their Western employers. These locals, of course, would not be a big bourgeoisie. Those who were successful would become junior partners, filling roles as junior and, in time, not-so-junior executives. The size of such an elite, and particularly its autonomy from Western employers, depends on how attractive the central European market is to large Western capital and the conditions under which Westerners would prefer this part of the world to Southeast Asia or Latin America.

Limits of the Class Formation: Internal Division by Age and Profession Within the Intelligentsia. In the previous three sections, we considered the possibilities for, and limits on, the assimilation of the cadre elite and its children into an intellectual class. But intellectuals themselves are also quite diversified and divided. Some benefit from the current political boom; others are left behind. Thus, they may not all be enthused by the prospects of the intellectual class formation.

We see divisions among the highly educated along generational and occupational lines. If these divisions become deep enough, they may prevent the formation of the new class.

One exciting new phenomenon is the emergence of a new young cohort of intellectuals as the vanguard of social and political change. One of the most radical and visible opposition movements in Hungary today is FIDESZ (Association of Democratic Youth). FIDESZ, a youth organization, won almost 10 percent of the popular vote in the 1990 national elections. Representatives of FIDESZ—young men (and very few women)—many of them under thirty, are now MPs—people of significant power and authority. The younger generation is also well represented in other political movements, such as SZDSZ (Association of Free Democrats) or MDF (Hungarian Democratic Forum), currently the largest party of the ruling center-right coalition government. Young people are even represented in the Communist party. The situation is similar to that of 1945–1949, when people in their twenties or early thirties suddenly became heads of government ministries, university professors, or members of the Academy of Sciences, largely because they were young enough not to have been compromised in any way in the ancien régime.

Today, a similar mechanism operates. A new generation of intellectuals has appeared. Speaking the new language like natives, they have burst energetically onto the political scene. To the older competitors with skeletons in their closets, they constitute formidable opposition for parliamentary seats, government offices, and academic posts. The older professionals who saved themselves from politics for decades, hoping ultimately to be rewarded for their political neutralism and professional competence, may feel particularly uncomfortable about being bypassed by this new younger generation. This younger cohort of intellectuals not only feels more comfortable in the new, highly politicized atmosphere but also looks with suspicion on the formerly politically neutral technocrats, whom it regards—because of their silence or lack of public protest—as perhaps collaborators with the Communists.

There may also be an occupational division within the intelligentsia threatening this new class project. In the 1970s and 1980s, the technocratic intelligentsia appeared to be the most serious candidate for power sharing with the bureaucracy; however, with the most recent developments, the humanistic intellectuals are taking the lead. Historians, poets, and novelists play a crucial role in the leadership of the MDF. The SZDSZ is a club of extraordinary talent, made up of sociologists, economists, political scientists, and legal theorists. If the SZDSZ were not a political party, it could well be the National Academy of Social Sciences (with probably more social science talent than the Hungarian Academy of Sciences). About 90 percent of MPs in the new Hungarian parliament have university degrees, and half of them can use the title "doctor." Will the social scientist, humanistic intelligentsia ally itself with the technical intellectuals? Or will the technocrats turn away with annoyance and follow the technically skilled cadre elites who look for jobs abroad or in foreign firms in Hungary, leaving petty and—in their view—unimportant politics to these eggheads? We do not have answers to these questions, but Gouldner undoubtedly was right when he pointed out that the key criterion of the formation of the new class is the success or failure of the merger between what he called the technical intelligentsia and humanistic intellectuals.

Problems of Consciousness: The Victory of the Culture of Critical Discourse

We now turn to the second dimension of the formation of the class: Are there any indications that these agents described above are developing a consciousness adequate for claims for class power? Undoubtedly the most fundamental change in the transition to post-communism is discursive. The intelligentsia achieved a major victory over the bureaucracy by superimposing its own discourse, the culture of critical discourse, over that bureaucracy.

Communist bureaucratic domination could be characterized by a specific discourse. This cadre discourse was a new language that clearly set the limits of the political and intellectual agenda. It excluded from the domain of appropriate speech those issues that could cast doubt on the nature of bureaucratic domination. The characterization of this discourse needs a more careful analysis, but we can briefly indicate some of its features here. The Communist discourse presumed certain references to Marxism-Leninism but allowed discussion about proper or improper, correct or incorrect, interpretations of Marxism. In the post-Stalinist epoch, Marxisms of different sorts— a pluralism of Marxisms—were permissible. Certain phenomena, even non-Marxist reflections, were acceptable. The discourse operated within the general acceptance of socialism as the good society (although it did allow some discussion about more or less desirable forms of socialism) and capitalism as having to be overcome. The existence of the one-party system, however, could not be questioned. Since the 1960s, this discourse rehabilitated the concept of market, although only allowing speech about a socialist market economy. It was assumed that the nationalization of property rights was an irreversible process anyway.

The *samizdat* literature, the appearance of alternative thinkers (in Hungary, the dissidents of the late 1970s called themselves *máskéntgondolkodók*, or those who think differently), and the underground press were extraordinarily important because they undermined this discourse and created a new one, which set a completely new agenda for politics.

The 1980s can be understood as the great battle of discourses in which the cadre elite suffered a humiliating defeat. Today it would be embarrassing to try to speak of the old discourse. The change of the discourse was so drastic that even an academic Marxist discourse—which is perfectly legitimate in a French, English, or U.S. university—would not be respected or even listened to by a Hungarian audience.

Gouldner's term *the culture of critical discourse* offers a lot of insight in describing this new speech. It is, indeed, radically critical and deeply distrustful of claims made on the grounds of the office or authority based on the office of the speaker. One interesting effect is the challenge to Western-style academic or scholarly authority. During the 1980s, for instance, two different researchers claimed to have discovered a drug that cures cancer. The educated public remains totally distrustful of the academic or drug industry authorities who have reported that neither drug cures anything. The fact that these statements were made by office holders—a former president of the Hungarian Academy of Sciences and a distinguished medical researcher—is a sufficient ground to distrust them. Any set, bureaucratic procedure—in this case, the procedure for testing used by the drug industry— is suspicious when confronted by the free-floating critical imagination.

We are living in a world in which nothing is set, in which everything is fluid and changing. Every week sees a new blueprint on how to organize the economy, how to run medical institutions, how to build universities and organize culture: Hungary or Poland is living in the years of the orgy of critical thought. It appears there is virtually nothing that could not be done through a thought experiment. The power of critical thought seems to be limitless.

Paradoxically, this almost unconditional belief in the power of critical thought—in the ability to transform reality through thinking, through blueprints and model-building—sets limits on the critical nature of this critical thinking. There is an interesting moralizing quality in this critical thinking. Pedestrian empiricism pointing to the limits of change may be perceived as dangerous or even immoral. Gouldner somewhat missed this moralizing tendency in the culture of critical discourse. However, conservative thinkers of the early 1970s—such as Norman P. Podhoretz or Irvin K. Kristol—who also analyzed the power aspirations of intellectuals, point to the curious "ethical terror" implemented by the speakers of the culture of critical discourse. Thus, for instance, in debates about the Vietnam War, conservatives often complained bitterly that they could not conduct a truly rational discourse because the critical intelligentsia, on moral grounds, would not allow any discourse on the necessity of U.S. involvement in Southeast Asian politics. These conservatives probably identified an interesting feature of the culture of critical discourse, which may need further exploration.

Our concluding remark here is that no matter how critical or how moralizing the culture of critical discourse is in the post-Communist transition, the speakers of this culture emerge victorious. The most fundamental reason for the sudden collapse of Communist bureaucratic authority is probably that the cadre elite lost its tongue. The cadre elite now has to confront the critical intelligentsia on the latter's terms.

Usually, the collapse of communism is linked to its economic crisis. A more conventional Marxist analysis could reject our arguments above by suggesting that such a change of discourse is only the result of the economic crisis. We do not doubt that the discursive victory of the critical intelligentsia over the cadre elite is linked to the economic crisis and the inability of this elite to run the society and economy effectively. But we should have learned from Foucault that crisis itself is not completely outside the scope of discourse. The discourse not only reflects the underlying crisis to some extent but also creates it.

The New Structural Position:
Politocracy, or Intellectuals as Referees
or Play-Masters Between Bureaucracies
and the New Bourgeoisie

The third criteria of a class formation has something to do with the position occupied by the agents, who, with adequate consciousness, can be formed into a collective actor. No serious claim can be made about the formation of a class unless the analyst can identify a position from which these agents can exercise class power.

In *The Intellectuals on the Road to Class Power*, we believe we identified such a position in the institutions of the redistributive economy. In that book, our argument was that in a statist economy, the redistributor occupies a position that is analogous to that of property owners in a capitalist society. Both redistributors and property owners appropriate surplus from the direct producers, and both allocate this surplus in order to reproduce in an expanded manner the asymmetrical economic relationship between producer and appropriator. The successful capitalist becomes richer and employs even more workers, appropriating even more from those workers. The successful redistributor expands the state budget and increases the dependence of the producers on state subsidies and benefits. While the law of capitalist production is the attempt to maximize profit, the law of socialist production is to maximize redistributive power. We are now inclined to believe that this project of the technocratic intelligentsia to rationalize the socialist economy and to create the class power of planners-redistributors probably failed.

One of us wrote an auto-critique of our book during the mid-1980s.[14] According to this auto-critique, we did not foresee two processes with sufficient clarity during the early 1970s. First, in 1974, although we saw the counteroffensive of the ruling estate against the reform intellectuals, we did not anticipate this would last for an entire epoch. However, the cadre elite proved to be more stubborn than we anticipated by sabotaging the rationalizing reforms of socialism at the costs of risking its own existence. By the mid-1980s, the intelligentsias—in Hungary and Poland at least—were disappointed sufficiently to lose their belief in the reformability of communism, and they showed little interest in any compromise with the cadre elite. Second, it appeared that while the cadre elite stubbornly resisted the compromise with the intelligentsia, it proved to be more open to a petty capitalist development than we could imagine during the early 1970s. One could even suggest that this was used as an alternative to the big compromise with the intellectuals: Instead of sharing political power with the intelligentsia, the cadre elite opened up space for private ventures in the economy. In a sense, it opted for a "Spanish Road,"[15] a one-party system in combination with some capitalism.

These were, indeed, unanticipated developments during the decade between 1975 and 1985. But in light of the developments in Hungary since mid-1988, this strategy of the cadre elite did not work. It even backfired, and suddenly the intelligentsia seems to be emerging victorious from this struggle. It also appears that the intellectuals may have learned how to take advantage of the emergent petty bourgeoisification process that was initially designed to keep them out of power.

First, the Spanish Road scenario of the Communist bureaucracy proved to be an illusion. Capitalist development, especially a development that is sufficiently capitalistic to rescue the sinking ship of the statist economy, proved to be impossible without legal and political reform. The Communist bureaucratic elite, by doing nothing on the political and legal fronts, undermined the efficiency of its own petty capitalist development. It thus deepened the economic and resulting political and social crises that culminated in the political breakthrough that occurred beginning in mid-1989.

But the intellectuals not only achieved a major victory by forcing the cadre elite into political and legal reforms, which is deeper than any of the economic reforms it ever attempted; the intelligentsia also discovered the advantages of capitalist development that accrued in the meantime. In a sense, the intelligentsia discovered a role, or a position, for itself that is better suited to its transcendental nature: the role of teleological planner. As we saw it in *The Intellectuals on the Road to Class Power*, for the intellectuals to form a class around the position of redistributor, a high price was expected: It had to undergo a certain degree of bureaucratization. In the book we also saw the formation of the intellectual class as a dual process: as the result of the intellectualization of the bureaucracy and the bureaucratization of the intellectuals.

In the current post-Communist transition, the intelligentsia seems to have discovered a nonbureaucratized role for itself. Rather than becoming a class formed around redistributive power, it exercises power of its own as a politocracy or as a mediacracy.

This new position is opening up with the appreciation and acceptance of the duality of post-Communist social structure. While communism was a society with one master[16] (what we called the bureaucratic ruling estate), post-Communist society knows two masters. Under post-communism, the state bureaucratic elite has to learn how to live, and to some extent compete, with an emergent class of property owners. The intelligentsia, which suddenly opened the sphere of democratic politics for itself, dominates this sphere by monopolizing the discourse that sets the agenda for present and, particularly, for future politics. The intelligentsia finds this diversified, enlarged political space comfortable and begins to see its role as playing one master against the other, using the mechanisms of political democracy to keep both under control and to keep itself above both masters as the "super-master"— the master of the games, the referee.

While the bureaucratic ruling estate was more stubborn and not as smart as we anticipated, the intellectuals proved to be smarter than we thought they were. Not only did they achieve power, they also exploited the very institutions, or mechanisms, the cadre elite instituted to advance itself and obstruct the intellectuals. Furthermore, the intellectuals created a position in the social structure for themselves that better suits their nature.

In the very first stages of post-Communist transformation, the intellectuals primarily established themselves as a mediacracy. In Hungary today, about five hundred publishing houses exist, and people spend an extraordinary amount of money on books and newspapers. The mass media plays a key role in defining the core issues. Media campaigns defeated the government's plans to build a major dam on the Danube, to introduce a highway tax, and similar proposals. Intellectuals also play an unusually visible role in the media. For example, every night Channel 2 (there are just two television channels in Hungary) finishes its nightly broadcast with a debate among two to four social scientists on issues such as the question of the formation of the new elite, strategies and philosophies behind reprivatization, the role of Hungarian film in the world, and the like. Lasting for forty to forty-five minutes, this must be rather unimaginable for late-night U.S. television viewers. But this mediacracy is already preparing itself for the role of politocracy. The television debates proved to be training grounds for electoral campaigners. Millions watch them, much as people watch the World Wrestling Federation in the United States; but in Hungary, the victorious wrestlers emerge as MPs, senators, heads of government ministries, or ambassadors. These are more than shows; they are exercises of power. The new prime minister, the minister of defense, and the foreign secretary are all historians. A new elite is in the making that—we think—is not likely to be a new big bourgeoisie. This new elite is being recruited from among our own ranks, and the ones who speak the culture of critical discourse most fluently have the best chance of making it to the top.

If one thinks about it, this is not surprising. After all, we have never known a society without an elite, and who could play the role of the new elite if and when the bureaucracy disappears from the scene of history? The intelligentsia is the only serious candidate.

TRANSITORY PERIOD OF A NEW EPOCH?

Here we wish to discuss three alternative scenarios: bureaucratic restoration, bourgeois class domination, and intellectual class power. As we suggested before, the most difficult question is this: How long can such a power project last? Is it imaginable that intellectuals can form a class that can reproduce itself? Or are intellectuals only troublemakers who are good enough to undermine systems of authority but are unable to create their own? Can they serve only as intermediaries who will pave the way to the power of other new dominant classes? Is this post-Communist period indeed an entire historic epoch, or will it be only a brief interval until the restoration of a Communist social order or a transition to a bourgeois class rule?

So far, although we have little hard evidence to support our analysis, we have still basically remained on firm ground in trying to explain what is happening. In this last section, we face an adventurous task: We have to explore future scenarios. We will be brief and as cautious as we can in this venture.

We feel the least likely scenario is a Communist restoration. A conversion according to a Western capitalist model is more likely. Joining Europe or, more probably, fitting into the capitalist world system somewhere around the periphery—with some luck, at the semiperiphery and a consolidation of an intellectual class power—are both possible. The latter may have a greater chance.

The word *impossible* does not exist in the dictionary of a social scientist, but we regard a Communist restoration as nearly impossible in Hungary.

As we explained before, the bureaucratic ruling estate lost its ability and its will to rule. It has been assimilated in the intelligentsia and bourgeoisified in its habitus, or lifestyles. We do not see any domestic force that could present a serious threat of restoration. A dramatic, conservative turn in the Soviet Union would, of course, significantly slow the progress toward post-communism in Hungary, Poland, and Czechoslovakia. The possibility of such a change in the Soviet Union, particularly in light of the May–June 1989 events in China, cannot be excluded. But even with a China-like turn in the USSR, we fail to see how Hungary or Poland could return to a Communist model. Who are those sociologically identifiable agents who have a real interest in this process? Where are the credible economic or social blueprints that could promise a workable organization?

The second alternative is a transition to some kind of bourgeois class domination—as Hankiss puts it, the emergence of a new big bourgeoisie or some kind of dependent, Third World-like capitalist development in which the domestic social structure remains mainly proletarian while the bourgeoisie remains foreign. This alternative is possible but not likely. The domestic bourgeoisie is too weak and small to form a genuinely new elite. The Hankiss scenario of transforming the cadre elite into Rockefellers is also not particularly believable. We fail to see exactly what kind of political process would allow a redistribution of the national wealth into the hands of a few hundred thousand private property holders. There is no reason why the nonmanagerial cadre elite (those who are not managers of large state corporations but officials in party, state, and cultural institutions) would accept the fact that a few of them would become billionaires while the majority remains penniless.

Adding all this up, the most likely future seems to be one in which a new kind of balance will be created between bureaucracy and bourgeoisie (the latter being mostly rather petty, although some are likely to grow fast or function in conjunction with large Western or multinational corporations). In this combination of a bureaucratic and bourgeois structure, the intelligentsia may retain its dominant position as paymaster or super-master. After all, this would not be much different from the traditional central European experience in which the *Bildungsbürgertum* retained an edge over the *Besitzbürgertum*. The dialectic of central European *Verbürgerlichung* may just continue in the very way that it has unfolded in our modern history.

NOTES

1. In the book, we distinguish three epochs of socialist development. The first was Stalinism. We regard Milovan Djilas as the best theorist of the Stalinist social structure. During this epoch, the bureaucratic elite held a monopoly of power, ruled over a single hierarchy of bureaucratic elite, and ruled in an estate-like manner. In the USSR, this epoch began soon after the October revolution; in central Europe and China, around 1948–1949. It ended in most countries—although not in China—by the mid- or late 1950s.

The second epoch of socialism began with the death of the Charismatic leader. In the resulting legitimation crisis, the bureaucratic elite attempted to establish new principles of legitimation. It began to emphasize the ideal of scientific socialism and attempted to redefine the essence of socialism as a rational order, superior to capitalism because of its orderliness and scientific rationalism. *The Intellectuals on the Road to Class Power* is an analysis of this second epoch, in which the bureaucratic elite began to invite the technical intellectuals, if not the whole of the intelligentsia, to share power with them. In our book, we claim that under such circumstances, the disintegration of the estate type of domination of the bureaucratic elite and the formation of a new dominant class, which is likely to include the whole of the intelligentsia, began.

We believed that the formation of this new class would represent an entire historic epoch. We noticed, for instance, that during the early 1970s, in many countries the bureaucratic elite began to sabotage its deal with the intellectuals and launch a conservative counteroffensive, which later became known as Brezhnevism. Thus, we claimed that socialism, in which the intelligentsia will have power, will be a qualitatively new epoch—the third or mature epoch of socialism.

2. The term post-Communist is quite controversial. Andras Hegedus, for instance, recently criticized us for using this term. He, along with many of the conventional old and new Left, asks how a society can enter a post-Communist epoch without having experienced real communism. In our view, it is quite accurate to describe Russia since 1917 and central Europe since 1949 as Communist. These social experiences and experiments were attempts to create social and economic organizations that were as collectivistic as possible. These experiments failed, not because they were not sufficiently collectivistic but because they were excessively communistic. Current forces, which search for solutions to the contradictions accumulated during these experiments and will certainly limit collectivism, will search for more individualistic forms and values.

We could also use the notion of post-state socialism. But we prefer the term post-communism for two reasons: (1) Post-state socialism emphasizes the anti-statist elements in the current changes, but it does not capture their anti-collectivistic features. Thus, it allows more room for another wave of collectivistic utopianism, which we do not share. (2) Post-state socialism implies that the emergent new social formation will be a socialist one. We believe that it is not possible to tell at the moment if the notion of socialism will be useful for describing the future social formations in central Europe. These social formations may or may not be socialistic.

The concept of post-communism is a flexible one as far as the future is concerned. Post-communism may be a mature form of socialism (as we were likely to believe in 1974 in *The Intellectuals on the Road to Class Power*). This term is not as consistent as it might first appear. The distinction between socialism as an early stage and communism as a mature stage of social development appears quite late in Marx's own thinking, and it was codified to a dogma only under Stalin. In fact, in the Paris Manuscripts (Marx and Engels 1975) Marx calls the earliest stage of statist transformation "crude communism" and expects socialism to follow this crude communism as a restriction on, rather than the perfection of, statist collectivism. Although Marx's own terminology or thinking is rather insignificant in analyzing the current social realities of central Europe, we believe it is important to leave open the theoretical possibility that central Europe may become a mature form of socialism. In this scenario, although the significant role of the state is retained, collectivistic economic and social forces may be complemented by individualistic private forms.

3. Here, our inspiration comes primarily from Jeno Szucs (1983). He suggests that Europe historically can be divided into three regions. Central Europe represents—

according to Szucs—a qualitatively different configuration from both Russia and Western Europe. Populists of both right-wing and left-wing persuasions (exemplified in Hungary by Laszlo Nemeth and Istvan Bibo, respectively) typically used the notion of "third way," "third road," or "third side" to express their belief in the superiority of the central European way. Thus, they claimed the superiority of the Polish, Hungarian, Rumanian, Bulgarian, and Croatian civilizations and cultural, economic, and political institutions. From the mid-nineteenth century, and particularly during the inter-war years, such ideologies were rather popular in the whole region. Szucs used the idea of the "third historic region" in a descriptive, nonnormative way. His point is that central Europe is on a somewhat different trajectory of historical evolution from the other two regions of Europe. While central Europe is more backward than the West and more advanced than Eastern Europe (meaning Russia in a narrow sense or Eastern Christianity more broadly), it cannot only be described in terms of backward progress. It is also different. In this chapter, we use the term "third or central European way" in this descriptive manner, acknowledging the importance of the historical heritage for the present and the future.

4. In the paper "The Three Waves of New Class Theories" (Szelenyi and Martin 1988–1989), we speculated that each class formation can occur in three dimensions. In order to have a new class—not only an intellectual class but any new class at any point in history—one needs "agents" who are able and willing to occupy a new class position. One also needs new socioeconomic positions these agents can occupy. Finally, to act as a class from these positions, these new agents have to develop a new kind of consciousness. In this paper, we suggested that earlier power projects of the highly educated beginning in the late nineteenth century were unsuccessful, as no group of highly educated was able to form a class in all three dimensions. Thus, for instance, the "socially unattached" intellectuals of central and Eastern Europe, as far as agency was concerned, were quite formidable representatives of a class power project, but they did not have a proper new class position or an adequate consciousness. The bureaucrats or technocrats of the 1940s and 1950s claimed power from a new class position, but they were agents who were ultimately unable to act collectively as a class. Finally, the radical middle class of the 1968 phenomenon did indeed develop a radical new consciousness, which represented a formidable challenge to bourgeois cultural hegemony, but they were rather weak in terms of structural position and agency. We will organize our analysis according to these three dimensions and argue that the formation of the intellectual class is progressing in all three dimensions during the transition to post-communism.

5. The above characterization of Communist societies is somewhat ideal-typical, but due to limitations of time and space, we cannot pay enough attention to details. The state, of course, never achieved complete monopoly in the economy. Some private economic activity was always tolerated—if not legally, at least semi-legally. Private wealth was never completely eliminated as a dimension of social inequality, and even the Communist party had some rivals (opposition parties may even have existed in some countries). Still, it should be reasonably uncontroversial to say that, despite minor deviations, communism is indeed a statist economy with a single bureaucratic rank order and a near-power near-monopoly held by a single Marxist-Leninist party.

6. Here and in the rest of the chapter, we struggle with a linguistic problem. The term we would like to use is *Verbürgerlichung* in German, or *polgarosodas* in Hungarian. The notion of embourgeoisement or bourgeoisification does not fully and precisely capture the meaning of these words. The German *Bürger* or the Hungarian *polgar* simultaneously contain the meaning of bourgeois and *citoyen*—capitalist and citizen. For those who think in the German or Hungarian way, the English words

embourgeoisement or *bourgeoisification* (and their French equivalents) place undue emphasis on the "propertiedness" of those agents who undergo these processes. The German *Bürger* or *Verbürgerlichung* does not preempt the nature of the dialectics between private ownership and citizenship; thus, it is quite imaginable—at least in principle—that a fair degree of *Verbürgerlichung*, or *polgarosodas*, may occur without much private property—a society in the mind of a German or Hungarian thinker can be quite *bürgerlich* or *polgarosodott* even if it does not have much of a propertied class. Later in this chapter, we will use the distinction between *Bildungsbürgertum* (the educated middle class, which is bourgeois, or *bürgerlich*, primarily in terms of its habitus, lifestyles, consciousness, or commitment to pluralistic democratic institutions and civil liberties) and *Besitzbürgertum* (the propertied) as a characteristically central European distinction that presumes the openendedness or undetermined nature of the dialectical relationship between these two phenomena.

7. In our book, *Socialist Entrepreneurs* (1988), we documented at great length this process of embourgeoisement. For similar arguments about the emergence of a new petty (or not so petty) bourgeoisie and the emergence of a dual hierarchy (one based on bureaucratic rank, the other on private wealth or market capacities), see Ivan Szelenyi (1986–1987), where Kolosi describes the new Hungarian social structure with an L-shaped "model"; Elemer Hankiss (1989), Chapter 9, where Hankiss forecasts a "grand coalition" between the new bourgeoisie and the old cadre. For a good summary of the relevant Hungarian literature, see Imre Kovach (1988).

8. See Alvin Gouldner (1979).

9. From a purely methodological point of view, one can think of Marx in this respect. Marx, in analyzing the social character of the peasantry in "The Eighteenth Brumaire of Louis Bonaparte" (Marx and Engels 1979), suggested that the peasants do indeed form a class to the extent that they do certain things and have certain characteristics but that they cannot be regarded as a class in other respects.

10. Pal Juhasz (1983).

11. Agnes Horvath and Arpad Szakolczay (1989) report on the survey they conducted among some 200 so-called "instructors" of the different district party organizations in Budapest. (These "instructors" are full-time apparatchiks whose job is to advise and direct party organizations in firms and institutes in their districts.) Their data demonstrate the dramatic shift away from the cadre elite toward a new apparatus formed by professionals. While among the instructors who are 45 years old or older only 38 percent have college degrees, of the instructors who are 35 years old or younger the overwhelming majority (81 percent) holds a degree. In the older cohort, 24 percent of the apparatchiks came from nonprofessional jobs (manual work), while in the youngest cohort, this number decreased to 4 percent.

Sociologists who analyzed data on social stratification during the 1980s systematically noticed the narrowing gap between professionals and the cadre elite and the increasing importance of education, or cultural capital, in explaining social inequalities. Rudolf Andorka, the internationally most respected Hungarian mobility researcher, noted (1982) that the cleavage between members of the apparatus and university-trained professionals is shrinking. Tamas Kolosi (1984) repeatedly demonstrated that educational credentials are the most important variable in explaining inequalities in contemporary Hungary. He also noted that the importance of the cultural capital variable is increasing over time and seems to be greater than in any of the Western countries. A U.S. sociologist who analyzed the 1982 Hungarian income statistics survey, Robert Jenkins (1987), also identified educational credentials as a variable that is more important in Hungary than in the United States in predicting income distribution.

12. Szelenyi wrote about the ability of the elite to "commodify its bureaucratic privileges" in an earlier article. See Ivan Szelenyi and Robert Manchin (1987). Elemer Hankiss (1989) makes a similar point.

13. Janos Kornai (1980) calls the state socialist system of domination *paternalistic*. This is certainly the most insightful characterization of the Kadarist epoch in Hungary, but it is also useful for describing power elites in other Communist countries as well.

14. Szelenyi (1986–1987).

15. This term became very popular during 1989–1990 in both Hungary and Poland. In these recent debates, the *Spanish Road* indicated the possibility of a peaceful transition from authoritarianism to democracy, referring to the period following Franco. In the auto-critique, the term *Spanish Road* is used in a more ironic way. Here the point of reference is the last decade of Francoism, in which the Fallangist party adopts a policy of liberalism in the economy in exchange for retention of the political monopoly. It appeared, during the mid-1980s, that both the late Kadarist bureaucracy and Jaruzelski's bureaucracy were similarly inclined. Particularly in Kadarist Hungary, the Communists showed a great deal of tolerance toward small private businesses as long as they did not interfere with politics. They were, however, rather rigid toward the critical intelligentsia.

16. We owe the term "master" here to Max Nomad, who wrote, with a sense of humor, about the new class of intellectuals as the "new masters."

REFERENCES

Andorka, Rudolf. 1982. *Changes in Social Structure in Hungary*. Budapest: Gondolat Kiadó.

Gouldner, Alvin. 1979. *The Future of the Intellectuals and the Rise of the New Class*. Oxford: Oxford University Press.

Hankiss, Elemer. 1989. *East European Alternatives*, chap. 9. Budapest: Kozgazdasagi es Jogi Kiado.

Horvath, Agnes, and Arpad Szakolczay. 1989. *Senkifoldje—Or No-Man's Land*. Budapest: Akademiai Kiadó.

Jenkins, Robert. 1987. *Social Inequality in the State Socialist Division of Labor: Earnings Determination in Contemporary Hungary*. Ph.D. dissertation, University of Wisconsin.

Juhasz, Pal. 1983. "The Role of Agricultural Engineers in the Cooperatives." *Medvetanc* 1.

Kolosi, Tamas. 1984. *Stratified Society*. Budapest: Kossuth Kiadó.

Konrad, George, and Ivan Szelenyi. 1979. *The Intellectuals on the Road to Class Power*. New York: Harcourt Brace Jovanovich.

Kornai, Janos. 1980. *Economics of Shortage*. Amsterdam: North Holland Publishing Company.

Kovach, Imre. 1988. *Producers and Entrepreneurs*. Budapest: Tarsadalomtudomanyi Intezet, pp. 7–28.

Marx, Karl, and Friedrich Engels. 1975. "Economic and Political Manuscript of 1844." *Collected Works*, 3:229–346. New York: International Publishers.

———. 1979. "The Eighteenth Brumaire of Louis Bonaparte." *Collected Works*, vol. 11. New York: International Publishers.

Szelenyi, Ivan. 1986–1987. "The Prospects and Limits of the East European New Class Project." *Politics and Society* 7:103–144.

Szelenyi, Ivan, and George Konrad. 1988. *Socialist Entrepreneurs*. Cambridge: Polity Press.

Szelenyi, Ivan, and Robert Manchin. 1987. "Social Policy and State Socialism." In G. Esping-Anderson, L. Rainwater, and M. Rain, eds., *Renewal in Social Policy,* pp. 102–139. White Plains: Sharpe.

Szelenyi, Ivan, and B. Martin. 1988–1989. "The Three Waves of New Class Theories." *Theory and Society* 17.

Szucs, Jeno. 1983. "The Historical Regions of Europe." *Acta Historica,* nos. 2–4.

Intellectuals and the Politics
of Knowledge (Abstract)

Ivan Szelenyi

This paper explores the changes that occurred in intellectual-knowledge-power relations during the 1970s and 1980s. It reviews some of the theories that tried to make sense of these changes and, finally, tries to assess the prospects for the power aspiration of intellectuals during the 1990s.

My charge for this conference was broader. I was asked to discuss the question of the politics of knowledge in general and to locate the role, interest, and strategies of intellectuals in this broader picture (intellectuals being, of course, only one of the agents affected by politics of knowledge). We were all asked to link our analysis to the "great transformations" of our times, to changes such as the third industrial revolution and the like.

This assignment proved to be too complex for me. After a few unsuccessful attempts to paint an all-encompassing picture, I decided to narrow the focus of this paper to a *critical (or reflexive) sociology of intellectuals*. The twin questions such a critical sociology of intellectuals asks are these: (1) Do intellectuals have power aspirations? If yes, in what ways can they use knowledge to attain power of their own? and (2) To what extent do self-interests and, specifically, power aspirations of intellectuals affect—if they affect at all—the nature of knowledge that is being produced, processed, and disseminated by intellectuals?

The critical sociology of intellectuals represents a radicalization of the sociology of knowledge. It aims at a higher degree of self-reflexivity: in exploring the knowledge-power or knowledge-interest links, it wants to subject the knowledge producers themselves to critical scrutiny. Such a critical sociology of intellectuals intends to move beyond the assumptions that the knowledge producers *as* knowledge producers are neutral (think of Mannheim's [1972] sociology of knowledge and his notion of socially unattached intellectuals) or that they have only cognitive or emancipatory interests (think of Habermas's [1971] radical theory of knowledge) in the process of knowledge production. The critical sociology of intellectuals instead posits that knowledge producers as knowledge producers pursue self-interests and have power aspirations that intrinsically affect the way they produce discourse. As Gouldner (1979), the most powerful theorist of this reflexive sociology of intellectuals, put it, in this approach the camera is focused on the "cameraman" itself.

This emphasis on the cameraman does not imply that the whole story about knowledge and power or the politics of knowledge can be told in this way. There are at least two reasons for this: Knowledge is *not the only* and, in most historical circumstances, *not even the most important* source of power; furthermore, intellectuals also *do* pursue cognitive or emancipatory interests in the processes of producing, processing, and disseminating knowledge. All that a reflexive sociology of intellectuals can do is to complement other approaches in investigating the power-knowledge link by focusing on a previously underemphasized dimension, on the missing link in critical theory, on ourselves—with an ironic view—self-reflexively.

Within this more limited scope, this paper tries to achieve three aims. I start with a summary of the origins of the critical sociology of intellectuals and a few brief comments on social theories of the 1970s, which began to focus attention on the inseparability of knowledge-power and on the self-interest knowledge producers may pursue. I will locate "knowledge class theories"—theories that claim that in a post-industrial, information, or knowledge society (post-capitalist and post-Communist?), intellectuals, or knowledge monopolists, may perform an analogous role to that played by owners under capitalism or that played by the bureaucracy in Communist societies.

In this broader context, I will then offer a brief sociology of the knowledge analysis of these theories. I will show that these theories did reflect the changing significance of knowledge in social domination and economic growth under both capitalism and socialism. To put it ambitiously, I will try to show that there has been a "power project" of intellectuals (in Eastern Europe, linked to the reform movements of the 1960s; in the West, culminating in the radicalization of the educated middle classes during the late 1960s and early 1970s). My main hypothesis is that knowledge class theories or other radically self-reflexive theories of knowledge-power were theoretical reflections of such "projects" of intellectuals to promote their power aspirations; these theories were falsified by history because these projects were defeated both in the West and in Eastern Europe.

Finally, I will explore what the strategies and prospects of the highly educated may be after the fall of the knowledge class project. In the last section of the paper, I will focus my attention particularly on recent changes in socialist societies, the trend toward post-communism, the emergence of a socialist mixed economy with a significant private sector, the corresponding changes in social structure, and the emergence of a new entrepreneurial class. I argue that intellectuals, in this rather unanticipated turn toward post-communism, will play a crucial role and that a critical sociology of intellectuals as defined above may help us to understand their attitudes toward these changes, what they may or may not do as the process unfolds, and where they may fit in the emergent new alliances among classes and social forces. I am particularly fascinated by how the bureaucracy begins to learn the market ways of preserving its privileges and to carve out a space for itself and its children in the socioeconomic structure of post-communism. How are intellectuals adapting to the challenges of a market economy? Are they ready to accept the role of "professionals" a Western type of market economy would offer them? I am also fascinated by the complexity of intellectuals' attitudes toward embourgeoisement, the emergent new private sector. Many fear that the worst combination of both worlds—capitalist greed and bureaucratic corruption—may evolve. What, therefore, can be the role of intellectuals in this transition to post-communism? How may they renegotiate their place in the emergent new social space of the new social formation? I will try to deconstruct different discourses about reform from these perspectives. Finally, I end the paper with a brief note about the prospects of the power aspirations of intellectuals in the West.

REFERENCES

Gouldner, A. 1979. *The Future of Intellectuals and the Rise of the New Class.* New York: Oxford University Press, p. 9.
Habermas, Jurgen. 1971. *Knowledge and Human Interest.* Boston: Beacon Press, pp. 43–63; 301–317.
Mannheim, Karl. 1972. *Ideology and Utopia.* London: Routledge and Kegan Paul, pp. 137–146.

Comments

Seymour Martin Lipset

This interesting paper is a contribution to the sociology of intellectuals. But an effort at theory in any area requires clarity about key concepts, about definitions—in this case, the terms *class* and *intellectuals.* To speak of a knowledge class implies a group that has a common relationship to the occupational or economic structure or a distinct status position linked to shared attributes. In this case, these appear to be a common level of education, those who went to college, as evidenced by the survey data on which the paper draws.

Since Szelenyi is primarily interested in the relationship between intellectuals and power, focusing on the behavior of the college educated involves dealing with a large heterogeneous population that includes highly diverse elements. The college educated, however, are not a class in any sense of the term. To anticipate their role in political life requires distinguishing among different categories of the educated.

1. The intellectuals—the *creators* of knowledge, ideas, science, and art. While they expect to be supported for their work by society, the state, business, and the consuming public, they emphasize that only their fellow intellectuals may judge quality and achievement in any specific area. Evaluation of contributions to physics can only be made by physicists, to art by artists, to literature by writers, and so on. The highest awards—the Nobel Prizes or their equivalents—are given for originality, innovation, and creativity. Those who produce for rewards in the marketplace, for the

approbation of the prince or the public, are viewed by their fellows as "sellouts," as betrayers of their calling. The best way to distinguish between intellectuals and other knowledge-related practitioners is to ask whether those involved believe in art for art's sake. There is an inherent tension between intellectuals and society because laymen—politicians, the church, the wealthy, foundations, the consuming public, students, all those who pay the intellectuals—often play a major, sometimes decisive role in determining whether intellectuals can even work at their trade or secure adequate financial rewards.

2. The intelligentsia—the *users* and *appliers* of innovative intellectual works. These include teachers, journalists, engineers, most professionals— that is, experts—rather than creators. The borderline between the two categories is highly porous. A person may play both roles within the same occupational category—for example, a professor who is a teacher and a scholar, a composer who is a musician, an engineer who is also an innovative scientist. It is obviously possible to use the same talent in different occupations, such as a novelist who is also a journalist or a medical researcher who is a clinician.

The distinction is particularly relevant to academics. Almost everyone at this conference is both a scholar and a teacher. As a teacher, one may be creative and innovative in better presenting the ideas, knowledge, and information produced by scholars, including oneself. But such creativity is akin to that of a skilled worker rather than an intellectual. There are approximately six hundred thousand college professors in the United States. They are all members of the intelligentsia, what is basically meant by the term *new class*; only a small minority are intellectuals.

3. College students—the *apprentice* intellectuals and intelligentsia. They form both an audience for, and are potential shock troops of, the adult groups.

The knowledge class, as operationally employed by Szelenyi in this paper, includes all of the above plus, seemingly, others in middle-class occupations. It is an extremely heterogeneous category containing those in all the professions—managerial personnel, business people, and the like. Much of the political action, which interested Alvin Gouldner and concerns Szelenyi, goes on within this grouping rather than between this group and the rest of society. To discuss the politics of post-industrialism, it is necessary to distinguish among the knowledge strata.

Knowledge, as Gary Becker and Pierre Bourdieu have emphasized in different ways, is a form of capital much like other forms of skill. As capital, knowledge gives power. In Max Weber's terms, it increases life chances, the ability to affect the behavior of others and of society generally, and supplies those who have more of it with greater personal freedom, more ability to control, to determine their work and their own destinies. As *experts*, members of the intelligentsia may have considerable influence on power holders, on decision makers. Klaus Knorr, who dealt with foreign and military policy authorities in many Western countries, concluded in the mid-1950s that U.S. academics have more influence on such people than their compeers elsewhere because U.S. elites have been socialized to rely on expert advice. Conversely, in most European countries, where high status retains aspects of diffuse aristocratic standing, elites tend to think of themselves as generalists and pay less attention to functionally specific outside advice.

U.S. intellectuals not only have high prestige, as all the comparative surveys of occupational status indicate, but, as authorities in their fields, they have considerable influence. As I note in *Political Man* (Baltimore: Johns Hopkins University Press, 1981), U.S. intellectuals, who tend to have a comparative international frame of reference, fail to recognize that the symbols of high esteem given to creative intellectuals in many other countries that are post-feudal reflect the greater deference accorded all elites in more status-stratified societies, not a special esteem accorded intellectuals. Knorr emphasized that in France, the bulk of the members of the political class are alumni of the *grands écoles*, the special elitist colleges, and are uninterested in the views of outsiders, even when they are experts. The intellectuals are given great public recognition but are not much listened to by politicians and top civil servants. Similar points have been made about the relationships among elites in Britain.

Knowledge by those occupationally involved in public forms of communication may be used to develop and facilitate the acceptance of the hegemonic dogmas and beliefs—the values of the dominant strata—or to undermine them. Whether the phenomenon is conceptualized in Marxist or functionalist terms, it is obvious that there is a process of legitimation in every society. There are legitimating ideologies, legitimating doctrines. Who enunciates them? The answer is obvious: people who can communicate, write, and speak; those who have more knowledge.

The intellectuals and communicators among the intelligentsia, however, are not simply enunciators of hegemonic creeds. Every group in society has its own spokespersons, ideologists, journalists, and lawyers. Although the situation obviously varies considerably cross-nationally, the evidence suggests that intellectuals are more likely to oppose the hegemonic doctrines, the legitimating ideologies, than other strata. Szelenyi curiously ignores the considerable body of observation and, in recent years, of survey data that indicates that intellectuals have on occasion undermined social stability and hegemonic legitimacy through producing new values and criticisms.

John Adams sought to bar the visit in the 1790s of a group of French scientists, which included the subsequent founder of the DuPont Company, on the grounds that people such as they were responsible for the French Revolution and could corrupt the United States. Arinori Mori, the minister of education in Meiji Japan, advised his aristocratic cabinet colleagues that Japan required first-rate universities and centers of research if it were to become a modern industrial power. But, writing in the early 1870s, he warned them—based on reports brought back by investigators sent abroad— that universities, as institutions that foster originality and free communication, are inherently centers of disloyalty. To reduce their negative impact, he proposed that teachers' colleges be located at considerable distances from universities to prevent the universities from corrupting those training to teach in the elementary and high schools. Whitelaw Reid, the editor of the *New York Tribune*, wrote at about the same time in approving terms that the foremost role of the scholar in politics was to be a spokesman for the "radicals." Three decades later, in a speech at Stanford, he complained bitterly that scholars were just that—seditious, rebellious, unpatriotic (opposed to the Spanish-American war). And Richard Hofstadter noted in the mid-1960s that U.S. academics and intellectuals had been found in disproportionate numbers on the left of U.S. political life for the previous seventy-five years. His findings coincide with conclusions about the dominant themes in U.S. literature reported in the 1950s by his Columbia University colleague, Lionel Trilling. The latter emphasized that U.S. writers adhere to an "adversary culture," one that rejects the values of bourgeois society.

Two sociological economists or, if you will, economic sociologists, Thorstein Veblen and Joseph Schumpeter, well over a half a century ago, independently suggested an explanation for radicalism—anti-establishmentism—being endemic in the intellectual enterprise. Writing in 1919, Veblen argued that intellectual creativity involves rejection of the past, of what one has been taught, and is, in effect, a form of rebellion. He linked Jewish intellectual creativity and political radicalism together, as derived from the same conditions—their marginal outsider status—which makes them less disposed than insiders to uncritically accept the dominant paradigms. In the 1940s, Schumpeter, in analyzing the predisposition of intellectuals to undermine the status quo, advanced a similar argument. He also contended that the capacity to be original or innovative is related to opposition to the established.

The logic of these analyses would dictate the proposition that the more creative should be the more critical. A leading conservative (in the U.S. sense of the term), Friedrich Hayek, writing in "The Intellectuals and Socialism" in 1949, reported that the dominant tone among U.S. academics at the time was socialist, by which he meant New Deal statist liberalism. More surprisingly, given his own free-market commitments, he noted that the socialists were much more likely to be found among the best scholars. Subsequent survey data sustain his observations. Interviews with a random sample of 2500 U.S. social scientists, collected in the 1950s by Paul Lazarsfeld, indicated that, as a group, scholars were far to the left of other strata (17 percent had supported Henry Wallace, the Progressive party nominee, for president in 1948) and that the achievers among them, the research scholars, were the most left-oriented of all. A national questionnaire survey of sociologists conducted for Alvin Gouldner in the mid-1960s also found, to his surprise, that the upper-echelon members of the discipline were the most socially critical. (These findings are reported in an unpublished dissertation by Timothy Sprehe.) The same relationships between achievement and political and social orientations have been documented in abundant multivariate detail by Everett Ladd and myself, based on analyses of large national samples of academics in all disciplines taken in 1969 and 1975. Our 1977 survey of members of the major honorific societies, the National Academy of Sciences and the American Academy of Arts and Sciences, reveals that they are the most left of all academic groups sampled—more so than scholars at the leading research universities, who are in turn more liberal than their colleagues at less prestigious and less research-oriented schools.

The empirical hypothesis derived from the Veblen-Schumpeter theory is that intellectuals will oppose the established, not that they will be on the left. Or to paraphrase Arthur Schlesinger, to be a creative intellectual requires a socially critical outlook; those who support the status quo are engaged in public relations work. Criticism and anti-establishment orientations may take a right-wing as well as a left-wing form. In many Western countries, there has been an important, but usually minority, classically liberal (Adam Smith) or libertarian intellectual tendency, which in recent decades has challenged the strong government-planning, welfare-state liberal, social-democratic, or Communist orientations from a coherent anti-statist perspective. But in countries that had been long dominated by social democrats, such as Israel and Sweden in the 1960s; by authoritarian socialists, as in various African states; or by totalitarian Communist parties, the dominant tendency among intellectuals as revealed by polls in Western countries and oppositional behavior in dictatorships, has been anti-statist, frequently supportive of libertarian and free-market policies.

Intellectuals can also be differentiated along occupational or substantive lines. Among U.S. academics, for whom the most reliable data exist, those in the liberal arts are on the whole considerably to the left of the faculties of professional schools. This distinction, of course, corresponds in large part to the degree of intellectuality and emphasis on scholarly innovativeness. Scientists, orientated to the logic of their disciplines, are much more likely to be political critics than engineers, who deal with applied problems. The latter, like business school professors, are predominantly conservative. The social scientists (economists excepted), humanists, and theoretical scientists tend to be the most anti-establishment of all. Similar discipline variations distinguish the orientations of students as well.

The rest of the intelligentsia, the college educated, also varies in considerable part along the lines that differentiate the views of faculty. Those involved in work that is linked to the social sciences and humanities—such as journalism, the broadcast media, social work, libraries, and major segments of the civil service—tend to be disproportionately on the left. Conversely, the graduates of most professional schools are more likely to be found on the conservative side.

In discussing the new class, Szelenyi fails to note the relevant literature or make distinctions such as these. Basing himself on the survey analysis of Martin, he notes correctly that college graduates increasingly show up as political conservatives and vote Republican. But in the United States, with its massive college student cohort, a higher education background is closely linked to middle- or upper-class occupational position, not to membership in a new class and certainly not with being an intellectual. The many millions who have been to college include business managers, stockbrokers, the self-employed, realtors, car dealers, druggists, sales personnel, and on and on. Not surprisingly in an economically prosperous nation, they vote Republican and are conservative.

But the intelligentsia, linked to the intellectual world, remains more liberal politically. The election day exit polls, which have large samples running 10,000 or more, usually differentiate voters with post-graduate educations from those who stopped their studies with Bachelor's degrees. Invariably, up to and including 1988, those with advanced education are much more liberal than the others, often voting Democratic by 15 percent more than the college educated. Separately done complex secondary analyses of occupationally recoded survey data by Steven Brint and John McAdams document the link within the elites in occupation and new class reformist views. In a number of surveys of policy-relevant scientific and communications leadership groups, Stanley Rothman and Robert Lichter have reported a considerable degree of liberalism, even leftist radicalism, among these groups.

To sum up, Professor Szelenyi has contributed an important introduction to the analysis of the implications of the growth of the intelligentsia and the college educated in contemporary advanced industrial, post-industrial, post-materialist, scientific-technological, new class-dominated society. But on an empirical level, his paper is a discussion of the political reactions of the middle and upper strata, although only a portion of them derive their positions from intellectual capital. Education, his principal indicator of class position, correlates with liberal views on social issues, gender, race, civil liberties, and the environment but is not an independent determinant of orientation toward economic and class power policies. A better educated world is more disposed to be "greener" and socially egalitarian than one in which the overwhelmingly predominant source of capital is economic. But there is no emerging dominant new class, and the economy is not in the hands of the intellectuals. The intellectuals are agents of change, important ones, but they are not a class.

Comments

Klemens Szaniawski

I would like to elaborate on the kind of influence the intellectuals exercise in a country such as Poland. First, they use their expert knowledge. Szelenyi calls this simply *knowledge*, and its quality (theoreticity) is rightly stressed. In a very obvious way, expert knowledge is needed to solve problems that arise in political life: legal, economic, technical, social, and the like. This *is* power, no matter which side uses it in the political confrontation. Experts are needed, for instance, in negotiations such as those that preceded the breakup of the Communist establishment in Poland and that have occurred in the period since then.

Second, there is something that I will call intellectual know-how. By this I mean the ability to think abstractly, to organize data into a coherent whole, to articulate results in a clear and concise way, and so on. The distinction between expert knowledge and intellectual know-how is perhaps best exhibited by means of an example. One of Lech Walesa's ablest advisors during the period preceding the breakup of the Communist establishment was Gieremek, a historian who specializes in the French Middle Ages. He is extremely knowledgeable about, among other things, the milieu of thieves and prostitutes in Paris during François Villon's times. I doubt that this kind of expert knowledge was of much use to the leader of the trade union Solidarity, but his general intellectual know-how undoubtedly was.

Finally, there is the charisma. What the intellectuals have to say carries, as a rule, more weight than the same opinions have if they are expressed by other people. It is not only the question of their expertness but also of their integrity. In a social situation of general distrust, this is a nonnegligible quality. Thus, for instance, intellectuals can lend credibility to statements by public officials who would otherwise be believed by hardly anybody. This device has been used too often to be efficient; nevertheless, it still works, particularly in the case of people who have not compromised their names by just rubber stamping official declarations. In the case of Poland, a reason for the special charisma of intellectuals can perhaps be found in Polish history. In the nineteenth century, when the independent Polish state did not exist, the intellectuals—writers, poets, historians, even musicians and painters—maintained the national spirit and were in a sense responsible for the state of Polish consciousness. For this reason, they were treated with special respect, which probably was not accorded to intellectuals in some other countries.

The question arises as to what use the intellectuals have made of this special kind of power in the post-war period. What I am going to say on that topic applies to Poland, but I conjecture that it could be generalized to the other countries of Realsozialismus.

In the beginning of the post-war period, many intellectuals identified with the system. There were several reasons for that. I will not analyze this phenomenon, as Szelenyi describes it in broad outline. The important thing is that it was possible at the time to support the system while acting in good faith; for an intellectual, the problem of good faith has an obvious importance, as it is closely connected with his or her calling. The first disappointment came when the true face of Stalinism was partly disclosed in the early 1950s. The final disappointment occurred in 1968 with the invasion of Czechoslovakia and the reactionary takeover in Poland. For many intellectuals, it was the true end of Communist ideology. A few years later, cooperation between intellectuals and the working class began to take place. This evolution can be summarized by what philosopher Leszek Nowak had to say about his motives for joining the party and then leaving it in

1980. As he put it, he joined and left the party for the same reason: He wanted to be with the oppressed against the oppressors. Such evolution explains the fact that today, many leading intellectuals in the political opposition have a Communist past (which the party exploits in the attempt to discredit them in public opinion). This applies, of course, to the older generation (the age group over fifty).

It can be said that cooperation between intellectuals and the workers' movement is historically nothing new. Indeed, this is how the socialist parties were created. However, as a movement directed against the Communist establishment, it is a new phenomenon. In Poland, it can be dated back to the mid-1970s when the Committee for the Defence of Workers was created by a group of intellectuals. In 1980–1981, the cooperation was in a sense institutionalized: Pro-Solidarity intellectuals were represented by the Coordinating Committee of Learned and Artistic Societies. The committee and Solidarity worked together on a number of important issues, such as freedom of expression, access to the media, education, and health problems. At the Solidarity Congress in the autumn of 1981, agreements were signed for further cooperation. After the declaration of the martial law, independent intellectuals founded several bodies to act underground and take care of certain areas of national life, such as education, culture, and science. Again, this was done in partnership with Solidarity.

The above description applies to the more important part of the intellectual milieu—if not in terms of numbers, then in terms of weight. It is true, however, that there remain intellectuals faithful to the party, if not to its ideology. Many of them act as experts for the government; some are active in the party apparatus; certain others do the propaganda work. In a very real sense, they participate in macro-power. Their position *qua intellectuals* is rather precarious. They are bound by loyalty and party discipline to a system that is intellectually not defensible, at least by the kind of argument that was originally put forward to justify its introduction: greater economic efficiency and stability, providing for everybody's basic needs, respecting the rights of every individual, and the like. There being overwhelming evidence to the contrary, this kind of justification is no longer possible, at least intellectually. Of course, in propaganda anything is possible.

The only argument that seems to remain is that of social justice. Its use, however, is hampered by the fact that there is little to be just about. Indeed, a just distribution of want is all that can be realistically postulated. And even that has not been achieved. It comes as no surprise, therefore, that party intellectuals seek a rapprochement with the opposition and go so far as to question the basic tenets of the Leninist theory of socialism (one-party rule, state ownership of the means of production, the monopoly of Communist doctrine, and the like). They still pay lip service to Marxism, but very little follows from this in practical terms.

To conclude this short comment, I would stress once more the need for differentiation between independent intellectuals and party intellectuals, as their positions vis-à-vis macro-power are very different. They influence the course of events in very different ways. Party intellectuals participate in decision-making as experts for those who make decisions concerning the running of the state. Independent intellectuals exercise considerable influence on public consciousness, and, in at least one case (Poland), they are experts for a formidable social force—the Solidarity movement. This, too, is macro-power.

Do independent intellectuals constitute a homogeneous group? Only insofar as the opposition to the system goes. The more successful the opposition is, the more important the differences in outlook become. On this point, I agree with the analysis presented by Szelenyi. Many intellectuals of the leftist persuasion are far from enthusiastic about the changes toward a capitalist system of production and all the consequences thereof. On the other hand, there is a revival of conservative and nationalistic ideology in Poland. For the proponents of such views, the return to traditional (pre-war) political and economic systems would be welcome. It is here that interests begin to diverge and the opposition intellectuals cease to constitute one single group with respect to power.

Epilogue:
On the Possibility of a Field
of World Sociology

Pierre Bourdieu

Translated from the French by Loïc J.D. Wacquant

Sociology has this privilege—that it can take as an object its own functioning as a relatively autonomous social world and that it is thereby able to bring to rational consciousness at least some of the sociopolitical constraints that bear on scientific practice. Consequently, it can utilize the awareness and

---

After considerable hesitation, I have decided to leave my contribution to this volume in the deliberately tentative and oral form of my original address, in keeping with the spirit in which it was written and delivered. Having coorganized, with James Coleman, a conference bringing together scholars occupying often very distant positions in the space of the social sciences, I wanted to try to explicate the purpose and significance of this meeting and the functions it was to fulfill in my eyes. In agreeing to come to Chicago to cochair these discussions, my idea was to help open up—or to widen—a space of debate so as to demonstrate, experimentally as it were, that the progress of scientific reason in sociology hinges crucially on a transformation of the *social organization of scientific production and communication*.

Ex post, the enterprise seems to me to have been successful: I believe that it offers proof that social scientists who belong to very different, if not antagonistic, theoretical and methodological traditions, who come from different countries and different intellectual traditions, and who sometimes root for opposed political visions of social science, can *s'entendre*, as we say in French, that is, both *hear* one another and *agree* with each other, at least enough to enter into *constructive* dialogue. I hope that the publication of the proceedings of this conference will convince sociologists of the necessity, for the future of their discipline, of such confrontations whereby social science can avoid the false and costly alternative between, on the one hand, a cold war of position between opposed camps and, on the other, the anarchical exchanges of large national and international meetings, without relapsing into the fictitious and falsely progressive consensus imposed by an orthodoxy.

the knowledge it has of its own functioning, and of the negative or positive epistemological effects that ensue, to try to overcome some of the obstacles that stand in the way of scientific progress.

As the title of my chapter is rather obscure, I would like to state briefly the questions I will address: Does the sociological universe presently function in a manner of a *unified* scientific field on a world scale? Is it possible to contribute to the unification of this world sociology beyond the mere "growth and consolidation of an international scientific community" (Bottomore and Nisbet 1978, xiv), in particular by controlling the purely social effects of domination that are exercised under scientific guises? Is it possible to circumvent the barrier of the nationalisms that hinder the free circulation of ideas and set back the unification of a sociological problematic, that is, the formation of a worldwide space of social-scientific discussion and critique? Is it possible to create such a space of discussion unified around *purely scientific questions,* rather than to continue to perpetuate the sort of intellectual protectionism fostered by all forms of closure and division into theoretical, methodological, and national traditions and schools?

Max Weber (1978) reminds us that, in the art of warfare, the greatest progress originated not in technical inventions but in transformations of the social organization of the warriors, as for instance with the case of the invention of the Macedonian phalanx. One may, along the same line, ask whether a transformation of the social organization of scientific production and circulation and, in particular, of the forms of communication and exchange through which logical and empirical control is carried out would not be capable of contributing to the progress of scientific reason in sociology—and to do so more powerfully than the refinement of new technologies of measurement or the endless warnings and "presuppositional" discussions of epistemologists and methodologists. I have in mind here a scientific *politique*—that is, policy and politics—whose goal would be to foster scientific communication and debate across the many divisions associated with national traditions and with the fragmentation of social science into empirical subspecialties, theoretical paradigms, and methodological schools.

Although it is not, I believe, wholly circumstantial, my purpose in this chapter is to explicate the full meaning, the scientific raison d'être, of this peculiar scientific gathering. This conference is peculiar inasmuch as it brings together sociologists who belong to different nations, different generations, and—especially—very different, even antagonistic, theoretical and methodological traditions, not to mention wide differences in political vision. Indeed, it seems to me that, by convening sociologists who ordinarily do not communicate with one another—and who all too often do not even read one another—by forsaking, if only for a moment, the quasi-ritual strategies of mutual avoidance, mutual ignorance, and, perhaps, mutual contempt that routinely impose themselves upon the occupants of opposed positions in the scientific field, we have thrown one another—and ourselves—a challenge.

I would like to ground this *ethical and political challenge* (not to say gamble) by recapitulating some of the more general properties of the scientific field before proposing a summary characterization of the specificity of the sociological field. I will then briefly sketch the recent and present state of the field of sociology—or, better, of the distinct *fields* of national sociologies in the cases of the United States and France.

SOME PARTICULARITIES
OF THE FIELD OF SOCIOLOGY

The scientific field is a social microcosm partially autonomous from the necessities of the larger social macrocosm that encompasses it. This world is homologous to various other social universes—the economic field, the political field, the religious field, and so on (see Bourdieu et al. 1988; Bourdieu 1981, 1971)—that is, it is at once similar to them in a number of respects and crucially different in others. It is, on the one hand, a social world like all the others, and, as in the economic world, we can find in it capitals and monopolies, relations of force and struggles of interests, coalitions and alliances; we can even observe, as in international relations, imperialisms and nationalisms (Bourdieu 1990).

But, on the other hand, and against the self-proclaimed "strong program" in the sociology of science, we must emphasize that the scientific field is also a special world, a peculiar world (*un monde à part*) endowed with its own laws of functioning. All the properties that it has in common with the other fields take up specific forms (see Bourdieu 1975, 1991). For instance, no matter how fierce, competition within the scientific field remains bounded, if not by explicit rules, at least by the quasi-automatic regulations that result from the mutual control between competitors, which are such that social interests (such as the thirst for fame and recognition) are transformed into *Erkenntnisseinteressen*—interests in knowledge. In other words, the mutual control by competitors who have one another as consumers is such that the *libido dominandi*, which always enters for a part into the *libido sciendi*, is transformed into a *libido scientifica*—a pure love of truth to which the logic of the field, functioning in the manner of a mechanism of censorship and sublimation, assigns its legitimate goals and the legitimate means to reach them. The sublimated drives (*Triebe*) that define this specific *libido* apply to objects which are themselves highly purified. And no matter how violent and deadly they can be in reality, these compulsions cannot be separated, in their very existence and in the form of their fulfillment, from the practical knowledge of the requirements that are inscribed in the very logic of the field in which they express themselves.

In what ways is the case of sociology peculiar? We can see at once that sociology is in a unique situation. Due to the fact that he or she produces representations of the social world endowed with the authority of science, the sociologist is engaged willy nilly, whether he or she knows it or not, in the symbolic struggles for the imposition of legitimate principles of vision and division of the social world involving other specialists in symbolic production. (The Greeks called this common principle of vision and division *nomos;* I will come back to this notion in a moment.) This is why sociologists cannot obtain as easily as specialists in natural science the recognition of their autonomy, that is, of their monopoly over the truth of the social world that they claim, by definition, by claiming scientificity. Their rivals—both inside, as in the case of politicians, and outside, as with lay people—can always invoke against them common sense—that very common sense against which, like all scientists, sociologists must construct their representation of the social world. Sociology is an esoteric science that has all appearances of being exoteric. Therefore modes of producing representations of the world that would be discredited in other scientific domains can survive even in the highest positions in the sociological field as long as they are granted a social authority capable of offsetting their technical, logical, and empirical inadequacies.

Thus *sociology partakes at once of two radically discrepant logics:* the logic of the political field, in which the force of ideas is mainly a function of the power of the groups that take them to be true; and the logic of the scientific field, which, in its most advanced states, knows and recognizes only the "intrinsic force of the true idea" of which Spinoza spoke. Scientific communication in its ideal form differs from political communication in that the weight given to arguments, to problems and solutions, is not a function of the specifically *social* force of its advocates (it does not depend, for instance, on their number: Scientific debates are not adjudicated by means of physical confrontation or by majority rule). Scientific communication— and this is the more true the more autonomous the field—is a function of how well propositions and procedures conform to the rules of logical coherence and compatibility with observational evidence. On the contrary, in the political field, the propositions that win are those that Aristotle (in the *Topics*) called *endoxic*, that is, propositions that must be taken into account because people of importance, people who muster a lot of social power, would like them to be true. To say of a proposition or an opposition that it is endoxic is to say that it partakes of the *doxa*, that it belongs to common sense, to the ordinary vision of the world.

As such, endoxic propositions tend to impose themselves upon us even when they are in total or partial contradiction with experience and logic because they have behind them the power of a group. Endoxic propositions are *not probable but plausible* (in the etymological sense of the word) that is, liable to receive the assent and *applause* of the majority. Sociology partakes of the logic of the field of politics in that propositions that are logically inconsistent and incompatible with observation can survive in it, in con- tradistinction with what happens in the purest scientific fields (where no one today, for instance, would think of even trying to argue that the earth does not rotate around the sun).

One could thus show that a good number of the most prevalent antinomies in sociology, and particularly those that are predicated upon the opposition between the individual and the collective, owe their existence and their persistence in the sociological field to the existence of homologous oppositions within the political field, such as the opposition between individualism and collectivism or socialism. It is this same heteronomous logic, that of the confrontation of ideas reduced to a confrontation between *idées-forces*, that explains that in the struggles internal to the sociological field, some can, without discrediting or excluding themselves, call upon the oppositions of common sense—such as the distinction between the individual and society—to give strength to strategies aimed at characterizing as "totalitarian" the opponents of methodological individualism.

It would be easy to draw up a list of indicators of this heteronomy of sociology. In the academic space, as described by Kant in *The Conflict of the Faculties*, sociology stands closer to law and to the temporally dominant disciplines, those whose power is delegated by temporal powers, than to the scientific disciplines that recognize no criterion other than the rule of pure reason. Let me mention three such indicators of the heteronomy of sociology, going from the most to the least visible. First, there is the propensity unthinkingly to convert *social* problems into *sociological* problems (as, for instance, when the problem of inequality is transformed into that of status attainment or, today, the problem of the black subproletariat into the problem of poverty and the "underclass"), the tendency to smuggle into scientific discourse concepts (such as that of "profession," to which I will return) or antinomies (individual versus collective, achievement versus ascription, primordial versus constructed, etc.) directly borrowed from ordinary discourse and to employ as instruments of analysis notions that should be the very *objects* of analysis. There is also, and this is more subtle, the propensity to take as the principle of the hierarchy of scientific objects the social hierarchy from which they are drawn. For instance, it is easy to see that, with a few notable exceptions, specialists in the professions have more prestige within the profession of sociology than specialists in the black community or that specialists in intellectual history have more prestige than specialists in women's history. A last indicator, albeit one that is more difficult to use, is the fact that the social hierarchy of positions—the status of the university in which one teaches in the academic field—tends to contaminate the intellectual hierarchy of the occupants of these positions. (This is more difficult to interpret because those who owe their intellectual authority to their proximity to temporal powers can falsely believe, and make others believe, that it is their scientific quality that determines their weight in the scientific field.)

FROM "PROFESSION" TO THE INSTITUTIONALIZATION OF *ANOMIE*: NOTES ON THE RECENT EVOLUTION OF SOCIOLOGY

The unique status of sociology has perhaps never revealed itself more clearly than in the United States in the post–World War II era. Although the classic works of the new sociological Establishment were written and published before the 1940s, it is only after 1945 that the ambition to give sociology full respectability by constituting it into a *profession* crystallized. As George Homans (1986) recently showed in his article "Fifty Years of Sociology," it was in the 1930s and 1940s that the most decisive achievements of the new discipline were made, notably the new statistical techniques invented by Samuel Stouffer and Paul Lazarsfeld and the great theoretical constructions built by Talcott Parsons and Robert K. Merton. In the manner of Cicero when he offered a soft and spongy reinterpretation of Greek philosophers, Parsons brought together the classics of modern European social thought— Durkheim, Weber, and Pareto (overlooking Marx)—into a syncretic, rather than a synthetic, theory that claims to mark a new beginning for social theory and thereby to lay the foundations of a specifically American tradition, that is, of a tradition independent from Europe and from its founding fathers.

Indeed, it is no exaggeration to say that the universe of sociology, which had begun to function like a *field* in the interwar period—that is, as a space of competition, of struggles, and of genuine debate (there were also the Chicago school, Marxists, and many of the currents that were to emerge later in the so-called period of crisis)—this universe was soon organized into a veritable hierarchical corporate body, a *corporatio* unified around a common vision of science founded upon a few common principles and on a great many exclusions. Based on their preeminent university positions, the three great figures of the Capitoline triad of the American sociological Pantheon were able to dominate, both in the United States and in other major Western countries, not only teaching institutions but also official publication outlets, professional associations, and even—more or less directly—access to the resources necessary for empirical research. (It was also after 1945 that the sociopolitical function of sociology was fully recognized, in particular through the demands and the substantial grants governments thrust upon sociologists to study various social problems of the day, thus instituting them as organic intellectuals of the dominant class.)

The leaders of the sociological establishment thus succeeded in imposing a true intellectual *orthodoxy* by imposing a common corpus of issues, stakes of discussion, and criteria of evaluation. And this imposition proceeded on a global scale. For instance, in France each of the great masters had his own agent: Francois Bourricaud for Parsons, Henri Mendras for Merton, and Jean Stoetzel and Raymond Boudon for Lazarsfeld (see Bourdieu and Passeron [1967] for a fuller discussion of the links between French and American sociology at the time). With the combination of functionalist theory and positivistic methodology that, as Norbert Wiley (1985) showed, "pervaded the textbooks" for two or three decades, this mode of intellectual production that may be called *academic* in the strict sense (it is reminiscent of that of the French *Académie de peinture*, the Painting Academy of the nineteenth century), found the means to *mimic* what it took to be the major characteristic of a science worthy of the name—namely, the surface consensus that was to bestow on sociology the respectability of a discipline at long last non-controversial. In reality, this forced and artificial consensus was the *communis doctorum opinio* on which the authority of the whole medieval corporation of doctors, jurists, or theologians was based, and it has nothing to do with the agreement on domains of disagreement and on the processes and procedures capable of adjudicating disagreements that are at the basis of the scientific field.

I believe that the theory of professions, as it is expressed, for instance, in the article "Professions" written by Talcott Parsons (1968) for the 1968 edition of *The International Encyclopedia of the Social Sciences,* offers a very lucid expression of the *professional ideology* of these professionals that establishment sociologists aspire to be. In this article, professionals are characterized by their intellectual training and authority, which rests more on expertise than on political power; being free from dependence upon the state and governmental bureaucracy, they are guided by the search for the common good. This "collectivity orientation," which is mentioned in most definitions of professions, this disinterestedness, this altruism that justifies that they be granted the highest symbolic and material rewards, can also be found in the Mertonian representation of the scientific universe. In sum, we may legitimately see in the preconstructed notion of "profession" this conceptual ready-made that has elicited an endless ocean of discourses— less a description of a social reality than a practical contribution to the ongoing construction of sociology as a "profession," and a "scientific profession" to boot.

It is this mode of organization of the discipline that was challenged in the 1960s under the thrust of a dramatic morphological change. Just as in the nineteenth century the inflow of starveling art students attracted by the social and economic success of the famous *pompier* painters was one of the crucial factors behind the Impressionist revolution (Bourdieu 1987b), likewise the sudden growth experienced by the sociological "profession" in the 1960s was one of the determining factors behind what has ordinarily been described as a crisis of sociology. Morphological transformations resulting from the abolition of the *de facto* and *de jure numerus clausus,* which protected a corporation by guaranteeing the scarcity and thus the distinctiveness of its members, are very often at the roots of the transformations of fields of cultural production. They are at any rate the specific mediation through which the effects of broader economic and social changes work themselves out. (This is why we must reject, as a typical form of what I call the *short-circuit fallacy,* explanations that put in direct relationship changes that occur in specialized fields such as the sociological field and broader sociopolitical trends.) Indeed, many observers have noted the extraordinary expansion of the number of sociologists since the 1950s. Thus Howard Becker (1986), in a provocative paper entitled "What's Happening to Sociology?" points out that the number of sociologists officially tallied by the American Sociological Association went from 2,400 in 1950 to 15,500 in 1978. Likewise, in France, the number of sociologists jumped from about 200 to over 1,000 in the same time period. The *Association professionnelle des sociologues,* which uses a very broad definition of the "profession," recently counted 1,678 professional sociologists in both the public and the private sector. (To be more precise, in 1949, the Centre National de la Recherche Scientifique [CNRS] employed a grand total of merely 18 sociologists; in 1967, there were over 500 of them, including 112 at the CNRS, 135 at the Ecole Pratique des Hautes Etudes, and 290 in private research centers. This growth continued into the 1980s, when 261 sociologists worked for the CNRS.)

In this case, as in others, the effects of morphological change depend very strongly on the structure of the field in which they occur, and they thus display the different particularities of the different national contexts. In the United States, where publication and attendance at conferences are much stronger professional requirements, there occurred a proliferation of journals (which went from three truly national journals in 1950 to over fifty in 1978) as well as a multiplication of official meetings and informal conferences where papers are read, research discussed, information circulated, and so on. What really matters, however, is that everywhere the artificially united and hierarchicized system of the 1950s was superseded by a "polycentric" system (as Becker [1986] puts it) that cannot be controlled completely because of its very fragmentation and diversification and because of growing centrifugal forces. This morphological change has gone hand in hand with transformations in the composition of the student population—and of sociology students in particular—in terms of gender, social origins, and educational capital. Such transformations and all the contradictions they entail created conditions propitious to the protest movements of the 1960s and to the rise of feminism toward the end of the 1980s, all of which provided both inspiration and an eager audience for the questioning of the functionalist and positivist orthodoxy. The more decisive development of this period is, in my view, the emergence of a questioning of the symbolic foundations of social domination within the university field and the elaboration, through the medium of feminism in particular, of a *specific critique* liable to have practical effects, for instance upon rituals of deference and demeanor within the academic world, rather than a general critique aimed at abstract and distant revolutionary objectives in the manner of traditional Marxist critical discourse.

The main consequence of these changes, which have prompted the formerly dominant or their spokespersons to complain of a "crisis" (as Neil Smelser [1988] does in his recent "Introduction" to the new *Handbook of Modern Sociology*), is the questioning of the *nomos*, that is, the common principle of vision and division that the old orthodoxy was seeking to impose. Just as in the crisis of the academy and of academicism which gave birth to modern painting around the 1880s, legitimacy became fragmented, split, grounded in a multiplicity of criteria; the unique and unitary *nomos* was replaced by the anomie of competing principles of legitimation. The unified and hierarchical profession as a corporate body was replaced by a field of competition between sociologists struggling to impose competing principles of legitimation. One can understand in this way what the most perceptive observers of American sociology, such as Randall Collins '(1986; see also Gans 1989), have described as a profound malaise:

> [Today] *wide recognition* of intellectual accomplishment seems so much less likely to happen; persons who are elevated . . . can only satisfy the intellectual alliances of comparatively small parts of the total intellectual field and hence seem illegitimate to adherents of other specialties. Mathematical sociologists, historical Marxists (and non-Marxist historical sociologists, non-historical Marxists, etc.), phenomenologists, analysts of contemporary social problems, organizational researchers, and others seem scarcely to recognize the names of the eminent practitioners in specialties other than their own. . . . Hence the vituperation that permeates our intellectual life today, when members of one subfield look out at the specialties beyond.

This description of the American sociological field, which seems to me accurate, needs to be qualified and pushed further on three counts. First, although it speaks of the sociological field in the sense in which I use the term, it still seems to retain a nostalgic yearning for the notion of an integrated profession, which prevents it from understanding the full significance of new developments. Second, it may cause us to overlook the existence of a new socially based scientific power that has survived the crumbling of the functionalist orthodoxy. Never have the means of scientific production (and of the legitimate means of scholarly publication) been more concentrated in the hands of the positivist quantitativists (Bryant 1985). The domination the latter wield would no doubt be complete if they were to succeed in universally inculcating the idea, which encapsulates a "theodicy" of their scientific power, that methodology can substitute for theory and in striking a new hegemonic alliance between all manners of empiricist methodology (as represented, for instance, by status attainment research and new methods of log-linear analysis) and modernized versions of methodological individualism, that is, the theory of rational action immanent to neoclassical economics and that some scholars today are even trying to combine with a revamped Marxism (see Wacquant and Calhoun 1989). One of the effects of this potential new domination, and in my eyes the most dangerous and most harmful, is that it would lead us to ignore the full potency of a *structural statistics*, represented in the United States by network analysis and in France, Japan, and the Netherlands by correspondence analysis, thus undermining the possibility of a quantitative sociology that takes as its unit of analysis not individuals but institutions or, to be more precise, objective relationships between institutional or organizational positions. A third, germane shortcoming of Collins's analysis is that it tends to overlook, through an effect of ethnocentrism very characteristic of American sociologists, everything that occurs *outside* of the United States, which prevents it from fully understanding what really goes on *inside* the American field. As I indicated earlier, the sociological field has always been international, generally for the worse and rarely for the better. There has always existed an International of the members of the sociological Establishment of all countries who, for evident social reasons, traveled more and developed much wider and denser networks and who spontaneously entered into an agreement on a functionalist definition of the social function of sociology.

Today this sort of International of the dominant has taken new forms that I briefly evoked above and that I could not describe more fully here without lapsing into the "war of metatheories" that Randall Collins justly deplores. What must be emphasized is that intellectual strategies of borrowing are overdetermined or, better, contaminated by social strategies of importation: Theories, methods, analytic techniques are also *weapons*, and, if you allow me this desacralizing metaphor, the international circulation of ideas is always a traffic in arms—a traffic that sometimes borders on smuggling, as when borrowed ideas are left unacknowledged thanks to the lag in translations and to the ordinary ignorance of foreign languages. In other words, importing ideas (via translations, book reviews, prefaces, and similar sources) is one of the main weapons used in intellectual conflicts within national fields, especially when it comes to discrediting an established position (an orthodoxy), giving credit to a new position, and speeding up the ever-painful process of the primary accumulation of symbolic capital geared to subverting the existing intellectual hierarchy. The result is persistent and serious misunderstandings in the international circulation of ideas (Bourdieu 1990).

International intellectual exchanges, especially borrowings, tend to operate on the basis of structural homologies between national fields, that is, they operate not only among the dominant but also among the dominated in each national sociology, and with the same effects of interested and unconscious misunderstanding. Thus, just as in France the temporally (or socially) dominant sociologists (such as Stoetzel in the 1950s) could count on the American Establishment to secure and maintain their domination, likewise today a number of young researchers who occupy dominated positions in U.S. universities can refer to the great figures of critical European thought (Foucault, Habermas, and Derrida, among others) to challenge domestic sociological authorities. This sort of cross-circulation is the cause of enormous distortions; and one shivers to think of how certain members of the American sociological establishment view these oppositional theories when they know them only through gatekeepers who have a special interest in blocking their circulation or through the objections or "essays" of their students or their younger colleagues.

But these factors themselves lead to the internationalization of the sociological field through the internationalization of the struggles of which the field becomes the site. The new International of the dominant that has recently emerged around *Commentary* and *Commentaire* has gone from conservative to reactionary politics under the impact of the student movements of the late 1960s and of the collective trauma that these movements caused, from Berkeley to Paris and Berlin, to a whole generation of centrist or even liberal professors. The connections that were until then informal have become organized (a good instance of "constructed social organization" dear to James Coleman) around establishment foundations and neoconservative journals. And distinguished "society conservatism" (*conservatisme de salon*) has now given way to the kind of vulgar ultra-right-wing pledges and manifestos exemplified by Alan Bloom's tract on *The Closing of the American Mind.*

On the other hand, the International of the dominated, of the outsiders, brings together individuals and currents that have few principles of unification other than their marginality relative to the dominant current. (In its early days, the journal *Theory and Society* was typical of this mainly negative gathering of disparate tendencies.) Like avant-garde movements in literature and art, the International of the dominated brings together the marginals by excess and the marginal by default, which only time will sort out. In their reaction against the depoliticized vision and practice of Establishment sociology, they have often given up the very weapons they need, including sometimes science itself, as in the case of those who now partake of the new fad of epistemological nihilism. Epistemological couples—such as the opposition between quantitative and qualitative methods, structural and historical approaches, and subjectivist and objectivist perspectives—are endlessly reactivated by their rooting in social oppositions and thus function as so many "mirror traps." It is obvious, for instance, that by rejecting the use of advanced quantitative techniques of analysis, the self-proclaimed proponents of a critical sociology tend to accept the limitations inherent in their position, and they considerably weaken the critique with which they seek to oppose pure quantitativists. The same applies when critical sociologists limit their investigations to specialties that are perceived as inferior (race relations, women's issues, and similar topics) and leave to the dominant not only the methods that are held to be the noblest but also the empirical objects that are the most prestigious.

As always in such cases, opponents are united by a form of objective complicity. This can be seen most clearly in the case of the totally fictitious theoretical opposition between objectivist structuralism, which seeks to grasp objective structures with more or less sophisticated quantitative techniques (path analysis, network analysis, log-linear modeling), and all manners of constructivism that, from Blumer to Goffman to Garfinkel, seek to capture through so-called qualitative methods the representation that agents have of the social world and the contribution they make to the construction of that world. Yet another example is the opposition between a microphrenic "empirical research" totally severed from fundamental theoretical culture and a "theory" conceived as a separate specialty, most often reduced to a purely exegetical revisiting of canonical authors or to flat and academicist trend reports on "theoretical works" both badly read and badly digested (see Bourdieu 1988b for elaborations).

How are we to escape from the mutual reinforcement of these fictitious antagonisms that are favored by the dialectic of contempt responding to contempt? The questioning of every socially dominant principle of vision and division, if it has the unquestionable virtue of destroying the fictitious consensus that annuls discussion, must be accompanied by the building of organizational forms capable of countering the tendencies toward anomic fission inscribed in the multiplicity of modes of thinking and capable of making possible the regulated confrontation of contending points of views.

It is at this juncture that we must bring in a *realpolitik* of reason armed with the rational knowledge of the social mechanisms that operate within the sociological field (Bourdieu 1987a, 1988a). A point of view that perceives itself as such, that is, as a view taken from a point in a space of contending positions, is in a position to overcome particularity. It can do this in particular by entering into a rational exchange capable of effecting, through a regulated confrontation of differences of vision (which includes an awareness of the social determinants of these differences), a departicularization of particular points of view.

CONCLUSION

If there do not exist, *pace* Habermas, transhistorical invariants of communication, there certainly exist socially instituted forms of communication that are more or less likely to facilitate the production of the universal. Logic can be inscribed into a social relation of regulated discussion founded, to use Aristotelian language, upon a topic and a dialectic. These common places (*topoi*) are a visible manifestation of the communality of the problematic as an agreement on the grounds of disagreement with which no genuine discussion—as distinct from parallel monologues—can dispense. They make possible the collective construction of a mutual demand that defines the fundamental oppositions, theses and antitheses, of the discussion. We must work to build such a space of play not on the basis of moral prescriptions and proscriptions but by creating, as we collectively tried to do with this conference, the social conditions of a rational confrontation aimed at establishing not what Erving Goffman would call the *working consensus* of an orthodoxy sustained by complicity with the powers that be but at least a *working dissensus* founded upon the critical acknowledgment of compatibilities and incompatibilities. This space of regulated confrontation can be the fount of the freedom that sociologists can give themselves by *collectively* working to uncover the most specific social determinations that bear upon the functioning of the sociological field and thus upon their very thinking.

But such "undistorted" scientific communication will not come down from the pure world of ideas or from a moral commitment, as Habermas would seem to have us believe. The autonomy of the scientific field, which is the prerequisite of the autonomy of every scientist and thus of every sociologist, must be produced and reproduced through constant struggles based on the knowledge of the mechanisms that foster all forms of "distorted communication" or, more precisely, of symbolic violence. In short, in the realm of science as in the realm of politics, one can escape the alternative between the naively Hegelian or Kantian vision of politics only by offering a solution that I would label Machiavellian: Just as political virtue presupposes the establishment of a republic such that all citizens have a vested interest in civic virtue, scientific virtue presupposes the establishment of a scientific republic in which social scientists have a vested interest in scientific virtues. This means that to create this field of world sociology as an autonomous space of struggles, in which truth may be produced on condition that only scientific weapons are used will require protracted and involved social struggles.

Thus, to come back to the question I tried to answer in this chapter, presently there is no scientific *field* of world sociology for all the reasons I have discussed, but especially because purely social and political forces can still be efficacious in the sociological universe. There are still in this universe forms of scientific authority that are disguised, euphemized forms of political authority. The sociology of sociology can help us move toward a unified scientific field of world sociology by increasing our awareness of the socially based effects of domination that are exerted in that field and by promoting struggles aimed at controlling these effects and the mechanisms that produce them.

It bears emphasizing that this sociology of sociology is not an end in itself: If it is the alpha of any rigorous sociological practice, it is not its omega. Thus I must here clearly disassociate myself—and this is a way of making visible one of the positive effects of the internationalization of scientific debate—from the tradition of the philosophical critique (be it in the form of deconstruction or archeology) of texts, in particular of scientific texts, that originated in France (in particular in the works of Derrida and Foucault) and that, reinterpreted in the idiom of American "campus radicalism" realizes itself in a nihilistic questioning of science (e.g., Marcus and Fisher 1986, Rosaldo 1989, Latour 1987). In truth, the sociology of sociology as I construe it is the means of giving its full force to what Gaston Bachelard called "epistemological vigilance" and to arm the scientist against all the presuppositions he or she tacitly accepts as a social agent and that she is forever tempted unknowingly to reintroduce into her discourse. In other words, against the antiscientific use of the science of science, I advocate a scientific—but not a scientistic—usage of this reflexive science. By thus granting priority to scientific critique within the scientific field, I make no concessions to a form of narcissistic escapism, as those who are accustomed to more prophetic forms of political engagement would be liable to believe. Rather, to turn the burden of the argument around, it is precisely because I detect escapism in the gratuitous pledges of an abstract and hyperbolic revolutionarism that I hold as an absolute prerequisite of a politically responsible sociology the reflexive approach that leads the scientist to uncover the social roots of his or her political and scientific dispositions, investments in the field, and even the purest of theoretical choices.

This is why, far from being a specialty among others, the sociology of sociology is for me a fundamental dimension of sociological epistemology. It is the necessary prerequisite of any rigorous sociological practice. Indeed, it not only has the effect of heightening the lucidity of the scientist regarding the determinations that bear durably on his or her practices and, thereby, on a possible freedom from these determinations. It also supplies the principles of a *realpolitik* of reason (Bourdieu 1987a), that is, of a methodical line of action aimed at creating the conditions of the individual autonomy of scientists by increasing the collective autonomy of the scientific field from external forces and powers or, what amounts to the same, by strengthening the social mechanisms liable practically to impose the norms of rational communication within the scientific universe. It is on this condition, and on this condition only, that we can hope to produce sociological works capable of forcing symbolic violence into retreat, both within the field of social science and in the social world at large.

REFERENCES

Becker, Howard S. 1986. "What's Happening to Sociology?" Pp. 209–220 in Howard S. Becker, *Doing Things Together*. Evanston: Northwestern University Press.

Bottomore, T. B., and R. A. Nisbet. 1978. "Introduction." Pp. vii–xvi in *A History of Sociological Analysis*. New York: Basic Books.

Bourdieu, Pierre. 1971. "Genèse et Structure du Champ Religieux." *Revue Francaise de Sociologie* 12(3):295–334.

————. 1975. "The Specificity of the Scientific Field and the Social Conditions of the Progress of Reason." *Social Science Information* 14(6):19–47.

————. 1981. "La Représentation Politique. Eléments pour une Théorie du Champ Politique." *Actes de la Recherche en Sciences Sociales* 37:3–24.

————. 1987a. "Für eine Realpolitik der Vernunft." Pp. 229–234 in S. Müller-Rolli, ed., *Das Bildungswesen der Zukunft*. Stuttgart: Ernst Klett.

————. 1987b. "L'Institutionalisation de L'Anomie." *Cahiers du Musée National d'Art Moderne* 19–20 (June):6–19.

————. 1988a. *Homo Academicus*. Stanford: Stanford University Press.

————. 1988b. "Vive la Crise! For Heterodoxy in Social Science." *Theory and Society* (Special issue on "The Critical Futures of Sociology") 17:773–787.

————. 1990. "Les Conditions Sociales de la Circulation des Idées." *Romanistische Zeitschrift für Literaturgeschichte* 14:1–10.

————. 1991. "The Peculiar History of Scientific Reason." *Sociological Forum* 5: in press.

Bourdieu, Pierre, and Jean-Claude Passeron. 1967. "Sociology and Philosophy in France Since 1945: Death and Resurrection of a Philosophy Without Subject." *Social Research* 34 (Spring):162–212.

Bourdieu, Pierre, Salah Bouhedja, Rosine Christin, Claire Givry, and Monique de Saint Martin. 1988. *Eléments d'une Analyse du Marché de la Maison Individuelle*. Paris: Centre de Sociologie Européenne.

Bryant, Christopher G.A. 1985. "Instrumental Positivism in American Sociology." Pp. 133–173 in *Positivism in Social Theory and Research*. New York: St. Martin's Press.

Collins, Randall. 1986. "Is 1980s Sociology in the Doldrums?" *American Journal of Sociology* 91 (May):1336–1355.

Gans, Herbert. 1989. "Sociology in America: The Discipline and the Public." *American Sociological Review* 53 (February):1–16.

Homans, George C. 1986. "Fifty Years of Sociology." *Annual Review of Sociology* 12:xii–xxx.

Latour, Bruno. 1987. *Science in Action*. Cambridge, MA: Harvard University Press.

Marcus, George E., and Michael M.J. Fisher. 1986. *Anthropology as Cultural Critique.* Chicago: University of Chicago Press.

Parsons, Talcott. 1968. "Professions." Pp. 536–546 in D. L. Sills, ed., *The International Encyclopedia of the Social Sciences.* New York: MacMillan.

Rosaldo, Renato. 1989. *Culture and Truth: The Remaking of Social Analysis.* Boston: Beacon Press.

Smelser, Neil J. 1988. "Introduction." Pp. 9–19 in Neil J. Smelser, ed., *Handbook of Modern Sociology.* Newbury Park: Sage.

Wacquant, Loïc, and Craig Jackson Calhoun. 1989. "Intérêt, Rationalité et Culture. A Propos d'un Récent Debat sur la Théorie de l'Action." *Actes de la Recherche en Sciences Sociales* 78:41–60.

Weber, Max. 1978. *Economy and Society.* Berkeley: The University of California Press.

Wiley, Norbert. 1985. "The Current Interregnum in American Sociology." *Social Research* 52 (Spring):179–207.

About the Book
and Editors

As we approach the closing years of the twentieth century, the pace of technological innovation, the scope of economic changes, and accelerating sociopolitical transformations raise new questions about the future of societies and the ability of social theory to shed light on their structure, functioning, and trajectory.

Social Theory for a Changing Society addresses a broad range of issues arising from this nexus of transformations that reshape individuals and families, cities and landscapes, firms and bureaucracies, social groups and nation-states. Leading sociologists, with diverse conceptions of sociological theory and research, confront their conflicting visions and collectively assess the contribution of social science toward the elucidation of these transformations.

Contributors

James S. Coleman
Charles Sabel
Rosabeth Moss Kanter
Craig Calhoun
Paul DiMaggio
Thomas Luckmann
Charles E. Bidwell
Mary C. Brinton

James W. Stigler
Alessandro Pizzorno
Kenneth A. Shepsle
Kim Lane Scheppele
Aristide R. Zolberg
George Konrad
Ivan Szelenyi
Pierre Bourdieu

Pierre Bourdieu, professor at the Collège de France, and **James S. Coleman,** professor at the University of Chicago, are two of the leading figures in sociology today.